EU ENVIRONMENTAL AND PLANNING LAW ASPECTS OF LARGE SCALE PROJECTS

European Environmental Law Forum Series, Volume 2

EU ENVIRONMENTAL AND PLANNING LAW ASPECTS OF LARGE-SCALE PROJECTS

Edited by
Bernard VANHEUSDEN
Lorenzo SQUINTANI

intersentia
Cambridge – Antwerp – Portland

Intersentia Ltd
Sheraton House | Castle Park
Cambridge | CB3 0AX | United Kingdom
Tel.: +44 1223 370 170 | Fax: +44 1223 370 169
Email: mail@intersentia.co.uk
www.intersentia.com | www.intersentia.co.uk

Distribution for the UK and Ireland:
NBN International
Airport Business Centre, 10 Thornbury Road
Plymouth, PL6 7PP
United Kingdom
Tel: +44 1752 202 301 | Fax: +44 1752 202 331
Email: orders@nbninternational.com

Distribution for Europe and all other countries:
Intersentia Publishing nv
Groenstraat 31
2640 Mortsel
Belgium
Tel.: +32 3 680 15 50 | Fax: +32 3 658 71 21
Email: mail@intersentia.be

Distribution for the USA and Canada:
International Specialized Book Services
920 NE 58th Ave Suite 300
Portland, OR 97213
USA
Tel.: +1 800 944 6190 (toll free) | Fax: +1 503 280 8832
Email: info@isbs.com

EU Environmental and Planning Law Aspects of Large-Scale Projects

GPRC
Guaranteed
Peer Reviewed
Content

ISBN 978-1-78068-381-2
D/2016/7849/40
NUR 828

British Library Cataloguing in Publication Data. A catalogue record for this book is available from the British Library.

CONTENTS

Chapter 9.
Environmental Impact Assessment to Support Marine Innovation: The 'Rochdale Envelope' and 'Deploy & Monitor' in the UK's Ocean Energy Industry

PART IV. WATER

Chapter 10.
The Case for Smart Governance in European Water Law

INTRODUCTION

Bernard VANHEUSDEN* and Lorenzo SQUINTANI**

Following the patterns initiated by the First European Environmental Law Forum (EELF) Conference held in 2013 in Groningen, which focused on energy transition and energy security, the Second EELF Conference focused on the struggle of balancing economic development with environmental protection. Governments, companies, environmental associations and citizens all over the European Union (EU) are struggling with large-scale projects. On the one hand large-scale projects can contribute to economic development; on the other hand they often also raise environmental concerns. Because of their size and potential impact, large-scale projects usually lead to heavy debates and quickly become of great symbolic value. Consequently, large-scale projects are excellent examples of the difficulty to balance economic development with environmental protection.

The types of large-scale projects, planned as well as 'under construction' in the EU, are very diverse. One can think of all kinds of infrastructure projects (motorways, railways, waterways, stations, ports, airports, etc.), building projects (offices, housing projects, sports stadiums, redevelopment of brownfields, etc.), waste projects (incineration, landfill, etc.), energy projects (electricity and gas networks, wind farms, biogas installations, heat networks, extraction projects, etc.), climate projects (CDM projects, etc.), water projects, etc.

In order to promote the legal thinking about all kinds of environmental and planning law aspects of large-scale projects, Hasselt University and KU Leuven, Campus Brussels, jointly hosted from 10 to 12 September 2014 the Second EELF Conference, with the central topic 'Environmental and Planning Law Aspects of Large-Scale Projects'.

This book offers a selection of the contributions presented at the EELF Conference. We would like to thank the anonymous reviewers for their comments on the contributions published in this book.

* Associate Professor of Environmental Law, Faculty of Law, Hasselt University (Belgium).
** Assistant Professor of European and Economic Law, Faculty of Law, University of Groningen (the Netherlands).

Following the structure of the conference, the book is subdivided into six main themes: general; public participation; environmental impact assessment; water; nature; and land use.[1]

GENERAL

In Chapter 1 *Marcin Stoczkiewicz* focuses on environmental aspects of state aid for energy investment projects. The development of large scale energy projects – e.g. power stations, electricity transmission and distribution networks, gas pipelines, storages or terminals – usually depends on state aid granted for investment by the Member States. The EU state aid regulations are designed to protect competition on the internal market. However, as large scale projects funded by state aid can have a significant impact on the environment, environmental consequences may need to be taken into account during state aid assessment. The key question in this context is whether environmental aspects *must* or *may* be taken into account during the state aid assessment of the economic support for investment in energy projects. To address the question this chapter asks: (a) whether environmental consequences must/may be part of an assessment of whether the support measure constitutes State aid according to the meaning of Article 107(1) TFEU; and (b) whether environmental consequences must/may be a part of an assessment of the compatibility of the State aid measure with the internal market.

In Chapter 2 *Delphine Misonne* presents the new 2014 EU Regulation on the establishment of rules and procedures with regard to the introduction of noise-related operating restrictions at Union airports within a Balanced Approach. The new Regulation reflects typical concerns of the Chicago Convention on International Civil Aviation. There is a growing fear that local measures adopted for reducing noise nuisances due to aviation could, in the long run, limit airport capacity and development. The Regulation, as a consequence, proposes a peculiar approach to noise management. *Misonne* discusses whether it shall help or hurdle the action of public authorities, when in charge of protecting the environment.

Ludwig Krämer deals in Chapter 3 with the participation of the civil society in large projects in the EU. Large projects, such as for infrastructure, industrial installations, power plants or other purposes, have increased considerably in number in the last decades. The reasons for this development are greater mobility of persons, increased trade, globalisation, more free time and greater welfare. In Europe, the existence and the activities of the EU have largely contributed to this development. In particular, the policy decision in the early 1990s to develop trans-European networks in the area of energy, transport and telecommunication played an important role in this regard. The EU provisions on the Structural

[1] The summaries of the chapters below are based on the abstracts and the introductions delivered by the authors.

Funds provided for specific provisions for 'big projects' which were defined as having an investment volume of more than 25 million euros. Other projects to be mentioned are nuclear power plants, military projects, projects for sport events – Olympic Games (London 2012, Sochi 2014), motorsport races, international championships – and leisure installations such as Disneyland, Eurovegas, or pleasure parks, festivals and concert halls. *Krämer*'s contribution examines some environmental problems linked to such projects, in particular the transparency in the decision-making and the possibilities for civil society to participate in this process.

Chapter 4 contains a contribution by *Yixin Xu* on the sustainability of Clean Development Mechanism (CDM) projects. The significance of forest ecosystem services for the environment and human health has been increasingly debated by the contemporary international community. For its functions in combating climate change, forestry was incorporated into the United Nations Framework Convention on Climate Change (UNFCCC). However, the sustainability of forest projects hosted in developing countries under the CDM in the Kyoto Protocol to the UNFCCC has been questioned by scholars in terms of biodiversity conservation and poverty alleviation. Therefore, this chapter aims to analyse the sustainability of CDM forest projects with a focus on the regulation for the assessment of sustainability and the incentives of the participants.

PUBLIC PARTICIPATION

According to *Hendrik Schoukens* in Chapter 5, many politicians believe that environmental law has gone astray by providing the wider public and environmental NGOs with additional procedural environmental rights which could be used to block or at least delay large infrastructure projects. Because of their size and potential environmental impact, large-scale projects usually lead to polarised debates and quickly become of great symbolic value. In former days, the lack of substantial participatory rights and the limited access to courts in environmental cases, rendered large infrastructure projects virtually immune from successful legal challenges. At present, however, environmental NGOs and local action groups are increasingly eager to go to court in order to enforce their viewpoints, which leads to an increasing number of deadlock scenarios. One way to avoid deadlock scenarios is to take recourse to legal ratification of development consents. By including development consents in legislative acts, an increasing number of national and European governments, impatient with the many court challenges against large infrastructure projects, tried to bypass the allegedly rigid environmental impact assessment (EIA) rules. The ratification technique has clearly been gaining popularity throughout the past few years. This chapter addresses the multitude of thorny legal questions that pop up in the context of legislative validation for large infrastructure projects and unravel the many particularities it might have to confront. In particular, it tries to analyse to what extent the procedural demands enshrined in international and EU environmental are reconcilable with the parliamentary process.

In Chapter 6 *José Ignacio Cubero Marcos* and *Unai Aberasturi Gorriño* indicate that also in Spain the legislative power authorises projects and passes plans using the legislative act as an ordinary mechanism. This leads to a lot of controversies about projects or plans passed by law in Spain. In many cases the decisions have been adopted without an effective procedure to guarantee participation of the people concerned, because the legislative procedures do not include stages consisting in consultations or providing information from other administrations involved. As an example, the EIA procedure cannot be followed, which allows the legislative power to elude the analysis of the environmental impacts. Moreover, in Spain the right to appeal legislative acts is restricted, which hampers an effective control of the legislators' decisions on environmental issues. Both the Aarhus Convention and European law could be violated due to the discretionary powers attributed to the legislative power in Spain.

Viviana Molaschi aims in Chapter 7 at giving an overview of the level of public participation in environmental proceedings in Italy, with particular regard to the procedures concerning major works, which generally raise opposition from the communities involved (let us think of the NIMBY and the BANANA syndromes). These conflicts are quite often the effect of a lack of public participation in the decision-making process. One of the most well-known examples is given by the construction of the high speed railway line (known as TAV), to connect Turin and Lyon, which has aroused very strong protests, mostly as a consequence of the so-called DAD approach (Decide, Announce, Defend), and are still ongoing. Reflections on participatory guarantees in the environmental field entail the analysis of the implementation in the Italian legal system of the Aarhus Convention, which is a milestone in the evolution of environmental democracy. This chapter focuses on participatory rights, and, specifically, on the second pillar, whose implementation in Italy is investigated as to the Environmental Impact Assessment (EIA), especially when major works come into consideration, and the Strategic Environmental Assessment (SEA). The chapter also formulates some preliminary considerations on the diffusion in the environmental (and planning) field of the so called 'deliberative arenas', a new frontier of public participation in decision-making, analysing some experiences at a regional level.

ENVIRONMENTAL IMPACT ASSESSMENT

Cross-border oil and gas pipelines as large-scale projects, which stretch across international borders, have the potential to create substantial environmental risks. *Mehdi Piri Damagh* looks in Chapter 8 at the trans-boundary environmental impact assessment in cross-border oil and gas pipelines and what lessons can be learned from the 1991 Espoo Convention and the 2011 EU EIA Directive. The Espoo Convention and the EU EIA Directive contain a few relevant rules concerning trans-boundary EIA, and basically they encompass cross-border pipelines as large-scale projects, which require mandatory EIA. Nevertheless, the Espoo Convention and the EU EIA Directive mainly deal with projects with trans-boundary impacts, while the cross-border pipelines are indeed trans-boundary projects, which may also have trans-boundary impacts. The cross-border nature of such projects creates extra challenges compared with the normal trans-boundary EIA procedure for projects with trans-boundary effects. This issue increases the level of complexity of the trans-boundary EIA procedure. The chapter aims to provide a detailed analysis of the application of the Espoo Convention and the EU EIA Directive to large-scale cross-border projects, in particular cross-border pipelines. The chapter concludes that the Espoo Convention and the EU EIA Directive both are envisaged to deal with projects with trans-boundary impacts and not with trans-boundary projects. Therefore, conducting trans-boundary EIA for trans-boundary projects such as cross-border pipelines under the Espoo Convention and the EU EIA Directive may raise a few but important obstacles.

Chapter 9 explores the role of risk-based approaches to EIA in approving new developments in the marine environment. In particular, *Glen Wright* examines regulatory approaches applied to the United Kingdom's emerging ocean energy industry: the 'Rochdale Envelope' and 'Deploy and Monitor' approaches. This chapter represents the first substantial exposition of these concepts in the academic literature. It is argued that by utilising such approaches, in the context of additional reform and a complementary marine governance framework, EIA can contribute to a supportive regulatory environment that facilitates innovation whilst also protecting the marine environment.

WATER

David Salm argues in Chapter 10 that the Water Framework Directive (WFD) includes ambitious objectives that most Member States most likely will not meet. Since legislative action is unlikely and environmental goals should not be compromised, a realistic legal interpretation of Article 4 WFD is paramount. On 1 July 2015, the European Court of Justice delivered a judgment concerning some crucial aspects in European water law. This ruling will most likely significantly impair the admission of large scale projects throughout the European Union. Critically evaluating the ECJ's line of argument, *Salm* believes that the intention of European water law is to provide tools for smart governance rather than to make industrial projects virtually impossible.

Also, *Lisa Löffler* looks in Chapter 11 at the Water Framework Directive. Coal-fired power plants emit mercury, a heavy metal that is considered persistent, bio-accumulative and acutely toxic to human health, ecosystems, and wildlife. In order to avert the threat of mercury it has been added to the list of priority hazardous substances under Annex X of the WFD in 2001. During implementation of the WFD and its daughter directive, the Directive on Environmental Quality Standards in the field of water policy into national law, controversies about the compatibility of the permission of coal-fired power plants with EU water law intensified. In particular, the phasing-out of priority hazardous substances as required under Article 4(1)(a) 4th indent WFD is subject of on-going discussions in legal doctrine and case-law. This contribution analyses the legal implications of the phasing-out requirement. It is argued that Article 4(1)(a) 4th indent WFD is directly applicable in domestic law. In consequence, it prohibits the operation and permission of mercury emitting coal-fired power plants as of 16 December 2028.

One of the overriding problems of the 21st century is that of the protection and the sustainable use of the scarce water resources, which is intensified due to the climate-induced changes on water ecosystems. Population growth, economic activities, such as industry and agriculture that presuppose an increased use of water, and increasing urbanisation are, among others, significant drivers for an over-exploitation of the water resources in many regions, which often results in shortages of water availability. *Vicky Karageorgou* indicates in Chapter 12 that in such circumstances, demand-oriented measures are not entirely sufficient. Supply-oriented measures are also considered to be possible solutions to increasing water demand in areas which are not able to live within their ecological limits. Interbasin water transfers (IBTs) are regarded as one of the most prominent supply oriented solutions for coping with the above-described situations. Since the implementation of such projects presupposes large scale and significant interventions, the consequences arising from their realisation can be far-reaching not only from an environmental but also from a social and an economic point of view. The main aim of the chapter is to answer the central question of whether EU water law and EU environmental law in general provide either concrete rules or at least certain clear-cut criteria and other relevant instruments for assessing the permissibility of the IBTs as a possible solution for satisfying water demand in water-stressed regions. To this end, the chapter also analyses the experience gained through the implementation of certain relevant projects worldwide with a view to demonstrating the various issues triggered by their realisation.

NATURE

The continuing loss of biodiversity is an issue of global concern. Europe's biological diversity, in addition to displaying a number of important ecological characteristics, is testament to the millennial symbiosis between man and his natural environment. In effect, more than on any other continent, human activities have been shaping biodiversity over centuries. Ecosystems were relatively stable until the agricultural and industrial revolutions of the past two centuries. Today, however, biodiversity faces a major crisis at both global and European levels, the implications of which still have not been fully appreciated.

In order to reverse these negative trends, in 1979 the EU enacted the Birds Protection Directive and in 1992 the Habitats Directive. These directives are the cornerstones of EU nature conservation law, aiming at the conservation of the Natura 2000 network, a network of protected sites under these directives, and the protection of species.

Among the different provisions of the Habitats Directive, Article 6 has been giving rise to a steady flow of cases. It requires Member States to protect designated habitats, and provides for specific procedural requirements whenever projects or plans are likely to threaten those protected habitats. In shedding the light on the procedural requirements laid down under Article 6(3) and (4) of the Habitats Directive, a key provision for implementing the EU's system of protecting and preserving biological diversity in the Member States, *Nicolas de Sadeleer* attempts in Chapter 13 to emphasise the extent to which this atypical procedure reinforces the obligations stemming from the EIA and the SEA Directives. In sharp contrast to these two directives, which are entirely dedicated to impact assessments, only two sentences in Article 6(3) of the Habitats Directive relate to the appropriate assessment.

The protection regime for Natura 2000 sites and protected species is not absolute: Member States may, under certain conditions, allow plans or projects that can have an adverse impact on nature. In this case compensatory measures can play an important role on safeguarding the Natura 2000 network and ensuring the survival of the protected species. In Chapter 14 *Geert Van Hoorick* analyses whether taking compensatory measures is always obligatory, and discusses the aim and the characteristics (i.e. the naturalness) of compensatory measures, in relation to other kinds of measures such as mitigation measures, usual nature conservation measures, and former nature development measures, and to the assessment of the adverse impact caused by the plan or project and of the alternative solutions. These issues are discussed in light of the text of the legislation, the guidance and practice of the European Commission, (legal) doctrine and the judgments of the Court of Justice in the *Briels* case and (to a lesser extent) the *Acheloos River* case.

LAND USE

Elizabeth Dunn considers in Chapter 15 the nature of land use regulation in England and Wales and the significant role played by the courts in the context of the increasing influence of European legislation on the planning process. In particular, this article explores the discretion afforded to local decision-makers and the extent to which that discretion is respected by the courts. It looks at the legacy of the *Alconbury* case from 2001 regarding the compliance of the UK planning system with the European Convention on Human Rights. Consideration is also given to the prevalence of judicial review claims in the context of recent proposals for reform of the system including the new Planning Court for England and Wales.

Finally, in Chapter 16 *Iñaki Lasagabaster* and *María del Carmen Bolaño* look at public participation in the land management law-making process in the Basque Country (Spain), and at what the effects are on soil and other natural resources. Soil provides the main foundation for human activities and it is a matter of transversal nature. It affects a number of issues and regulations such as the ones that govern water, habitats, birds or waste. Despite the progress made by Land Management Law in the Basque Country, the most remarkable obstacle found is that Land Management Law does not apply to some large projects. Although, in reality, those projects have a major effect on land's development. This is the case, for instance, of the High Speed Train Project.

This book ends with a conclusion in which we try to place the findings from the various contributions into the broader perspective of the EU legal framework for achieving (quasi-)sustainability and the legal design of instruments aiming at (quasi-)sustainability. It concludes with a call for further research on instruments to achieve quasi-sustainability.

We wish you a pleasant and interesting read, and we look forward to meeting you at one of the next EELF Conferences.

PART I
GENERAL

CHAPTER 1

ENVIRONMENTAL ASPECTS OF STATE AID FOR ENERGY INVESTMENT PROJECTS

Marcin STOCZKIEWICZ*

1. INTRODUCTION

1.1. THEMATIC CONTEXT AND SCOPE OF ANALYSIS

The European law rules on State aid are of considerable importance to the energy sector given the traditionally high level of involvement of governments in energy production and supply.[1] The development of large-scale energy projects – e.g. nuclear or coal-fired power stations, major hydropower plants, electricity transmission and distribution networks, gas pipelines, storage, gas or oil terminals – frequently depends on the State aid granted for investment by the Member States. Granting State aid to develop energy projects could affect competition on the internal energy market. Therefore State aid is in principle prohibited under Article 107(1) of the Treaty on the Functioning of European Union ('TFEU' or 'Treaty')[2] but can be allowed by the European Commission if certain conditions under Articles 107(2) or 107(3) TFEU are satisfied. The State aid rules, Articles 107–109 TFEU, are found in Title Seven, Chapter One (named 'Rules on Competition') of the Treaty. The TFEU provides that the European Union shall have exclusive competence in the area of establishing competition rules necessary for the functioning of the internal market.[3] EU State aid regulations were not established to protect the environment and do not have environmental objectives. However, as State aid for energy investment projects

* Dr Marcin Stoczkiewicz is senior lawyer and head of Climate & Energy Program at non-governmental organisation ClientEarth.

1 *L. Hancher*, State aid, in C. Jones (ed.), EU Energy Law, Volume II: EU Competition Law and Energy Markets, 2007, p. 549.

2 OJ 2012 C326/51 of 26.10.2012.

3 Article 3(1)(b) TFEU.

could have indirect significant impacts on the environment, the environmental consequences may need to be taken into account during State aid assessment.[4]

The growing importance of EU climate and energy legislation has caused several specific legal problems where environmental law and State aid law interact, e.g. in the scope of free allowances for power stations under EU Emission Trading System; exemptions from environmental taxes or charges; aid for Carbon Capture and Storage projects and aid for renewable energy, energy efficiency or Combined Heat and Power projects.[5] In addition, several environmental conditions are included in the Commission's soft law State aid documents. Indeed, the European Commission adopted the Community Guidelines on State Aid for Environmental Protection of 2008 as part of the first Climate and Energy Package.[6] Also adopted were the Guidelines on State aid for environmental protection and energy 2014–2020 (EEAG).[7] These should be understood as being applicable to the EU climate and energy policy up to 2020, confirmed by the text of EEAG, which refers in the 'Introduction' to the Europe 2020 strategy. It goes on: 'To this end, a number of headline targets have been set, including targets for climate change and energy sustainability: (i) a 20% reduction in EU greenhouse gas emissions from 1990 levels; (ii) raising the share of EU energy consumption produced from renewable resources to 20%; (iii) a 20% improvement in the EU's energy-efficiency compared to 1990 levels.'[8] In terms of the second climate and energy package, EEAG states that '[o]n 22 January 2014 the Commission proposed the energy and climate objectives to be met by 2030 in a Communication "A policy Framework for climate and energy in the period from 2020 to 2030" (the 2030 Framework). The pillars of the 2030 Framework are: i) a reduction in greenhouse gas emissions by 40% relative to the 1990 level; ii) an EU-wide binding target for renewable energy of at least 27%; iii) renewed ambitions for energy efficiency policies; and iv) a new governance system and a set of new indicators to ensure a competitive and secure energy system.'[9]

In the context of this chapter, 'energy investment projects' are understood to be public or private projects which are likely to have significant effects on the environment within the meaning of Directive 2011/92/EU of the European

---

4 *C. Quigley QC*, European State Aid Law and Policy, 2nd ed., 2009, pp. 270–293; *E. Kutenicova & A.T. Seinen*, Environmental Aid, in W. Mederer, N. Pesaresi and M. van Hoof (eds.), EU Competition Law, Volume IV: State Aid. Book Two, 2008, pp. 851–961.

5 *L. Hancher, supra* note 1, pp. 579–585, 642–655; *M. Stoczkiewicz*, State aid for energy undertakings in EU law, 2011 [in Polish], pp. 95–130, 158–164, 241–247; *M. Stoczkiewicz*, The Emission Trading Scheme in Polish Law. Selected Problems Related to the Scope of Derogation from General Rule for Auctioning in Poland, YARS 2011 (4:4), pp. 95, 96 et seq.

6 *E. Kutenicova & A.T. Seinen, supra* note 4, p. 851.

7 OJ 2014 C200/1. See: *P. Nicolaides & M. Kleis*, A Critical Analysis of Environmental Tax Reductions and Generation Adequacy Provisions in the EEAG 2014–2020, EStAL 2014 (4), pp. 636, 637 et seq. *M. Villar Ezcurra*, EU State Aid and Energy Policies as an Instrument of Environmental Protection: Current Stage and New Trends, EStAL 2014 (4), pp. 665, 667 et seq.

8 EEAG, para. 3.

9 EEAG, para. 4.

Parliament and of the Council of 13 December 2011 on the assessment of the effects of certain public and private projects on the environment,[10] as listed in its Annex I, points 2, 3, 14, 16, 20, 21, 22, 23 or in Annex II, points 3, 10(i).[11] All of these kinds of projects could be recognised as 'large-scale projects' in the common sense.

Pursuant to Article 107(1) TFEU, any aid granted by a Member State or through State resources in any form, which distorts or threatens to distort competition by favouring certain undertakings or the production of certain goods, in so far as it affects trade between Member States, is incompatible with the internal market. However, the prohibition of State aid under the TFEU is not absolute. State aid for energy investment projects may be compatible with the internal market, and therefore permissible, in a number of cases. First, certain aid is declared by Article 107(2) TFEU to be compatible with the internal market. Secondly, the Commission has discretion under Article 107(3) TFEU to determine that certain aid is compatible with the internal market. Thirdly, the Council, pursuant to Article 107(3)(e) TFEU may decide that other categories of aid may be permissible.[12] There is no doubt that Article 107(3)(c) TFEU is the broadest legal basis by which State aid for energy investment projects can be declared to be compatible with the internal market. It allows the Commission to consider as compatible with the internal market State aid 'to facilitate the development of certain economic activities within the European Union, where such aid does not adversely affect trading conditions to an extent contrary to the common interest.'

EEAG constitutes detailed rules on the application of Article 107(3)(c) of TFEU to aid for environmental protection and energy. Several requirements

---

10 OJ 2012 L26/1.

11 Thermal power stations and other combustion installations with a heat output of 300 megawatts or more; nuclear power stations and other nuclear reactors including the dismantling or decommissioning of such power stations or reactors; installations for the reprocessing of irradiated nuclear fuel; extraction of petroleum and natural gas for commercial purposes where the amount extracted exceeds 500 tonnes/day in the case of petroleum and 500,000 cubic metres/day in the case of gas; pipelines with a diameter of more than 800 mm and a length of more than 40 km for the transport of gas, oil; carbon dioxide (CO_2) streams for the purposes of geological storage; construction of overhead electrical power lines with a voltage of 220 kV or more and a length of more than 15 km; installations for storage of petroleum, petrochemical products with a capacity of 200,000 tonnes or more; storage sites pursuant to Directive 2009/31/EC; installations for the capture of CO_2 streams for the purposes of geological storage pursuant to Directive 2009/31/EC from installations covered by Annex I, or where the total yearly capture of CO_2 is 1.5 megatonnes or more; industrial installations for the production of electricity, steam and hot water (projects not included in Annex I); industrial installations for carrying gas, steam and hot water; transmission of electrical energy by overhead cables (projects not included in Annex I); surface storage of natural gas; underground storage of combustible gases; surface storage of fossil fuels; industrial briquetting of coal and lignite; installations for the processing and storage of radioactive waste (unless included in Annex I); installations for hydroelectric energy production; installations for the capture of CO_2 streams for the purposes of geological storage pursuant to Directive 2009/31/EC from installations not covered by Annex I.

12 *C. Quigley QC*, *supra* note 4, p. 125.

included in EEAG suggest that environmental consequences of projects that are beneficiaries of State aid should be taken into account during the assessment of the compatibility of measures in question. Specific conditions are provided in respect of aid to energy from renewable sources, energy efficiency, district heating, Carbon Capture and Storage, aid to energy infrastructure, aid for generation adequacy and aid in the form of tradable permit schemes.[13]

1.2. KEY QUESTIONS AND THE STRUCTURE OF AN ANALYSIS

Any further legal reflection in the context of State aid and the environment should start with the question of whether environmental aspects must, or eventually may, be taken into account during State aid assessment of the economic support for investment in potentially environmentally harmful projects. There are two parts to this question. First, whether the measure in question constitutes State aid. Second, if the answer to the first question is positive, whether the State aid measure is compatible with the internal market. Taking environmental aspects into account could have significant consequences for both questions. In the following sections an analysis will be conducted to examine: (i) whether environmental aspects must/may be part of an assessment of whether the support measure constitutes State aid within the meaning of Article 107(1) TFEU, and (ii) whether environmental aspects must/may be a part of an assessment of the compatibility with the internal market of the State aid measure.

The structure of this chapter is adapted to the questions mentioned above. First, the relationship between competition policy and environmental policy as established in TFEU is described. As EU environmental policy and competition rules have separate, specific legal bases and objectives, a question of consistency of these rules arises. So, next the analysis is conducted to define to what extent the 'polluter pays' principle and the integration clause act to integrate State aid law with environmental protection. Subsequently, special emphasis is given to an analysis of the integration clause in the context of State aid case-law and in the context of EEAG. Finally, the conclusions of the analysis are presented.

2. EU ENVIRONMENTAL POLICY AND STATE AID RULES

Articles 191 and 192 TFEU constitute the legal basis for the environmental policy of the European Union. Article 191(1) TFEU also fixes specific environmental

[13] EEAG, section 3.

objectives.[14] In terms of State aid, Articles 107–109 TFEU are included in Title Seven, Chapter One (named 'Rules on Competition') of the Treaty. Pursuant to Article 3(3) of the Treaty on European Union (TEU):[15] 'The Union shall establish an internal market. It shall work for the sustainable development of Europe based on balanced economic growth and price stability, a highly competitive social market economy, aiming at full employment and social progress, and a high level of protection and improvement of the quality of the environment.' Both 'highly competitive social market economy' and 'high level of protection and improvement of the quality of the environment' are objectives of the Union and their legal status is equal. In the case of any conflict between these objectives, the Union's authorities are committed to seeking agreement between them and implementing them as far as possible.[16] It is worth noting that the Treaty's competition policy rules, and especially its State aid rules, do not include any environmental objectives. The converse is also true: the Treaty's environmental provisions do not incorporate objectives oriented around a highly competitive social market economy. In summary, EU environmental policy and competition rules have separate, specific legal bases and specific objectives, yet there is no good basis for the assertion that they are not legally equal; something which may lead to the (false) conclusion that EU State aid policy and EU environmental policy are clearly separated.

3. 'POLLUTER PAYS' AND 'INTEGRATION' AS PRINCIPLES LINKING ENVIRONMENTAL OBJECTIVES WITH COMPETITION RULES

There are two principles of the Treaty linking environmental protection objectives and requirements with competition rules and their enforcement: (i) the 'polluter pays' principle, established by Article 191(2) TFEU; and (ii) the 'integration' clause established by Article 11 TFEU. Although the precise legal nature of these principles is debatable (for example, whether they are legally binding or constitute general guidelines),[17] there is no doubt that both principles are applicable to Union policies, and especially to competition policy.

---

14 Article 191(1) TFEU: 'Union policy on the environment shall contribute to pursuit of the following objectives – preserving, protecting and improving the quality of the environment; protecting human health; -prudent and rational utilisation of natural resources; -promoting measures at international level to deal with regional or worldwide environmental problems, and in particular combating climate change.' See: *L. Krämer,* EU Environmental Law, 7th ed., 2011, pp. 8–14.

15 OJ 2012 C326 of 26.10.2012.

16 139/79, *Maizena GmbH*, para. 23; C-44/94, *National Federation of Fishermen's Organisations*, para. 37.

17 See: *L. Krämer, supra* note 14, pp. 14–16; *R. Macrory* (ed.), Principles of European Environmental Law, 2004; *N. de Sadeleer,* EU Environmental Law and the Internal Market, 2014, pp. 21–89.

3.1. THE 'POLLUTER PAYS' PRINCIPLE AND STATE AID

There is no need here to rehearse the jurisprudence relating to the polluter pays principle in the Treaty and in secondary environmental legislation.[18] The polluter pays principle is particularly important in the EU State aid policy. The European Commission is responsible for the practical implementation of the polluter pays principle with regard to State aid. In order to ensure legal certainty, unify practices and limit the scope of its own discretion, the Commission has issued several 'soft law' instruments on State aid for environmental protection. In 1994, the Commission adopted the first Community Guidelines on State Aid for Environmental Protection,[19] followed by the Guidelines of 2001,[20] and by the Guidelines of 2008.[21] At present, the most recent guidelines are EEAG. All these guidelines have made explicit reference to the polluter pays principle. In the meaning of the Guidelines of 2008, the polluter pays principle means that the costs of measures to deal with pollution should be borne by the polluter who causes the pollution, unless the person responsible for the pollution cannot be identified or cannot be held liable under Community or national legislation or may not be made to bear the costs of remediation. Pollution in this context is the damage caused by the polluter by directly or indirectly damaging the environment, or by creating conditions leading to such damage to physical surroundings or natural resources.[22] The Commission has assumed that ultimately the polluter pays principle would be fully implemented and the entire environmental costs would be internalised.

The currently-in-force EEAG states: 'the polluter pays principle or "PPP" means that the costs of measures to deal with the pollution should be borne by the polluter who causes the pollution'[23] and next 'In Respect for the "polluter pays principle" ("PPP") through environmental legislation ensures in principle that the market failure linked to negative externalities will be rectified. Therefore, State aid is not an appropriate instrument and cannot be granted insofar as the beneficiary of the aid could be held liable for the pollution under existing Union or national law'.[24] This wording clearly shows that in EEAG the polluter pays principle has been introduced to prohibit some State aid instruments on the grounds that they are not compatible with the internal market. Indeed, within the scope of State aid for environmental protection, only the aid which is either consistent with the polluter pays principle or constitutes a particularly justified

18 See: *L. Krämer, supra* note 14, pp. 26–27; *J.H. Jans & H.H.B. Vedder*, European Environmental Law, 3rd ed., 2008, pp. 43–45.
19 OJ 1994 C72 of 10.03.1994.
20 OJ 2001 C37 of 03.02.2001.
21 OJ 2008 C82/I of 01.04.2008.
22 OJ 2008 C82/I of 01.04.2008, para. 70.24.
23 EEAG, section 1.3, para. 28.
24 EEAG, section 3.2, para. 44.

exception to this principle is allowed.[25] It shows how the polluter pays principle connects State aid control with environmental policy.[26]

3.2. INTEGRATION PRINCIPLE AND STATE AID

Nevertheless, the main question in the context of State aid and the environment is whether environmental aspects must, or eventually may, be taken into account during State aid assessment of the economic support for investment in projects which could have significant positive or negative impacts on the environment. The European Court of Justice in the landmark ruling of 22 December 2008, C-487/06 P, *British Aggregates* analysed the problem of the application of the integration principle to State aid law. In the case of 13 September 2006, T-210/02, *British Aggregates v. Commission*, the Court of First Instance upheld a Commission decision (863/01) which had – on the basis of its nature and scheme – considered the imposition of a levy on only certain category of aggregates (aggregate levy) used as construction material to be justified. Certain aggregates considered as being environmentally friendly were exempted from the scope of this levy. In its ruling the Court of First Instance concluded that the Commission did not commit a manifest error of assessment in concluding that the exemption from the scope of the aggregate levy of certain aggregates having a better environmental impact was justified. Taking into account the general environmental objectives pursued, the Court of First Instance concluded that the exemption appeared 'reasonably' justified by the nature and the general scheme of the aggregate levy.[27] The Court of First Instance argued that in exercising their powers in relation to environmental policy, 'it is open to the Member States to introduce sectoral environmental levies in order to attain those environmental objectives'. In particular, the Member States are free, 'in balancing the various interests involved, to set their priorities as regards the protection of the environment and, as a result, to determine which goods or services they are to decide to subject to an environmental levy.' Next, the Court of First Instance concluded that, in that legal framework, 'it is for the Commission, when assessing an environmental levy for the purposes of the Community rules on State aid, to take account of the environmental protection requirements referred to in Article 6 EC' (now Article 11 TFEU). According to the Court of First Instance, that conclusion is justified in the light of Article 6 EC (Article 11 TFEU), which 'provides that those requirements are to be integrated

25 *M. Stoczkiewicz*, The polluter pays principle and State aid for environmental protection, JEEPL 2009 (6:2), p. 196.

26 See more: *M. Stoczkiewicz*, *supra* note 25, pp. 171, 172 et seq.; *N. de Sadeleer*, State Aids and Environmental Measures: Time for Promoting the Polluter Pays Principle, Nordic Journal of Environmental Law 2012 (1), pp. 3, 5 et seq.

27 *K. Van de Casteele & M. Hocine*, Favouring certain undertakings or the production of certain goods. Selectivity, in W. Mederer, N. Pesaresi & M. van Hoof (eds.), EU Competition Law, Volume IV: State Aid, 2008, p. 261; *N. de Sadeleer*, *supra* note 17, pp. 450–451.

into the definition and implementation of, inter alia, arrangements which ensure that competition is not distorted within the internal market'.[28]

This ruling has been the subject of criticism on the grounds that the concept of selectivity was misunderstood.[29] Most criticised was the Court's of First Instance interpretation of Article 6 EC (Article 11 TFEU). The question is whether the integration of environmental protection in other Union policies has to be taken into account only when it is being considered whether a State aid measure can be justified, or also when considering the upstream question of whether a measure constitutes State aid in the first place. It was underlined that so far the Commission has only taken Article 6 EC (Article 11 TFEU) into account when assessing the compatibility of a State aid with the common market.[30]

Also Advocate General Mengozzi in his opinion in the case C-487/06P made comments critical of the Court of First Instance judgment. Advocate General Mengozzi observed: 'The approach taken by the Court of First Instance … is highly innovative as compared with the Community case-law on the application of the selectivity criterion and, more generally, of the concept of aid within the meaning of Article 87(1) EC (Article 107(1) TFEU). It is, in fact, settled case-law that neither the fiscal nature nor the economic or social aim of the State measure at issue, nor the environmental protection objectives with it pursues are sufficient to exclude it from the ambit of prohibition laid down in Article 87 EC (Article 107 TFEU). … Neither the competence enjoyed by the Member States in matters relating to taxation or the environment, nor the principle laid down by Article 6 EC (Article 11 TFEU) of the integration of environmental protection requirements into definition and implementation of Community policies, justifies the wholesale removal of public measures that could distort competition from the ambit of the supervisory power conferred on the Commission by the Treaty rules on State aid. In particular, it seems to me that compliance with Article 6 EC (Article 11 TFEU) does not require the environmental objectives of a measure to be taken into account for the purposes of its classification under of Article 87(1) EC (Article 107(1) TFEU), since the requirements that those objectives be integrated into the Community monitoring of State aid can easily be satisfied by taking them properly into consideration when it comes to assessing the measure's

28 Opinion of Advocate General Mengozzi delivered on 17 July 2008, Case C-487/06P, paras. 92–93.

29 See more: *M. Stoczkiewicz*, State aid for energy undertakings in EU law, 2011 [in Polish], pp. 253–263.

30 See: *C. Arhold*, The 2007/2008 Case Law of the European Court of Justice and the Court of First Instance on State Aid, EStAL 2008 (3), p. 466; *J. Lohrberg*, Clarifications on the Application of the EC State Aid Rules to Fiscal Measures Aimed at Environmental Protection. Note on Case T-2010/02, BAA v. Commission, EStAL 2007 (3), pp. 538, 539 et seq.; *M. Honore*, Selectivity and Taxation – Reflections in the Light of Case C-487/06P, British Aggregates Association, EStAL 2009 (4), pp. 527, 529 et seq.

compatibility with the Common Market under Article 87(3) EC (Article 107(3) TFEU).'[31]

The European Court of Justice in its judgment of 22 December 2008 in Case C-487/06P followed the Opinion of Advocate General Mengozzi and referred the case back to the General Court.[32] The European Court of Justice ruled that: 'It is true, as the Court of First Instance pointed out in paragraph 117 of the judgment under appeal, that it is for the Commission, when assessing, in the light of the Community rules on State aid, a specific measure such as an environmental levy adopted by Member States in a field in which they retain their powers in the absence of harmonisation measures, to take into account of the environmental protection requirements referred to in Article 6 EC (Article 11 TFEU), which provides that those requirements are to be integrated into the definition and implementation of, inter alia, arrangements which ensure that competition is not distorted within the internal market. It should also be born in mind that protection of the environment constitutes one of essential objectives of the Community. ... However, the need to take account of requirements relating to environmental protection, however legitimate, cannot justify the exclusion of selective measures, even specific ones such as environmental levies, form the scope of Article 87(1) EC (Article 107(1) TFEU) ... as account may in any event useful be taken of the environmental objectives when the compatibility of the State aid measure with the common market is being assessed pursuant to Article 87(3) EC (Article 107(3) TFEU).'[33]

Further clarification in this aspect was made by the General Court in the recent judgment in the case of *Castelou Energia v. Commission*.[34] The General Court in its ruling in case T-57/11 has confirmed the applicability of the integration principle and polluter pays principle to the State aid assessment: 'It is true that it has been sentenced that by assessing aid in accordance with EU legislation on State aid the Commission should take into account its requirements on environmental protection, stated in Article 11 of the TFEU (above in point 30 sentence British Aggregates vs. The Commission, EU:C:2008:757, point 90, 92; 8 Sept 2011. The Commission vs. The Netherlands, C-279/08 P Court Reports EU:C:2011:551, point 75; and especially taking the rule 'the polluter pays' into account, being a part of the appeal sentence from 16 July 2014 Germany vs. The

---

31 Opinion of Advocate General Mengozzi delivered on 17 July 2008, Case C-487/06P, paras. 95–96,102.

32 The *British Aggregates* saga finished by the judgment of the General Court of 7 March 2012 in Case T-210/02 RENV where the General Court annulled the Commission decision no. 863/01. See: *G. Lo Schiavo*, The General Court Reassess the British Aggregates Levy: Selective Advantages 'Permeated' by an Exercise on the Actual Effects of Completion? EStAL 2013 (2), pp. 384, 385 et seq.

33 Case C-487/06P, paras. 90–92.

34 Judgment of the General Court of 3 December 2014, Case T-57/11, *Castelou Energia v. Commission*.

Commission, T-295/12, EU:T:2014:675, point 61).'[35] However, the General Court expressed a narrowing interpretation of the previous case-law: 'The European court found this duty on the side of the Commission in the case that if aid was accomplished for goals on environmental protection it can be regarded as being coherent with the internal market, based on Article 107(3) (b) or (c) of the TFEU. By assessing the support mechanism that has no environmental goal, the Commission is not obliged to take environmental rules into consideration when researching the support and implementation procedures that are not bond to it. The support in favour of environmental protection can, pursuant to Article 107(3) (b) or (c) of the TFEU be declared as compatible with the internal market, but support that has severe negative impact for the environment does not have to, for this reason, deconstruct the creation of the internal market. While environmental protection must be integrated into the policy description and implementation of the EU Law, including the lines stating the implementation of an internal market (Article 11 TFEU; see also arrest 13 Sept 2005, Commission, Council, C-176/03, Jurispr., EU:CL2005:542, para. 42), it is not in fact seen as a part of the internal market, described as an area without internal borders, in which free movement of traffic, goods, people, services and capital is allowed (Article 26(2) TFEU). Taken from the juridical formulation above, in which the extent of the Commission's framework on the State aid procedure is extended to other provisions than Article 107 TFEU, especially para. 3, and to ensure the coherence of the State aid procedure provisions and the specific provisions of the European law, the European court leads the obligation to follow other regulations than the State aid procedure regulations, limiting them to regulations that have a negative impact on the internal market.'[36] In my opinion, the General Court has assumed a very narrow approach to integration principle in State aid policy. This narrowing approach doesn't have appropriate ground in the Treaty. The Treaty does not differentiate application of integration of environmental protection requirements in different parts of competition policy, and especially does not limit integration of environmental requirements to competition assessments of measures that have environmental goals. The General Court's approach could deprive the integration principle of its real importance in the scope of State aid policy and shouldn't be confirmed by future settled case-law.

Both rulings (C-487/06P and T-57/11) are essential for State aid and environmental protection. It could be concluded, simplifying the statement, that environmental objectives cannot change the notion of what State aid is and therefore cannot be included in the assessment of whether a particular measure constitutes State aid within the meaning of Article 107(1) of the TFEU. Environmental rules must be considered in the scope of assessing compatibility of the State aid measure with the internal market pursuant to Article 107(3) of the TFEU, if the measure

[35] Case T-57/11, para. 188.

[36] Case T-57/11, paras. 188–189.

has an environmental goal. Nevertheless, in a case where the measure does not have an environmental goal, environmental rules must be included during the assessment of compatibility of the State aid measure with the internal market pursuant to Article 107(3) of the TFEU only when specific support mechanisms are so closely tied with the goal that the eventual incompatibility of it with the previous provisions influence the compatibility of the support mechanism with the internal market.

As a consequence, further considerations will be limited to an analysis of the compatibility requirements adopted by the Commission in EEAG.

4. STATE AID FOR ENERGY INVESTMENT PROJECTS IN ENVIRONMENT AND ENERGY GUIDELINES 2014–2020

4.1. GENERAL REMARKS

Environmental requirements are included in several guidelines and regulations adopted by the Commission,[37] but there is no doubt that EEAG have the largest scope of application and significance for large-scale energy investment projects.[38] The integration of environmental protection requirements into EEAG has two aspects: (i) 'positive integration' – compatibility conditions which support EU environmental protection policy; and (ii) 'negative integration' – compatibility conditions which avoid State aid measures lead to environmental harm.

4.2. POSITIVE INTEGRATION

Environmental goals constitute an important part of the 'Introduction' of EEAG. Pursuant to recital (3) of EEAG: 'The Europe 2020 strategy focuses on creating the conditions for smart, sustainable and inclusive growth. To that end, a number of headline targets have been set, including targets for climate change and energy sustainability: (i) a 20% reduction in Union greenhouse gas emissions

---

37 Communication from the Commission, Guidelines on certain State aid measures in the context of the greenhouse gas emission allowance trading scheme post-2012, OJ 2012 C158/4; Commission Regulation (EU) No 651/2014 of 17 June 2014 declaring certain categories of aid compatible with the internal market in application of Articles 107 and 108 of the Treaty, OJ 2014 L187/1.

38 Guidelines on certain State aid measures in the context of greenhouse gas emission allowances are limited to the certain type of State aid measure with very limited scope of application. See: *G. Catti De Gasperi*, Making State Aid Control 'Greener': The EU Emissions Trading System and its Compatibility with Article 107 TFEU, EStAL 2010 (4), pp. 785, 786 et seq.; *M. Stoczkiewicz*, Free Allocation of EU Emission Allowances to Installations for Electricity Production from a State aid Perspective, Environmental Economics, 2012 (3:3), pp. 99, 100 et seq.

when compared to 1990 levels; (ii) raising the share of Union energy consumption produced from renewable resources to 20%; and (iii) a 20% improvement in the EU's energy-efficiency compared to 1990 levels. The first two of these nationally binding targets were implemented by 'The climate and energy package'. In recital (4) of EEAG the future goals of EU climate and energy policy are described: 'On 22 January 2014 the Commission proposed the energy and climate objectives to be met by 2030 in a Communication "A policy Framework for climate and energy in the period from 2020 to 2030" (the 2030 Framework). The pillars of the 2030 Framework are: i) a reduction in greenhouse gas emissions by 40% relative to the 1990 level; ii) an EU-wide binding target for renewable energy of at least 27%; iii) renewed ambitions for energy efficiency policies; and iv) a new governance system and a set of new indicators to ensure a competitive and secure energy system.'

According to recital (5) of EEAG 'The headline targets mentioned in recital (3) are particularly important for these Guidelines.' In the recitals which follow such aims as 'shift towards a resource-efficient and low-carbon economy', 'reducing use of resources', 'fight against climate change', 'limit the environmental impacts of the use of resources' and 'reduce greenhouse gas emissions in line with 2050 roadmap' are mentioned as a basis for compatibility conditions.[39]

In EEAG the Commission sets out the compatibility conditions under which aid for energy and environmental protection may be considered compatible with the internal market under Article 107(3) TFEU. By establishing common assessment principles, general compatibility conditions[40] and specific compatibility conditions of State aid for renewable energy projects,[41] energy efficiency and cogeneration projects,[42] Carbon Capture and Storage projects[43] and aid in the form of tradable permits,[44] EEAG introduces the presumption that State aid for such projects granted in accordance with these conditions will be considered compatible with the internal market. It is worth noting that the Commission itself is bound by its own guidelines.[45]

4.3. NEGATIVE INTEGRATION

Even more significant from an environmental point of view is the following general condition set out in EEAG with reference to the settled case-law of the CJEU: 'If a State aid measure or the conditions attached to it, including its financing

[39] EEAG, paras. 5–6, 8–9.
[40] EEAG, section 3.1–3.2.
[41] EEAG, section 3.3, paras. 107–137.
[42] EEAG, section 3.4, paras. 138–151.
[43] EEAG, section 3.6, paras. 160–166.
[44] EEAG, section 3.10, paras. 234–236.
[45] Case C-313/90, *CIRFS v. Commission*, para. 36; Case C-351/98, *Spain v. Commission*, para. 53; Case C-409/00, *Spain v. Commission*, para. 95.

method when it forms an integral part of it, entail a non-severable violation of Union law, the aid cannot be declared compatible with the internal market.'[46] The importance of the following general environmental requirement should also not be underestimated: 'To avoid that State aid measures lead to environmental harm, Member States must also ensure compliance with EU environmental legislation, including in particular the need to carry out an environmental impact assessment when it is required by EU law and ensure all relevant permits.'[47] At the current stage of development of the EU law, this requirement of EEAG should be understood in the light of the CJEU ruling in the *BUPA* case: 'the Commission may take into account the relevant provisions that do not strictly concern the State aid, only when some aspects considered as aid are so closely tied with the subject that the eventual incompatibility of it with the previous provisions influence the compatibility of the support mechanism with the internal market'.[48]

Additionally, EEAG establishes several specific compatibility conditions with reference to EU environmental legislation directed at preventing negative environmental impacts of the State aid measures. A few examples can be noted in this context. When granting aid for the production of hydropower, Member States must respect Directive 2000/60/EC (Water Framework Directive) and in particular Article 4(7) thereof, which lays down criteria in relation to allowing new modifications of bodies of water.[49] A core principle of Union legislation on waste is the waste hierarchy which prioritises the ways in which waste should be treated, as described in Article 4(1) of Directive 2008/98/EC (Waste Framework Directive). The State aid for energy from renewable sources using waste, including waste heat, as input fuel can make a positive contribution to environmental protection, provided that it does not circumvent the waste hierarchy principle.[50] Investment aid for the relocation of undertakings to new sites for environmental protection reasons is considered compatible with the internal market if, inter alia, the following conditions are met: the undertaking must comply with the strictest environmental standards applicable in the new region where it is to be located and the beneficiary can be an undertaking established in an urban area or in a special area of conservation designated under Directive 92/43/EEC (the Habitats Directive) which lawfully carries out an activity that creates major pollution and which, on account of its location, must move from its place of establishment to a more suitable area, or an establishment or installation falling within the scope of Directive 2012/18/EU (the Seveso III Directive).[51] The Commission considers also that aid granted to allow adaptation to future Union standards has in principle an

46 EEAG, section 3.1, para. 29, sentence 1 with the reference to case C-156/98 *Germany v. Commission*, para. 78; C-333/07 *Regie Networks v. Rhone Alpes Bourgogne*, paras. 94–116; Joined Cases C-128/03 and C-129/03 *AEM and AEM Torino*, paras. 38–51.

47 EEAG, Recital 7.

48 T-289/03, *BUPA and Others v. Commission*, para. 132.

49 EEAG, section 3.3, para. 117.

50 EEAG, section 3.3, para. 118.

51 EEAG, section 3.11, paras. 238–239.

incentive effect, including where the standard has already been adopted but is not yet in force, provided it incentivises the realisation of the investment long before the standard enters into force. This will be taken to be the case if the investment is implemented and finalised at least one year before the Union standards enter into force. In this context 'Union standard' means a mandatory Union standard setting the levels to be attained in environmental terms by individual undertakings, or the obligation under Directive 2010/75/EU (Industrial Emission Directive) to use the best available techniques (BAT).[52]

The review of EEAG clearly shows that environmental objectives are integrated in EEAG by making environmental requirements an important part of the conditions establishing the compatibility of a measure with the internal market.

5. CONCLUSIONS

EU environmental policy and EU competition rules have separate, specific legal bases, distinct objectives and separate pieces of secondary legislation. However, these two areas of EU legislation and policy do not operate independently of one another. There are two principles of the Treaty linking environmental protection objectives and requirements with competition rules and their enforcement: (i) the 'integration' clause in Article 11 TFEU and (ii) the 'polluter pays' principle in Article 191(2) TFEU. The application of the integration principle to State aid law means that environmental aspects should be taken into account during assessment of State aid for environmental and energy projects. Environmental objectives cannot change the notion of what State aid is and therefore cannot be taken into account in the assessment of whether a particular measure constitutes State aid within the meaning of Article 107(1) of the TFEU. Environmental rules must be considered in the scope of the assessment of compatibility of the State aid measure with the internal market pursuant to Article 107(3) of the TFEU, if the measure has an environmental goal. In a case where the measure does not have an environmental goal, environmental rules must be taken into consideration during the assessment of compatibility of the State aid measure with the internal market pursuant to Article 107(3) of the TFEU only when some aspects of considered aid are so closely tied with the subject that the eventual incompatibility of it with the previous provisions influences the compatibility of the support mechanism with the internal market.

The Commission has integrated environmental objectives with State aid control in EEAG by setting up environmental requirements as an important part of the conditions which a measure must satisfy if it is to be deemed compatible with the internal market. Integration of environmental protection with State aid

[52] EEAG, section 3.2, para. 53 and section 1.3, para. 19(3).

control in the scope of EEAG can be classified as twofold: (i) 'positive' integration – where compatibility conditions support EU environmental protection policy and (ii) 'negative' integration – where compatibility conditions prohibit State aid measures which lead to environmental harm.

CHAPTER 2

THE NEW 2014 REGULATION ON NOISE-RELATED RESTRICTIONS AT EU AIRPORTS

Help or Hurdle to Noise Management?

Delphine MISONNE*

1. INTRODUCTION

Noise and airports: this is a long story, especially in Europe. A story about how to reconcile the general interest linked to the use of air space with the rights of those who suffer the consequences of the noise emissions that are generated during take-off and landing. Aircrafts are noisy vehicles indeed and they often generate nuisances when flying at low heights. Member States have for long been faced with that issue, which is particularly critical when airports are not ideally located, by being much too close to heavily populated urban areas. As a consequence, many States have already developed substantial mandatory measures aimed at avoiding or mitigating noise due to airport activities, with more or less success. Due to an ever-increasing public sensitivity, case-law is flourishing, both internally and internationally, around issues of human rights, of home protection and of the protection of a healthy environment, in relation to day and night flights.[1]

* FNRS Research Associate, Saint-Louis University Brussels, Belgium. The author can be contacted at delphine.misonne@usaintlouis.be.

1 See for instance, ECtHR, *Hatton and others v. the United Kingdom*, judgments of 2 October 2001 (Chamber) and 8 July 2003 (Grand Chamber); ECtHR, *Powell and Rayner v. the United Kingdom*, judgment of 21 February 1990; *F. Tulkens*, Nuisances sonores, droits fondamentaux et constitutionnels belges : développements récents, Revue trimestrielle des Droits de homme, 2005, pp. 279–298; *V. Staelens*, Geluidshinder door nachtvluchten versus mensenrechten. Analyse van de Belgische situatie in het licht van de Straatsburgse rechtspraak, NjW 2004, pp. 218–227; *T. Hauzeur*, Les nuisances sonores générées par l'aéroport de Bruxelles-National: chronique de jurisprudence, Aménagement-Environnement, 2008 (2), pp. 72–95; *F. Tulkens*, Le droit des riverains dans la défense de la qualité de leur environnement sonore, in CEDRE (dir.), Le bruit des avions. Aspects juridiques, Brussels, Bruylant, 2002, pp. 133–163; *L.G. Zambrano*, Balancing the Rights of Landowners with the Needs of Airports: The Continuing Battle over

To a point that, from another point of view, noise-related measures have turned out to be seen as a threat to airport development and even as the possible cause of capacity shortage in Europe. A very topical subject in 2014, in that very regard, is the adoption of a new Regulation aimed at revising the rules on restricting operations at an EU airport because of noise, Regulation (EU) No 598/2014 of the European Parliament and of the Council of 16 April 2014 on the establishment of rules and procedures with regard to the introduction of noise-related operating restrictions at Union airports within a Balanced Approach.[2] The new regulation, which is based on the Transport Title of the Treaty on the Functioning of the European Union,[3] shall enter into force on 13 June 2016.

This contribution proposes an insight into that Regulation, which nicely fits the general theme of the present book on *Environmental and Planning Law Aspects of Large-Scale Projects*. After an introduction (1. Introduction), the first section explains the content and recent modifications of the current framework, while paying attention to the influence of the International Civil Aviation Organization in that evolution (especially through the notion of 'balanced approach') and to relevant case-law at European Union level (2. Current framework). In a second section, the contribution describes the content of the new Regulation and explains its main new requirements, including those having an impact on the decision-making processes when adopting the so-called 'noise-related operating restrictions' (3. New regulation). The third section of the contribution consists in an assessment of the environmental dimension of the Regulation, which is based on the Transport Title of the Treaty on the Functioning of the European Union. Does the new Regulation offer a potential to contribute to a better protection of citizens against noise due to airport activities, an issue that has turned out to be very sensitive in the European Union? Or shall it, on the contrary and quite paradoxically at first sight, rather upset and complicate the task of public authorities in balancing conflicting interests, would they wish to give an appropriate weight to their positive obligations regarding the protection of human rights against excessive acoustic nuisances? (4. Assessment).

Noise, J. Air L. & Com. 2000–2001 (66), p. 445; *F. Hampson*, Restrictions on rights of action and the European Convention on Human Rights: the case of Powell and Rayner, in The British Yearbook of International Law, 1990, LXI, pp. 279–310.

2 Regulation (EU) No 598/2014 of the European Parliament and of the Council of 16 April 2014 on the establishment of rules and procedures with regard to the introduction of noise-related operating restrictions at Union airports within a Balanced Approach and repealing Directive 2002/30/EC, OJ 2014 L173/65.

3 Article 100(2), according to which '[t]he European Parliament and the Council, acting in accordance with the ordinary legislative procedure, may lay down appropriate provisions for sea and air transport. They shall act after consulting the Economic and Social Committee and the Committee of the Regions'.

2. CURRENT FRAMEWORK

2.1. INFLUENCE OF ICAO

The regulation does not pop up in a vacuum. It repeals, with effect from 13 June 2016, a 2002 Directive on precisely the same issue (the introduction of noise-related operating restrictions at Community airports), which did itself repeal a former Regulation, the so-called 1999 'Hushkit Regulation', which did also found its roots in another frame.[4] The mainspring of that evolution is to be found in the rules promoted at international level, within the International Civil Aviation Organization (ICAO), a UN specialised agency founded by the Chicago Convention of 1944,[5] due to the fact noise by aircraft has in the last two decades turned out to be quite a contentious issue, by means of the impact noise-related restrictions could have on economic activities.

The trend is clear but not smooth. The 1999 'Hushkit Regulation'[6] was done away with under pressure from ICAO members. The Regulation, because it systematically banned the registration of 'recertified aircrafts', those aircrafts meeting noise-limitation requirements only through 'hushkitting',[7] was fiercely criticised abroad. US carriers, often flying quite noisy aircrafts fitted with these mufflers, saw it as a clear threat of protectionism. Actions were soon brought before the ICAO,[8] and also before the European Court of Justice, through a preliminary ruling. The Regulation did not resist the heavy political pressure.[9] It was replaced, in 2002, by a new Directive, Directive 2002/30 of the European Parliament and of the Council of 26 March 2002 on the establishment of rules and procedures with

---

4 Before the Regulation came into effect, the Community had adopted three directives imposing limits on aircraft noise emissions: Council Directive 80/51/EEC of 20 December 1979 on the limitation of noise emissions from subsonic aircraft (OJ 1980 L18/26), as amended in particular by Council Directive 83/206/EEC of 21 April 1983 (OJ 1983 L117/15); Council Directive 89/629/EEC of 4 December 1989 on the limitation of noise emission from civil subsonic jet aeroplanes (OJ 1989 L363/27); and Council Directive 92/14/EEC of 2 March 1992 on the limitation of the operation of aeroplanes covered by Part II, Chapter 2, Volume 1 of Annex 16 to the Convention on International Civil Aviation, second edition (1988) (OJ 1992 L76/21), as amended by Council Directive 98/20/EC of 30 March 1998 (OJ 1998 L107/4). See, on air transport and the environment, *P. Thieffry*, Droit de l'environnement de l'Union européenne, Brussels, Bruylant, 2011, pp. 1120–1126.

5 See www.icao.int.

6 Council Regulation (EC) No 925/1999 of 29 April 1999 on the registration and operation within the Community of certain types of civil subsonic jet aeroplanes which have been modified and recertified as meeting the standards of volume I, Part II, Chapter 3 of Annex 16 to the Convention on International Civil Aviation, third edition (July 1993) (OJ 1999 L115/1).

7 Specific technical devices, the so-called hushkits, are added to airplanes in order to allow them to change categories, among those established by the Chicago Convention, from the noisiest to the less noisy, while still being quite polluting.

8 The United States filed a complaint at the ICAO under Article 84 of the Chicago Convention. See Archives of the US Department of State, http://2001-2009.state.gov/r/pa/prs/ps/2002/9006.htm.

9 *A. Knorr & A. Arndt*, 'Noise wars': the EU's 'Hushkit Regulation', Bremen Universität, Globaliesierung der Weltwirtschaft, 2002.

regard to the introduction of noise-related operating restrictions at Community airports.[10] This without waiting for the judgment of the European Court, which actually fully confirmed the legality of the Hushkit approach.[11]

The uproar caused by the 1999 EU Regulation forced the ICAO to clarify its position on noise reduction policies. States were developing very different approaches to the issue, from the most flexible to the most restricting. The uncoordinated approach of individual airports led to cumulative disputes.[12] It is the reason why the international agency came out, quite at the same moment, with its new 'balanced approach' concept, which immediately rooted in the fresh 2002 Directive.

2.2. BALANCED APPROACH

The 'balanced approach' is jargon that sounds like having something to hide and it does indeed. It sounds nice and harmless but it pursues a very specific agenda: discourage the adoption of constraining noise-related restrictions, that could heavily bear or air transport companies. Before adopting such measures, one should assess all possible alternatives. Priority must be given to cost-effective measures, which are not necessarily identical for all airports. This should all be decided and verified on a case-by-case basis.

The concept emanates from Resolution A33-7, adopted by the 33rd ICAO Assembly, in 2001, which calls upon all ICAO Contracting States and International Organizations 'to recognize the leading role of ICAO in dealing with the problem of aircraft noise' and, implicitly, to be more open to global standards. It is in that package on environmental protection that a reference to the need to adhere to a 'balanced approach' is made.[13] Details were provided later, in 2004, in a Guidance Document.[14]

The balanced approach concept of aircraft noise management comprises four principal elements and requires a careful assessment of all different options to mitigate noise, including reduction of aeroplane noise at source, land-use planning and management measures, noise abatement operational procedures

---

[10] OJ 2002 L85/40.

[11] Case C-27/00 and C-122/00, 12 March 2002, *Omega Air Ltd*: 'The Council did not commit a manifest error of assessment in its choice of criteria by taking account of the fact that the by-pass ratio appears more workable because it requires fewer tests and measurements, both in terms of design and control' (§72).

[12] *M. Murphy et al.*, Study on the Balanced Approach to Noise Management and its Influence on the Economic Impact of Air Transportation, German Institute of Air Transport and Airport Research, 2011.

[13] See all documents at: www.icao.int/Meetings/AMC/MA/Assembly%2033rd%20Session/plugin-resolutions_a33.pdf.

[14] ICAO, Guidance on the Balanced Approach to Aircraft Management, Doc. 9829AN/451, revised in 2007.

and operating restrictions, without prejudice to relevant legal obligations, existing agreements, current laws and established policies.

One of the key features of the approach is that noise policy should not target single solutions but use any combinations of solutions as the most appropriate option to solve the cause of problems.[15] The approach is described as a process, which needs to be complied with. That process requires careful assessment of four elements, which are not proposed in a hierarchy but horizontally, apparently equal. Still, according to commentators, operating restrictions should not be applied as a first resort, but only after consideration of the benefits to be gained from other elements in a manner 'that is consistent with the balanced approach, even if all elements are to be considered equally'.[16] If quiet aircraft technology can significantly reduce the noise footprint of aircraft, the severity of noise problems would actually mostly depend on individual airport's locations and markets and should be assessed distinctly, on a case-by-case basis.[17] Land-use planning can, for instance, be quite successfully used in order to avoid the annoyance about aircraft noise.[18]

2.3. NEW AVENUE FOR LITIGATION

The 2002 Directive imposed Member States to adopt a balanced approach in dealing with noise problems at airports in their territory.[19] It also required that, when considering operating restrictions (understood as noise related action that limits or reduces access of civil subsonic jet aeroplanes to an airport), 'the competent authorities shall take into account the likely costs and benefits of the various measures available as well as airport-specific characteristics'.[20] These new provisions fuelled new litigation, at the initiative of air transport operators, showing first hints about how the new balanced approach, besides helpfully guiding public authorities, could perhaps also hinder them in their environmental protection tasks, when trying to adopt measures that could reduce the noise impact of airport activities.

---

15 *F. Netjasov*, Contemporary measures for noise reduction in airport surroundings, Applied Acoustics, 2012 (73), pp. 1076–1085.

16 *M. Murphy et al.*, *supra* note 12, p. 11; *R. Girvin*, Aircraft noise-abatement and mitigation strategies, Journal of Air Transport Management, 2009 (15), pp. 14–22.

17 Ibid.

18 *M. Murphy et al.*, *supra* note 12, p. 75, giving the example of how Belgium's Liège Airport is often mentioned as a best practice example in the light of the balanced approach.

19 Art. 2. 'An approach under which Member States shall consider the available measures to address the noise problem at an airport in their territory, namely the foreseeable effect of a reduction of aircraft noise at source, land-use planning and management, noise abatement operational procedures and operating restrictions'.

20 Arts. 2 and 3.

In Belgium, a 2002 Royal Decree[21] imposed strict bans on nightlights above the Brussels area, in order to dampen the nuisances resulting from the activity of a large airport located in the close vicinity, whose awkward position up North imposes aircrafts to take off above the densely populated city centre. The European Commission immediately questioned the ban before the European Court of Justice, on the very basis of a breach of the 'balanced approach'.[22] In support of its action, the Commission complained that, during the period granted to the Member States for transposition of the Directive and while the latter was already in force, the Kingdom of Belgium adopted the Royal Decree of 14 April 2002, which, as regards the operating restrictions imposed on certain types of aeroplanes, follows the approach adopted by Regulation No 925/1999, which had already been repealed, and not that chosen by the Directive, which takes the 'balanced approach' on board. The Court explains that, although it is true that, in adopting the new Directive, the Community legislature was pursuing the objective of reducing noise pollution generated by aeroplanes, as with the adoption of Regulation No 925/1999, the fact remains that the implementing measures envisaged by those two pieces of legislation are '*radically different*'. Under the Directive, the reduction of noise emissions is the result of a balanced approach on noise management in each airport, whereas the provisions of Regulation No 925/1999 aim to prevent deteriorations of the overall noise impact by imposing operating restrictions on civil subsonic jet aeroplanes according to another criterion. As a consequence, the court declared that Belgium was in breach of the new 2002 Directive and of the duty to cooperate in good faith.[23]

Later on, it is also on basis of the same 'balanced approach' that the legality of fines, that had been imposed on air companies, which did not comply with noise quality standards, was tested before the European Court, via a preliminary ruling. The question was whether the concept of 'operating restriction' in Directive 2002/30/EC had to be interpreted as including rules imposing limits on noise levels, as measured on the ground, to be complied with by aircraft overflying areas located near the airport and providing that any person responsible for exceeding those limits may incur a penalty. In short: could environmental quality standards, specific to noise, be assimilated to operating restrictions? With the consequence that these restrictions would need to comply with the specific consultation and cost-benefit requirements that are imposed under Annex II of the 2002 Directive. The Court, interestingly, declares that the 'balanced approach' concept functions under European law on basis of a hierarchy: 'Recital 10 in the preamble to that Directive states that the balanced approach constitutes a policy approach to address aeroplane noise, including international guidance for the introduction of operating restrictions on an airport-by-airport basis. The "balanced approach"

21 OJ, 17.04.2002.

22 Case C-422/05, *Commission v. Belgium* [2007] ECR I-4749. V. *Bouhier*, CJCE, 14 juin 2007, (Commission c. Belgique), Revue des affaires européennes, 2007–2008, pp. 421–428.

23 Referring to former Article 10 EC Treaty.

to aircraft noise management … comprises four principal elements and requires careful assessment of all different options to mitigate noise, including reduction of aeroplane noise at source, land-use planning and management measures, noise abatement operational procedures and operating restrictions, without prejudice to relevant legal obligations, existing agreements, current laws and established policies.[24] It follows that operating restrictions are applicable only when any other noise management measures have failed to achieve the aims of Directive 2002/30, as laid down in Article 1'.[25]

According to the Court, environmental legislation, such as that at issue in the main proceedings, imposing limits on maximum noise levels, as measured on the ground, to be complied with by aircraft overflying areas located near the airport, does not itself constitute a prohibition on access to the airport in question. It observes that, in any event, the adoption of a method consisting in measuring on the ground the noise produced by an aircraft in flight constitutes an element of a balanced approach in that it is capable of providing more data to help reconcile the competing interests of people affected by noise nuisance, of economic undertakings that operate aircraft and of society as a whole. But the judge also considers that it cannot, however, be ruled out that such legislation, in view of the relevant economic, technical and legal contexts to which it belongs, can have the same effect as a prohibition on access. If, indeed, the limits imposed by that legislation are so restrictive as to oblige aircraft operators to forgo their business operation, such legislation would amount to prohibition of access and would constitute, therefore, 'operating restrictions' within the meaning of that directive. As a consequence, the Court declared that national environmental legislation imposing limits on maximum noise levels, as measured on the ground, to be complied with by aircraft overflying areas located near the airport, does not itself constitute an 'operating restriction' within the meaning of that provision, 'unless, in view of the relevant economic, technical and legal contexts, it can have the same effect as prohibitions of access to the airport in question', and left the referring court with the task to determine whether the measures adopted by the local authorities have such effects.[26]

When asked in an interim 2008 assessment[27] about how happy they were with the 2002 Directive and its balanced approach, Airport authorities were doubtful. Many airports operators indicated that the Directive did not help them

---

24 With note: 'see, in particular, Case C-442/05 Commission v Belgium [2007] ECR I-4749, paragraph 38'.

25 Case C-120/10, 8 September 2011, *European Air Transport v. College d'environnement de la Région de Bruxelles-Capitale,* para. 34, paras. 24 and 25.

26 Case C-120/10, 8 September 2011, *European Air Transport v. College d'environnement de la Région de Bruxelles-Capitale,* para. 34.

27 Report from the Commission to the Council and the European Parliament of 15 February 2008 – Noise Operation Restrictions at EU Airports (Report on the application of Directive 2002/30/EC) (COM (2008) 66 final).

much.[28] The Directive had not directly influenced the noise management around their airport. What the Directive enabled was already possible under national law. By contrast, several airports said that the Directive made the process of noise management around the airport more onerous due to the requirements of its Annex 2.[29] This annex, as already mentioned, requires a consultation and an assessment of the costs and benefits of alternative means of reducing noise around the airport. The airport operators even mentioned the fear that airlines might sue them easily, under the argument that the Annex 2 measures would not have completely been adhered to. Not less importantly, the Directive did not help reducing the number of people affected by noise, particularly at night. That number did not even stabilise; it has increased since the Directive came into force.[30]

3. NEW REGULATION

3.1. *RATIO LEGIS*

In such a puzzling context, why bother adopting a new Regulation on noise-related restrictions?

The initiative emanates from a December 2011 European Commission 'Better airports' package initiative. The package was clearly focused on addressing capacity shortage at Europe's airports and contained three legislative proposals: one on slots, one on ground handling and one on noise.[31] The main focus is not environmental protection but the facilitation of air transport.[32] The tone is set: 'the introduction of operating restrictions may have a substantial impact on business and operations, as it restricts access to an airport. Hence, the process leading to a decision on noise-related operating restrictions should be consistent, evidence-based and robust to be acceptable for all stakeholders'.[33] The wish to avoid conflicts with ICAO is confirmed: 'this regulation aims to apply noise-related operating

28 This in particular for the German and UK airports, according to the Commission Report, that does not give any further detail.

29 According to the Commission Report, p. 4, that does not give any further detail (no specific data).

30 §11, p. 13, Conclusions of the 2008 Commission report.

31 Proposal for a Regulation of the European Parliament and of the Council on the establishment of rules and procedures with regard to the introduction of noise-related operating restrictions at Union airports within a Balanced Approach and repealing Directive 2002/30/EC of the European Parliament and of the Council COM (2011) 828 final.

32 This explains the legal base of the Regulation: Article 100(2) TFEU.

33 Proposal for a Regulation of the European Parliament and of the Council on the establishment of rules and procedures with regard to the introduction of noise-related operating restrictions at Union airports within a Balanced Approach and repealing Directive 2002/30/EC of the European Parliament and of the Council, COM (2011) 828 final – 2011/0398 (COD), explanatory memorandum, §2.

restrictions of the Balanced Approach in the EU in a consistent manner which should greatly reduce the risk of international disputes in the event that third country carriers are impacted by noise abatement measures at airports in the Union. In addition, competent authorities will be in a better position to phase-out the noisiest aircraft in the fleet. The proposed regulation will repeal Directive 2002/30/EC which was instrumental in bringing an international dispute to an end and set the first steps in the harmonisation of noise management policies, including tackling the noisiest aircraft of that time. However, the instrument needs to be adapted to the current requirements of the aviation system and the growing noise problem'. The new motto is 'robust'. All steps in the assessment process will be clarified in order to ensure a more consistent application of the balanced approach across the Union. The proposal 'aims to strengthen the basic logic of the ICAO Balanced Approach by making a stronger link between its pillars and by clarifying the different steps of the decision-making process when considering operating restrictions'.

The Regulation is more focused on detail and process, on what to assess and who to consult. Far beyond the general requirement for Member States to adopt the balanced approach in dealing with noise problems that characterised the former Directive, the new Regulation fixes the procedural steps that have to be followed in order to adopt noise-related restrictions. It imposes a heavy consultation process that shall ban any possibility of a rush in the future, for the adoption of noise-related measures having a possible impact on the access to an airport. In that regard, the legislation still bears the marks of very tense discussions between the European Commission and the Member States, as to who should have the last say in choosing the most appropriate restricting measures.

3.2. OPERATING RESTRICTIONS

The 598/314 Regulation only applies to Member States in which an airport with more than 50,000 civil aircraft movements per calendar year is located and when the introduction of noise-related operating restrictions is being considered at such an airport.

The adoption of 'operating restrictions' clearly remains the central issue.

An operating restriction is a *noise-related action* that *limits access to or reduces the operational capacity* of an airport, including operating restrictions aimed at the withdrawal from operations of marginally compliant aircraft at specific airports as well as operating restrictions of a partial nature, which for example apply for an identified period of time during the day or only for certain runways at the airport.[34] A 'noise-related action' means 'any measure that affects the noise climate around airports, for which the principles of the Balanced Approach apply,

[34] Art. 2.6.

including other non-operational actions that can affect the number of people exposed to aircraft noise'.[35]

This means in short that any measure that affects the noise climate around airports, from the moment it limits access to or reduces the operational capacity of an airport, can potentially qualify as an 'operating restriction'. The scope of the notion is consequently quite large. This even if the definition slightly changed, by comparison to Directive 2002/30/EC,[36] 'in order not to delay the implementation of operational measures which could immediately alleviate the noise impact without substantially affecting the operational capacity of an airport. Such measures should therefore not be considered to constitute new operating restrictions'.[37]

A night time flight ban is a clear and classical illustration of what is meant by an operating restriction,[38] as is a runway that is being closed, due to the noise nuisance it generates, or a quantitative limitation in the yearly maximum of take-off and landing movements at the airport. There are quite a few possibilities.

Would a change in air routes planning also fall within than definition (turn sooner to the left, or more to the right …)? Not necessarily. It all depends if it does limit access to the airport or reduce its operational capacity.

3.3. A PROCESS UNDER CLOSE SUPERVISION

Under the new Regulation, the process of adopting operating restrictions is made extremely heavy. In other circles, one would no doubt raise the issues of simplification and unnecessary red tape. Here, the trend is in the reverse order: towards a more and more burdensome regime for the public authorities.

From the mere observation of its content, the Regulation's main implications can be summed up as such:

- it shall slow down the process of adoption of operating restrictions;
- it shall make local authorities accountable to the European Commission for the adoption of such restrictions, even if only through the need to answer its objections;
- it shall impose cost-benefit analyses and intense consultation processes that, if not complied with, could lead to judicial review.

---

35 Art. 2.5.

36 '"Operating restrictions" shall mean noise related action that limits or reduces access of civil subsonic jet aeroplanes to an airport. It includes operating restrictions aimed at the withdrawal from operations of marginally compliant aircraft at specific airports as well as operating restrictions of a partial nature, affecting the operation of civil subsonic aeroplanes according to time period', Art. 2(e).

37 According to the preamble.

38 See for instance, on night bans, *J. Farber et al.*, Night flight restrictions and airlines responses at major European airports, CEDelft, September 2012, 55 p.; TO70 Aviation & Environment, Night time restrictions at Amsterdam-Schiphol: an International comparison, The Hague, 2004.

3.3.1. *Notifications*

Before introducing an operating restriction, such as a night ban, the competent authorities must give six months' notice to the other Member States, the Commission and the relevant interested parties, according to Article 8 of the new Regulation. They must explain, in their notification, the reasons for introducing the operating restriction, the noise abatement objective established for the airport, the measures that were considered to meet that objective, and the evaluation of the likely cost-effectiveness of the various measures considered, including, where relevant, their cross-border impact. At the request of a Member State or on its own initiative, the Commission may, within a period of three months after the day on which it receives notice, review the process for the introduction of an operating restriction. Where the Commission finds that the introduction of a noise-related operating restriction does not follow the process set out in this Regulation, it may notify the relevant competent authority accordingly. The relevant competent authority shall examine the Commission notification and inform the Commission of its intentions before introducing the operating restriction.

This new notification requirement is the result of a fierce negotiation. Initially, the proposal gave a plain veto right to the Commission, as can be read from the following wording: 'at the request of a Member State or on its own initiative, and without prejudice to a pending appeal procedure, the Commission may scrutinise the decision on an operating restriction, prior to its implementation. Where the Commission finds that the decision does not respect the requirements set out in this Regulation, or is otherwise contrary to Union law, it may suspend the decision'.[39] *Excessive and against the subsidiarity principle*, was the answer, at the occasion of the national parliament's scrutiny of the compliance with the subsidiarity principle. Such a veto would clearly lead to a deterioration of the protection of the citizens. As expressed by the Austrian authorities,[40] 'the primary objective pursued by the Commission is to overcome the perceived capacity shortages at European airports. The issue of noise abatement is of secondary importance in this context, as reflected in the overriding importance attributed to cost efficiency in the proposal. Hence, there is cause for concern that the proposed version would lead to a deterioration of the noise situation for people living in the surroundings of airports. In return for an increase in capacity, the Commission is willing to accept a reduction in the level of protection for the resident population, which is not acceptable'. What more, 'noise-related operating restrictions are often agreed upon after protracted negotiations among all stakeholders, representing a delicate compromise between the groups concerned. If the Commission had the right to interfere with such arrangements, this would unnecessarily contribute

---

39 Former version of Art. 10.

40 European Affairs Committee of the Federal Council of 12 April 2012 to the European Parliament and the Council pursuant to Article 23f (4) of the Austrian Constitution, available at: ipex.eu.

to a further alienation between the EU bodies and the citizens, and violate the autonomy of local decision-making, a principle recognised by Union law'. Other Parliaments did also firmly reject the proposal.[41]

Even if the Commission has now been denied the possibility of a veto, it still keeps the possibility to review the process for the introduction of an operating restriction and, where it finds that the introduction of a noise-related operating restriction does not follow the process set out in the Regulation, to ask for explanation. The intrusion of the European Commission into a dynamic that was so far left to local authorities and domestic arrangements is a new requisite, that shall turn out to be one of the cornerstones of the new regime. When one knows how politically sensitive these airport-related noise issues are already at domestic level, it remains to be seen how constructive the intervention of that new actor shall be, when re-examining the agreements obtained between local authorities, sometimes with much efforts, in the light of the new Regulation.

The notification process is also bound by a six-month long standstill obligation: 'Before introducing an operating restriction, the competent authorities shall give to the Member States, the Commission and the relevant interested parties six months' notice'.[42] Six months – a very long deadline if without any possible nuance, without any consideration of possible pending judgments or other legal constraints.[43]

The future shall not be made of rushed decisions. React slowly, a first step towards wiser solutions?

3.3.2. *Extensive Consultations*

Dialogue is often profitable for finding balanced solutions. Understanding each other's concerns, discovering possible win-win options – who would oppose the idea of large consultation processes, when facing the need to solve sensitive issues? The Regulation goes very far in that direction. It even mentions the possibility of a mediation process, 'organised in a timely and substantive manner',

---

41 See reasoned opinion by the Bundesrat of the Federal Republic of Germany/by the French Senate/by the House of Representatives of the Kingdom of the Netherlands on the proposal for a regulation of the European Parliament and of the Council on the establishment of rules and procedures with regard to the introduction of noise-related operating restrictions at Union airports within a Balanced Approach and repealing Directive 2002/30/EC of the European Parliament and of the Council (COM (2011) 828 – C7-0456/2011 – 2011/0398(COD)). See *J. Weissenberger*, New rules on EU airport noise restrictions, Library briefing of the European Parliament, 5 February 2013.

42 Art. 8(1).

43 Such as what happened in 2014 when a Belgian Tribunal imposed a penalty on the Federal authorities to quickly remediate the illegality of the 'Wathelet plan', which reorganised flight routes above the Brussels airport area. The judge ordered the Belgian state to adapt the Wathelet flight plan within the following 3 months, with the threat of a fine of 50,000 euros per day (and a maximum of 36.5 million euros). See for instance, 'Court orders adaptation of Brussels flight plan', http://deredactie.be/cm/vrtnieuws.english.

between a very broad range of possible stakeholders, offering the promise of intense brainstorming sessions. Interested parties are, in that regard, according to Article 6: local residents living in the vicinity of the airport and affected by air traffic noise, or their representatives, and the relevant local authorities; representatives of local businesses based in the vicinity of the airport, whose activities are affected by air traffic and the operation of the airport; relevant airport operators; representatives of those aircraft operators which may be affected by noise-related actions; the relevant air navigation service providers; the Network Manager, as defined in Commission Regulation (EU) No 677/2011, where applicable, the slot coordinator.

These stakeholders must also be given the possibility to submit comments, three months before the possible adoption of new operating restrictions.[44] Added to the other notification processes mentioned under Article 8, this means that the competent authority shall have a most important charge in networking and communication, which shall necessarily become central to its activity.

3.4. BALANCED BUT ALSO COST-EFFECTIVE APPROACH

If there is a noise problem, that noise problem must be identified in accordance with Directive 2002/49/EC of 25 June 2002 relating to the assessment and management of environmental noise. The new Regulation draws a clear and necessary link to the pre-existing 'environmental noise Directive',[45] which, even if it does not impose any emissions limits, is a key instrument in guiding Member States in their assessment of the acoustic quality of the environment. The noise directive is helpful in assessing the noise problems, but the choice of solutions is locked to the application of the new Regulation: measures that could lighten the noise burden must be proposed according to the balanced approach.

Within the framework of the new Regulation, the balanced approach is redefined as 'the *process* developed by the International Civil Aviation Organization under which the range of available measures, namely the reduction of aircraft noise at source, land-use planning and management, noise abatement operational procedures and operating restrictions, is considered *in a consistent way* with a view to addressing the noise problem in the *most cost-effective* way on an *airport-by-airport basis*'.[46]

---

44 Art. 6(d).

45 Directive 2002/49/EC of the European Parliament and of the Council of 25 June 2002 relating to the assessment and management of environmental noise – Declaration by the Commission in the Conciliation Committee on the Directive relating to the assessment and management of environmental noise, OJ 2002 L189/1226.

46 Art. 2.3, emphasis added.

An explicit division in two categories also complements it: on the one hand, the usual measures. On the other hand, the measures that cannot be applied as a first resort.

> 'Member States must ensure that, when noise-related action is taken, the following combination of available measures is considered, with a view to determining the most cost-effective measure or combination of measures:
> (a) the foreseeable effect of a reduction of aircraft noise at source;
> (b) land-use planning and management;
> (c) noise abatement operational procedures;
> (d) *not applying operating restrictions as a first resort*, but only after consideration of the other measures of the Balanced Approach.'[47]

The available measures may, if necessary, include the withdrawal of marginally compliant aircraft.[48] Member States, or airport managing bodies, as appropriate, may offer economic incentives to encourage aircraft operators to use less noisy aircraft during the transitional period referred to in point (4) of Article 2. Those economic incentives shall comply with the applicable rules on State aid. Moreover, a necessity test is imposed. Needless to say, measures or a combination of measures taken in accordance with this Regulation for a given airport shall not be more restrictive than is necessary in order to achieve the environmental noise abatement objectives set for that airport. Operating restrictions shall be non-discriminatory, in particular on grounds of nationality or identity, and shall not be arbitrary.

What is a cost-effective measure? According to the requirements of Annexe II, the elements that must duly be taken into account for assessing the cost-effectiveness of envisaged noise-related operating restrictions are, to the extent possible, in quantifiable terms:

- the anticipated noise benefit of the envisaged measures, now and in the future;
- the safety of aviation operations, including third-party risks;
- the capacity of the airport;
- *any effects* on the European aviation network.

---

47 Art. 5.3, emphasis added.

48 As specified by Art. 2.4: '"marginally compliant aircraft" means aircraft which are certified in accordance with limits laid down in Volume 1, Part II, Chapter 3 of Annex 16 to the Convention on International Civil Aviation signed on 7 December 1944 (the Chicago Convention) by a cumulative margin of less than 8 EPNdB (Effective Perceived Noise in Decibels) during a transitional period ending on 14 June 2020, and by a cumulative margin of less than 10 EPNdB following the end of that transitional period, whereby the cumulative margin is the figure expressed in EPNdB obtained by adding the individual margins (i.e. the differences between the certificated noise level and the maximum permitted noise level) at each of the three reference noise measurement points defined in Volume 1, Part II, Chapter 3 of Annex 16 to the Chicago Convention.'

It is only 'in addition' and if they wish to do so that competent authorities *may take due account of the following factors*:

- the health and safety of local residents living in the vicinity of the airport;
- environmental sustainability, including interdependencies between noise and emissions;
- any direct, indirect or catalytic employment and economic effects.

The exercise can hardly be described as fairly balanced. The semantic demonstrates a clear bias against a due and fair taking into consideration of the societal benefits that can flow from a healthier and less noisy environment, even through transport policy.

The order in which provisions are presented in the legislative text do also give indications about how the operating restrictions should be perceived. It is noticeable that, even before presenting the process leading to the adoption of possible operating restrictions, the Regulation first imposes on the Member States the creation of a specific right of appeal against these measures: 'Member States shall ensure the right to appeal against operating restrictions adopted pursuant to this Regulation before an appeal body other than the authority that adopted the contested restriction, in accordance with national legislation and procedures'.[49] This could be interpreted as the indication of a prejudice. Those measures are not welcome and are potentially highly contentious. Is it a sort of diplomatic language, meant to reassure foreign trade partners and the ICAO?

3.5. AUTHORITIES THAT ARE INDEPENDENT FROM ALL STAKEHOLDERS

The adoption of the true operating restrictions (but not of the other measures falling within a balanced approach) falls within the remit of a specific competent authority which shall be 'independent of any organisation which could be affected by noise-related action. That independence may be achieved through a functional separation'.[50] This is a new requirement. According to the preamble, 'the competent authority responsible for adopting noise-related operating restrictions should be independent of any organisation involved in the airport's operation, air transport or air navigation service provision, or representing the interests thereof and of the residents living in the vicinity of the airport'.[51] The required independence is independence from all possible stakeholders. From now on, that quite logical requirement of objectivity shall be made judiciable and accountable

[49] Art. 4, Right of Appeal.
[50] Art. 3(1) and (2).
[51] Paragraph 13 of the preamble.

for. But how shall such independence be formalised? Does it entail the creation of new decentralised agencies? Not necessarily, at least according to the preamble, as it declares that 'this should not be understood as requiring Member States to modify their administrative structures or decision-making procedures'.[52]

4. ASSESSMENT

The adoption of noise-related restrictions shall be a heavy test to pass in the future, once the new Regulation shall enter into force. There is a clear wish to place them under control, but not only under the control of competent local authorities. The EU Commission, on the one hand, the representatives of aircrafts operators, on the other hand, shall all intensively be heard. Together with many other interested parties. Much ado, about allowing people to sleep soundly at night.

The logic of the Regulation is specific: seduce the ICAO and its partners. Make sure that public authorities understand that noise insulation can also be a solution, that airports are better located if they are not too close to cities, to understand that heavy airplanes are noisier than lighter ones? They did know that already, for long. The key point in the Regulation is to make the process of adopting true restrictions on access and capacity much trickier.

On the positive side, the heavy procedural requirements and consultations might help re-technicalise the debate, on issues where the margin of appreciation of public authorities is so large. It has long been recognised that processes and studies, in these highly sensitive matters, are important. Governmental decision-making processes concerning complex issues of environmental and economic policy such as in the case of night bans must necessarily involve appropriate investigations and studies in order to allow them to strike a fair balance between the various conflicting interests at stake. However, this does not mean that decisions can only be taken if comprehensive and measurable data are available in relation to each and every aspect of the matter to be decided. This has been settled in another context, by the European Court of Human Rights, in the case *Hatton*.[53] But it sheds light on a crucial question: could an operating restriction be considered illegal as listed in Annexe II, § 1, by the mere fact that a stakeholder was not consulted or if some elements are missing in the cost-effectiveness exercise?

The Regulation is not balanced. This explains the serious concern that new rules on aviation noise could fall short of what is needed to protect people living

52 On the possible autonomy of independent administrative authorities, see for instance: *E. Slautsky*, Droit européen, Constitution et autorités administratives indépendantes, APT, 2012, pp. 95–113; *P.O. De Broux*, Introduction à la décentralisation administrative : évolutions théoriques et pratiques politiques, in P. Jadoul, B. Lombaert and F. Tulkens (dir.), Le paraétatisme, Brussels, La Charte, 2010, pp. 2–32.

53 European Court of Human Rights, *Hatton*, Grand Chamber, 8 July 2003, § 128.

near airports.[54] The cost-effectiveness exercise does not take the health and environmental concerns very seriously. This can be observed from the fact that nothing is provided for framing the possible deletion of a pre-existing operating restrictions, the suppression of a night flight ban for instance. The introduction of restricting measures is submitted to a heavy consultation process and to cost-benefit assessment, but their deletion? This is a potentially detrimental gap, as the revision of noise-related operating restrictions, which were already introduced before 13 June 2016, is foreseen: 'they shall remain in force until the competent authorities decide to revise them in accordance with this Regulation'.[55] These elements demonstrate a narrow-minded approach to how transport policies should integrate the protection of the environment and of citizen's health against noise, an issue that ranks high among the environmental causes of ill-death today in the European Union.[56]

Another puzzling element is the insistence on an airport-by-airport approach, a reduction in scope that looks quite awkward when one knows how competitive airports can be with each other and how important it could be to enlarge the scale of the debate in order to propose solutions. 'Consistent application of the balanced approach should identify the most cost-effective solutions, tailor made to the specific airport situation'. The message is that a general ban on noisy aircraft at larger scale is not the way forward. But where shall then discussions take place, between close regions or neighbouring States, on how to best organise the air traffic between their competing airports? Was it not also worth looking at that larger scale, in order to better promote aviation network efficiency?

Rather a hurdle, is the conclusion. Is this the price of compliance with global international standards?

[54] www.airportwatch.org.uk/2014/07/new-eu-rules-on-airports-seen-as-too-timid-to-reduce-extent-of-aircraft-noise/.

[55] Art. 14.

[56] Noise in Europe, European Environmental Agency, 2014.

CHAPTER 3

THE EU AND THE PARTICIPATION OF CIVIL SOCIETY IN LARGE PROJECTS

Ludwig KRÄMER

1. INTRODUCTION

Large projects, such as for infrastructure, industrial installations, power plants or for other purposes, have increased considerably in number in the last decades. The reasons for this development are greater mobility of persons, increased trade, globalisation, more free time and greater welfare. In Europe, the existence and the activities of the European Union have largely contributed to this development. In particular, the policy decision in the early 1990s to develop trans-European networks in the area of energy, transport and telecommunication played an important role in this regard.[1] The EU provisions on the Structural Funds provided for specific provisions for 'big projects' which were defined as having an investment volume of more than 25 million euros. Other projects to be mentioned are nuclear power plants, military projects, projects for sport events – e.g. Olympic Games (London 2012, Sochi 2014), motorsport races, international championships – and leisure installations such as Disneyland, Eurovegas, or pleasure parks, festivals and concert halls.

The following lines will examine some environmental problems linked to such projects, in particular the transparency in the decision-making and the possibilities for civil society to participate in this process.

2. LARGE PROJECTS IN EU ENVIRONMENTAL LAW

The environmental policy in Europe developed since the early 1970s a particular concern for large projects. This process was in particular driven by the activities and measures of the European Union. However, since the fall of the Berlin wall,

1 See now Articles 170–172 TFEU.

the financial support given to projects in non-EU countries by the European Investment Bank (EIB) and the European Bank for Reconstruction and Development (EBRD), later on the accession negotiations led to a considerable spill-over of EU policies and legislative measures on non-EU countries; this process is not yet finished, if one thinks of the Balkan States or countries such as Ukraine or Moldavia.

The first measure to mention is the requirement of an environmental impact assessment (EIA) for large infrastructure and other projects which was introduced in 1985, and subsequently extended and fine-tuned.[2] This EIA required an examination of the direct and indirect, secondary, cumulative, short, medium and long-term, permanent and temporary, positive and negative effects which a project might have on the environment.[3] The impact assessment has to be made, before the permit for the realisation of the project is granted. Though the EU legislation does not explicitly require that the large projects which come under the Directive require a permit, this consequence follows indirectly from the phrasing of the Directive and was in the meantime confirmed by the EU Court of Justice.[4]

The impact assessment procedure requires that the 'public concerned' obtains the possibility to comment on the proposal as it was submitted for permitting to the public authorities. Though this possibility was, right from 1985 onwards, drafted in a way that the public concerned had an individual right to participate and that the permitting procedure was defective if this right was impaired, it needed the entry into force of the Aarhus Convention[5] and a series of judgments of the EU Court of Justice, before this individual right was generally recognised.[6]

For projects with transboundary impacts, the EU Directive of 1985 had provided an intergovernmental cooperation instead of the right of citizens to participate in the decision-making process; France had insisted in this provision because it did not want citizens from neighbouring countries participating in the decision-making process on its nuclear power plants, which France had frequently placed at the border of other countries. This concept of intergovernmental cooperation was taken over by the Espoo Convention 1986[7] which only provided for such cooperation, but did not provide for individual citizens' rights to participate.

---

2 Directive 85/337, OJ 1985 L175/40; at present, Directive 2011/92 on the assessment of the effects of certain public and private projects on the environment, OJ 2012 L26/1, applies, with amendments introduced by Directive 2014/52, OJ 2014 L124/1.

3 See Directive 2011/92, *supra* note 2, Annex IV fn. 1.

4 Court of Justice, C-215/06, *Commission v. Ireland* [2008] ECR I-4911.

5 The Aarhus Convention on access to information, public participation in decision-making and access to justice in environmental matters, Aarhus 1998, was ratified by the EU by Decision 2005/370, OJ 2005 L124/1. According to Article 216 TFEU, it is binding on the EU institutions *and* on its 28 Member States and prevails over secondary EU law.

6 Court of Justice, C-72/12, *Altrip*, judgment of 7 November 2013; C-463/11, *L. v. M.*, judgment of 18 April 2013. Directive 2011/92, *supra* note 2, Article 10a.

7 Espoo Convention on environmental impact assessment in a transboundary context, Espoo 1991. The Convention was ratified by the EU by an unpublished decision of 15 October 1996.

In contrast to this, the Aarhus Convention[8] gave participation rights to all persons concerned and did not differentiate between projects with national and with transboundary environmental impact. Though the Convention was ratified by all EU Member States, by the EU itself and by some other 20 countries, its provisions have not yet led to the full recognition of a right of citizens to participate in the decision making of projects in another State. Rather, Article 7 of EU Directive 2011/92 and the Espoo Convention continue to be applied.

EU law also provided for a permit requirement for large industrial installations, in the beginning only with regard to air emissions and water discharges,[9] but subsequently also for waste generation and other impacts on the environment.[10] The lists of projects which come under Directives 2011/92 and 2010/75 are very largely identical. Also with regard to the permitting procedure, there is a right of the public concerned to participate in the decision-making process.[11]

3. PARTICIPATION AND CONSULTATION

In legal terms, 'participation' is much broader than 'consultation'. Consultation is the possibility of the public to comment on a specific proposal within a specific time-span. No differentiation is made between the general public and the public which is concerned by a project, a plan or a programme. At what time the consultation takes place is left open. What the administration makes of the comments is a matter for the administration. It need not give any follow-up, explain its final choice or otherwise justify its final decision.

Participation is the possibility to make comments or submit information, analyses or opinions on a specific project, plan or programme. In order to do so, the administration which intends to take a decision on the project, plan or programme shall:[12]

- submit information to the public concerned as early as possible, when all options of the envisaged administrative decision are still open;
- inform the public concerned what environmental information relevant to the proposed activity is available;
- inform on the application for a decision which had been made (if any), a description of the foreseeable environmental impacts, the measures to

8 Aarhus Convention, *supra* note 5, Articles 3(9) and 6.

9 Directive 84/360 on the combatting of air pollution from industrial plants, OJ 1984 L188/20.

10 See Directive 96/61 on integrated prevention and pollution control, OJ 1991 L257/26; Directive 2008/1 on integrated pollution and prevention control, OJ 2008 L24/8; and presently Directive 2010/75 on industrial emissions (integrated pollution prevention and control), OJ 2010 L334/17.

11 Directive 2010/75, *supra* note 10, Article 11.

12 These obligations are derived from Articles 6 and 7 of the Aarhus Convention.

prevent or reduce negative environmental effects, and an outline of the main alternatives that were studied;
- provide the information in an adequate, timey and effective manner so that the public is able to comment;
- give reasonable time-frames for the submission of opinions;
- inform of the time and venue of any public hearing which is organised;
- take due account of the submissions, comments and opinions; and
- once the administrative decision is taken, give the reasons and considerations which led to that decision.

For projects, a non-technical summary also has to be made available.

'Participation' implies that the public concerned has the appropriate knowledge of the application. All legal texts therefore provide for extensive information of the public concerned. This may be illustrated by the obligation which the competent authorities have, when they receive a permit application for a project.[13] Then they are obliged to the public concerned of the application, the nature of the possible decision, the public authority responsible for making the decision and details of the procedure, in particular what environmental information relevant to the project is available. Furthermore, they have to make available:

- a description of the site and the physical and technical characteristics of the project, including an estimate of the expected residues and emissions;
- a description of the significant effects of the project on the environment;
- a description of the measures envisaged to prevent or reduce the effects;
- a non-technical summary;
- an outline of the main alternatives studied by the applicant; and
- the main reports and advice issued to the public authorities.

At EU level, the Commission published, in 2002, a Communication on consultation which was limited to the above-mentioned elements of a communication.[14] The ratification of the Aarhus Convention by the EU did not lead to any substantive change in the Commission's policy. In particular, consultations take normally place in one language (English, less frequently French) which makes the process inaccessible for those who do not master the language.

Very soon after the adoption of the EU legislation on environmental impact assessment, it became clear that the political or administrative decision to permit an infrastructure project or an industrial or other installation was often taken before the application for a permit was introduced. In order to ensure effective

[13] Example taken from Directive 2010/75, *supra* note 10, Article 24 and Annex IV.

[14] Commission, Towards a reinforced culture of consultation and dialogue. General principles and minimum standards for consultation of interested parties by the Commission, COM (2002) 704. Neither the European Parliament nor the Council provide for a systematic participation or consultation of the concerned public.

public participation also in such cases, the Aarhus Convention included a right to participation concerning plans and programmes relating to the environment.[15] This participation had to take place 'when all options are open and effective public participation can take place'. The EU followed pace and introduced, in 2001, a requirement for an environmental impact assessment for plans and programmes. However, the relevant Directive[16] only referred to such plans and programmes which formed the basis for subsequent projects that had to undergo an environmental impact assessment under EU law, not for all plans relating to the environment, and is thus not in full compliance with the Aarhus Convention.

4. PARTICIPATION IN EU LARGE, IN PARTICULAR TRANS-EUROPEAN PROJECTS

All these provisions of EU law, including those of the Espoo and the Aarhus Conventions – which had become by virtue of their ratification by the EU, part of EU law – did not change the basic approach that the permitting of large projects remained the responsibility of national authorities. The fact that in many cases, a large project would, in practice, never have been realised without the financial support of the EU Structural Funds, the EIB or the EBRD, did not change this reality. The reason for this approach is obvious: the public authorities of a (Member) State could realise the project also without the financial support of those institutions, for example by finding financial support from other sources.

For large projects under the EU Structural Funds legislation, the Member State is obliged to submit to the European Commission information on the project.[17] The Commission shall examine the information supplied and may refuse the approval of the project only on grounds that the independent external quality review identified 'significant weaknesses' of the project. Any 'approval' only concerns the co-financing of the project by the EU. Regulation 1303/2013 is silent on participation questions. Article 6, though, declares that 'Operations supported by the ESI Funds [these are the Funds mentioned in the title of Regulation 1303/2013] shall comply with applicable Union law and national law relating to its application'. Participation of the public shall thus be ensured at the level of the EU Member States.

Generally, it can be confirmed that the permitting procedures for large projects and thus the participation provisions depend exclusively on national law.

15 Aarhus Convention, Article 7.

16 Directive 2001/42 on the assessment of the effects of certain plans and programmes on the environment, OJ 2001 L197/30.

17 Regulation 1303/2013 laying down common provisions on the European Regional Development Fund, the European Social Fund, the Cohesion Fund, the European Agricultural Fund for Rural Development, and the European Maritime and Fisheries Fund, OJ 2014 L347/320, Articles 100–102. A large project is a project with investment costs of 50 or 75 million euro.

Nevertheless, EU law has, in recent years, considerably influenced the national provisions. The requirement of realising an environmental impact assessment for projects, before a permit is granted, was already mentioned. Of particular interest are the provisions of Articles 170–172 TFEU on trans-European networks. These provisions intended to promote the realisation of projects in the area of transport, energy and telecommunications which had a trans-national character. As administrative cooperation between Member States was frequently hampered by different strategic approaches, different political and financial priorities, and other obstacles, EU secondary legislation progressively interfered in the planning and permitting process of trans-European projects, as will be demonstrated hereafter. Examples from the trans-European energy and transport regulations may illustrate this.

4.1. TRANS-EUROPEAN ENERGY PROJECTS

Regulation 347/2013 deals with the guidelines for trans-European energy infrastructure;[18] in this regard, the term 'guidelines' is somehow misleading, as the provisions of the Regulations are binding.[19] The Regulation provides for an EU list of projects of common interest, which is prepared by twelve regional groups[20] and adopted by the Commission.[21] The first list was established in 2013 on the basis of suggestions by regional groups which are said to have consulted stakeholders;[22] it is to be updated every two years.[23] The inclusion of a project in the EU list establishes the necessity to realise the project, subject to its exact location, routing and the used technology (Article 7). The project shall obtain the highest possible national priority and 'shall be considered to be considered as being of public interest from an energy policy perspective and may be considered

---

18 Regulation 347/2013 on guidelines for trans-European energy infrastructure, OJ 2013 L115/39.

19 Also the fact that Article 172(2) TFEU requires that guidelines which relate to the territory of a Member State shall require the approval of the Member State concerned, is without relevance, as this approval must be deemed to have been given with the adoption of the Regulation.

20 The regional groups are composed of representatives of the Member States concerned, the EU Commission, the Agency for Cooperation of Energy Regulators, and professional organisations. Only the Member States and the Commission vote; see Regulation 347/2013, Annex III.

21 Regulation 347/2013, *supra* note 18, Article 3; the criteria for establishing the list are laid down in Article 4. In the meantime, the Commission adopted Delegated Regulation 1391/2013, OJ 2013 L349/28 which contains the first EU list of some 242 energy projects of common interest.

22 See Regulation 1391/2013, *supra* note 21, Recital 4: 'In the context of the Regional groups, organisations representing relevant stakeholders, including producers, distribution system operators, suppliers, consumers, and organisations for environmental protection, were consulted'.

23 Projects which are part of that list include the construction and reinforcement of electricity lines and gas pipelines, interconnectors, internal lines, storage projects for electricity, for gas and liquefied natural gas (LNG), air energy and hydro-pumped projects, construction and extension of transformers, substations, LNG terminals, and oil terminals.

as being of overriding public interest provided that all the conditions' set in Directives 92/43 and 2000/60 are fulfilled.[24]

The permit procedure is split into a 'pre-application procedure' which dates from the start of the permit procedure and the acceptance of the application by the competent authority, and a 'statutory permit granting procedure' which dates from the acceptance of the application and the decision on it (Article 10). Together, these procedures shall not exceed 42 months. Before the beginning of the pre-application procedure, at least one public consultation on the project shall be organised, in particular in order to find the most suitable location and trajectory of the project (Article 9(4). The wording of the Regulation – the consultation 'shall be carried out by the project promoter, or, where required by national law, by the competent authority' – indicates that the consultation be preferably made by the promoter.

Member States must appoint one national competent authority to facilitate and coordinate the permit granting process (Article 8). Annual reports on progress of the project shall be submitted to the Commission. Where delays occur, they have to be explained. And where 'significant implementation difficulties' appear, a European coordinator may be appointed to eliminate problems – in particular those between different Member States (Article 6).

The provisions of Directive 2011/92 on public participation in an environmental impact assessment of a project were not explicitly changed by Regulation 347/2013. This includes the taking-over, in Article 9(6), of the error in Directive 2011/92, according to which for transboundary projects, only an inter-governmental cooperation with the neighbouring State shall take place.[25] Indeed, as mentioned above, that provision of Directive 2011/92 was superseded by Articles 3(9) and 6 of the Aarhus Convention which gives an own, fundamental right of participation to every citizen who is concerned, independent of his citizenship, nationality or domicile. The Aarhus Convention prevails over Directive 2011/92 as well as over Regulation 347/2013.

While not explicitly stated in Regulation 347/2013, it may be expected that the process of public participation in future will be organised by the project promoter and not by the public authorities. This follows from the fact that the promoter shall 'prepare a report summarising the results of activities [not of 'his' activities!] related to the submission of the application including those activities that took place before the start of the permit granting procedure ... Due account shall be taken of these results in the comprehensive decision' on the permit application.[26] If this interpretation is correct, it means that the public authorities will, in projects coming under Regulation 347/2013, hear of the public concern only via the filter of the project promoter.

[24] Regulation 347/2013, *supra* note 18, Article 7(8).

[25] See Directive 2011/92, *supra* note 2, Article 7.

[26] Regulation 347/2013, *supra* note 18, Article 9(4).

4.2. TRANS-EUROPEAN TRANSPORT PROJECTS

The trans-European network in the transport sector is more integrated. New guidelines for the transport network were adopted[27] which establish two transport networks concerning railways, inland waterways, road, maritime transport and motorways of the sea and airports: a comprehensive network which lists the projects that are to be realised by 2050, and a core network for those transport projects which are 'of highest strategic importance' and shall be realised by 2030. Regulation 1315/2013 lists, in the form of maps, the projects which come under the two networks. The projects are structured in nine European corridors; for each corridor, a European coordinator was appointed by the Commission which shall facilitate and promote the realisation of the projects. The Coordinator shall be assisted by a 'Corridor Forum', the composition of which is decided upon by the Member States concerned by the corridor.[28] For projects in each corridor, a plan shall be elaborated which shall be approved by all Member States concerned.

For each project, Member States 'may' appoint a single contact authority for the purpose of facilitating and coordinating the process of granting permits. As regards the environment, Regulation 1315/2013 limits itself in mentioning that the projects shall respect existing EU environmental law, including Directives 92/43 (habitats and species), 2000/60 (water), 2001/42 (strategic impact assessment), 2009/147 (birds) and 2011/92 (environmental impact assessment). The projects shall also be resilient to climate change and environmental disasters.

4.3. CONCERNED CITIZENS AND TRANS-EUROPEAN PROJECTS

Participation, states Article 6(4) of the Aarhus Convention, shall take place early, 'when all options are open and effective public participation can take place'. If one looks at the present state of affairs for the large trans-European energy and transport projects, one wonders what this means in reality.

For example in the energy sector, the project of common interest listed in Commission Regulation 1391/2013, under no. 2.3.2, provides for an interconnection line for electricity between Aubange (Belgium) and Bascharage/Schifflange (Luxembourg). Project 1.3 provides for an interconnection between Endrup (Denmark), Niebüll and Brunsbüttel (Germany). A look at the geographical map shows that the routing for both electricity lines is more or less fixed by the different end points. What can thus the public concerned still participate in?

[27] Regulation 1315/2013 on Union guidelines for the development of the trans-European transport network, OJ 2013 L348/1.

[28] Regulation 1315/2013, *supra* note 27, Article 46.

The common interest project 8.1.2 provides for the realisation of 'one of the following LNG terminals: Finngulf LNG, Paldiski LNG, Tallinn LNG, Latvian LNG'. In this regard, Regulation 1391/2013 has the character of a plan, as apparently there was a decision to build a LNG terminal, but it is not yet decided, where exactly this project will be realised.[29] Under the Aarhus Convention, Article 7, as well as under Regulation 1367/2006,[30] Articles 2(e) and 9, there should have been 'early and effective' participation of the public concerned with regard to such planning. However, neither the draft regional energy lists were submitted to a participation procedure of the public concerned;[31] nor was Regulation 1391/2013 submitted to any form of participation procedure.

The decision on projects of common interest in the transport sector is even more arbitrary: the projects of common interest are laid down in Regulation 1513/2013. There is no mention of any discussion at regional or local level, whether this or that project should be included, this or that city selected as the 'urban node', etc.

For both energy and transport projects, the citizens concerned may thus, when it comes to the permitting stage of the individual projects, raise concerns about the exact location of the project and may, at best, reach a displacement by some meters. However, the realisation of the project as such cannot be questioned any more, as it is fixed by EU legislation which, in turn, is based on the concerned Member State's explicit agreement.

The Espoo Convention – let it be repeated, it is part of EU law – provides that for transboundary projects also the zero alternative be examined, which means the option not to realise a project. EU Directive 2011/92 does not go as far, but only requires an examination of alternatives. Both provisions are, in the light of the content of Regulations 347/2013 and 1315/2013, in practice no longer relevant.

This means in clear terms that EU infrastructure planning restricts the possibilities of the public concerned to participate in decision-making on projects or plans and programmes. The 'technocratic' concern for accelerating and streamlining the permitting process for such projects very largely prevailed over concerns to have a democratic decision-making process, as it had been developed under the Aarhus Convention and Directives 2011/92 and 2001/42 and Regulation 1367/2006. It is not surprising that in view of this approach to citizen participation in decision-making on projects that have an impact on the

---

29 Tallinn is the capital of Estonia. Paldiski is an Estonian city 50 km west of Tallinn. 'Finngulf' refers to the places of Ingaa or Porvoo in Finland; 'Latvia' apparently means the construction of an LNG terminal somewhere in Latvia.

30 Regulation 1367/2006 on the application of the provisions of the Aarhus Convention on access to information, public participation in decision-making and access to justice in environmental matters to Community institutions and bodies, OJ 2006 L264/13.

31 Regulation 1391/2013, *supra* note 18, mentions in Recital 4 that 'in the context of the work of the Regional Groups … organisations for environmental protection were consulted'. Whether these organisations were 'concerned' or not, is not mentioned. Also, the Recital refers to consultations, not to a participation process.

environment, citizens mainly adopt a NIMBY attitude: the project should be realised 'Not In My BackYard'.

4.4. WAYS AHEAD

The discussion on public participation in decision-making on projects, plans and programmes that relate to the environment can, however, not end here. Indeed, the individual citizen who is concerned by a trans-European project will mainly act in his own, personal interest and will normally have a limited concern for greater socio-economic considerations. What can he seriously argue about when there is a reflection to build a gas pipeline between Belgium and the United Kingdom or a motorway between Paris and Warsaw? Normally, he does not have enough information on the environmental impacts which such projects will have on fauna and flora, water, land use and other assets. And the Commission, which is, whether it likes it or not, in the driving seat for realising trans-European projects, has abstained until now from descending to the local level and inform the local population, concerned by the project, of the general European interest in realising it. It leaves this task to the national authorities which, in turn, delegate that task to even lower instances.

This leads to a gap between local concerns and European interests. The heavy discussions in Germany concerning the construction of the Stuttgart railway station as part of a trans-European railway project are an eloquent example of what such lack of communication can lead to.

It is obvious that there is some need of transboundary European planning of energy and transport infrastructure; even if the EU would disappear tomorrow, this need would still continue to exist. The question is therefore not to stop trans-European transport or energy projects with the argument that the existing provisions on citizen participation are not complied with. Rather, the problem to solve is the compliance of the trans-European projects with Article 11 TFEU, according to which environmental requirements – of which citizen participation are a significant part – must be integrated into the definition and implementation of the Union policies in the energy and transport area. If one takes this legal requirement of EU policy seriously, one will have to admit that the consultation of the citizens concerned only after the adoption of Regulations 347/2013 on energy infrastructure, Regulation 1391/2013 on energy projects of common EU interest and Regulation 1315/2013 on transport infrastructure comes too late. An effective input of the citizens during the permitting procedure is not possible any more.

In the energy sector, the EU has set up twelve regional energy groups. These groups are composed of government representatives of the Member States concerned, and of professional operators in the energy sector. Representatives of civil society should also be represented in such groups. They should have the specific task of ensuring that environmental organisations and the general public in the regions concerned be informed in time of plans to realise energy projects of common interest. Such an approach would avoid the present unpleasant situation that only energy suppliers and other economic operators who are active in the energy sector, are informed at an early stage of the envisaged trans-European projects and are capable to bring their (vested) interests into the discussion. Effective European, trans-boundary planning requires an open, democratic and transparent planning and decision-making process, not an approach which is limited to discussions between interested groups and the administration and which is, hence, better qualified as technocratic.

Another option would be to set up, in addition to the regional group mentioned before, an advisory group of civil society representatives which would have access to the same information – studies, planning considerations, policy reflections, etc. – as the regional group and which would be in charge to initiate, stimulate and drive the discussion of the public concerned by the planning and by the different projects which are considered. The above-mentioned case of the construction of an LNG terminal in Finland, Latvia or Estonia is a good example: why should the public concerned in these three countries not be able to express opinions at the stage of planning, suggest the making of studies or exploration tests or draw the attention on aspects which were, until now, less considered by the engineers in charge of finding the best suitable place? This would not only be a legal requirement of Directive 2001/42 and of the Aarhus and Espoo Conventions, but would allow the taking into consideration of environmental concerns at an early stage of the planning and permitting procedure.

It would also be possible for the Commission to appoint, for each of the twelve regional groups, an environmental coordinator whose task would be to ensure early and effective information and participation of the public concerned in the process of realising the trans-European energy projects. In the same way as the environmental representatives in the regional group or the environmental advisory body, such a coordinator would have to liaise with the public concerned and ensure that the procedure is less technocratic and more transparent and that early and effective participation of the public concerned in the projects planning, permitting and implementation stage is possible.

In the transport sector, no such regional groups for the nine trans-European corridors appear to exist. However, the need to better inform and let participate the public concerned in the planning, permitting and implementation of the trans-European projects also exists in the transport sector. Here the necessity to ensure a more efficient participation of the public concerned is even greater than in the energy sector, because there is a common transport policy under the EU Treaties which leads to more uniform and streamlined decisions at EU level; hence, the weight of the technocratic element in this policy sector is greater and needs to be better balanced against the interests of the public concerned. Therefore, it would have been necessary, as a minimum, that environmental representatives are members of the different Corridor Forums mentioned in

Article 46 of Regulation 1315/2013, though such a membership does not appear sufficient yet, in order to ensure effective participation of the public concerned in the decision-making process of trans-European transport projects.

It is not overlooked that only few environmental organisations and, more broadly, civil society organisations and bodies have the necessary personal and financial resources to assume the task of actively participate in the trans-European energy and transport planning and permitting process. However, this cannot be an obstacle to moving into the direction which is suggested here. European and national institutions and bodies who develop plans, programmes and projects to realise the trans-European energy and transport infrastructure are also responsible for ensuring that this process takes place in democratic-transparent and not in technocratic secretive forms. It is well known that the environment has no voice; as trans-European energy and transport projects always affect the environment, it is the task of those who advance such trans-European projects to ensure that the environment obtains the opportunity to voice its concern – be it through concerned citizens or environmental organisations. The final decision on how to balance in a concrete case the environmental and the project promoter interests remains with the public authorities. But these public authorities must ensure that they hear both promoters and citizens, and thus avoid one-sided decisions.

5. CONCLUSION

1. Transparency and citizen participation in large projects which are realised in the context of the trans-European energy and transport networks is at present very unsatisfactory. The essential decisions in both sectors are taken at EU level, before the national permitting process begins.
2. For trans-European energy and transport projects, the concerned citizens therefore have only marginal possibilities of voicing their concern during the permitting process.
3. Citizen participation in transboundary projects is not organised in the form which is required by the Aarhus Convention – an individual right of concerned citizens to participate – but is based on intergovernmental cooperation.
4. The European Commission would be well advised to consider new forms of environmental and/or civil society participation earlier in the process at European level, where projects of common EU interest are selected and where considerable financial resources are made available. The almost total absence of environmental considerations in the present decision-making process on trans-European energy and transport infrastructure is not compatible with Article 11 TFEU.

CHAPTER 4

FROM HOST TO INVESTOR: ENHANCING THE SUSTAINABILITY OF CDM FOREST CARBON PROJECTS

Yixin Xu*

1. INTRODUCTION

Serving the ultimate goal to 'stabilize GHGs concentrations in the atmosphere at the level that would prevent dangerous, human-induced climate change', the UNFCCC has originally recognised forests as both terrestrial sinks and sources of greenhouse gases (GHGs) since 1992.[1] On the one hand, forests are so-called 'sinks' because the vegetation and soils contained in forests can absorb and store GHGs, particularly carbon dioxide (CO_2), from the atmosphere through the photosynthesis process.[2] Therefore, enhancing forests conservation and planting more trees can reduce atmospheric GHGs and mitigate climate change.[3]

On the other hand, forests can be called 'sources' of GHGs emissions because the CO_2 absorbed by the forests can be released back into the atmosphere through natural respiration or by human actions such as logging, biofuel consumption and artificial forest fires.[4] This means that the forest storage of the CO_2 is not

* Yixin Xu is a PhD student at the Erasmus University Rotterdam, the Netherlands, supported by a scholarship from the China Scholarship Council. E-mail: xu@law.eur.nl. Special thanks to my supervisor Prof. Michael Faure, who has given valuable comments and advice on my paper and PhD research.

1 Article 2, Article 4(1)(d), Article 4(1)(c) UNFCCC, adopted at the 'Rio Earth Summit' in 1992 and entered into force on 21 March 1994, full text available at: http://unfccc.int/essential-background/convention/items/6036.php.

2 *R.K. Dixon, A.M. Solomon, S. Brown, R.A. Houghton, M.C. Trexier, & J. Wisniewski,* Carbon pools and flux of global forest ecosystems, Science, 1994 (263), p. 185, 187 et seq.

3 *R.T. Watson, I.R. Noble, B. Bolin, N.H. Ravindranath, D.J. Verardo & D.J. Dokken,* Land use, land-use change and forestry: a special report of the Intergovernmental Panel on Climate Change, Summary for Policymakers, 2000, p. 4.

4 *S. Brown, I.R. Swingland, R. Hanbury-Tenison, G.T. Prance & N. Myers,* Changes in the use and management of forests for abating carbon emissions: issues and challenges under the Kyoto Protocol. Philosophical Transactions of the Royal Society of London. Series A: Mathematical, Physical and Engineering Sciences, 2002 (360), p. 1953, 1594 et seq. *A. Golub, T. Hertel, H.L. Lee, S. Rose & B. Sohngen,* The opportunity cost of land use and the global potential for

permanent. This non-permanence feature brings challenges and uncertainties to measure forest emission reductions accurately and leads to a controversial negotiation process on this issue.[5]

After the UNFCCC, the Kyoto Protocol to the UNFCCC incorporated land use, land use change and forestry (LULUCF) activities as a method for the committed industrialised countries to comply with their GHGs emission reduction commitments.[6] However, subsequently, the Marrakech Accords narrowed down the scope of legitimate LULUCF projects hosted in developing countries. Firstly, it stipulates that only afforestation and reforestation (A/R) projects in developing countries can produce measurable CERs in the CDM regime.[7] Afforestation and reforestation refer to tree planting activities on lands without forests for at least 50 years or lands which used to be forests before 1989.[8] Activities reducing emissions from deforestation and forest degradation plus the conservation, sustainable management of forests and enhancement of forest carbon stocks in developing countries (REDD+) were excluded from the CDM and have remained undecided in the negotiations since 2005.[9] Secondly, it stipulates that the CERs from CDM A/R projects have temporary validities and limits the maximum amount of the CERs that can be used from CDM A/R projects to meet the commitments for the first commitment period (2008–2012) to five percent.[10]

---

greenhouse gas mitigation in agriculture and forestry, Resource and Energy Economics, 2009 (31), p. 299, 300 et seq.

5 *N. Höhne, S. Wartmann, A. Herold & A. Freibauer,* The Rules for Land Use, Land Use Change and Forestry Under the Kyoto Protocol – Lessons Learned for the Future Climate Negotiation, Environmental Science & Policy, 2007 (10), p. 353, 359 et seq.

6 Article 3, Kyoto Protocol, 37 ILM (1998) 22, was adopted in 1997 and came into force on 16 February 2005, full text available at: http://unfccc.int/resource/docs/convkp/kpeng.pdf (hereinafter Kyoto Protocol). The industrialised countries are listed in the Annex I to the UNFCCC, their commitment for the first commitment period from 2008–2012 is listed in the Annex B to the Kyoto Protocol, their commitment for the second commitment period from 2013–2020 is listed in the Doha amendment to the Kyoto Protocol. The Doha amendment was adopted in 2012, has been ratified by 23 countries and has not entered into force. See more about Doha amendment at: http://unfccc.int/kyoto_protocol/doha_amendment/items/7362.php.

7 Article 3, Kyoto Protocol, *supra* note 6, para. 13, 14, D. Article 12, Annex, Definitions, Modalities, Rules and Guidelines Relating to Land Use, Land-Use Change and Forestry Activities under the Kyoto Protocol, Decision 11/CP.7. See more at the UNFCCC official website, LULUCF – Developments at past COP and SB sessions: http://unfccc.int/methods/lulucf/items/3063.php.

8 Definition, Decision 16/CMP: '(b) "Afforestation" is the direct human-induced conversion of land that has not been forested for a period of at least 50 years to forested land through planting, seeding and/or the human-induced promotion of natural seed sources; (c) "Reforestation" is the direct human-induced conversion of non-forested land to forested land through planting, seeding and/or the human-induced promotion of natural seed sources, on land that was forested but that has been converted to non-forested land. For the first commitment period, reforestation activities will be limited to reforestation occurring on those lands that did not contain forest on 31 December 1989.'

9 REDD+ related UNFCCC documents trace back to COP 11, 2005, see more at: http://unfccc.int/methods/lulucf/items/6917.php.

10 Para. 7(a), (b), Decision 17/CP.7. Modalities and Procedures for a Clean Development Mechanism as Defined in Article 12 of the Kyoto Protocol: http://cdm.unfccc.int/EB/rules/modproced.html.

As a cost-effective compliance method, the CDM was adopted in the Kyoto Protocol. The CDM allows industrialised countries to invest in projects hosted in developing countries and to purchase cheaper certified emission reductions (CERs) from the projects.[11] In the meantime, the developing countries can benefit by receiving finance and/or advanced technologies from the investing countries. This process fulfils the other goal of the CDM: to assist sustainable development in developing countries.[12]

Currently, the sustainability assessment of CDM projects is conducted at the second stage of the CDM Project Cycle procedure. The CDM Project Cycle provides guidance of the monitoring of the implementation of all CDM projects including forest projects.[13] Previous literature about the sustainability assessment of the CDM forest projects could be divided into two groups.

First of all, the extensive discussions about the general contribution of CDM to sustainable development argue that the CDM projects fail to assist sustainable development in developing countries.[14] This part of literature, nonetheless, lacks a focus on forest projects, which are even excluded in some studies because of the forests' ecological features and the high uncertainty of relevant data.[15] With regards to the regions studied, some scholars have studied Africa and Latin America, but few focus on Asia.[16] Secondly, the literature on forests governance also provides valuable insights about monitoring forest sustainability. However, few focus on forest projects under the CDM legal regime. Regionally speaking,

---

11 Article 12(3)(b) Kyoto Protocol, *supra* note 6.

12 Article 12(2) Kyoto Protocol, *supra* note 6.

13 For more information about the CDM Project Cycle, see: http://cdm.unfccc.int/Projects/diagram.html. For more information about CDM's other projects sectors see the CDM official website: https://cdm.unfccc.int/Projects/projsearch.html.

14 *L. Schneider,* Is the CDM Fulfilling Its Environmental and Sustainable Development Objectives? An Evaluation of the CDM and Options for Improvement, Öko-Institut for Applied Ecology, 2007 (248), p. 1685; *K.H. Olsen,* The Clean Development Mechanism's Contribution to Sustainable Development: A Review of the Literature, Climatic Change, 2007 (84), p. 59. *K.H. Olsen & J. Fenhann,* Sustainable Development Benefits of Clean Development Mechanism Projects: A New Methodology for Sustainability Assessment Based on Text Analysis of the Project Design Documents Submitted for Validation, Energy Policy, 2008 (36), p. 2819; *C. Sutter & J.C. Parreño,* Does the Current Clean Development Mechanism (CDM) Deliver Its Sustainable Development Claim? An Analysis of Officially Registered CDM Projects, Climatic Change, 2007 (84), p. 75; *J. Alexeew, L. Bergset, K. Meyer, J. Petersen, L. Schneider & C. Unger,* An Analysis of the Relationship Between the Additionality of CDM Projects and their Contribution to Sustainable Development. International Environmental Agreements: Politics, Law and Economics 2010 (10), p. 233.

15 *M. Jung,* Host Country Attractiveness for CDM Non-Sink Projects, Energy Policy, 2006 (34), p. 2173, 2174 et seq.

16 *C. Figueres,* Institutional Capacity to Integrate Economic Development and Climate Change Considerations. An Assessment of DNAs in Latin America and the Caribbean, Inter-American Development Bank, 2004, p. i; *H. Winkler, O. Davidson &, S. Mwakasonda,* Developing Institutions for the Clean Development Mechanism (CDM): African Perspectives, Climate Policy, 2005 (5), p. 209; *L. Morera, O. Cabeza & T. Black-Arbeláez,* The State of Development of National Clean Development Mechanisms Offices in Central and South America, in OECD (ed.), Greenhouse Gas Emissions Trading and Project-based Mechanisms, 2004, pp. 30–39.

some forest scholars discuss forest management in Southeast Asia.[17] However, China, a major host country of CDM forest projects, has not been included in these studies.

To contribute to filling the literature gaps, this chapter discuss the sustainability of the CDM forest projects and put particular attention to the major host developing countries including China, Colombia and India. Following the new tool published by the CDM Executive Board for describing the sustainable development co-benefits of the projects, this study considers sustainable development and forest sustainability consisting of three aspects: social, economic and environmental.[18]

Within the limited literature which sheds light on the sustainability of CDM forest projects, some scholars questioned the projects' environmental sustainability and claim that many CDM forest projects cause harm to local lands and biodiversity conditions by the plantation of harmful trees or by unintentionally increasing illegal logging in unprotected forests.[19]

With reference to the social-economic impacts of the projects, firstly, some scholars pointed out that the state has preferentially granted land titles to key corporations rather than to smallholders, which directly or indirectly causes the exclusion of poor, non-documented tenant farmers and rural populations.[20] Secondly, many contracts for the CDM forest projects have arrangements about using large-scale industrial tree plantations to replace original agricultural activities. Some study claims that industrial tree plantations provide less employment than agricultural activities and such arrangement may, therefore, have difficulties in sufficiently providing local formers' livelihood.[21] Thirdly, a

17 *B. Cashore & M.W. Stone*, Can Legality Verification Rescue Global Forest Governance?: Analyzing the Potential of Public and Private Policy Intersection to Ameliorate Forest Challenges in Southeast Asia, Forest Policy and Economics, 2012 (18), p. 13.

18 CDM, Voluntary Tool for Describing Sustainable Development Co-Benefits (SDC) of CDM Project Activities or Programmes of Activities (SD Tool), http://cdm.unfccc.int/Reference/tools/index.html. The three-pillars definition is also adopted in the Forest Principles, A/CONF.151/26 (Vol. III), Report of The United Nations Conference on Environment and Development, www.un.org/documents/ga/conf151/aconf15126-3annex3.htm; *OECD*, Guideline on Sustainability Impact Assessment, 2010, p. 4; *Forest Stewardship Council*, FSC Principles and Criteria for Forest Stewardship, FSC-STD-01-001 V5-1 EN, 2014, p. 2.

19 *M. Ma, T. Haapanen, R.B. Singh & R. Hietala*, Integrating Ecological Restoration into CDM Forest Projects, Environmental Science & Policy, 2013, p. 143, 145 et seq. *Greenpeace*, What Accelerate the Drought in Guangxi? – The Secret of the Fast-Growing Eucalyptus Forest, 20 April 2010, www.greenpeace.org/china/zh/news/stories/forests/2010/04/gx-plantation-story/. *Fern*, Sinking the Kyoto Protocol: The links between forests, plantations and carbon sinks, 2000, p. 1, 9 et seq. *A. Long*, Global Climate Governance to Enhance Biodiversity & Well-Being: Integrating Non-State Networks and Public International Law in Tropical Forests, Environmental Law, 2011 (41), p. 95, 131 et seq.

20 *M. Kröger*, The Expansion of Industrial Tree Plantations and Dispossession in Brazil, Development and Change, 2012 (43), p. 947, 948 et seq.

21 *R. Carriere, L. Lohmann & L. Lohmann*, Pulping the South: Industrial Tree Plantations and the World Paper Economy, 1996, p. 102.

new form of colonialism is deemed to be happening.[22] Because through a forest carbon project contract, the needs and rights of indigenous peoples will be frozen in the coming decades. Their lands are used by developed countries to make up for their previous or future GHGs emissions and themselves are left no choice but to leave their hometown to make a living elsewhere.

Therefore, to promote the sustainability of CDM forest project in terms of biodiversity conservation and poverty alleviation, this chapter proposes to enhance the current CDM sustainability assessment regulation and practices from a law and economic perspective. The rest of the chapter is structured as follows.

Based on a legislative analysis and case studies, section 2 will firstly discuss the current regulatory and private sustainability assessments practices in detail and examine the existing problems. Furthermore, section 3 will review previous literature and possible solutions from a law and economics perspective. Subsequently, in section 4, a new suggestion is proposed from the perspective of the investors of the projects. Lastly, section 5 will briefly conclude the main points of this chapter.

2. CURRENT REGULATORY AND PRIVATE SUSTAINABILITY ASSESSMENT

Under the CDM rules, it is compulsory for the projects to pass the host developing country's assessment on whether the project assists sustainable development.[23] Moreover, there are also projects that additionally employ international private forest certification schemes to test the projects against self-design sustainability criteria and practices. Recently, in response to the considerable criticism on the contribution of the CDM projects to sustainable development, the CDM Executive Board (CDM EB) approved an international sustainability assessment tool.[24] Through this tool, a CDM project could elaborate its co-benefits for sustainable development from social, economic and environmental perspectives on a voluntary basis. The following texts will separately discuss these sustainability assessments in detail.

---

22 *A. Agarwal & S. Narain,* Global Warming in An Unequal World: A Case of Environmental Colonialism, 1991, pp 16–17.

23 Para. 1, CDM EB 16 Report, Annex 6, Clarification on elements of a written approval, http://cdm.unfccc.int/EB/016/eb16repan6.pdf, p. 1.

24 Carbon Market Watch News, New Sustainable Development Tool Is A Small Step Forward, 9 April 2014.

2.1. HOST COUNTRIES' REGULATORY SUSTAINABILITY ASSESSMENT

The regulatory sustainability assessment of host developing country is currently conducted at the National Approval stage of the CDM project cycle.[25] This section will first briefly introduce the main players and the stages of the CDM project cycle. Secondly, it will focus on the sustainability assessment at the National Approval stage.

2.1.1. The Main Project Players and CDM Project Cycle

The CDM Project Cycle is formulated by neatly structured CDM rules including standards, methodologies and guidelines. The CDM rules deprive from the general principles in the UNFCCC and KP. Detailed regulations of the CDM are decided at the Conference of the Parties (COP) and Conference of the Parties serving as the Meeting of the Parties to the Kyoto Protocol (CMP). Rules about practical and technical issues are further developed by the CDM Executive Board (CDM EB), including most standards, methodologies, guidelines and templates. The CDM EB was established by the decision of the first session of the CMP.[26]

The CDM project cycle works as a monitoring procedure and also a guide for the project players to follow. Pursuant to the CDM rules at each stage, projects are assessed by various monitoring entities at national and international levels. Accordingly, the project players have different tasks according to the criteria at different stages.

In a CDM project, there are four main players. Firstly, the public or private entities from the Annex I countries act as the investors or the buyers of the CERs. The investors aim to pay a lower price for the same amount of GHGs emission reductions that would otherwise be produced in their home countries. Secondly, the 'project developer' manages the project and sells the CERs. The project developer is largely a private or public entity with professional knowledge in writing Project Design Document (PDD) or in promoting, managing and representing the project.[27] Regardless of the identity of the project developer, the country where the project is located is the host country of the CDM project. The host country has to be a developing country, which would receive finance and/or advanced technologies from investing countries. The third type of players

---

25 For more information about the CDM Project Cycle, see: http://cdm.unfccc.int/Projects/diagram.html. For more information about CDM's other projects sectors see the CDM official website: https://cdm.unfccc.int/Projects/projsearch.html.

26 Para. 5, Annex, Decision 3/CMP.1, Modalities and Procedures for a Clean Development Mechanism as Defined in Article 12 of the Kyoto Protocol, FCCC/KP/CMP/2005/8/Add.1, full text available at: http://unfccc.int/resources/docs/2005/cmp1/eng/08a01.pdf, p. 6, 8 et seq. See more CDM rules and reference at https://cdm.unfccc.int/Reference/index.html.

27 World Bank, BioCarbon Fund Experience: Insights from Afforestation and Reforestation Clean Development Mechanism Projects, 2011, p. 140.

is the landowners of the project, which is also called the project's stakeholders. The identities of the stakeholders vary pursuant to the national land-use laws. The fourth type of players consists of the international and national monitoring entities, which govern the performance of the CDM projects. Except for the monitoring entities, other players are regarded as project participants.[28]

For all CDM projects, there are seven stages in the CDM project cycle to obtain certified emission reductions (CERs) and afterwards the CERs can be transferred to the investors. The seven stages are project preparation, national approval, validation, registration, monitoring, verification and issuance.[29] At the preparation stage, a Project Design Document (PDD) will be developed by the project developer according to the PDD template published by the CDM demonstrating detailed information about the project including geographical and environmental information.[30] The PDD is one of the most significant documents of CDM projects. It is the basis to apply for approvals and verifications.

The second stage in the CDM project cycle is the National Approval, where the project documents including PDD will be assessed at the national level by the designated national authorities (DNA). This part will be further elaborated in the next section. At the third stage, validation, the PDD will be submitted to a Designed Operational Entity (DOE) to be reviewed against the CDM requirements.[31]

The DOEs can be either domestic legal entities or international organisations accredited by the CDM EB for CDM projects of specific sectors.[32] The DOEs act like the extended arm of the CDM EB and have a contractual relationship with the project developer. If a DOE is in favour of the project, the project will go to stage four, registration, in which the CDM EB and the public will review the project against the CDM requirements.[33]

At stage five, monitoring, the project participants monitor the implementation of the project against the approved methodology in the PDD. At stage six, verification, the DOE will verify the emission reductions generated by the project. A project successfully verified by the DOE will receive the issuance of CERs from the CDM EB at stage seven.

---

28 CDM, Glossary: CDM terms, Version 07.0, CDM-EB07-A04-GLOS, p. 16.

29 See CDM official website, CDM Project Cycle: https://cdm.unfccc.int/Projects/diagram.html.

30 There are in total 5 types of PDD template on the official website of CDM and two special forms for CDM A/R project activities. They are CDM-AR-PDD-FORM, https://cdm.unfccc.int/filestorage/e/x/t/extfile-20140625145508804-PDD_form06.pdf/PDD_form06.pdf?t=SFN8bmE1ZWZlfDAoSsUOrM3Om6yA_cNnAYWX and CDM-SSC-AR-PDD-FORM for small scales CDM A/R projects, https://cdm.unfccc.int/filestorage/e/x/t/extfile-20140625145538274-PDD_form08.pdf/PDD_form08.pdf?t=WUh8bmE1ZWZtfDB7GjeA2oGHv4ZRTx-1p5c_.

31 CDM validation and verification standard, Version 07.0, https://cdm.unfccc.int/filestorage/e/x/t/extfile-20140624190900494-accr_stan02.pdf/accr_stan02.pdf?t=YXh8bmE3bjBmfDCUk-aZawyZr7IvW7DA5EeS.

32 See CDM official website, Governance, DOE, https://cdm.unfccc.int/EB/governance.html.

33 Afforestation and Reforestation Projects under the Clean Development Mechanism: A Reference Manual, 2013, p. 19.

As discussed above, there are three types of monitoring entities in the CDM project governance. At stage two, the project will be assessed against national laws by authorised national entities from the host country and the investing countries. At subsequent stages, the project will be assessed by international entities (DOE and CDM EB) against internationally binding CDM rules. Serving the ultimate goal of the UNFCCC, the specific CDM rules focus on monitoring GHGs emissions reductions. Therefore, the requirements are mainly about the production and assessment of credible emission reductions, rather than the assessment of the sustainability of the projects.

2.1.2. Regulatory Sustainability Assessment in the National Approval Procedure

As discussed above, at the second stage of the CDM Project Cycle, National Approval, the project will be evaluated by the Designated National Authorities (DNAs) of the countries involved in the project.[34] The countries involved in a CDM project normally include one developing country which hosts the project and at least one developed country which invests in or purchases CERs from the project.

The national authorities of the investing parties and of the host party have different tasks when assessing the participants and the project under the CDM rules. An investing country's authority will examine whether their domestic participants are voluntary.[35] If an investing country's authority approves the project and the participation of its domestic participant, it will issue a Letter of Approval indicating that the investing country has ratified the Kyoto Protocol and the participation is voluntary.[36]

As for the host country, its national authority will not only assess the voluntary participation of its domestic participants but also assess whether the project assists the host country in achieving its sustainable development goals.[37] A letter of approval from a host country shall indicate that the host country has ratified the Kyoto Protocol, the participants are voluntary and it confirms the contribution of the project to sustainable development.[38]

Only with positive statements in the letters of approvals from both sides, a project can move to the subsequent stage of the CDM Project Cycle. To acquire the approval letters from the involving countries, the project proponent has to comply with relevant national requirements of each involving countries. In practice, the national authorities of the parties have discretion in stipulating their national requirements. The CDM rules only regulate what issues shall be stated in

34 CDM, Designated National Authorities, http://cdm.unfccc.int/DNA/index.html.

35 Para. 1, Annex 6, CDM EB 16 Report, Clarification on Elements of a Written Approval, p. 1.

36 *Ibid.*

37 *Ibid.*

38 *Ibid.*

the letter of approval and do not prevent the host countries from conducting the national assessment according to their national laws.

The national authorities can have additional requirements and assess on other issues that are not required by the CDM. In fact, the national approval procedure has evolved diversely in different countries.[39] The sustainability assessments of host developing countries emerge with their own characteristics in the approval procedures and requirements.[40] This part will be further discussed in the next section.

As discussed above, the CDM rules do not contain detailed requirements for the sustainability of projects. Therefore, the international entities do not conduct substantial reviews on the projects' design and implementation on sustainable issues. Nevertheless, a formality review is required. According to the CDM PDD template, an environmental impact analysis and a socio-economic impact analysis of a CDM project are required to be demonstrated in the PDD of a CDM afforestation and reforestation project.[41] Moreover, if the host country requests the project proponent to conduct an environmental impact assessment, the project developer has to conduct such an assessment.[42] However, the international entities only review whether the analysis is presented and whether an assessment is conducted. They will not assess whether the analysis or the assessment is accurate, sufficient or credible.

In summary, from the discussion above, we can see that only the host country has the authority and responsibility to assess the sustainability of a CDM project in the CDM Project Cycle. The following section will provide a critical review of the host countries sustainability assessment. With limited resources, this research focuses on cases from three major host countries: China, India and Colombia, because these three countries were among the five countries with most CDM forest projects, biggest project area and most CERs production by August 2014.[43] To avoid repetitive introduction of their national approval procedures, the discussion will focus on their existing problems in the assessments.

---

39 *M.L.R. Chaparro,* DNA structure and CDM project approval process in five Latin American Countries: Argentina, Brazil, Chile, Mexico, and Peru, CDM Investment Newsletter, 2006 (2), pp. 7–10.

40 *R. Tewari,* Mapping of Criteria set by DNAs to Assess Sustainable Development Benefits of CDM Projects, 2012, p. 4.

41 Section D & E, CDM-AR-PDD-FORM, Version 08.0, revised and issued on 9 March 2015, p. 19.

42 Para. 132, Annex 1, Clean Development Mechanism Validation and Verification Manual, CDM EB 55 Report, p. 26.

43 According to the data provided in the PDD on the CDM official website: https://cdm.unfccc.int/Projects/projsearch.html.

2.1.3. *Problems of Host Countries' Sustainability Assessments*

Limited theoretical and empirical research has shed light on the problems of host countries' sustainability assessments under CDM rules.[44] Continuing the discussion above about the host countries' sustainability assessment, the following text will draw upon existing literature and identify the main factors that lead to the failure of many host countries in maintaining the sustainability of CDM forest projects.

First of all, based on an empirical study of India, Schneider (2008) pointed out two problems that may exist in the host countries' sustainability assessment. Firstly, when an internationally unified definition for sustainable development is lacking, the assessing criteria of some host countries appear to be too broad and poorly enforced. Schneider (2007) criticised India's criteria for sustainability assessment as being very ambitious. Its criteria cover many aspects such as poverty alleviation, environmental sustainability and technology developments. However, very few CDM projects initiated at early stages comply with all the criteria in practice. Projects' data indicate that most approved projects put economic attraction as the priority.[45]

Secondly, when a host developing country vies for a larger market share of the global carbon market, projects that are more economically profitable and with less financial risks will prevail in receiving the national approval of the host developing country.[46] Enforcing sustainable requirements would increase the cost for project management.[47] Conversely, those CDM forest projects carried out in an unsustainable manner may bring more short-term profits for local governments and communities.[48] Therefore, the host countries may intentionally dilute their sustainability assessments to attract more foreign investment.

Thirdly, two cases in Panama and Colombia reflect that it is urgent for host countries to address another problem in their sustainability assessments: the absence of *ex-post* monitoring mechanism during and after the implementation

---

44 *L. Schneider,* Is The CDM Fulfilling its Environmental and Sustainable Development Objectives? An Evaluation of the CDM and Options for Improvement. Öko-Institut for Applied Ecology, 2007 (248), p. 1685; *S. Subak*, Forest Certification Eligibility as a Screen for CDM Sinks Projects, Climate Policy, 2002 (2), p. 335, 339 et seq. *Carbon Market Watch,* The Mandate to Protect Human Rights in the CDM (Newsletter No 17), 4 July 2011. *A. Vorner & O. Sogandares,* Press Release: UN's Offsetting Project Barro Blanco Hampers Panama Peace-Talks, Carbon Market Watch, 15 March 2012. *J. Chen & J.L. Innes*, The Implications of New Forest Tenure Reforms and Forestry Property Markets for Sustainable Forest Management and Forest Certification in China, Journal of Environmental Management, 2013 (129), p. 206, 207 et seq.

45 *L. Schneider, supra* note 14, p. 46.

46 *Ibid.*, p. 47 et seq.

47 *J. Fehse*, Forest Carbon and Other Ecosystem Services, Synergies between the Rio Conventions, in David Freestone, Climate Change and Forests: Emerging Policy and Market Opportunities, p. 60.

48 *L. Tacconi,* Decentralization, forests and livelihoods: theory and narrative, Global Environmental Change, 2007 (17:3), p. 344.

of the forest carbon projects. The host countries' sustainability assessment is conducted at an early stage of project preparation or implementation based only on a document review of the project design. The current CDM legal regime is unclear about the host countries' authority on *ex-post* monitoring after the Letter of Approval (LoA) is granted.

In a case at Barro Blanco, Panama, a CDM forest project turned to have severe negative impact on biodiversity.[49] An environmental group asked to withdraw the approval and questioned the accuracy of the conducted environmental impact assessment. In another case in Colombia, the government sought the right to withdraw the letter of approval for registered CDM projects because of a controversy on human rights issues in a CDM forest project.[50] At the 69th meeting of the CDM Executive Board, it was recommended that a host country should be able to withdraw its LoA if a project is proven to have a harmful impact on sustainable development.[51] However, the CDM EB stated its point of view that the suspension of a LoA is up to each of the relevant parties of the project, and it is not for the Board to control or to comment on.[52]

The CDM's attitude indicates that the value of the produced CERs in the international carbon market is not directly affected by the sustainability of a CDM project. The current CDM legal framework does not contain international ex-post sanctions or punishments on the CDM projects for sustainable issues. Without further supervision during or after the project implementation, the actual contribution of the projects may vary from what is planned.

Fourthly, some regulatory sustainability assessments of the host countries show a lack of assessment on the compensation plans for indigenous peoples. CDM forest projects normally occupy a large area of land, which may previously be used by indigenous peoples to conduct unsustainable, short-term rotation forest activities.[53] Sustainable plantations with minimised fertiliser and longer rotations may end up with less income for the local communities.[54] In many CDM forest projects, local communities receive compensations or revenues for providing land for the projects for a certain period. However, once the project

49 *A. Vorner & O. Sogandares*, Press Release: UN's Offsetting Project Barro Blanco Hampers Panama Peace-Talks, Carbon Market Watch, 15 March 2012.

50 *Carbon Market Watch*, the Mandate to Protect Human Rights in the CDM (Newsletter No 17), 4 July 2011.

51 Report of the High-Level Panel on the CDM Policy Dialogue, Climate Change, Carbon Markets and the CDM: A Call to Action, Executive Summary, 2012, p. 6.

52 Annual report of the Executive Board of the Clean Development Mechanism to the Conference of the Parties serving as the meeting of the Parties to the Kyoto Protocol, Eighth session, Doha, 26 November to 7 December 2012, FCCC/KP/CMP/2012/3 (Part I), para. 101. See more at UNFCCC Secretariat, Withdrawal or Suspension of Letters of Approval: Fourteenth meeting of the CDM DNA Forum, 2012, p. 3.

53 *J. Chen & J.L. Innes*, The Implications of New Forest Tenure Reforms and Forestry Property Markets for Sustainable Forest Management and Forest Certification in China, Journal of Environmental Management, 2013 (129), p. 206, 207 et seq.

54 *S. Subak*, Forest Certification Eligibility as a Screen for CDM Sinks Projects, Climate Policy, 2002 (2), p. 335, 339 et seq.

is terminated, local people may just go back to their original ways of forests exploitation. Moreover, insufficient compensation within the project period may increase leakage. This means that if the compensation within the project period is not fairly contracted and is not enough for the local people to live on, it is likely that the local people will commit illegal logging or unsustainable forestry activities on unprotected lands outside the project area. Therefore, the sustainability assessment of host countries should also assess the compensation plans for indigenous peoples to ensure a sustainable livelihood for them when conserving environmental sustainability in CDM forest projects.

Fifthly, the sustainability assessment of some host developing countries is lack of transparency, such as China. According to a CDM Country Guide for China, the national approval for CDM projects is not conducted by China's DNA, the National Development and Reform Commission.[55] The DNA facilitates the procedures for approving CDM projects in China. Its higher authority, the National CDM Board, supervises the approval of CDM projects. It is an expert team who actually assesses the project documents and decides to request a resubmission of the application or to reject an application.[56] Neither the composition of the team nor the sustainability criteria used by the team is revealed in the documents or relevant websites.[57]

2.2. PRIVATE FOREST CERTIFICATION SCHEMES IN CDM FOREST PROJECTS

Except for the host country's regulatory sustainability assessment, private sustainability certification schemes are also applied in CDM forest projects. The private forest certification schemes have been developed since early 1990s, due to the ecological features and large scales of forest projects. The schemes are normally implemented by special entities and have been widely applied not only in CDM forest projects but also in other forest activities around the world.[58] Among the numerous forest certification schemes at national, regional or international level, only two of them prevail in the CDM forest projects practices. They are the Climate, Community and Biodiversity (CCB) standard and the Forest Stewardship Council (FSC).

---

55 Institute for Global Environmental Strategies & Chinese Renewable Energy Industries Association (eds.), CDM Country Guide for China, 1st ed., 2005, p. 2.

56 *K. Iyadomi*, CDM Country Fact Sheet: China, IGES Climate Policy Project / CDM Programme, 2008, p. 3.

57 *R. Tewari*, Mapping of Criteria set by DNAs to Assess Sustainable Development Benefits of CDM Projects, 2012, p. 32.

58 Non-forest CDM projects mainly apply the Golden Standards to assess projects' sustainability. See more at *M.A. Drupp*, Does the Gold Standard label hold its promise in delivering higher Sustainable Development benefits? A multi-criteria comparison of CDM projects, Energy Policy, 2011 (39), p. 1213.

Until August 2014, among 55 CDM A/R projects, 13 (23.6%) were certified by private forest certification schemes.[59] Six of them are certified by the CCB and another seven certified by the FSC. Additionally, there is one project claiming being operated by the companies certified by the Pan-European Forest Certification (PEFC).[60] Another one mentions that it will apply FSC best practices but does not claim to be certified by the FSC.[61]

Many articles have discussed the legitimacy, reputation and acceptability of private forest certificate schemes including Raines (2003), Barnett (2006) and Deephoust and Carter (2005).[62] However, this section focuses on the credibility of the private forest certification schemes in CDM forest projects in the market, namely to what extent such private sustainability assessment can reflect the true status of the project's sustainability. To do so, this section selects the two dominating forest certification schemes as study subjects: the CCB and the FSC. This section will first discuss how the market of private forest certification schemes works in general. Then it will particularly focus on the CCB and the FSC. Eventually, it will review the pros and cons of the private forest certificate schemes in CDM forest projects from a law and economics perspective.

2.2.1. The Market of Private Forest Certification Schemes

Private forestry certification schemes are conducted in a market environment. In contrast with regulatory sustainability assessment, the private certification schemes are applied on a voluntary basis. It is the project developer who decides whether to hire an independent entity to perform a sustainability assessment, which indicates the project's potential benefits and risks at social, environmental and economic aspects.

Private forest certification schemes originally emerged in the market to provide standards and monitoring services to the wood industries. Driven by consumers' interests on the environmental and social impacts of wood products (including timber, paper pulp and biofuel), the projects voluntarily choose a

59 Based on the information documented in the PDD of registered projects on the CDM official website. Relevant documents are available at: https://cdm.unfccc.int/Projects/projsearch.html.

60 Project 4957: Securitization and Carbon Sinks Project, Chile, registered on 3 January 2012, the PDD is available at: https://cdm.unfccc.int/Projects/DB/ICONTEC1309467081.51/view.

61 Project 3233: Argos CO2 Offset Project, through reforestation activities for commercial use, Colombia, registered on 17 February 2011, the PDD is available at: https://cdm.unfccc.int/Projects/DB/TUEV-SUED1261416776.52/view.

62 *S.S. Raines*, Perceptions of Legitimacy and Efficacy in International Environmental Management Standards: The Impact of the Participation Gap, Global Environmental Politics, 2003 (3), p. 47. *D.L. Deephouse & S.M. Carter*, An Examination of Differences between Organizational Legitimacy and Organizational Reputation, Journal of Management Studies, 2005 (42), p. 329. *M.L. Barnett*, Waves of Collectivizing: A Dynamic Model of Competition and Cooperation over the Life of an Industry, Corporate Reputation Review, 2006 (8), p. 272.

certificating entity and pay for the assessing services.[63] The assessing entities are mostly non-governmental organisations (NGOs). Once contracted, the private institution gains the authority for decision-making, setting criteria, monitoring and verification.[64] Certification from a credible certification entity would prove the projects' sustainability to the host countries, investors and the consumers of wood products. Although, there is no superior authority overseeing the conducts of the assessing entities, they are supervised by the market and influence each other.

In CDM forest projects, project developers may seek to prove the sustainability of the projects, the generated CERs and wood products to the host countries, investors and the consumers of wood products. In some cases, the investors directly request the project developers to obtain such a certificate as an additional condition to the investment. For instance, the World Bank Biocarbon Fund requires financed CDM A/R projects to be certified against the CCB.[65]

To enter national markets, international forest certification institutions like FSC need to obtain legitimacy in national jurisdictions. The assessing schemes need to adapt to the local socio-economic contexts and to face local competitors. The empirical studies of Cashore et al. (2004) on the emergence of the FSC in the US and the Europe show the interaction between the international forest certification scheme FSC and the local competitors.[66] In developing countries, there is limited existence of certified forests.[67] Van Kooten et al. (2005) revealed several reasons for this phenomenon and concluded a few motivations for firms in developing countries to seek forest certification.[68]

2.2.2. *Forest Stewardship Council*

The Forest Stewardship Council (FSC) was established in 1993 and was the earliest transnational forest certification scheme that emerged to promote sustainable forest management (SFM).[69] The FSC is governed by members including environmental NGOs such as WWF and Greenpeace, business and social

63 *S. Subak, supra* note 54, p. 337 et seq.

64 *T.M. Smith & M. Fischlein,* Rival Private Governance Networks: Competing to Define the Rules of Sustainability Performance, Global Environmental Change, 2010 (20), p. 511.

65 *Z. Salinas & E. Baroudy,* BioCarbon Fund Experience: Insights from Afforestation and Reforestation Clean Development Mechanism Projects, World Bank, 2011, p. 31.

66 *B.W. Cashore, G. Auld & D. Newsom,* Governing through markets: Forest certification and the emergence of non-state authority, 2004, pp. 59–218.

67 *B. Cashore & M.W. Stone,* Can Legality Verification Rescue Global Forest Governance?: Analyzing the Potential of Public and Private Policy Intersection to Ameliorate Forest Challenges in Southeast Asia, Forest Policy and Economics, 2012 (18), p. 13, 14 et seq.

68 *G.C. Van Kooten, H.W. Nelson & I. Vertinsky,* Certification of Sustainable Forest Management Practices: A Global Perspective on Why Countries Certify, Forest Policy and Economics, 2005 (7), p. 857.

69 *S. Bell & A. Hindmoor,* Governance without Government? The Case of the Forest Stewardship Council, Public Administration 2012 (90), p. 144, 145 et seq.

organisations, companies and individuals.[70] Its ultimate objective is to develop 'environmentally appropriate, socially beneficial and economically viable' forest management.[71] To ensure that the environmental, social and economic values are fairly weighted by different interest groups and economic powers, the FSC uses a voting mechanism, in which the votes of the members are equally designated to three groups: environmental, social and economic chambers. Within each chamber, the members are distributed to two sub-chambers: the North and the South with equal amount of votes.

To understand the operational structure of the FSC, the following text draws upon the discussions of Subak (2002) and Angelstam et al. (2013).[72] The FSC's international headquarter certifies institutions in different regions or countries in the world and set up regional or national offices with more local experience and expertise. The FSC only set the standards for forest practices and let third parties carry out the assessments.[73]

The FSC International sets out 10 principles from environmental and social-economic perspectives.[74] The principles incorporate opinions of the consumers of wood products, environmentalists and private forest managers.[75] These 10 principles will be further elaborated and supplemented by the national or regional offices, taking into account the local context of particular countries or regions.

The third parties accredited according to the FSC accreditation requirements can implement the standards to forest projects and issue certificates independently and individually under the supervision of the Accreditation Service International of the FSC. There are two main steps in the certifying process. The first step is the project plan review, ensuring that the forests activities are designed with desirable environmental and social characteristics. The second step is an auditing process, which aims at monitoring the implementation of the project.

2.2.3. Climate, Community and Biodiversity Standard

The Climate, Community and Biodiversity (CCB) standard is provided by the Climate, Community and Biodiversity Alliance (CCBA). By July 2014, the CCBA partnership is joined by five international NGOs. They are the Care for global poverty alleviation,[76] the Conservation International for nature protection for

---

70 FSC, Governance: https://ic.fsc.org/governance.14.htm.

71 FSC, Our Vision and Mission: https://ic.fsc.org/about-us.1.htm.

72 *P. Angelstam, J.M. Roberge, R. Axelsson, M. Elbakidze, K.O. Bergman, A. Dahlberg & J. Törnblom,* Evidence-Based Knowledge versus Negotiated Indicators for Assessment of Ecological Sustainability: The Swedish Forest Stewardship Council Standard as a Case Study, Ambio, 2013 (42), p. 229, 230 et seq.

73 FSC, Accreditation Program: https://ic.fsc.org/accreditation.28.htm.

74 FSC, FSC Principles and Criteria for Forest Stewardship, FSC-STD-01-001 V5-1 EN, 2014, p. 3.

75 *S. Subak, supra* note 54, p. 337 et seq.

76 The Care, official website: www.care.org/about.

human well-being,[77] the Nature Conservancy for ecologically important lands and waters and the most pressing conservation threats at the largest scale,[78] the Wildlife Conservation Society for wildlife and wild habitats across the world,[79] Lastly, the Rainforest Alliance for 'conserving biodiversity and ensuring sustainable livelihoods by transforming land-use practices, business practices and consumer behaviour'.[80]

The CCB identifies land-based projects design and implementation based on three elements: global climate change mitigation, local communities' socio-economic benefits and biodiversity conservation.[81] The CCBA website is not clear about who made the CCB standards under which procedure. Notwithstanding, the CCB standards are highly regarded by the World Bank Biocarbon Fund, which require financed CDM forest projects to apply CCB standards to verify the non-carbon benefits for local farmers and local environments.[82] World Bank Biocarbon Fund contracted 21 projects over 16 countries and 5 regions by November 2011.[83]

2.2.4. Problems of Private Forest Certification Schemes in CDM Forest Projects

The first problem associated with the private forestry certification schemes is that the assessing target is also the buyer who pays for the assessing service. Therefore, the assessing entity may diminish their assessing quality to attract more clients (race to the bottom). Schneider (2007) claimed that such format of race to the bottom is more likely to happen in a highly competitive market with a weak sanction scheme.[84]

The lack of supervision is another problem of the private forestry certification schemes. The private certification schemes are not legally constrained to any authorities or sanctions. For them, a default would not be easily detected and does not necessarily lead to any sanction.

Thirdly, Melo et al. (2013) considered that the technocracy of private certification schemes imperil their assessing capacities.[85] Because of the privileges of scientific expertise and the standardised monitoring systems, cultural and intrinsic values are usually neglected. Indigenous peoples' participation in

---

77 Conversation International, official website: www.conservation.org/about/Pages/default.aspx.

78 Nature Conservancy, official website: www.nature.org/about-us/index.htm?intc=nature.tnav.about.

79 Wildlife Conservation Society, official website: www.wcs.org/about-us.aspx.

80 Rainforest Alliance, official website: www.rainforest-alliance.org/about.

81 CCB, Climate, Community & Biodiversity Standards, 3rd edition, 2013, p. 1.

82 *Z. Salinas & E. Baroudy, supra* note 65, p. 31 et seq.

83 According to the CDM official website, there are in total 55 CDM forest projects by February 2014.

84 *L. Schneider, supra* note 14, pp. 5–6.

85 *I. Melo, E. Turnhout & B. Arts.* Integrating Multiple Benefits in Market-Based Climate Mitigation Schemes: The Case of the Climate, Community and Biodiversity Certification Scheme, Environmental Science & Policy, 2014 (35), p. 49, 50 et seq.

decision making and implementation are often not clearly defined, such as the CCB Standards, which reduce the equity and transparency of the certification schemes.

2.3. CDM VOLUNTARY TOOL FOR DESCRIBING SUSTAINABLE DEVELOPMENT CO-BENEFITS

At the 70th session of the CDM Executive Board meeting, a voluntary tool for describing sustainable development co-benefits was approved by the board.[86] This tool was developed under the decisions of the CMP7. This tool provides a platform for the project proponents to highlight the co-benefits of CDM projects on a voluntary basis. The tool can be applied and updated at any time in the life of a CDM activity. It maintains the authority of the host countries to define national sustainable development criteria and to assess project accordingly.[87]

The tool is a template that the project operating entity can fill in to reflect a project's co-benefits in sustainable development in social, economic and environmental aspects.[88] As far as the environment is concerned, the tool assesses a project's benefits in improving air, land, water and natural resources conservation, including biodiversity. Regarding social impacts indicators, this tool includes employment, health and safety, education and welfare. Under the economic section, business growth, energy, technology transfer and national economic independence are selected as indicators.

Several drawbacks of the tool were pointed out by Olsen (2012) and the Carbon Market Watch (2012).[89] First of all, the application of the tool is voluntary. Projects with less or no contributions on sustainable development may choose not to apply the tool. Secondly, the accessibility of the tool is limited to project coordinating or managing entities. Other parties, for instance, the indigenous peoples at a forest project area, have no right of filling in or of supplementing the tool. Thirdly, the information about the co-benefits provided by the project coordinating or managing entities is not necessarily verified by an independent third party. The credibility of the information is not guaranteed. Fourthly, negative impacts are excluded from the tool. The projects are not required to

---

86 CDM Executive Board Seventieth Meeting Report, 2012, para. 82.

87 Decision 8/CMP7, Further Guidance Relating to the Clean Development Mechanism, FCCC/KP/CMP/2011/10/Add.2, para. 5, p. 6.

88 The projects sustainable development co-benefits description reports is available at: http://cdm.unfccc.int/Reference/tools/index.html.

89 *K.H. Olsen*, CDM Sustainable Development Co-Benefit Indicators, Measuring the Future We Want – An International Conference on Indicators for Inclusive Green Economy/Green Growth Policies, United Nations Environment Programme (UNEP), December 2012, Geneva; Carbon Market Watch, The CDM Sustainable Development Tool: Why 'Highlighting' Will Not Deliver (Newsletter No 20), 12 July 2012.

report their negative impacts in the tool. Lastly, there is also no indicator in the tool reflecting the involvement of local stakeholders in a project.

3. SUGGESTIONS PROPOSED BY PREVIOUS SCHOLARS

To look for possible solutions to enhance CDM forest projects' environmental sustainability in developing countries, this research draws insights from three sources of literature: first of all, the literature with specific focus on the ecological restoration of CDM forest projects; secondly, research about the sustainability of CDM projects. Lastly, studies about the sustainability of forest projects under any legal framework. The proposals in the literature could be categorised as below.

3.1. INTERNATIONAL VERSUS NATIONAL REGULATORY APPROACH

Some scholars propose to use international regulatory resolution to enhance CDM projects' sustainability. Ma et al. (2013) suggested integrating ecological restoration into CDM forest projects.[90] Muller (2007), Olsen and Fenhann (2008) recommended applying international approaches such as rent extraction and text analysis.[91] However, developing countries refuted international intervention on sustainability arguing that applying international standards on this issue would impinge on their sovereignty.[92] In the new CDM validation and verification standards revised in April 2014, the power is still left with the host Party who can request the project participants to conduct an environmental assessment and who will eventually consider the significance of the impacts.

Other scholars prefer national level regulation but not from developing countries. Fehse (2008) suggests that to protect forest ecosystem services national law is the best level for rule-making and criteria setting with international guidance as a supplementary source.[93] Zhang et al. (2011) argued for the use of ecological criteria to develop CDM projects in China.[94] In fact, the Marrakech Accords states that, 'there is no "one size fits all" formula'. Capacity building

---

[90] *M. Ma et al., supra* note 19, pp. 145–147.

[91] More details see, *K.H. Olsen & J. Fenhann, supra* note 14. *A. Muller,* How to Make the Clean Development Mechanism Sustainable – The Potential Of Rent Extraction, Energy Policy, 2007 (35), p. 3203.

[92] *C. Figueres,* Sectoral CDM: Opening the CDM to the Yet Unrealized Goal of Sustainable Development, McGill Int'l J. Sust. Dev. L. & Pol'y, 2006 (2), p. 5, 11 et seq.

[93] *J. Fehse, supra* note 47, p. 48.

[94] *Y. Zhang, S. Ulgiati, X. Dong & D. Pfahler,* Using Ecological Criteria to Develop CDM Projects in Zhifanggou Valley, Loess Plateau, China, Agriculture, Ecosystems & Environment, 2011 (141), p. 410.

including sustainable developing must be country-driven, considering 'the specific needs and conditions of developing countries, reflecting their national sustainable development strategies, and primarily to be undertaken by and in developing countries in accordance with the provisions of the Convention.'[95]

Although national level regulation is considered the best, the institutional capacity and financial resources of developing countries for criteria setting and enforcement is still considered to be problematic and inadequate.[96] The theoretical discussion about the Environmental Kuznets Curve shows that it is more effective and has significantly lower transaction costs to implement environmental regulation in developed countries, where transparent information, advanced science and technology are more available.[97] Therefore, there is a call to build up international payments, regulated either by international organisations, by developed countries, or by a combination of both levels.[98]

3.2. PROMOTING INCENTIVES FOR CONSERVING FORESTS ECOSYSTEM SERVICES

In response to the call for compensation to indigenous people for conserving forests, the following reasons explain the incentives for unsustainable forest activities. First of all, as Fehse (2008) claims, under the current framework, the revenue from the sale of forestry carbon credits is less than other kinds of carbon credits. The current carbon trading schemes have not provided enough incentives for forest conservation.[99] Wood products with sustainability certification do not have a clear price premium.[100] The return for forestry projects is still low even after adding the revenues from commercial plantations.[101]

Additionally, the cost of sustainable CDM forest projects is higher than other types of CDM projects. Because trees take years to grow, forestry projects expect returns in the distant future. Consequently, project developers may face high insurance fees and higher requirements for finance.[102] Considering the attributes

95 Para. 5, Annex, Framework for capacity-building in developing countries, the Marrakesh Accords, FCCC/CP/2001/13/Add.1: http://unfccc.int/resource/docs/cop7/13a01.pdf, p. 8.

96 *J. Fehse*, *supra* note 47, p. 62.

97 *J. Strand*, Environmental Kuznets Curves: Empirical Relationships between Environmental Quality and Economic Development, 2002, pp. 5–10. *M. Faure & J. Smits* (eds.), Does Law Matter? On Law and Economic Growth, Cambridge-Antwerp, Maastricht European Private Law Institute Working Paper No 2011/35, pp. 386–388.

98 *J. Fehse*, *supra* note 47, p. 62.

99 *K.H. Olsen & J. Fenhann*, *supra* note 14, p. 2822.

100 *G.C. Van Kooten, et al.*, *supra* note 68, p. 860.

101 *Ibid.*, p. 60.

102 *S. Subak*, *supra* note 54, p. 337.

above, many investors choose other types of CDM projects with a shorter project period.[103]

Thirdly, forests implemented in an environmentally sustainable manner have less carbon storage in a project period than industrial trees monoculture plantations.[104] The amount of carbon storage are closely related to the trees' growth rate, plantation density and rotation frequency. Sustainable forest plantations turn out to have slower growth and a longer rotation period than industrial tree plantations. Whether healthier plantation would make up the shortage in carbon sequestration is still uncertain. Considering this conflict between carbon storage and ecosystem services in forests, if the UNFCCC only recognises measurable emission reductions as profitable project products, project participants would be highly motivated to choose the monoculture plantation of industrial trees rather than sustainable plantations.[105]

To restructure the project participants' incentives and promote sustainable forest activities, several regulatory proposals were proposed by scholars. Firstly, to promote sustainable CDM forest projects, offset mechanisms with better design and implementation should be provided to deliver optimal incentives. One way to do so would be to accumulate finance from international beneficiaries. Tacconi (2007) asserted that the costs of forests conservation are borne by the local community, while the benefits are enjoyed by the international communities.[106] The local or international beneficiaries of sustainable forests have not fully realised the significance of forestry conservation and the risks of harmful plantation and deforestation.[107]

Secondly, Fehse (2008) suggested that to create the incentives for protecting forests ecosystem services, regulation would be more effective than a voluntary approach, such as offsetting mechanisms or command-and-control regulations.[108] Some may argue that detailed regulation is not applicable, because the benefits on sustainable development are not quantitatively measurable. However, Olsen and Fenhann (2008) proposed that, since some sustainable development benefits are qualitatively measurable, the veracity of the benefits claimed by the project developers should be reviewed.[109] From the discussions above, it seems an obligatory international off-setting or compensating mechanism and an

---

103 *T. Sebastian, P. Dargusch, S. Harrison & J. Herbohn,* Why Are there so Few Afforestation and Reforestation Clean Development Mechanism Projects?, Land Use Policy, 2010 (27), p. 880, 881 et seq.

104 *S. Subak, supra* note 54, p. 339.

105 See more about the conflict between forests ecosystem conservation and industrial tree plantation at *S. Rousseaux,* Carbon Sinks in the Kyoto Protocol's Clean Development Mechanism: An Obstacle to the Implementation of the Convention on Biological Diversity?, Environmental Law Review, 2005 (7), p. 1.

106 *L. Tacconi, supra* note 48, p. 344.

107 *K.H. Olsen & J. Fenhann, supra* note 14, p. 2820.

108 *J. Fehse, supra* note 47, p. 62.

109 *K.H. Olsen & J. Fenhann, supra* note 14, p. 2830.

obligatory monitoring mechanism on the veracity of the claimed sustainable benefits are necessary for promoting sustainable CDM forest projects.

3.3. *EX-POST* ENVIRONMENTAL SUSTAINABILITY ASSESSMENT

To prevent poor sustainability performance, Subak (2002) suggested that ex-post punishment could be designed, either to suspend issued verification or to discount generated carbon credits until relevant requirements are met again.[110] However, Subak (2002) also pointed out that such regulations are difficult and expensive to implement because they could jeopardise project returns and increase insurance costs.[111]

Currently, the CDM has regulations about verification during and after project implementation. The first time of verification of a CDM forest project should be decided by the project participants, and afterwards, the verification will be conducted every five years until the end of the crediting period.[112] However, the current verification is only a review of the removal of carbon.

In this matter, the private forest certification schemes are more advanced than host countries' regulatory assessment. The FSC provides certificates that are valid for only five years and after that annual surveillance audits will be conducted by the FSC certification body to verify continued compliance. If certified forests are deemed to be worsening social or environmental conditions, the FSC would suspend their certificates.[113] Appeals against suspension decisions are allowed in the FSC system. A successful appeal would lead to a withdrawal of the suspension.[114]

3.4. INCREASE LOCAL PARTICIPATION AND POWER DECENTRALISATION

Multiple scholars and authorities have stated a point of view of increasing local participation and enhancing power decentralisation for forest and environment conservation. Ostrom and Nagendra (2006) believe that transferring decision-making power to local farmers and increasing local autonomy will increase the probability of local people complying with the rules and monitoring each other

110 S. *Subak*, *supra* note 54, p. 346.
111 *Ibid.*
112 Decision 3/CMP.1, Modalities and Procedures for a Clean Development Mechanism as Defined in Article 12 of the Kyoto Protocol, Annex, para. 63, FCCC/KP/CMP/2005/8/Add.1, p. 6.
113 FSC, Resolute Forest Products' FSC Forest Management Certificates to Be Suspended, 18 December 2013.
114 FSC, Statement by Forest Stewardship Council on Lifting of Suspension of FSC Certification for Swedwood Karelia, 11 March 2014.

in reducing deforestation and forest degradation.[115] The European Commission also stressed that 'public participation in decision-making' is essential to environmental assessment procedures.[116] Melo et al. (2014) asserted that the participation of the local farmers or stakeholders may enhance the equity and transparency of the certification schemes and counteract the market orientation and technocracy.[117]

However, Oates and Schwab (1988) brought a concern that local decision-making may lack of incentives for restoring long-term environmental benefits for future generations because of the mobility of the descendants.[118] Oates and Schwab offered two solutions to solve this problem. Firstly, national policies should be combined with local decision-making to better represent future generations. Secondly, capitalise local properties in a way that the value of its surrounding environment in future will be reflected in the current price of the properties.

In addition, Tacconi (2007) pointed out that potential negative environmental impacts associated with local participation and power decentralisation are not necessarily avoided, unless the following issues are clearly regulated: authority and responsibility assignment between various levels of governance, participatory planning, monitoring objectives, financial support and sanctions linked with environmental criteria.[119]

4. POLICY ANALYSIS

To solve the existing problems in the current regulatory and voluntary sustainability assessment schemes for CDM forest projects, by referring to proposals from previous literature, this research provides suggestions to promote the sustainability of CDM forest projects from an investor's perspective. One solution would be for investing countries to execute a sustainability (environmental or social impact) assessment of CDM forest projects at the National Approval stage of the CDM project cycle ('the investor's approach'). The investor's approach induces sustainability assessment as a mandatory requirement for the domestic project investors in investing countries. The investing countries have full authority in regulating their own national approval procedure and in deciding whether a domestic investor can obtain a Letter of Approval.

---

115 *E. Ostrom & H. Nagendra*, Insights on Linking Forests, Trees, and People from the Air, on the Ground, and In the Laboratory, Proceedings of the National Academy of Sciences, 2006 (103), p. 19224.

116 European Commission, Environmental Assessment: http://ec.europa.eu/environment/eia/home.htm.

117 *I. Melo et al., supra* note 85, p. 54.

118 *W.E. Oates & R.M. Schwab*, Economic Competition Among Jurisdictions: Efficiency Enhancing Or Distortion Inducing?, Journal of Public Economics, 1988 (35), p. 333, 351 et seq.

119 *L. Tacconi, supra* note 48, p. 346.

The investor's approach could incorporate the above suggestions at a national level by adopting specific requirements. For instance, same as Ma et al. (2013) departing from ecological concerns, Zhang et al. (2011) argued for the use of ecological criteria at a national level for the development of CDM projects in China.[120] Moreover, it could apply the proposed methods of Muller (2007), to use national profit tax for rent extraction.[121] In addition, the investing countries can also apply the text analysis approach proposed by Olsen and Fenhann (2008) to review the project design documents (PDD) at the national level.[122] This text analysis approach qualitatively assesses the sustainability of the projects based on the information provided in the text of the PDD, which reflects the social, environmental and geographic characteristics of the local area and the unique interest of the local community. However, as mentioned by Olsen and Fenhann (2008), the PDD is formulated by the project applicants, hardly any negative impacts of the project would be provided and the credibility of the provided information is without third-party verification.[123]

Furthermore, the investing countries could also make use of private forest certification schemes. Private forest certification entities may perform better for issues that demand expertise and constant human resources such as *ex-post* monitoring and compensation plans for local forest-dependent communities. By requiring project proponents to obtain relevant certificates from private forest certification schemes, the assessing costs could be allocated to the project proponents. Regarding the criticism on the lack of public participation of private forest certification schemes, the national authorities could incorporate public participation procedure in the national approval process to counteract relevant shortcomings.

Lastly, developed investing countries can employ their existing national or regional assessing practices to design the national sustainability assessments for CDM forest projects. If assessing both environmental and social impacts is too costly, the governments can take smaller steps to start from only environmental impact assessment or social impact assessment. For instance, the European Commission has already required that individual and public projects and programmes co-financed by the EU have to comply with the Environmental Impact Assessment (EIA) and Strategic Environmental Assessment (SEA) Directives.[124] EU Member States could extend the scope for EIA and SEA practices to CDM projects financed by their domestic investors.

---

120 *Y. Zhang, S. Ulgiati, X. Dong & D. Pfahler*, Using Ecological Criteria to Develop CDM Projects in Zhifanggou Valley, Loess Plateau, China, Agriculture, Ecosystems & Environment, 2011 (141), p. 410.

121 *A. Muller, supra* note 91, p. 3203.

122 *K.H. Olsen & J. Fenhann, supra* note 14, p. 2830.

123 *Ibid.*

124 Directive 2011/92/EU of the European Parliament and of the Council of 13 December 2011 on the Assessment of the Effects of Certain Public and Private Projects on the Environment;

Focusing the sustainability assessment with the investors may have the following advantages. First, this approach could avoid the barriers of negotiating internationally unified sustainability assessment criteria. Second, the investor's approach is a national-level legal procedure to be applied in a project-specific manner. The unique social and environmental characteristics of the project site could be better considered in this manner than an internationally standardised apply-to-all manner. Third, as an additional assessment on top of the host countries' regulatory sustainability assessment, this approach does not decide the project's sustainability for CDM registration, therefore does not infringe the sovereignty of developing countries. The investing countries may merely assess and refuse their domestic participants. Lastly, compared with host developing countries, industrialised developed countries have more experience in environmental regulations, more transparent information, more advanced science and technologies to facilitate an effective implementation of environmental protection measures.[125]

Parallel with the investor's approach and the host countries' sustainability assessment, international entities like the CDM EB can publish several voluntary tools or guidelines as complementary sources of standards. One way to do this would be to categorise the tools and guidelines into different levels taking into account the various institutional capacities and contexts of different assessing countries. One category could contain tools and guidelines with basic sustainability requirements and applicable for countries with low capacities, namely, least developed countries. Meanwhile, there could be another two categories with higher sustainability standards that are applicable for countries with higher income including high-income developing countries and developed countries. Categorised voluntary tools or guidelines allow countries to choose according to their own conditions and provide optimal or best practices which would contribute to the harmonisation of various national standards.

With reference to monitoring the performance of sustainability assessment, the risk of 'race to the bottom' may also exist among investing countries. Some developed countries may lower their national approval criteria to reduce their costs for purchasing emission reductions from developing countries. However, this research argues that some investing countries' governments have less motivation to lower their criteria to obtain more economic interests than the host developing countries for the following two reasons. Firstly, the public finance from the governments or public entities of developed countries is mostly in the form of concessional loans or grants that require very low interest or no repayment.

Directive 2001/42/EC of the European Parliament and of the Council of 27 June 2001 on the Assessment of the Effects of Certain Plans and Programs on the Environment.

125 *M. Faure & J. Smits* (eds.), Does Law Matter? On Law and Economic Growth, Cambridge-Antwerp, Maastricht European Private Law Institute Working Paper No 2011/35, pp. 386–388. *J. Strand*, Environmental Kuznets Curves: Empirical Relationships between Environmental Quality and Economic Development, 2002, pp. 5–10.

Such investors would have more incentives to ensure a desirable project result rather than gaining economic interests. The World Bank Biocarbon report (2011) confirms this point of view that CDM forest projects initiated by public finance aim at a better social and environmental performance.[126]

Additionally, the investors' approach may create a regulatory competition among investing countries national approval procedures, which would lead to a 'race to the top' and the performance of an investing country's sustainability assessment will be 'trading up'. Drawing upon insights from Vogel (2004) and Sonnenfeld (2002), it is assumed that if any developed country starts adding a sustainability assessment requirement to the national approval procedure, their reputation in promoting developing countries social and environmental conditions will spread.[127] There is a possibility that NGOs and international communities, as the public reviewer, will start to evaluate the investing countries' sustainability assessment. In the meantime, developing countries, as the recipient of investments may develop preference for investors from investing countries with better sustainability performance in CDM forest projects.

Moreover, regarding the costs for sustainable assessment, adding this requirement to the national approval procedures of the investing countries will increase the costs of their domestic investors. The additional expenses not only result from the implementation of the assessment but also from the upgraded forest plantation and management to pass the assessment. In line with Tacconi (2007), this is a reallocation of costs to investing countries, which are part of the international beneficiaries of the forest ecosystem services.[128] Sustainable forest plantations bring lower returns and less carbon storage in the short term compared with industrial tree plantations. To incentivise people to conduct more sustainable CDM forest projects, more financial values should be given to forestry emissions reductions with potentially higher sustainability benefits. However, currently, there are more financial constraints on CDM forest carbon projects than other type of CDM projects, such as a maximum amount of one percent and temporary validity as discussed earlier.[129] However, this issue is not only about projects' sustainability but also about the value of the emission reductions, which needs to be further studied and may be solved from an international perspective under the UNFCCC regime.

---

126 *Z. Salinas & E. Baroudy*, *supra* note 65, pp. 90–92.

127 *D. Vogel & R.A. Kagan* (eds.), Dynamics of Regulatory Change: How Globalization Affects National Regulatory Policies, 2004, p. 3. *D.A. Sonnenfeld*, Social Movements and Ecological Modernization: The Transformation of Pulp and Paper Manufacturing, Development and Change, 2002 (33), p. 1, 12 et seq.

128 *L. Tacconi*, *supra* note 48, p. 344.

129 See *supra* note 10.

5. CONCLUSION

This chapter firstly briefly introduced the host countries' regulatory sustainability assessment of the CDM forest projects, the private forest certification practices and the voluntary CDM tools. Subsequently, it identified the existing problems in current regulation and practices and reviewed previous proposals addressing relevant problems. Finally, this chapter provided suggestions from an investors' perspective to solve existing problems and to enhance the sustainability of CDM forest projects. It recommends investing countries to apply sustainability (environmental or social impact) assessment on CDM forest projects at the National Approval stage of the CDM project cycle as a mandatory requirement for domestic investors to obtain the Letter of Approval ('the investor's approach').

Furthermore, this chapter firstly discussed the advantages of this investor's approach compared with the host developing countries' national approach and with an international approach. Subsequently, it analysed the potential risks and the monitoring of the performance of the sustainability assessment of the investing countries. Lastly, it discussed the redistribution of the cost for the sustainability assessment of CDM forest projects.

Through applying the investors' approach, some developed countries would share part of the cost of promoting sustainable CDM forest projects. However, investing countries that are not interested in CDM forest projects will still not bear any costs, although they are also the international beneficiaries. Therefore, further international regulatory reform is needed to redefine the value of Certified Emission Reductions generated by sustainable forest projects to mobilise more financial sources for sustainable forest activities in developing countries.

PART II
PUBLIC PARTICIPATION

CHAPTER 5
LEGISLATIVE VALIDATION IN TIMES OF ENVIRONMENTAL DEMOCRACY:

Going Beyond the Deadlock or a Road to Nowhere?

Hendrik SCHOUKENS*

'What is a rebel? A man who says no: but whose refusal does not imply a renunciation.'
Albert Camus

1. INTRODUCTION

'It's tragic that we have protest groups talking about "this ancient woodland" ... It's bollocks. They're not campaigning for forests, they're not campaigning for butterflies. They pretend to be, but what they're really furious about is that their house prices are getting it'.[1] These are the uncompromising words of Boris Johnson, the current Mayor of London and common media figure, when he was asked to give his view of the opponents to the High Speed 2(HS2), the UK's £50bn+ high-speed rail project to speed up travel between London and Birmingham - and eventually Manchester and beyond.[2] According to the proponents of this massive development project, the HS2 link is necessary to alleviate overcrowding on routes in and out of London and will be an engine for economic growth for the north of England. As it often goes in such cases, the opponents of the project refute these claims and argue that the Y-shaped HS2 railway project is a 'disastrous white

* PhD Candidate, Ghent University, hendrik.schoukens@ugent.be.

1 HS2 opponents are Nimbys who only care about house prices, says Boris Johnson, *The Telegraph*, 28 April 2014, www.telegraph.co.uk/news/uknews/road-and-rail-transport/10794224/HS2-opponents-are-Nimbys-who-only-care-about-house-prices-says-Boris-Johnson.html.

2 More information on the HS2 project is available at the following governmental website: www.gov.uk/government/organisations/high-speed-two-limited.

elephant' to which there are better and less harmful alternatives.[3] According to the anti-HS2 campaigners, the promise of 'growth, jobs and productivity', rests on fiddled economics.[4] Obviously, Boris Johnson's statements are deliberately provocative as they were meant to serve a political purpose. In the spring of 2014, the 'hybrid bill' paving the way for the HS2 high-speed rail link was up for vote in the House of Commons. By claiming that opponents of HS2 are simply 'pretending' to have an environmental objection when they in fact are 'furious' about house prices decreasing because of the £50 billion railway route, Boris Johnson probably hoped to mop up the last pockets of resistance against what is to become the UK's biggest development project of the coming decades.

It would be easy to dismiss the statements of Boris Johnson as simple election-year politicking or populism. As a matter of fact, he is but one of the many politicians who believe that environmental law has gone astray by providing the wider public and environmental NGOs with additional procedural environmental rights which could be used to block or at least delay large infrastructure projects. The latter discourse is symptomatic of the shifted attitude towards environmental law these days. Captured by the paradigm of economic growth, which has pushed the rate of environmental degradation to unprecedented levels, the narrative has profoundly changed from ambitious environmentalism to deregulation. Because of their size and potential environmental impact, large-scale projects usually lead to polarised debates and quickly become of great symbolic value. In former days, the lack of substantial participatory rights and the limited access to courts in environmental cases rendered large infrastructure projects virtually immune from successful legal challenges. The affected public was often forced to buy the governmental rationale behind such projects. At present, however, environmental NGOs and local action groups are increasingly eager to go to court in order to enforce their viewpoints, which leads to an increasing number of deadlock scenarios. This fallout has the potential of damaging the hard-won reputation of several bedrock principles of international and EU environmental law.

In this respect, the 1998 Aarhus Convention – or to give its full name, the UNECE Convention on Access to Information, Public Participation in Decision-making and Access to Justice in Environmental Matters[5] – is sometimes quoted as one of the main triggers of the 'excessive' administrative burden and cumbersome delays large infrastructure projects are facing across Europe these days. As is widely known, the Aarhus Convention is grounded on the assumption that a wider involvement of individuals and environmental NGOs

---

3 *R. Read*, HS2 is a disastrous white elephant, *The Ecologist*, 12 May 2014, www.theecologist.org/blogs_and_comments/commentators/2387190/hs2_is_a_disastrous_white_elephant.html.

4 See in this respect: www.iea.org.uk/in-the-media/press-release/hs2-highly-unlikely-to-transform-the-north.

5 Convention on Access to Information, Public Participation in Decision-making and Access to Justice in Environmental Matters, done at Aarhus, Denmark, 25 July 1998 (the Aarhus Convention). The Aarhus Convention entered into force on 1 October 2001.

in environmental matters, if supplemented by effective access to justice, can lead to significant improvements in environmental protection.[6] By undertaking to guarantee a series of 'citizens' rights in relation to the environment', essentially of a procedural nature, the European states signatory to the Convention wished to encourage what they described in the ministerial declaration of the Aarhus Conference, as 'responsible environmental citizenship', acknowledging that 'an engaged, critically aware public is essential to a healthy democracy'.[7] In that regard, the quintessential third pillar of the Aarhus Convention, laid down by Article 9, aims at providing environmental NGOs and citizens with the necessary access to justice in order to assist in the enforcement of environmental law.

Yet, in spite of the promising statements, the Aarhus Convention, alongside other seminal instruments of EU environmental law, has turned into the proverbial 'nemesis' of many business people and politicians. While the European Community/European Union, which ratified the Aarhus Convention back in 2005,[8] promulgated additional rules obliging the Member States to revise their existing planning policies and provide broad access to justice to enforce the rights of access to information and public participation guaranteed by the Union rules on Environmental Impact Assessment (EIA) and Integrated Pollution Prevention and Control (IPPC) procedures,[9] the application thereof on the ground appeared far from simple. Coming to grips with this new reality, in which citizens and environmental NGOs play an important role in the environmental decision-making process, proved to be harder than expected. Empowering citizens and environmental NGOs might have been a 'buzz phrase' in the early 1990s, but according to some it also led to increasing paralysis. In the face of intractable opposition against large infrastructure projects, planning authorities have an increasing tendency to return to a 'business as usual' policy, whereby little to no respect is paid to the input provided by the civil society. By consequence, environmental NGOs and citizens grew increasingly disillusioned with the lack of meaningful participation throughout the planning procedures. They frequently turned to the court in order to enforce their environmental rights, which are safeguarded by EU directives, such as the EIA and Strategic Environmental

6 See more extensively: *J. Watts*, The Aarhus Convention: a Driving Force for Environmental Democracy, Journal for European Environmental and Planning Law, 2005 (2).

7 *M. Pallemaerts*, Introduction, in M. Pallemaerts, The Aarhus Convention at Ten. Interactions and Tensions between Conventional International Law and EU Environmental Law, 2011, p. 3.

8 Council Decision 2005/370/EC of 17 February 2005 on the conclusion on behalf of the European Community, of the Convention on access to information, public participation in decision-making and access to justice in environmental matters [2005] OJ L124/1.

9 Directive 2003/35/EC of the European Parliament and of the Council providing for public participation in respect of the drawing up of certain plans and programmes relating to the environment and amending with regard to public participation and access to justice Council Directives 85/337/EEC and 96/61/EC [2003] OJ L257/26.

Assessment (SEA) Directives[10] and the EU nature directives.[11] The absence of any escape to this vicious circle led to an increasing paralysis, especially in the context of large infrastructure projects, where often various and opposing stakes are at play.[12]

As among others evidenced by the HS2 case, one way to avoid deadlock scenarios is to take recourse to legal ratification of development consents. By including development consents in legislative acts, an increasing number of national and European governments, impatient with the many court challenges against large infrastructure projects, tried to bypass the allegedly rigid EIA rules. On the surface, such practices seemed to be in line with EIA Directive, which under one of its core provisions states that projects that are adopted by a specific legislative act are exempted from the assessment requirements under EU law. However, the question arose to what extent the technique of legislative validation of planning consents was compatible with the additional procedural requirements set out by the Aarhus Convention. Rushing a development consent through parliament, and thereby circumventing the generic EIA and participation requirements that are enshrined in the Aarhus Convention, seems to be at odds with the recent progress towards environmental democracy. But is that also true in cases where a profound debate has taken place on the desirability of the purported large infrastructure development which goes beyond a rubberstamp? And to what extent are courts capable and willing to scrutinise the parliamentary debate in order to check whether the elected representatives were able to properly examine the proposed project? Ultimately, the use of legislative ratification of planning permits implicates the more fundamental question as to how such techniques can be aligned with the provisions on access to justice under the Aarhus Convention, as implemented in EU law.

This chapter addresses the multitude of thorny legal questions that pop up in the context of legislative validation for large infrastructure projects. In particular, it tries to analyse to what extent the procedural demands enshrined in international and EU environmental are reconcilable with the parliamentary process. To put things in perspective, this chapter starts out by briefly addressing the general requirements on EIA, participation and access to justice under EU law, as interpreted by the Court of Justice of the EU in its recent case law. Subsequently, focus shifts to the recent legal proceedings concerning, among others, extension and refurbishment works for regional Belgian airports. These proceedings provide

---

10 Directive 2011/92/EU on the assessment of the effects if certain public and private projects on the environment [2011] OJ L26/1 (EIA Directive); Directive 2001/42/EC of the European Parliament and of the Council of 27 June 2001 on the assessment of the effects of certain plans and programmes on the environment [2001] OJ L197/30 (SEA Directive).

11 European Parliament and Council Directive 2009/147/EC on the conservation of wild birds [2009] OJ L20/7; Council Directive 92/43/EEC on the conservation of natural habitats and of wild fauna and flora [1992] OJ L206/7 (Habitats Directive).

12 *F. La Camera*, Economy, Ecology and Environmental Democracy, in M. Pallemaerts, *supra* note 7.

us with an excellent case-study on the margin left for legislative validation within the context of EU environmental law, especially since the Court of Justice was asked to shed light on the acceptability of ratified building permits in light of the procedural environmental rights that are included in the Aarhus Convention. The rulings of the Court in the latter case serve as a benchmark when assessing the outcome of the legal challenges against the HS2 hybrid bill before the UK Supreme Court in the last section of this chapter. Throughout the analysis, the specific conditions that need to be fulfilled when ratifying development consents in legislative acts are analysed in more detail.

2. LEGISLATIVE VALIDATION, EIA AND AARHUS: '*CECI N'EST PAS UNE PIPE?*'

2.1. THE BASICS OF EIA IN THE EUROPEAN UNION: THE BACKBONE OF SUSTAINABLE SPATIAL DEVELOPMENT?

It is commonly understood that the EIA rules play a seminal role in tackling the adverse impacts of bigger and smaller projects on the environment and biodiversity. Thus it is not surprising to hear EIA, together with SEA, being referred to as the '*jewel in the crown*' of environmental policy. At the time, when we were still the European Economic Community, EIA had been introduced by Council Directive 85/337/EEC of 27 June 1985 on the assessment of the effects of certain public and private projects on the environment.[13] The latter directive and its subsequent amendments[14] have been codified by Directive 2011/92/EU (EIA Directive).[15] On 15 May 2014, the newly amended Directive (2014/52/EU), which aimed not only to reduce the alleged administrative burden associated with EIA but also to improve the level of environmental protection, entered into force.[16] In general, EIA is a procedure aimed at assessing impacts of a project on the environment before its implementation. The fundamental purpose of EIA is to make decisions more environmentally sensitive.[17] While the outcome of EIA is, in sharp contrast to the appropriate (habitat) assessment under Article 6(3) of the

13 Council Directive 85/337/EEC of 27 June 1985 on the assessment of the effects of certain public and private projects on the environment [1985] OJ L175/40.

14 See amongst others *supra* note 9.

15 The original Directive 85/337/EC on the assessment of impacts of certain public and private projects was amended in 1997 by Directive 97/11/EC and in 2003 by Directive 2003/35/EC. The latter amendment sought to align the provisions on public participation and access to justice with the Aarhus Convention.

16 Directive 2014/52/EU of the European Parliament and of the Council of 16 April 1014 amending Directive 2011/92/EU on the assessment of the effects of certain public and private projects on the environment [2014] OJ L124/1.

17 *M. Lee*, EU Environmental Law Challenges, Change and Decision-Making, 2005, p. 171.

Habitats Directive, not binding upon the permitting issuing authorities,[18] they are required to gather prior information on the potential negative projects on the environment and to integrate them in the decision-making process.

EIA rules, if properly applied and enforced, are capable of giving a strong impetus for planning authorities to revise the current spatial development strategies and ultimately propagate a more sustainable planning policy. Yet the EIA Directive does not establish substantive environmental standards. It merely lays down essential procedural requirements. Under the EIA Directive, the core obligation incumbent upon a project developer is to provide the competent authorities the necessary information on the environmental impact of the purported project, which will be compiled in the EIA report.[19] In a subsequent stage, the environmental authorities and the public must be informed and consulted on the content of the EIA report. The latter obligations are included in Article 6 of the EIA Directive which, in order to effectively implement the participatory rights set out by the second pillar of the Aarhus Convention, was amended in 2003 with the requirements that notices to the public shall be made available electronically[20] and that the Member States shall provide for reasonable timeframes for the procedures, being no less than 30 days.[21] Finally, the competent authority decides, taking into consideration the results of consultations. The public is informed of the decision afterwards and can challenge the decision before the national courts.

2.2. ACCESS TO JUSTICE IN RELATION TO EIA RULES

Initially, no explicit provisions were mentioned under the EIA Directive as regards to access to justice. Even so, long before the EU ratification of the EIA Directive, the Court of Justice had already clarified that, under the so-called 'direct effect' doctrine, Member States are required to allow individuals from relying on the core provisions of the EIA Directive, such as Article 4(2) and 2(1), in order to set aside national or regional legislation or measures which do not conform to the requirements set out by the latter.[22] This being the case, it was apparent that the principles of direct effect and effective judicial protection would in themselves not be able to ensure an effective implementation of the provisions on access to justice, as enshrined in Article 9 of the Aarhus Convention.

With the inclusion of Article 10a, which has been renumbered to Article 11 of the EIA Directive back in 2011, the European legislator hoped to bring Union

18 See, for instance, with respect of EIA under EU environmental law: Case C-420/11 *Leth* [2013], para. 46.

19 The exact content of the EIA report is enlisted in Annex IV of the EIA Directive.

20 Article 6(2) EIA Directive.

21 Article 6(6) and (7) EIA Directive.

22 See amongst others: Case C-73/95 *Kraaijeveld* [1995] ECR I-5403, para. 56.

law in line with Article 9(2) and (4) of the Aarhus Convention. Under Article 11 of the EIA Directive, the Member States are required to offer certain access to justice rights to 'public concerned', which is defined as 'the public affected or likely to be affected by, or having an interest in, the environmental decision-makings; for the purposes of this definition, non-governmental organizations promoting environmental protection and meeting any requirements under national law shall be deemed to have an interest'.[23]

First and foremost Member States are, in line with what is provided by Article 9(2) of the Aarhus Convention, required to offer the public concerned access to a review procedure before a court of law or another independent and impartial body to challenge both the substantive or procedural legality of decisions, acts or omissions subject to the public participation of the EIA Directive. Those who belong to the public concerned can either be individuals or environmental NGOs having a sufficient interest or, alternatively, maintaining the impairment of a right. While Article 11(3) leaves it to the Member States to determine what would constitute a sufficient interest and/or impairment of a right, it must be reiterated that environmental NGOs which fulfil the criteria mentioned in the aforementioned definition shall also be deemed to comply with the latter standing requirements. Pursuant to Article 11(4) of the EIA Directive, Member States are still allowed to maintain the pre-existing procedural requirements of administrative law, such as the requirement of exhaustion of administrative review procedures prior to recourse to judicial review procedures. In addition, it is stressed that, in line with Article 9(4) of the Aarhus Convention, any national or regional procedural rules shall be fair, equitable, timely and not prohibitively expense. However, in contrast to the implementation efforts in relation to Article 9(2) and (4), so far no explicit implementation measures have been taken at EU level to implement Article 9(3) of the Aarhus Convention, which includes a separate right to file a public interest law suit in environmental cases. The legislative proposal made in 2003 by the European Commission to implement Article 9(3) of the Aarhus Convention has never managed to gather sufficient support amongst the Member States to get adopted.[24]

In spite of the political stalemate on the latter proposal, the Court of Justice has lately been very proactive in advocating for a wider access to justice in environmental cases at national court level, both in cases that fall under the ambit of the EIA Directive and cases that go beyond it. When faced with interpretation questions concerning Article 11 of the EIA Directive, the Court of Justice consistently adopted a rather generous attitude towards standing for environmental NGOs and individuals in EIA-related cases. Whereas the progressive stance of the Court was in itself not that much of a surprise,

23 See also Article 2(5) of the Aarhus Convention.

24 Proposal for a Directive of the European Parliament and of the Council on access to justice in environmental matters, COM [2003] 624 final, 24 October 2003.

especially given its earlier progressive case law on the principle of 'direct effect' in environmental cases,[25] the Aarhus Convention, and the EU recent implementation efforts, certainly provided additional legal ammunition in the strive for more environmental democracy. Time and time again, the Court of Justice overruled restrictive national standing rules which blocked access to national courts for the public concerned, including environmental NGOs.

One of the first rulings worth mentioning in this regard is the 2010 ruling of the Court of Justice in *Djurgården*, in which the latter deemed the Swedish standing criteria for environmental NGOs, requiring the latter to have at least 2000 members, to contravene Article 11 of the EIA Directive.[26] Possibly most compelling was the Court's ruling in *Trianel*, where it was held that both EU environmental law and the Aarhus Convention preclude the use of a '*Schutznorm*' which does hinder environmental NGOs from relying before national courts on the infringement of a rule flowing from EU environment law and intended to protect the environment.[27] In its more recent case law, the Court also underlined that the public concerned must be able to invoke any procedural defect in support of an action challenging the legality of a decision which falls under the scope of the EIA Directive.[28] In a similar vein, the Court of Justice underlined the importance of the right for the public concerned to ask the national court or a competent and impartial body to order interim measures, pending a definitive decisions on the lawfulness of a permit in light of EU environmental law, in order to guarantee the effectiveness of the judicial review.[29] In two recent cases which dealt with the costs of access to justice which have traditionally been very high in the United Kingdom's various jurisdictions, the Court further clarified that the term 'not prohibitively expensive' must be interpreted so that the cost of proceedings must not appear, in certain cases, to be objectively unreasonable.[30]

As regards Article 9(3) of the Aarhus Convention, the notable 2011 ruling of the Grand Chamber of the Court of Justice in *Lesoochranárske zoskupenie VLK* certainly cannot be left unaddressed.[31] Whereas the Court denied direct effect to Article 9(3) of the Aarhus Convention, it underscored that Article 9(3) of the Aarhus Convention, although drafted in broad terms, still aimed to ensure effective environmental protection.[32] The judgment was welcomed by many as

---

25 See, more recently, the ruling of the Court of Justice in *Janecek*. Case C-237/07 *Janecek* [2008] ECR I-6221, paras. 34–42.

26 Case C-263/08 *Djurgården* [2010] ECR-9967.

27 Case C-115/09 *Trianel* [2011] ECR I-3673, para. 46.

28 Case C-72/12 *Altrip* [2013], paras. 53 and 54.

29 Case C-416/10 *Križan* [2013], para. 109.

30 Case C-530/11, *Commission v UK* [2014]; Case C-260/11 *Edwards* [2013].

31 Case C-240/09 *Lesoochranárske zoskupenie VLK* [2011] ECR I-1255. See more on this: *Eliantonio, M.*, Case note on case C-240/09 Lesoochranárske zoskupenie and case C-115/09 Trianel Kohlekraftwerk, CML Rev., 2012 (49), pp. 767–791.

32 *Ibid*, para. 46.

a bold step towards more effective judicial protection in environmental matters within the ambit of EU environmental law.[33]

Taking stock of the recent case law developments, which will also help to set the scene for the subsequent analysis, it becomes apparent that the Court of Justice cannot be accused of unwillingness to take into account the Aarhus Convention, and the EU's implementing rules, as yardstick against which well-established national rules, such as the German '*Schutznorm*' were measured. In spite of the absence of a new directive in order to further harmonise the national efforts in implementing Article 9(3) of the Aarhus Convention,[34] national efforts to limit access to justice in environmental cases proved to be ever more cumbersome and complex, opening the pitch for environmental NGOs and citizens that did not agree with the outcome of the decision-making process for projects that are subject to the EU EIA rules. For instance, in *Trianel* the Court stated that environmental NGOs are carriers of 'interests' and 'rights' that are derived from EU environmental law and thus should enjoy protected status, which almost comes down to according environmental NGOs automatic standing.[35] While the Court of Justice does not go that far in demanding from the Member States to establish a system of popular action ('*actio popularis*'), its recent case law does significantly curtail the margin to manoeuver that is left for the Member States. At any rate, it is now firmly established that the reference to criteria under national procedural law in the EIA Directive cannot serve as an excuse for introducing or maintaining such strict criteria that they effectively bar all or almost all environmental NGOs from challenging acts or emissions that contravene environmental law. Henceforth the scene seemed set for the advent of a true environmental democracy in the EU, as put forward by the Aarhus Convention.

2.3. THE EXEMPTION OFFERED BY ARTICLE 1(4) OF THE EIA DIRECTIVE

Being faced with an increase of deadlock scenarios for project developments, it is by no means surprising to note that Member States and planning authorities were eager to find ways around the strict participation requirements set out by the EIA Directive. Planning authorities did not need to look far for inspiration. In recent

33 See most recently: *J.-F. Brakeland*, Access to justice in environmental matters – developments at EU level, published in the Gyoseiho-kenkyu, 2014 (5), http://greenaccess.law.osaka-u.ac.jp/wp-content/uploads/2014/05/arten-brakelandup.pdf. See also in this regard: *J. Darpö & Y. Epstein*, Thrown to the Wolves – Sweden Once Again Flouts EU Standards on Species Protection and Access to Justice, Nordic Environmental Law Journal, 2015 (7).

34 See also in this regard: *J. Darpö*, Effective Justice?, Synthesis report of the study on the Implementation of Articles 9.3 and 9.4 of the Aarhus Convention in the Member States of the European Union, 2013, http://ec.europa.eu/environment/aarhus/access_studies.htm.

35 *Trianel*, *supra* note 27, paras. 55–59.

years, a long-forgotten provision of the EIA Directive, which allowed Member States to derogate from the EIA requirements for projects which are adopted by specific legislation, gained considerable airplay amongst planning authorities, both at national and regional level.

This exemption, which is included in Article 1(4) of the EIA Directive,[36] liberates projects covered by the latter directive, from compliance with the assessment procedure, including the participatory and access to justice rights that are attached to it, whenever the objectives of EIA, including that of supplying information, are achieved through the legislative process. The latter provision is not a standalone clause. It also has its counterpart in the Aarhus Convention, where Article 2(2) explicitly excludes 'bodies or institutions acting in a legislative capacity' from the definition of 'public authority'. According to the Implementation Guide to Aarhus Convention, the rationale for this exclusion is the following: 'elected representatives are in theory directly accountable to the public through the election process'.[37] On the surface, this reasoning seems convincing and logical in the context of environmental decision-making. At the same time, it must be highlighted that nothing excludes Member States from deciding to extend the participation and access to justice rights to the legislative process.[38] The Aarhus Convention merely sets out minimum requirements, just as is the case with EU environmental law.[39]

In spite of the apparent attractiveness of this loophole for 'detailed legislation', its application on the ground remained modest at best. Indeed, up until recently most national and regional planning authorities deemed it to be a highly impracticable solution for the increasing number of deadlock scenarios in the context of large infrastructure projects. To understand why, we have to briefly explore the critical appraisal of Article 1(4) of the EIA Directive in the early case law developments at EU level. In its landmark ruling of 16 September 1999 in *World Wildlife Fund*, which concerned the airport of Bolzano, a former military airport which Italian authorities planned to transform into an airport which can be used commercially, the Court of Justice clarified that, in order to render the exemption included in Article 1(4) applicable, two specific conditions need to be fulfilled.

The first condition requires the details of the project to be adopted by a specific act of legislation, whereas the second condition requires the objectives

[36] Before the codification of the EIA Directive by Directive 2011/92/EU this exemption clause was included in Article 1(4) of the EIA Directive.

[37] United Nations Economic Commission for Europe, The Aarhus Convention: An Implementation Guide, 2nd ed., 2014, p. 49 (Aarhus Implementation Guide), www.unece.org/environmental-policy/treaties/public-participation/publications/public-participation/2013/aarhus-convention-implementation-guide-second-edition-text-only-version.html.

[38] *Ibid.*

[39] Article 193 of the TFEU (ex-Art. 176 EC) allows Member States the option to maintain or take more stringent measures. These measures need to be compatible with the primary Treaty provisions and must be reported to the Commission.

of the EIA Directive, including that of supplying the necessary information on the potential environmental effects of the proposed construction works, to be achieved throughout the legislative process.[40] Subsequently, the Court of Justice held that whenever it is a legislative act, instead of a decision of the competent authorities, which grants the developer the right to carry out the project, that act must be specific and display the same characteristics as the development consent. The latter entails that the legislative act must lay down the project in a sufficiently precise and restrictive manner so as to include, like development consent, following their consideration by the legislature, all the elements of the project relevant to the EIA.[41] By contrast, when further studies are necessary after the adoption of the project in question, as was the situation in the Italian case, the requirements of Article 1(4) are not deemed to be fulfilled. In other words, when faced with a choice between an automatic presumption that the legislative process complies with the objectives of the EIA Directive and a more restrictive approach, whereby the exemption only applies whenever it has been ascertained that it observes the objectives of the EIA Directive, the Court of Justice clearly opted for the latter.

Authors like Krämer rightly submitted that the Court's rationale implied that, whenever application is being made of the exemption clause, the legislature, before adopting the act, is obliged to examine the direct and indirect effects of the project.[42] In addition, it has also been contended that the Court's reference to the sixth recital of the EIA Directive indicated that also in the case of a specific act of national legislation the public affected by the project must have the opportunity to express an opinion on the project.[43] Henceforth, the potential benefits of the application of the exemption clause seemed to be ephemeral at best. In the end, the legislature still needed to comply with the basic procedural requirements set out by the EIA Directive for generic permitting procedures. In its ruling in *Linster*, just two years later, the Court of Justice reasserted the latter viewpoint.[44]

Against the backdrop of this case law it appeared safe to conclude that the application of Article 1(4) did not make that much difference on the ground. In fact, it has only been applied in a limited number of cases in subsequent years.

To use the words of Advocate General Léger in *Linster*: 'By making an exception for cases where a project is adopted by a legislative act, the Community legislature did not intend to lay down a formal criterion enabling Member States to exclude such projects from an assessment of their environmental impact and from the requirement to inform and consult the public concerned merely on the

[40] Case C-435/97 *World Wildlife Fund* [1999] ECR I-5613, paras. 56 and 57.
[41] *Ibid.*, para. 59.
[42] *L. Krämer*, Casebook on EU Environmental Law, 2003, p. 66.
[43] *Ibid.*
[44] Case C-287/98 *Linster* [2000] ECR I-6917, para. 49.

basis of the nature of the act in question and the status of the authority which adopted it'.[45]

Reminiscent of Magritte's famous painting '*Ceci n'est pas une pipe*', the previous case law developments seemed to indicate that the exemption clause included in Article 1(4) of the EIA Directive did not bring about tangible benefits for planning authorities in comparison with the ordinary environmental decision-making procedures. In other words, the exemption turned out to be no exemption at all.

3. STRICT JUDICIAL SCRUTINY: AARHUS SHOWS ITS TEETH TO THE WALLOON REGION (IN THEORY ...)

3.1. THE RE-EMERGENCE OF ARTICLE 1(4) IN A BELGIAN LARGE INFRASTRUCTURE CASE

In light of the above, it is to be noted that the Court of Justice seemed particularly keen on preserving the effectiveness of the EIA Directive. Indeed, a more lenient interpretation would probably give rise to situations where planning authorities would increasingly resort to the exemption clause in order to circumvent the generally applicable EIA rules. Therefore, opting for the legislative detour appeared to be no longer a viable solution for national planning authorities that, out of fear of additional delays and legal obstacles, were unwilling to comply with the generic EIA rules and the comprehensive consultation and participation modalities attached thereto.

While it remained uncertain whether the above-featured reading of the Court's case law was the correct one, the tool of legal ratification disappeared from the radar for more than a decade in the context of spatial planning projects. However, only to re-emerge with more force in the case law developments of the Court of Justice from 2011 onwards. In spite of the clear-cut language used by the Court of Justice in its previous jurisprudence, the exact confines of the duties of the legislature when opting for a legislative validation of a development consent were not yet crystal-clear. A lot of compelling legal questions remained unanswered. For instance, is the legislature allowed to simply ratify development consent that had been subject to a prior EIA or is Article 1(4) only complied with when Member of Parliaments (MPs) are effectively capable of discussing an re-examining the provided environmental information? And, perhaps more importantly in light of the requirements of national constitutional law, to what extent it is for the national courts to review the quality of the parliamentary debate and the extent to which it complied with the objectives of the EIA Directive?

---

[45] Opinion Advocate General Léger, Case C-287/98 *Linster* [2000], para. 114.

In a Belgian case, pertaining to, among others, the expansion of the airports of Bierset (Liège) and similar projects affecting the airport Charleroi (Brussels South) and railway links to them, the latter issues needed to be addressed in more detail. The proceedings centred on a Parliamentary Decree, in which the Walloon Parliament had 'ratified' various planning consents, some of which had already been granted in 2003.[46] The ratification was deemed necessary since, in the Walloon Government's view, the purported works were grounded on 'overriding reasons in the general interests'. In order not to see its projects delayed or even derailed by 'mere' procedural flaws and defects, the Walloon Government decided to ratify the issued construction permits for the planned works. Accordingly, it took the instrument of legal ratification to a whole other level, beyond the ambit of the EIA Directive. In itself, such strategy was not novel within the Belgian context. Back in the early 2000s, in pre-Aarhus times, the Flemish government had already successfully pulled off this 'trick', when it ratified the building permits for the construction of a large tidal block in the Port of Antwerp (the so-called 'Deurganckdok'). All the legal challenges that had been launched against the Flemish decrees were dismissed by the Belgian Court of Arbitration, as the present Belgian Constitutional Court was named before 2003.[47]

Since the ratification of the development consents had deprived both the Belgian Council of State of its jurisdiction and the applicants of their interest in having the permits annulled, the opponents of the projects were left but with one option: challenging the ratified permits before the Belgian Constitutional Court. And this is exactly what happened. Yet somehow the Walloon Government had more trust in the judgment of the latter court, seeing that the competence of the Constitutional Court is in essence limited to constitutional issues. Ultimately, the Decree was directly attacked before the Constitutional Court back in 2008. At the same time, however, the Constitutional Court was confronted with several preliminary references issued by the Council of State, which centred on the constitutionality of the Walloon Decree. The Constitutional Court, being faced for the first time ever with questions concerning the compatibility of legal ratifications with the EIA Directive and the Aarhus Convention, finally decided to refer several questions of interpretation to the Court of Justice in 2010.[48] Earlier on, by its decisions of 27 March and 31 March 2009, the Council of State had already done the same in some of the cases in which the legality of the permits had been challenged.

---

46 Article 5 to 17 of the Walloon Decree of 17 July 2008 (*Official Gazette* 25 July 2008).

47 See among others: Court of Arbitration, 26 June 2002, no. 2002/116. See also: *J. Vanpreat*, Decretale validatie bij infrastructuurprojecten: een pleidooi voor de herziening van de rechtsbescherming, Tijdschrift voor Bestuurswetenschappen en Publiek Recht, 2012, p. 115.

48 Belgian Constitutional Court, case no. 30/2010, 30 March 2010, www.const-court.be/.

3.2. '¡*NO PASARÁN!*' SAYS THE COURT IN LUXEMBOURG AND THE BELGIAN CONSTITUTIONAL COURT IN BRUSSELS

As could have been expected from the analysis above, the Grand Chamber of the Court of Justice displayed the usual strict rigor when assessing the Walloon decree in the light of the EIA Directive and the Aarhus Convention in its rulings of respectively 18 October 2011 (*Boxus*)[49] and 16 February 2012[50] (*Solvay*). In order to fully grasp the ins and outs of the debate surrounding the alleged rigidity of the Court's case law in relation to Article 1(4) of the EIA Directive, a critical analysis of the two aforementioned landmark rulings is required.

The first issue to be decided upon by the Court of Justice was the applicability of the exemption clause in a constellation where a regional decree aimed at merely ratifying pre-existing development consents for large infrastructure works. The Court of Justice did so in remarkably clear words. After having briefly reiterated the two conditions at play in this regard, the Court, following the view of Advocate General Sharpston,[51] decided to focus more on the second limb of the twofold test. While it is clear that the Walloon Decree, which in itself did not lay down the project in detail,[52] does not comply with the first condition of Article 1(4) of the EIA Directive, the Court still decided to zoom in on the content of the information that had to be made available to the Walloon Parliament in order for the exemption to apply. More in particular, the Court of Justice held that the MPs must have at their disposal virtually all information on the environmental effects of the project that should otherwise be included in the EIA.[53] In this regard, the Court underlined that sufficient due regard needs to be given to Article 5(3) and Annex IV of the EIA Directive, which laid down the minimum information to be provided by a project developer in an EIA.[54] As such, the Court granted some leeway to national or regional parliaments by acknowledging that the legislature can, when adopting the final act authorising a project, take advantage of the information gathered during a prior, administrative procedure.[55] However, the Court of Justice explicitly ruled that a legislative act which does no more than simply 'ratify' a pre-existing administrative act, by merely referring to overriding reasons relating to the general interest without a substantive legislative process

49 Joined cases C-128/09 to C-131/09, C-134/09 and C-135/09 *Boxus* [2011] ECR I-9711.

50 Case C-182/10 *Solvay* [2012]. See also more extensively: *M. Delnoy,* Cour de justice de l'Union européenne – La validité des actes législatifs d'autorisation de projet au regard des exigences procédurales de la directive E.I.E. et de la Convention d'Aarhus: les arrêts des 18 octobre 2011 (Boxus) et 16 février 2012 (Solvay) de la Cour de justice de l'Union européenne relatifs au DAR, Amén. 2012, p. 153.

51 Opinion Advocate General Sharpston, Joined cases C-128/09 to C-131/09, C-134/09 and C-135/09 *Boxus* [2011], paras. 75 and 76.

52 *Ibid.*, para. 74.

53 *Boxus*, *supra* note 49, para. 43; *Solvay*, *supra* note 50, para. 37.

54 *Boxus*, *supra* note 49, para. 43; *Solvay*, *supra* note 50, para. 37.

55 *Boxus*, *supra* note 49, para. 44; *Solvay*, *supra* note 50, para. 38.

enabling those conditions to be fulfilled having first been opened, cannot be regarded as a specific legislative act for the purposes of Article 1(4) of the EIA Directive.[56] Since this had been the case for the Walloon decree, its survival chances were severely limited after the Court's rulings.

In itself, practices whereby the Parliament is merely used as a rubber-stamp for the government's spatial planning policy, are to be avoided. Interestingly, the Court of Justice did not pronounce itself on the legality of the Walloon Decree. Yet, in order to further guide the national courts, the Court issued some additional criteria to be observed when assessing the validity of the Walloon Decree. In checking whether the legislative act at issue complied with the requirements set out by Article 1(4) of the EIA Directive, the national court needs to take account of both the content of the legislative act adopted and of the entire legislative process which led to its adoption, including the preparatory documents and the parliamentary decree.[57]

Whereas the Court's stance on the first question can, in spite of its potentially far-reaching implications for national constitutional and procedural law, hardly be called surprising, the bigger question was how the provisions on judicial protection, among others contained in Article 9(2) and (4) of the Aarhus Convention, are to be interpreted in the context of legislative validation. Or, in other words, does the presence of a legislative act limit the scope of assessment available for the competent national courts? How to sanction the improper use of the exemption clause? Here, the Court of Justice was basically asked to clarify to what extent its progressive stance towards access to justice in environmental cases before the national courts (see *supra*) was also applicable in the context of legislative validation. Let us, for clarity's sake, briefly recap the thorny legal situation at play in the Walloon Region. Due to the ratification of the development permits, the Belgian Council of State was no longer competent to assess the formal and substantive legality of the permits, as was required by Article 9(2) of the Aarhus Convention. At the same time, however, the Belgian Constitutional Court seemed to lack full competence to carry out the latter test, since it could merely review the constitutionality of legislative acts. It was apparent that, in spite the Member States' procedural autonomy when implementing the provisions on access to justice, such a constellation could hardly be deemed reconcilable with the objectives of the Aarhus Convention.[58] Thus the Court of Justice was asked to choose sides. Would the procedural autonomy of the Member States prevail or, alternatively, would environmental rights trump well-established national procedural rules? The Court opted for the latter stance. Indeed, in the Court's view, a legislative act which did not comply with the requirements set out by Article 1(4) of the EIA Directive, must be challengeable before a national court

56 *Boxus*, *supra* note 49, para. 45; *Solvay*, *supra* note 50, para. 39.
57 *Boxus*, *supra* note 49, para. 47; *Solvay*, *supra* note 50, para. 41.
58 *Boxus*, *supra* note 49, para. 52; *Solvay*, *supra* note 50, para. 47.

or another independent and impartial body as to its substantive or procedural legality, in order to avoid that Article 9 of the Aarhus Convention and Article 11 of the EIA Directive would lose all effectiveness.[59]

This being the case, the Court of Justice did not go any deeper into the specific division of competences between the Belgian Council of State and the Constitutional Court, nor did it examine more into detail whether the Constitutional Court, if competent, can fully assess the compatibility of the Decree with the criteria set out by Article 1(4) of the EIA Directive. If anything, the Court of Justice underlined that, if no review procedure is available under national law, any national court before which an action falling within its jurisdiction is brought, would have the task of carrying out the review of the legislative act in light of the aforementioned requirements and, if necessary, should disapply the legislative act.[60]

Hence, if the jurisdiction of the Belgian Constitutional Court were to be limited to merely verifying compliance with constitutional principles per se, other national courts, including the Council of State, would have the task of carrying out the latter view and, if necessary disregard the legislative act.[61] A logical yet daunting statement, especially in light of the Member States' procedural autonomy.

By underscoring the importance of effective judicial review in the context of a legislative ratification, the Court of Justice has added another important layer to its already stringent approach to legislative validation. It can be inferred from the latter judgments that the Aarhus Convention serves as an additional guardian of the effectiveness of the EIA-rules. However, in order to fully assess the impact of the case law of the Court of Justice in this respect, it is appropriate to also take into account the final outcome of the lawsuit before the Belgian national courts, especially since it is illustrative for the complexities to which the case law of the Court of Justice might lead. Ultimately, the Belgian Constitutional Court took up the implicit hints by the Court of Justice and decided to quash the Walloon Decree in its ruling of 22 November 2012, thereby liberating the Council of State or any other national court from the burdensome task to transgress its own jurisdiction in order to accommodate the rationale underpinning the preliminary rulings of the Court of Justice in *Boxus* and *Solvay*.[62] Although it passed relatively unnoticed in the Belgian legal literature, the ruling of the Belgian Constitutional Court warrants closer analysis, especially since it is, to my knowledge, the first national

---

59 *Boxus, supra* note 49, para. 53; *Solvay, supra* note 50, para. 48.

60 *Boxus, supra* note 49, para. 55; *Solvay, supra* note 50, para. 50.

61 Opinion Advocate General Sharpston, *supra* note 51, para. 100.

62 Belgian Constitutional Court, case no. 144/2012, 22 November 2012, www.const-court.be/. See more extensively: *T. Bombois,* La jurisprudence de la Cour constitutionnelle relative à l'article 9 de la Convention d'Aarhus garantissant l'accès à la justice en matière environnementale, Amén. 2013, p. 61; *M. Delnoy & R. Smal,* La délivrance ou ratification par le législateur de permis d'urbanisme ou d'environnement au regard du droit européen et de la Convention d'Aarhus, JDE 2014, p. 50.

ruling in which a national court was asked to scrutinise the parliamentary process that has led to the adoption of a ratification act in the light of EU and international environmental law.

So how did the Belgian Constitutional Court handle the matter? Interestingly, the Constitutional Court initiated its reasoning by laying down the limits of its own direct jurisdiction, which is basically confined to reviewing legislative acts in respect of Articles 10, 11 and 23 of the Constitution.[63] It had to concede that its own jurisdiction did not match the criteria set out by the Aarhus Convention and the EIA Directive.[64] The Council of State's jurisdiction, by contrast, does easily comply with the latter requirements. However, due to the legislative validation of the permits, the jurisdiction of the Council of State had been removed. Such potential difference of treatment for the affected public could only have been justifiable if the legislative act complied with the requirements set out by Article 1(4). Accordingly, the Constitutional Court reviewed to what extent the Walloon decree observed the requirements set out by Article 1(4) of the EIA Directive.[65] In this respect, the Belgian Constitutional Court explicitly admitted that, in order to comply with the criteria set out by the Court of Justice, it needed to overstep the traditional competences that had been conferred upon it by the Belgian Constitution. As such, the Court did not devote many words to the latter and rather succinctly concluded that, given the limited role of the MPs of the Walloon Parliament throughout the legislative process, the Walloon decree breached the requirements set out by Article 1(4) of the EIA Directive.[66] Ultimately, the Walloon decree was annulled, which granted the Belgian Council of State, after more than 10 years of legal proceedings, competence to adjudge the legality of the building permits in the pending cases.

3.3. THE IRONY OF IT ALL?

Before touching upon the wider consequences of the above depicted rulings of the Court of Justice, which were later supplemented by the 2012 ruling in *Nomarchiaki*,[67] it needs to be highlighted that, by the time of the ruling of the Belgian Constitutional Court, most of the construction works, with the exception of some works that were planned in a Natura 2000 site, had already been carried out. This was amongst others the case for the light metro project in Charleroi. Other works, such as the extension and refurbishment works of the regional airports of Charleroi (Brussels South) and Liège-Bierset have been substantially completed by now. Moreover, in a first string of decisions, dating from June 2014,

63 *Ibid.*, para. B.9.3.
64 *Ibid.*, para. B.9.4.
65 *Ibid.*, para. B.13.
66 *Ibid.*, para. B.14.1.
67 Case C-43/10 *Nomarchiaki Aftodioikisi Aitoloakarnanias* [2012], paras. 76–91.

the Belgian Council of State dismissed all the legal arguments raised against the permits that had been granted for some of the construction works on the regional airport of Charleroi (Brussels South).[68]

Against the backdrop of the provisional outcome of the legal proceedings so far, the following five observations are in order.

First – focusing on the practical effect of the legal proceedings in the Walloon case – attention needs to be drawn to the long delays which the applicants had to face before being able to finally prompt the Council of State to a complete judicial review of some of the development consents. The length of legal proceedings is often overlooked by legal scholars, but in many cases the availability of smooth court procedures is seminal in order to safeguard the effectiveness of any judicial review. Having regard to the particular circumstances of the case – which included several preliminary references to both the Constitutional Court and the Court of Justice of the EU – the extensive time lag appears plausible. However, whereas the preliminary references might serve as partial justification for the extensive time gap between the issuance of the permits and the first decisions on the merits of the case, they still fail to explain why it lasted ten years before a first complete review of the legality of the development consents could be carried out. This in itself does not seem to be in line with the rationale underpinning Article 9(4) of the Aarhus Convention, according to which it must be ensured that the available review procedures are, in any event, fair, equitable, timely and not prohibitively expensive. Given the fact that many of the construction works have already been substantially accomplished, it is safe to conclude that the majority of the pending and or new challenges against the granted permits have lost their purpose, even if they are, legally speaking, still in order. Admittedly, it is not excluded that, in the event of a future annulment of one of the building permits, a national court might order the removal of alleged illegal construction works. However, practice learns that courts will be very reluctant to pass such harsh sentences, especially in the context of large infrastructure projects which have been financed by public funds. Evidently, opting for a legislative validation of permits does not in itself rule out the possibility of timely judicial review, nor does it preclude interim relief, if necessary. The Walloon Decree, however, could be quoted as a prime example of how legislative validation can be misused in order to block effective and timely judicial review in the context of large infrastructure projects.

Second – as to the content of the above-discussed rulings – it needs to be observed that the Court of Justice not only seemed keen on safeguarding the effectiveness of the EIA Directive but, in doing so, also reasserted the importance of an all-encompassing judicial review for projects falling within the scope of the EIA Directive. The central conclusion arising from this is the eagerness of the Court of Justice to put a halt to practices by which national legislatures seek to

[68] See, among others, Belgian Council of State, 26 June 2014 (Application No 227.902, 227.903, 227.904).

avoid scrutiny by rushing the development permits through parliament. Merely ratifying pre-existing permits in order to overcome potential EIA defects or flaws seems to be ruled out by the strict stance of the Court of Justice. Arguably *Boxus* and *Solvay* are the first two cases in which the Court of Justice was able exemplify how the access to justice rights are to be applied in the context of legislative validation. By demanding a comprehensive judicial review of legislative acts that do not comply with the requirements set out by Article 1(4) of the EIA Directive, the Court avoids that the exemption clause would turn into a major loophole in EU environmental law. To that end, the Court did not shy away from obliging the national courts to set aside national procedural rules in order to avoid that Article 9(2) and (4) of the Aarhus Convention would lose all its effectiveness. This is somehow reminiscent of the Court's earlier jurisprudence in *Simmenthal II*[69] and *Factortame*,[70] in which the Court clarified that directly applicable Community law provisions create legal rights which are enforceable by individuals, regardless of any contrary national procedural law. While the Court's take might appear far-reaching in itself, since it pushes national courts to the limits of their jurisdiction (or even beyond), it indeed seems to be the only viable way to safeguard the effectiveness of the procedural environmental rights.

Third – and widening the view further – the Court's stance appears all the more justified in the light of the provisional outcome of the proceedings in the Belgian case so far. In hindsight, the distrust towards the Council of State seemed to be at least partially misplaced. Although the Walloon government was particularly wary of the rigidity of the Council of State when assessing the legality of administrative acts, the Council's first take on the applications filed against the building permits did so far not lead to an annulment of the permits. While it remains hard to predict the outcome of the other pending annulment proceedings before the Council of State, the effect of a possible annulment on the ground would be limited at best since most of the projects have already been realised. This preliminary conclusion goes to the heart of much of the debate that is surrounding EU environmental law at present. Take for instance the Habitats Directive, which is often portrayed by its opponents as a 'rigid piece of legislation' that is, by virtue of its prohibitive nature, incapable of smoothly integrating nature conservation interests in a spatial planning process. In spite of the few 'hard cases' that have made the headlines in some Member States, the image of EU nature conservation law as 'ultimate bottleneck' for project development needs some adjustment in light of the fairly limited amount of projects that ultimately had to be cancelled due to biodiversity-related concerns.[71] It a similar vein, the 2009 report on the application and effectiveness of the EIA Directive

69 Case C-106/77 *Simmenthal* [1978] ECR I-629.

70 Case C-213/89 *Factortame* [1990] ECR I-2433.

71 See for more extensive information: *R. Beunen & M. Duineveld,* Divergence and Convergence in Policy Meanings of European Environmental Policies: The Case of the Birds and Habitats Directive, International Planning Studies, 2010 (15:4), pp. 321–334.

highlights that the EIA process in many Member States does not comply with the requirements set out by the latter Directive.[72] Inadequate screening practices and the use of unreasonably high thresholds help to explain why many projects are still excluded from prior assessments, while the EIA process at national level is often characterised by the poor quality of EIA and inapt practices for public participation. Improper EIA procedures are still a pervasive problem throughout many Member States. Thus, it remains safe to say that, instead of depicting the EIA Directive as a trigger for unnecessary administrative burden, a stronger emphasis is to be placed on a proper and more correct implementation of the EIA Directive. Paradoxically, high quality EIAs and meaningful and early participation might offer a more viable pathway to legal certainty than an increased application of the cumbersome exemptions clauses present in the EIA Directive.

Fourth – taking an even broader view now – it is to be noted that the restrictive view emanating from the case law of the Court of Justice does not seem to rule out the use of the exemption clause for legislative acts in itself. One might even portend that the Walloon case represented the best imaginable test case for the Court of Justice to underline its commitment to ensuring the effectiveness of the European EIA rules. Indeed, in the Belgian case it could easily be established that the Walloon parliamentary procedure, which basically came down to a mere formal ratification procedure, did not come forward to the objectives of the EIA Directive. As was also demonstrated by the subsequent ruling in *Nomarchiaki*, the Court of Justice does in itself not rule out the use of the exemption clause for legislative acts, provided that appropriate information was available at the time of adoption. This being the case, the strict stance of the Court of Justice will obviously further limit the attractiveness of the exemption clause, since it puts down a string of demanding requirements to be fulfilled. In this respect, it is to be noted that, aside from the latter observations, other EU environmental directives do not contain a similar exemption clause, which even further reduces the added value of the latter exemption clause. In many instances, a large infrastructure project will be subject to both a prior EIA and an appropriate assessment, for instance due to its location in the vicinity of a Natura 2000 site. As was affirmed by the Court of Justice in the *Solvay* case, the obligations incumbent on the Member States by virtue of Article 6(3) of the Habitats Directive do not differ when the plans or projects are approved by a legislative authority.[73] Thus, no short cuts will be available in such scenarios.

This brings me to my *fifth* and *final* comment, which also serves as introduction to the last section of this chapter. It touches upon the rather stringent test that has been put forward by the Grand Chamber of the Court of

[72] European Commission, Report from the Commission to the Council, the European Parliament, the European Economic and Social Committee and the Committee of the Regions. On the application and the effectiveness of the EIA Directive (Directive 85/337/EEC, as amended by Directives 97/11/EC and 2003/35/EC, COM(2009)378 final (Brussels 2009), 5–6.

[73] *Solvay*, *supra* note 50, paras. 68–70.

Justice for national courts in assessing whether the legislative process complies with the objectives of the EIA Directive. According to the Court of Justice, the national courts have to scrutinise the entire legislative process which led up to the adoption of the legislative act at issue. In doing so, the Court of Justice rightly underscored that legislative validation and judicial review are not mutually exclusive. While the Belgian Constitutional Court did not find it troublesome to check the parliamentary debate and the preparatory documents which preceded the adoption of the Walloon decree, the application of such a test might not be as straightforward in other jurisdictions, where, for instance, legislative acts are not challengeable before a constitutional court. So far, the latter requirements have not generated a lot of debate. However, it is worth pondering how the Belgian Constitutional Court would have applied the latter test in a constellation where the permits had been thoroughly discussed in the Walloon Parliament. While the Court of Justice itself did not elaborate extensively on the criteria to be used in this respect, both Advocates General tried to provide the national courts with additional guidance in this regard. Advocate General Sharpston underscored that, in assessing whether the legislative procedure comes forwards to the fundamentals of the EIA Directive, due regard needs to be taken of, among others, 'the process'. This entails that the national courts need to check whether, among others, the preparation time and discussion time were sufficient for it to be plausible to conclude that the people's elected representatives were able to properly examine and debate the proposed projects.[74] Advocate General Kokott highlighted that the 'legislature ... [should perform] its democratic function correctly and effectively'. Likewise she also underlined the need to clarify whether the legislature 'was able to properly examine and debate the environmental effects of the project'.[75] In the Belgian case, the performance of such assessment was relatively unequivocal since no genuine debate had been allowed on the specific content of the ratified permits. However, in general, national courts will be very reluctant in scrutinising the parliamentary process leading up to the adoption of a legislative act validating an administrative consent. Probably many judges will such an exercise to a form of undesirable judicial activism which might run counter to constitutional bedrock principles, such as the separation of powers and the sovereignty of the parliament.[76] And thus other, more troublesome questions are coming to the fore. For instance, how to assess whether the quality of a parliamentary debate in itself matches the standards of the EIA Directive? Will this only be the case whenever the act at issue was subject to an elaborate parliamentary debate? And what about the emergence of the system of strict party discipline, which is underpinning most coalition governments in Europe?

74 Opinion Advocate General Sharpston, *supra* note 51, para. 84.

75 Opinion Advocate General Kokott, Case C-43/10 *Nomarchiaki Aftodioikisi Aitoloakarnanias* [2012], paras. 136–137.

76 See also in a similar vein: *D. Hart QC*, Aarhus shows its teeth to Belgium, http://ukhumanrightsblog.com/2011/10/31/aarhus-shows-its-teeth-to-belgium/.

4. A MORE GENEROUS APPROACH: UK SUPREME COURT ENDORSES THE HS2 HYBRID BILL

4.1. A NEW TWIST TO A LONG-STANDING DEBATE ...

The latter questions are throwing yet another, more challenging hypothesis in the mix. Indeed, a scenario in which a development consent for a large infrastructure project has been subject to a legislative validation which was the result of a parliamentary process that went beyond 'formal ratification', would arguably pose a greater challenge for national courts. The recent HS2 case, which already served as an introduction to this chapter, and revolved around the construction of the HS2 high-speed rail link in the UK, provided the recently established UK Supreme Court with a first-class opportunity to shed light on the compatibility of a comprehensive legislative validation effort with the requirements set out by international and European environmental law. On the surface, the judgment of 22 January 2014 does serve as a logical follow-up to the ruling of the Belgian Constitutional Court of 22 November 2012.[77] However, in many aspects, the reasoning of the UK Supreme Court differs from the approach adopted by the Belgian judges. To understand why, we first need to take a closer look at the factual background of the case, which is to be distinguished from the above-discussed Belgium case on several counts.

The starting point, however, is quite similar. As was the case in the Walloon Region, the UK Government proved unwilling to opt for the generic administrative procedures in relation to what was to become the major construction project of the coming decades. On 10 January 2012 it issued the Command Paper High Speed Rail: Investing in Britain's Future – Decisions and Next Steps (DNS), which set out the UK Government's strategy for the promotion, construction and operation of HS2 and its detailed proposals for Phase 1 of the route from London to the West Midlands. In spite of the significance of the DNS on the further decision-making process for a nationally significant infrastructure liable to cause environmental effects over a widespread area, the UK Government decided to adopt it without first conducting an assessment of and publication on how the proposals compared in environmental alternatives to the reasonable alternatives. At the same time, the UK Government decided to obtain development consent for HS2 through two hybrid bills in Parliament. Henceforth, the decision concerning HS2 was to be taken not by administrative means but by way of the enactment of a so-called 'hybrid bill'.

[77] *R. (on the application of HS2 Action Alliance Limited) (Appellant) v. The Secretary of State for Transport and another (Respondents), R. (on the application of Heathrow Hub Limited and another) (Appellants) v. Secretary of State for Transport and another (Respondents), R. (on the application of Hillingdon London Borough Council and others) (Appellants) v. The Secretary of State of Transport (Respondent)* [2014] UKSC 3 (hereafter: 'Judgment UK Supreme Court 2014').

Basically, a hybrid bill is a public bill which affects a particular private interest in a manner different from the private interests of other persons or bodies of the same category or class. A hybrid bill has to go through a similar procedure as a public bill, but with an additional select committee stage after the second reading in each House, at which objectors whose interests are affected by the bill may petition against the bill and be heard. It is important to underline that, under the parliamentary procedure as envisaged by the Government back in 2012, matters that go to the principle of the bill, such as the business case for HS2, alternatives for the high-speed rail project and alternative routes for Phase 1, will not be considered by the selection committee.[78] The principle of the bill could in theory be re-opened at third reading, but that debate will also be subject to the Government whip. In addition, due regard must be given to the fact that the bill will be accompanied by an environmental statement (EIA), which must contain all the relevant information on the environmental effects of the purported works.[79]

However, in spite of the safeguards present in the legislative procedure, the opponents of the projects claimed the DNS to be adopted in glaring breach of the SEA Directive. In addition, they portended that the Parliament's consideration of HS2 would not comply with the more general requirements set out by international and EU law. More in particular, the critics questioned whether the Parliament's consideration of HS2 would be a satisfactory decision-making procedure in terms of EU environmental law. It was also feared that the EIA in itself would not look into other reasonable alternatives, which normally would have been taken care of at the level of a SEA.

As to the second point of contention, being the compatibility with the EIA Directive, the opponents put forward no fewer than three distinct lines of argumentation. *First*, they submitted that since there was no free vote to be expected in Parliament on the hybrid bill for HS2 – due to the so-called 'whipping of vote' (party discipline) and collective ministerial responsibility at second and third reading – there will be no sufficient room left for a proper consideration of the environmental effects of the purported project. *Second*, it was contended that the EIA would be so voluminous and complex that MPs will not be able to consider it properly throughout the normal legislative procedure. In their view, it would be implausible to suggest that all or even a majority of the MPs who vote on the bill will have been able to fully assess the environmental impact of the project. *Third*, it was stated that the limited participation provided for in the confines of the so-called select committee does not comply the public participation standards propagated by Article 6(4) of the EIA Directive since it does not allow for any consideration of the principle of the bill.[80]

78 *Ibid.*, paras. 57–58.
79 *Ibid.*, paras. 59–60.
80 *Ibid.*, paras. 70–73.

By including these arguments in their legal challenges against the HS2 project, the opponents urged the UK judges to express their opinion on the quality of the legislative procedure to which the hybrid bill for HS2 would be subject. Contrary to the above-discussed Belgian case, the lawsuit had been initiated by some anti HS2-action groups before the legislative procedure was effectively started. After having been dismissed by the Court of Appeal in July 2013, some opponents – among others HS2AA and LBH – pursued the UK Supreme Court which was, for the first time in its history, confronted with several arguments related to legislative validation in the context of the EIA Directive.

4.2. UK SUPREME COURT OPTS FOR A MIDDLE GROUND

The question now arose whether the newly established UK Supreme Court would be as willing as the Belgian Constitutional Court in applying the strict scrutiny test that has been put forward by the Court of Justice in its previous case law. In the UK, where a more restrained approach towards EU law is being upheld and traditionally a lot of weight is given to constitutional principles governing the relationship between Parliament and the Court, such strict scrutiny might even be less plausible than on the continent.

A logical starting point is the section of the ruling which addresses the first claim of the appellants. Here, the UK Supreme Court unanimously held that the DNS did not 'set the framework for development consent' within the meaning of the SEA Directive and thus did not need to be subject to a prior SEA. In light of the subsequent analysis, it is interesting to point out that, according to Lord Carnwath JSC, who wrote this section of the Supreme Court judgment, the UK Parliament is sovereign and thus cannot be subject to any *de jure* constraint, even if the *de facto* reality is that MPs could be influenced by the DNS to grant development consent for the HS2 proposal that it adopts.[81]

As far as the second argument was concerned, the UK Supreme Court first had to get round some substantial constitutional issues. For one, it remained unclear whether the strict scrutiny test, as allegedly required by the Court of Justice, was in itself compatible with the long-established constitutional principles governing the relationship between Parliament and the courts, as reflected in Article 9 of the Bill of Rights 1689. This also makes the ruling interesting from a broader perspective. Lord Reed, who wrote the judgment on this point, adopted a rather pragmatic stance, which allowed him to assess the arguments of the applicants, without losing sight of the constitutional principles, such as the separation of powers. In his view, the EIA Directive did not require strict scrutiny that might impinge upon the above-mentioned principles.[82] In particular, he distinguished

[81] *Ibid.*, paras. 36–42.
[82] *Ibid.*, para. 79.

the more reluctant level of scrutiny required by the Court of Justice in its recent rulings in *Boxus* and *Nomarchiaki* from the more progressive stance adopted by the Advocates General in the same cases. In this respect, Lord Reed highlighted that the comprehensive test put forward by Advocate General Kokott in *Nomarchiaki*[83] and Advocate General Sharpston in *Boxus*,[84] had not been explicitly endorsed by the Court of Justice in its final rulings. Thus, along these lines, the appellants could not rely on the latter statements in order to require the Court to carry out a substantive qualitative assessment of the legislative process which would lead to the adoption of the hybrid bill. Moreover, if anything, Lord Reed assumed the latter statements' focus to be upon the ability of the legislature to examine and debate the proposed project, rather than upon a qualitative assessment of the legislature's actual consideration of the proposal.[85]

To further understand the outcome of the case, it is important to consider that Lord Reed inferred from the case law of the Court of Justice that it is ultimately the responsibility of the national court to determine whether the legislative act at issue complies with the conditions at play in the context of Article 1(4). Hence it remains for the UK Supreme Court itself to decide whether the decision to adopt the project through a legislative act was the outcome of a substantive legislative process, and whether appropriate information was available to the MPs at the time when the project was adopted.

It is important to keep in mind that Lord Reed was fully aware of the implications of the recent jurisprudence of the Court of Justice on the topic of legislative validation. This is strikingly illustrated by the section of the judgment in which the participation requirements were tackled more into detail. Here, Lord Reed stated that, whenever the exemption clause included in Article 1(4) is applicable, neither the participation requirements included in Article 6(4) of the EIA Directive, nor the judicial review test that is included in Article 11 of the EIA Directive have to be observed. Or, as Lord Reed puts it: 'exemption from the requirements of the Directive cannot be conditional upon compliance with them: otherwise, there would be no exemption'.[86] In doing so, the UK Supreme Court partly went against the established view, according to which the participation requirements also have to be observed throughout the legislative process.[87] In support of the latter stance, Lord Reed explicitly referred to the Opinion of Advocate General Sharpston in *Boxus*, in which it was submitted that where a decision is reached by a legislative process, the participatory requirements are deemed to be observed since the legislature itself is composed of democratically elected representatives of the public. In the Advocate General's view, 'when the

83 *Supra* note 75.
84 *Supra* note 51.
85 Judgment UK Supreme Court, *supra* note 77, para. 112.
86 *Ibid.*, para. 91.
87 *L. Krämer*, *supra* note 42.

decision-making process takes place within such a body, it benefits from indirect, but nevertheless representative, public participation'.[88]

Taking all this into consideration, Lord Reed now turned to the crux of the matter. In spite of his earlier observations, in which he had explicitly refuted a qualitative assessment of the legislative process, the applicants' arguments relating to the alleged incapability of the hybrid bill procedure in achieving the objectives of the EIA still needed to be tackled. In this respect, Lord Reed made some compelling observations as regards the interplay between party politics and the EIA Directive, which transcend the context of this particular case.

First and foremost, Lord Reed rejected the applicants' view that the requirements of Article 1(4) of the EIA Directive are only complied with when there is a 'free vote' on the development consents. Or, to put it differently, a decision of the Parliament can only be deemed compatible with the objectives of the EIA Directive whenever the MPs are allowed a free vote, regardless of their party allegiance or of their membership of Government. Lord Reed took the view that Article 1(4) is indeed based on the premise that the objectives of the EIA Directive can be achieved where the decision is made by a legislative body. On the surface, the latter appears logical and reasonable since, in his view, party and government politics do not hinder MPs to carefully consider environmental information.[89] Either way, no support could be found in the recent case law of the Court of Justice to debunk the latter presumption. Likewise, Lord Reed held that, also within the framework of EU environmental law, no universal rule exists that permit issuing authorities or decision-makers must possess the independence and impartiality required of a court or a tribunal. With reference to case law of the German Constitutional Court and Article 10(4) of the Treaty on the European Union, which provides that 'political parties at European level contribute to forming European political awareness and to expressing the will of citizens of the Union', Lord Reed reasserted the legitimate role parliamentary parties are playing in the democratic decision-making process.[90] He drew further support for this viewpoint by stressing out that there is no single requirement in the EIA Directive which requires the consent on an infrastructure project to be influenced solely and decisively by environmental information.[91]

After having reiterated that the separation of powers is a fundamental aspect of most if not all constitutions of the Member States, Lord Reed held that nothing either in the text of Article 1(4) of the EIA Directive or in the case law of the Court of Justice requires national courts to review the quality of the parliamentary debate and the extent to which MPs participated in it. A contrary view would be at odds with the principle of the separation of powers.

---

88 Opinion Advocate General Sharpston, *supra* note 51, para. 54.
89 Judgment UK Supreme Court, *supra* note 77, para. 100.
90 *Ibid.*, paras. 103–107.
91 *Ibid.*, para. 107.

In its final considerations, Lord Reed held that there is no reason to suppose that the MPs will be unable to properly examine and debate the HS2 project. In this respect, he pointed out that the sheer size of the EIA, which ultimately is a reflection of the gigantic scale of the project, is not determinative since it can be expected to include a non-technical summary of the information.[92] Additionally, he underlined that the MPs will have the necessary information available well in advance of the second reading debate on the bill. And, in any event, due regard also had to be given to the long-standing political debate that had been taking place between proponents and opponents of the HS2 project, which, at least partly, also focused on its environmental impact.[93] Given the allegedly unambiguous case law of the Court of Justice on the topic of legislative validation, the UK Supreme Court finally did not seem it necessary to make a preliminary reference to the Court of Justice before reaching a decision on this matter.[94]

The central conclusion arising from this analysis is that the UK Supreme Court, by endorsing Lord Reed's stance, had achieved a practical middle ground, allowing it, on the one hand, to take into account the criteria set out by the Court of Justice as regards the room left for legislative validation in the scope of the EIA Directive, and, on the other hand, not to impinge upon the traditional principles which are underpinning UK constitutional law.

4.3. COMMON SENSE OR SPLENDID ISOLATION?

So far, so good for the HS2 project. According to the Department for Transport, the multibillion pound project programme would be able to continue 'as planned', with the government's approach to the environmental impact 'fully vindicated'. Since then, Parliament's second reading of the hybrid bill for Phase 1 took place on 28 April 2014 and was approved by 452 votes to 41. The hybrid bill for Phase 2 will be prepared for January 2015.[95] Still, in spite of the dismissal of all substantial legal challenges before the national courts, the HS2 opponents have not given up their battle to halt the railway project. In the wake of the dismissal of their case by the UK Supreme Court, they stated that a complaint will be made to the European Commission to say that the UK Government has not complied with its obligations under EU environmental law. In the meantime a complaint has been filed with the Aarhus Compliance Committee, in which it was submitted that the outright refusal by the UK Government to make the decision to go ahead with the HS2 project (the so-called 'DNS') subject to prior consultation and participation constitutes, in itself, a clear violation of Article 7 of the Aarhus

92 *Ibid.*, paras. 113–114.
93 *Ibid.*, para. 115.
94 *Ibid.*, para. 117.
95 See for more information: http://en.wikipedia.org/wiki/High_Speed_2#Hybrid_bill.

Convention. On 2 July 2014 that complaint has been declared admissible by the Aarhus Compliance Committee.[96]

Although the UK Supreme Court's approach is remarkably more reluctant in its interpretation of Article 1(4), especially set out against the allegedly progressive approach of the Belgian Constitutional Court, a lot can be said in favour of the rationale that was applied in the ruling of 22 January 2014.

First, the UK Supreme Court might have logics and common sense at his side in opting for a more pragmatic approach towards the topic of legislative validation. Indeed, the ultimate consequence of having an exemption clause present in the EIA Directive would be to accept that whenever a large infrastructure project will pass a comprehensive legislative procedure which complies with the basics of EIA, the project is exempted from the EIA rules. Otherwise Article 1(4) of the EIA Directive would amount to a pointless provision, with no tangible effects on the ground. Moreover, it seems legitimate to allow national or regional parliaments to have the final say on the acceptability of projects of regional or national scale. Even Advocate General Sharpston appeared ready to accept that the required participation might indirectly take place via the democratically elected representatives of the public. It also seems inconsistent to assume that politicians at lower instances, which issue permits for industrial activities and projects of a more average scale, are capable of properly examining a full-fledged EIA, while the same would not hold for MPs in a national parliament. And, while it is true that the strict party discipline is prone to significantly reducing profoundness of the political debate on the acceptability of major infrastructure projects, the HS2 case in itself indicated that, even in a system allegedly characterised by strict party discipline, some MPs are still susceptible to other influences and feel strong enough to vote against the official party line. Whereas the rise of party discipline and the dominance of political parties in recent decades has altered the outlook of politics in many countries, including the UK, it did not bar backbenchers from voting against the policy lines of their respective parties in earlier years. In that regard, it is interesting to point out that Lord Reed, when writing this section of the UK Supreme Court judgment, explicitly referred to a recent study that found that MPs on the Government benches had voted against the whip in 43% of divisions during the first 18 months of the Cameron Government.[97] To illustrate this point even further, reference could be made to the fact that, at the time of the second reading, 30–40 Conservative 'rebels' still felt optimistic that they could block the passing of the hybrid bill.

Second, by holding that EU law does not require the Parliament to meet the level of scrutiny the appellants asked for, the UK Supreme Court did not go

96 Preliminary determination of admissibility of communication to the Aarhus Convention Compliance Committee concerning compliance by the United Kingdom with article 7 of the Convention in relation to the proposed construction of the 'High Speed 2' railway (ACCC/2014/100), 2 July 2014.

97 Judgment UK Supreme Court, *supra* note 77, para. 64.

explicitly against the rationale upheld by the Court of Justice in its previous case law. One must indeed not lose sight of the simple fact that the EIA Directive does not explicitly require a development consent to be influenced solely and decisively by environmental information. Admittedly, it can be submitted that the UK Supreme Court's view stands at odds with the more stringent approach that was advocated for by, among others, Advocate General Kokott. Still, the latter viewpoint had not been explicitly supported by the Court of Justice in its final ruling. Admittedly, the Court of Justice indicated in *Boxus* that quickly rushing a development consent through parliament does not comply with the requirements set out by Article 1(4) of the EIA Directive. Having said this, it evidently will be harder to put forward minimum criteria for a scenario in which a project has been subject to a comprehensive parliamentary debate. One might take into account the preparation time and discussion time devoted to it. Again, driving a permit through Parliament in a nightly session might obviously not be in line with the criteria of the EIA Directive.[98] However, whenever a court is asked to declare in advance whether a parliamentary procedure would be capable of meeting the requirements of EU environmental law, such assessment would evidently require a more activist approach from the judges. Indeed, how exactly should national courts measure the quality of a parliamentary debate in the light of the criteria of the EIA Directive? And, even assuming that this would be possible, would this ultimately lead to stricter qualitative criteria for parliamentary debates on large infrastructure projects in comparison with an average parliamentary debate on the topic of fair taxes and rising inequality?

Third – and perhaps most importantly – it is to be noted that the UK Supreme Court had to walk a thin line in adjudging legal challenges which aimed to use the EIA Directive as a benchmark for the legality of an Act of Parliament. In essence, the applicants' claims indirectly challenged one of the cornerstones of parliamentary democracy, by submitting that party politics and party discipline jeopardise the objectives of the EIA Directive. In its judgment, the UK Supreme Court had to strike a balance between ensuring the effectiveness of EU environmental law on the ground, on the one hand, and not losing sight of the bedrock principles of the UK constitutional order, on the other hand. Things were not quite as simple as in the Walloon case, especially taking into account the particular sensitivity in the UK for the relationship between fundamental constitutional rules and EU law. By upholding that Article 1(4) did not have to be construed so that it requires national courts to assess the quality of the parliamentary debate, Lord Reed ostensibly chose the easy way out. He clearly intended not to open a new Pandora's box in this regard. Rejecting the strict scrutiny test that was advocated for by the appellants, the UK Supreme Court could keep away from troublesome constitutional riddles. In this respect, it is not unimportant to underline Lord Reed's dictum, in which he held that EU law's status within the UK legal order

98 See also in this regard: *D. Hart QC*, *supra* note 76.

is attributable to the European Communities Act 1972.[99] As already observed by Elliot, this dictum serves a warning shot that, if it came down to a show off, UK constitutional law, and more in particular Article 9 of the Bill of Rights 1689 might prevail over EU environmental law.[100] In the light of the further observations made by Lord Neuberger and Mance in this regard, the primacy of EU law might appear more qualified than so far had been assumed in the UK. In their view, it is certainly 'arguable (and it is for United Kingdom law and courts to determine) that there may be fundamental principles, whether contained in other constitutional instruments or recognized at common law, of which Parliament when it enacted the European Communities Act 1972 did not either contemplate or authorize the abrogation'.[101] Some authors have submitted that the obiter passage of the last two judges should be read as an implicit caution that, if one is to assume that EU environmental law overrides fundamental constitutional rules, such as parliamentary sovereignty and the separation of powers, UK's acceptance of EU law might have to be reconsidered.[102] Obviously, another solution would consist in the UK leaving the EU and/or withdrawing from the Aarhus Convention. Taking stock of the rising Euroscepticism in UK politics, such a prospect might not be that farfetched as may first appear.

Notwithstanding the elegance with which the UK Supreme Court ultimately wanted to reconcile parliamentary sovereignty with the fundamentals of the EIA Directive and the Aarhus Convention, the outcome of the HS2 case leaves a bitter taste in the mouth of many propagators of the concept of environmental democracy. Indeed, as has been highlighted among others by Pallemaerts, the ultimate aim of the Aarhus Convention is to increase the openness and democratic legitimacy of government policies on environmental protection, and to develop a sense of responsibility among citizens by giving them the means to obtain information to assert their interest by participating in the decision-making process, to monitor the decisions of public bodies and to take legal action to protect their environment.[103] Taking into account the major influence of lobbyists and pressure groups, mainly financed by large corporations and industrial interests, on the legislative process, one might indeed ponder whether the parliamentary decision-making process is still capable of matching the bold objectives underpinning international and EU environmental law. Seen from this angle, the rationale used by the UK Supreme Court in its recent ruling clearly goes against the basic foundations of the concept of 'environmental democracy', which underpins the Aarhus Convention. In essence, the term 'environmental

99 Judgment UK Supreme Court, *supra* note 77, para. 79.

100 See more extensively: *M. Elliot,* Reflections on the HS2 case: a hierarchy of domestic constitutional norms and the qualified primacy of EU law, http://ukconstitutionallaw.org/2014/01/23/mark-elliot-reflections-on-the-hs2-case-a-hierarchy-of-domestic-constitutional-norms-and-the-qualified-primacy-of-eu-law/.

101 Judgment UK Supreme Court, *supra* note 77, para. 207.

102 See *supra* note 100.

103 *M. Pallemaerts, supra* note 7, p. 4.

democracy' reflects the increasing recognition that environmental issues and concerns must be addressed by their outcome, not just by governments and industrial sectors.[104] Moreover, as already indicated by the above-featured case law of the Court of Justice, EU law has been eroding natural sovereignty for quite some time now. It could be argued that parliamentary sovereignty is not under threat since the strict judicial review, upon which the opponents of HS2 built their case, is the result of the deliberate actions of the UK Parliament itself that has ratified the Aarhus Convention back in 2005. In a way, the UK Supreme Court judgment heavily relies on the classical view on representative democracy, whereas the Aarhus Convention urged international community to go beyond the traditional approach in the sphere of environmental decision-making. Yet, while the hybrid bill procedure still grants MPs whose constituencies are affected by the HS2 project to speak up against the project, the likelihood of success is severely limited by the fact that the project was supported by the two major political blocks in the UK Parliament. Arguably the objectives of the Aarhus Convention would have been better achieved by rendering the governmental decision to go ahead with the project subject to a prior SEA. In that light, it is perhaps not surprising to see that the opponents of the projects zoom in on that aspect in their recent complaint before the Aarhus Compliance Committee. Indeed, while the hybrid bill is to be accompanied by an EIA, the latter will not consider other reasonable alternatives to the high speed rail project and alternatives for Phase 1. If anything, it was probably the lack of meaningful participation on the DNS that sparked off the intense judicial battle over the HS2 project in the first place. Given the scale of the project, providing meaningful participation and consultation on the reasonable alternatives and routes could have avoided some of the judicial mayhem the HS2 project had to face up until now.

5. CONCLUDING REMARKS

Returning to the title of this chapter, it can be concluded that the answer to the question whether legislative validation and environmental democracy are friends or foes is still open. On the surface, Article 1(4) of the EIA Directive remains an attractive option for large infrastructure projects. Even if the objectives of EIA need to be safeguarded through the legislative process, the application of Article 1(4) holds the promise of less judicial scrutiny and participation via representation in Parliament. In times of increasing opposition to large infrastructure projects, it is not surprising to note a surge in the application of this exemption clause. Yet, as demonstrated above, the recent case law of the Court of Justice has clearly narrowed down the leeway for Member States when opting for the route of legislative validation. The progressive stance of the Court of Justice

[104] S. *Hazen*, Environmental democracy, www.ourplanet.com/imgversn/86/hazen.html.

must certainly be welcomed. In the absence of such case law, the exemption tool of Article 1(4) of the EIA Directive would probably turn into one of the favourite techniques for governments and planning authorities to bypass the generic EIA-requirements or to cure defects related to that. However, by obliging the national courts to take into account the entire legislative process leading up to the adoption of the act, the Court of Justice, perhaps unconsciously, shifted the boundaries of EU environmental law into the constitutional realm.

Throughout the course of this analysis, it has become apparent that, rather than adding further refinements, the rulings of the Court of Justice in *Boxus* and *Solvay* made things more complex for national courts. Constitutional bedrock principles, such as the sovereignty of parliament and the separation of powers, have entered the scene as possible obstacles to the allegedly strict scrutiny test that appears to be required by the recent case law developments at EU level. This is strikingly exemplified by the national jurisprudence that has been treated in this chapter. On the surface, the rationales used by the Belgian Constitutional Court, on the one hand, and the UK Supreme Court, on the other hand, seem hard to reconcile. The former appeared remarkably willing to apply strict scrutiny when screening the legislative debate leading up to the adoption of a Walloon Decree, whereas the latter explicitly deferred from subjecting UK Parliament to the strict assessment required by the judges in Luxembourg. Some might see in this antagonism an illustration of the different attitudes towards EU law and its interplay with national constitutional law. Others might point to the different roles of the Belgian Constitutional Court and the UK Supreme Court in their respective jurisdictions. Indeed, the topic of legislative validation might lead to a more reluctant approach in Member States which do not have a constitutional court competent to assess the constitutionality of national laws or decrees. However, taking into account the distinct factual background of both cases and the distinct legal traditions, the truth might be more prosaic. In essence, the Belgian Constitutional Court had the easy task of carrying out an assessment of a parliamentary procedure in which little to no attention was paid to the environmental effects of the ratified permits, whereas the UK Supreme Court had the more troublesome task to decide in advance upon the acceptability of the legislative procedure that needed to be observed for the HS2 project. Hence the allegedly conflicting approaches to legislative validation can probably not entirely be blamed to their respective legal traditions.

Considering the wide array of interests at stake, it is hard to come up with clear-cut conclusions. Ultimately, this debate touches upon a more fundamental issue. That is the exact implications of the concept of environmental democracy. Acknowledging the Aarhus Convention's wide ranging objectives, some authors saw the environmental democracy and justice as 'a testing ground for efforts to transcend traditional models of representative democracy'.[105] It is clear that

105 *M. Pallemaerts, supra* note 7, p. 4.

the presence of a clause allowing national parliaments to exempt infrastructure projects from the generic environmental procedural rights that are linked to EIA is capable of significantly compromising the achievement of the participatory environmental society the Aarhus Convention is striving towards. While it is true that the Aarhus Convention also contains an exemption for legislative acts, the generous use thereof in order to validate development consents for specific infrastructure projects and circumvent the participation requirements set out by Articles 6 and 7 seems hard to reconcile with the objectives of the Convention itself. In times of environmental deregulation, it might seem a distant dream, yet, ultimately, doing away with the exemption clause present in Article 1(4) of the EIA Directive could be the most appropriate solution to avert further legal mayhem in the future. Only if environmental democracy is observed in every single sphere of decision-making will it be able to make a noticeable difference on the ground.

CHAPTER 6

CONTROVERSIES ABOUT PROJECTS OR PLANS PASSED BY LAW IN SPAIN

Environmental Impact Assessment, Right to Take Part and Access to Justice on Environmental Issues

José Ignacio CUBERO MARCOS and Unai ABERASTURI GORRIÑO*

1. INTRODUCTION

The power of law, as an instrument for expressing people's desires by means of political representatives, has become a source of troubles and controversies, when the aim is to authorise a project or pass a plan affecting environmental matters. In countries like Spain, today the legislative power does not give people any guarantee for participation in the procedures related to authorise infrastructures or industries. The Legislative Chambers have not passed yet a regulation that permits and promotes public participation on subjects as relevant as impacts either on human health or biodiversity. Paradoxically, the institution where the democratic sovereignty is exercised can put obstacles and barriers that hamper a true control and surveillance on laws, which citizenship should carry out in a democratic state. This problem also concerns regulatory compliance according to the Aarhus Convention. Furthermore, The European Union approved a Directive on Environmental Impact Assessment, according to which certain steps and requirements must be fulfilled to guarantee the public participation in procedures whose object is to authorise projects. However, the Spanish legislation has failed to transpose that Directive when Parliaments – in the extent of State and the

* Dr José Ignacio Cubero Marcos and dir. Unai Aberasturi Gorriño, University of the Basque Country/Euskal Herriko Unibertsitatea. This work is a product corresponding to the research project called 'Derechos fundamentales, ordenación del territorio y medio ambiente' funded by the Department of Education and Universities of the Basque Country's Government.

regional authorities – decide to pass a draft with effects on the environmental issues.

Another controversy relates to the access to jurisdiction. In some states of the EU, Laws passed by the Legislative Chamber can only be annulled by the Constitutional Court, because it is the only one that has the jurisdiction to override laws. The right to appeal a Law in this case is very limited. For instance, in Spain only 50 senators, 50 congressmen, the Ombudsman and the President of government are entitled to impugn a Law. Regional parliaments can also submit an appeal, as long as the Law invades the powers or competencies of their regional authorities. Aarhus Convention, signed by European Union and all the Member States, does not apply to the legislative acts. Nevertheless, it is necessary to distinguish between a project or activity that requires a particular implementation, and a Law that states a general regulation that do not dispose resources and sufficient information related to single projects or plans applying to a smaller area. Public administration, instead, has more means and information, because it knows the places and their needs with more precision. It could happen that Parliament commits a fraud of Law, in order to avoid public participation and the possibility of appealing the Law by the people concerned.

In that sense, this chapter presents three goals: the first one focuses on how the mentioned controversies and problems are been faced and solved both by the CJEU and the Spanish Constitutional Court; the second one consists in bringing the contradictions that can be deducted from sentences, and showing the possible solutions accomplishing the current regulations, especially in the extent of the European Union Law; lastly, proposals will be presented in order to prevent more conflicts and legal actions before courts and bring clear criteria regarding this controversy. The final aim is to make the Aarhus Convention (international regulation) and European Union Directives compatible, regarding the right to participate on environmental issues, with domestic law, which could need a constitutional reform.

In terms of methodology, on one hand, legislative documents are showed and explained. As an issue regulated by different institutions, sources correspond to an international convention (Aarhus), European Union Directives and Spanish legislation. On the other hand, the interpretation given by jurisdictions both in European Union and Spain is examined to check how the courts have fulfilled the requirements laid down by those legislations and find out controversies, problems or contradictions. All of them can appear in practice, so the analysis is not limited to the theory and general discussions related to the constitutional law, but the objective focuses on achieving future solutions when lawsuits happen. Finally, proposals and solutions are outlined in order to search for some coherency in this complex scenario.

2. THE RIGHT TO PARTICIPATE ON ENVIRONMENTAL MATTERS

2.1. AARHUS CONVENTION

The rules on this matter cannot be very exhaustive, because the effective application depends on the Convention signatory states' legislations and peculiarities. Nevertheless, substantive guarantees are binding upon in the Member States. Regarding participation, procedures to authorise projects and plans are distinguished. The rules of the Convention can be implemented only for the projects of activities provided by Annex I. All of them produce an intensive impact on elements of the environment, like water, air, sea, biodiversity and soil. The public authorities must fulfil some requirements to guarantee the effective participation during the decision-making process, whose final object consists in permitting or not the project or activity.[1]

Firstly, the public authorities must publish information and, in case people apply for data about the environmental issues, they must supply them. Information must be related to the settling activity and the project, which contains the environmental impacts and alternatives or measures proposed by promoter. Furthermore, they must give all citizens information about how they can take part in the decision-making process, like the steps, terms, organisms and institutions before which they can present allegations and the procedure modality, that is to say, whether it consists in a public consultation, an audience or an informative meeting.[2] In that sense, the public authorities which carry out the procedure must provide information about how people can complain about provided information, what obligations the authorities must fulfil and the procedure to obtain all requested data. It means that, if the institutions or the public authorities are forced to provide information, concerned citizens have the right to complain about it before the courts.[3]

Secondly, the time to participate in procedures is very relevant, because people should know as soon as possible what risks are involved in the new activity, not only for the environment but also for their health. If participation is delayed and

---

1 *S. Davies*, In name or nature? Implementing international environmental procedural rights in the post-Aarhus environment: a Finnish example, Environmental Law Review (ELR), 2007, pp. 191 and 192. *G.H. Salomons & G. Hobberg*, Setting boundaries of participation in environmental impact assessment, Environmental Impact Assessment Review (EIAR), 2014 (45), p. 73.

2 *J.A. Razquin Lizarraga & A. Ruiz de Apodaca Espinosa*, Información, participación y justicia en materia de medio ambiente. Comentario sistemático a la Ley 27/2006, de 18 de julio, 2007, p. 54. *I. Lasagabaster Herrarte*, Participación y protección del medio ambiente, in García Ureta, A. (coord.), Estudios de Derecho ambiental europeo, 2005, pp. 39 and 40.

3 *M. Hourdequin, P. Landres, M.J. Hanson & D. Craig*, Ethical implication of democratic theory for U.S. public participation in environmental impact assessment, EIAR, 2012 (35), p. 41. *N. Hartley & C. Wood*, Public participation environmental impact assessment – implementing the Aarhus Convention, EIAR, 2005 (25), p. 334.

the basis of project have been consolidated, it will be very tough for the concerned people to put pressure on public institutions in order to adopt other solutions or alternatives, included banning the project.[4] It is for that reason that the Aarhus Convention lays down that States must allow people to deliver all information within a reasonable period of time, analyse and submit proposals or allegations. Usually, publishing a complaint in the newspaper or appearing in the media are more effective than making allegations based on technical criteria in one of the stage of the procedure. It is indispensable to give the people concerned time to prepare the observations or consult to experts, so that the rest of the persons involved can support their demands.[5]

Thirdly, the public authorities must give people the opportunity to allege what is convenient for their interests in connection with the project. Other participation mechanisms can be provided, like public consultation or audience. It depends on how states regulate the procedure. It looks logical that oral procedure with interventions or presentations made by the concerned citizens are more open, efficient and transparent, so that people can comprehend all issues and formulate questions immediately. In the Basque Country, for example, the Soil Law enforces municipalities to approve a participation programme according to which the steps are established. Thus, authorities can manage the procedure to pass an urban plan, and it does not involve any limit about the modality of participation.[6] Finally, the results of the decision-making procedure must be published and the authorities should take them into account. If they do not agree with the presented allegations, they must give the reasons why they have been rejected.[7]

To finish, the procedure to approve plans must not comply with all those requirements to guarantee participation. Article 6(3), (4) and (8) must only be applied. So, it is not necessary to publish information or supply it to people about the project; the measures or alternatives adopted; the procedure's stages and terms to participate or to get information.[8] Regarding the projects and plans passed by law, the Convention points out that the judicial and legislative powers must not meet the mentioned requirements on public participation. A question

---

4 *B. Jadot*, Les cas dans lesquels une enquête publique doir être organisée en matiére d'urbanisme et d'environnement: l'inexorable évolution, in B. Jadot (dir.), La participation du public au processus de décision en matiére d'environnement et d'urbanisme, 2005, pp. 133 and 134. Articles 6.3 and 4. See also, *A. Pigrau Solé & S. Borrás Pentinat*, Diez años del Convenio de Aarhus sobre el acceso a la información, la participación y el acceso a la justicia en materia de medio ambiente, in A. Pigrau Solé (dir.), Acceso a la información, participación pública y acceso a la justicia en materia de medio ambiente: diez años del Convenio de Aarhus, 2008, pp. 33–39.

5 The Aarhus Convention: Articles 6.3 and 4. Regarding these, see also *E. Zaccai, L. Frendo & T. Bauler*, Etudes d'incidences sur l'environnement et participation du public en région wallonne, in B. Jadot, *supra* note 4, p. 275.

6 *J.I. Cubero Marcos, M. Iturribarria Ruiz & I. Lasagabaster Herrarte*, Acceso a la información, participación y acceso a la justicia en materia de medio ambiente, 2009, p. 82.

7 Aarhus Convention, Articles 6, 8 and 9.

8 *D. Renders*, Les obligations qui incombent á l'administration après avoir procédé á une enquête publique, in B. Jadot, *supra* note 4, p. 209.

should be asked: is the legislative power competent to pass all the projects and plans, or must only be the executive power or the administration responsible for permitting projects or approving plans? It is the key to understand why this issue is so problematic to adjust to some legal systems.[9]

2.2. EUROPEAN UNION LAW

As the European Union ratified the Aarhus Convention, a new regulation might be adapted to the new scenario. So, the 2003/35 Directive was passed to regulate the right to participate in decision-making procedures affecting the environment. This legislation does not provide any difference between plans and projects.[10] The above-mentioned criteria are repeated by this Directive, by pointing out the four steps or requirements, but plans and projects seem to belong to the same category. This failure has not hampered that states have introduced distinctions concerning the applicable rules.[11]

Directive 2014/52/EU, which modifies Directive 2011/92, related to the environmental impact assessment (EIA) for public and private projects, does not provide anything about projects passed by law. According to its Explanatory Memorandum, the Member States must try to achieve the goals on public consultation as established in the previous Directive, when a legislative procedure is followed.[12] That means that it is not necessary to apply all the rules about participation that EIA Directive lays down for the rest of projects not passed by a legislative act. However, this broad discretionary power of the internal authorities is confirmed because the same Directive points out that the Member States can exclude the application of its rules on public consultation, in case they decide to authorise projects using a legislative act. Additionally, states must deliver information to European Commission if they do not respect the current procedure related to effective participation in the EIA procedure every two years since 2017.[13]

---

9 *N. Pérez Sola*, La tutela judicial del medio ambiente: estado de la cuestión, in G. Ruiz-Rico Ruiz, et. al (coords.), Derecho ambiental. Análisis jurídico y económico de la normativa medioambiental de la Unión Europea y española: estado actual y perspectivas de futuro, 2007, p. 306.

10 Directive 2003/35/EC of the European Parliament and of the Council Directive of 26 May 2003 providing for public participation in respect of the drawing up of certain plans and programmes relating to the environment and amending with regard to public participation and access to justice Council Directives 85/337/EEC and 96/61/EC, OJ L156/17, Article 2.2.

11 *C. Nadal*, Pursuing substantive environmental justice: The Aarhus Convention as a pillar of empowerment, Environmental Law Review, 2008 (10), p. 33.

12 Directive 2014/52/EU of the European Parliament and of the Council Directive of 16 April 2014 amending Directive 2011/92/EU on the assessment of the effects of certain public and private projects on the environment Text with EEA relevance, OJ L124/1.

13 Directive 2011/92, modified by the Directive 2014/52, *supra* note 13, Article 2.5.

European Union law omits a reference to the procedures directed to pass a regulations or laws with effects on the environment. It is logical because the Union lacks competencies to change internal rules in matter of administrative organisation, procedures and the type of rules. Even so, the guarantees provided by the Aarhus Convention cannot be forgotten, as it has been mentioned above. Whereas neither the Participation Directive nor EIA Directive contemplates the possibility of linking legislative and administrative procedures, the CJEU, by resolving a dispute concerning the Information Access Directive, linked both to the legislative and administrative procedure. It declared the documents and information obtained from a previous administrative action, and used by Parliament in order to pass a Law, could be considered object of the obligation upon public authorities to provide information, although Directive 2003/4[14] does not force the legislative power to supply that information.[15] As they are data disposed by the public authority – in this case public administration – the public authority itself should deliver it to the Parliament. In virtue of the same Directive, the States can decide not to implement obligations enforcing to give information when it is submitted to the legislative power, as long as the legislation provides an appeal against the legislative act.[16]

2.3. SPANISH LEGISLATION

According to the 27/2006 Law, the regulation and procedure is different for the projects and the plans. The procedure directed to grant the permission has its specific rules, as it happens with the EIA or the plans to manage hydraulic resources. Regarding the regulation of the second ones, the Law distinguishes some plans, related to nitrates, wastes and batteries, whose procedures must lay down similar guarantees to which have been mentioned for the Aarhus Convention. The other plans – not referring to wastes, nitrates and batteries – are passed without implementing the requirements stated by Aarhus Convention.[17] For example, the obligations on previous information before participating and early participation steps are been excluded for that plans. Lastly, the procedure to approve certain plans which require environmental impact assessment (strategic assessment) or other ones referred to civil protection or labour risks, is regulated by its specific rules.

---

[14] Directive2003/4/EC of the European Parliament and of the Council Directive of 28 January 2003 on public access to environmental information and repealing Council Directive 90/313/EEC.

[15] Case C-204/09, *Flachglas Torgau* [2012], para. 51.

[16] *B. Jadot, supra* note 4, p. 145.

[17] *A. Pallarés Serrano*, La participación pública en materia de medio ambiente, in A. Pigrau Solé (dir.), *supra* note 6, pp. 309–312.

In the light of the 27/2006 Law, the legislative institutions or Parliaments are not considered public authority, so they must not fulfil the requirements on participation or access to jurisdiction. The reason is that, in order to adjust that regulation to internal rules of the Parliaments – state and regional – it should be reformed and it would be necessary to achieve a wide consensus between different ideologies and political parties, which nowadays looks very tough. Furthermore, the right to take part during the procedures aimed at passing plans or regulations is restricted to people with legitimate interests and certain NGOs, which must be subjected to some requirements that will be commented (see below).[18]

However, the regional parliaments have passed laws establishing the right of every person to impugn any administrative measure, act or regulation. This provision extends greatly the people's power to control public authorities and builds upon the expanded concept of the environment, because damaging it or its elements can suppose an assault on human being's health and life conditions.[19] In fact, some judgments emitted by the European Court of Human Rights have recognised the right to private and family life due to omissions or faults committed by the public authorities on environmental issues. For example, not adopting adequate measures to prevent from bothering noises or smells involves a breach of the right to private life and a violation of Article 8 of the European Convention of Human Rights.[20] Having said that, it could seem that the regional authorities have invaded state's competencies, but, as regulations refer to the administrative procedure, they could extend to the regional authorities powers for execution of the legislation on environmental issues. In that case it would be compatible with the Spanish Constitution.

3. THE EFFECTS OF THE PROJECTS AND PLANS PASSED BY A LEGISLATIVE ACT BOTH ON THE ENVIRONMENTAL IMPACT ASSESSMENT AND THE STRATEGIC ENVIRONMENTAL ASSESSMENT

Firstly, the foundation of the environmental impact assessment is explained, because it is convenient to find out whether legislative power disposes all the technical and material resources to carry out an assessment of physical elements of the environment. Secondly, from a legal point of view and regarding the legislative procedure, it could be questioned whether it is adequate for the

18 Article 17.1 of Law 27/2006 of 18 July, about the access to information, the right to participate and access to Justice on environmental matters.

19 *J.A. Razquin Lizarraga & A. Ruiz de Apodaca*, *supra* note 2, pp. 333–339.

20 Between many of them, ECtHR, *López Ostra v. Spain*, para. 58 or *Hatton v. United Kingdom*, para. 97.

concerned peoples' right to take part and for the coordination between other administrations as well. Finally, the controversy about the single legislative acts is raised in the light of the Spanish Constitutional Court's jurisprudence. It is a relevant topic because the conditions for the intervention of the legislative power should be determined in order to avoid encroachment of competences.

3.1. THE FOUNDATION OF THE ENVIRONMENTAL IMPACT ASSESSMENT

Before carrying out or settling an activity with effects on the environment, public authorities must grant promoter a permission or authorisation. During the procedure directed to give those permissions, public authorities must make an assessment taking into account environmental criteria. For that purpose, the project, as well as containing the object of activity, the emplacement and data related to promoters, has to include a description of the impacts of the activity on environmental elements, like water, sea, soil, air or biodiversity.[21] This information cannot be ignored by the public authority in charge of authorising the project and it is indispensable for it to make a correct assessment. The damage prompted to the environment must be reduced as much as it is possible. Public authorities have to examine the risks for the environment and public health. Therefore, private agents which previously submitted the project must include the alternatives or measures to reduce the effects of activity on the environment.[22] They use technical criteria, based on biological, chemical or geological aspects, but they make sure that human conditions of life and ecological balance are protected as much as possible. People and interested NGOs require public authorities to be informed about these issues so they can challenge the decisions.[23]

Information provided by the promoter of the project is used to make a previous assessment by the promoter. So, it should be adequate and precise. For example, in case some impacts were not included in the draft, promoter would not have to adopt any measure to correct the effect produced, but they can be necessary. Prevention principle would be ignored and damages to the environment would be generated until public authorities decide carry out an

21 *A. García Ureta*, Marco jurídico del procedimiento de evaluación de impacto ambiental: el contexto comunitario y estatal, 1994, pp. 227–234; *J. Agudo González*, Evaluación de impacto ambiental: problemas jurídicos, Revista de Derecho Urbanístico y Medio Ambiente, 2000 (176), pp. 321–324. *J. Rosa Moreno*, Régimen jurídico de la evaluación de impacto ambiental, 1993, pp. 168 and 169.

22 *G. García-Álvarez García*, Acceso a la información, participación y acceso a la justicia en cuestiones ambientales: del Convenio de Aarhus a la sentencia Boxus, Revista Aragonesa de Administración Pública, 2013 (14), pp. 467 and 468.

23 *C. Hatton, P. Castle & M. Day*, The environment and the law – does our legal systema deliver access to justice? A review, ELR, 2004 (6), p. 244.

investigation or inspection.[24] The previous exam allows the public authority to analyse the risks for the environment and, it any damage is caused, it should been corrected from its origin. For that, new technologies or protection adequate mechanisms are required and they have been included in the project.[25] The administrative procedure consists in supplying all of that information and criteria to all interested people and implicated administrations and authorities, so that they can submit allegations and oppose the project. In this moment the requirements for participation come into play.[26]

Nevertheless, a question has been made: are the mentioned steps and basis complied during the legislative procedure? Or do Parliaments dispose sufficient means to analyse and assess all those technical criteria or formulated alternatives? In Spain, for example, the Legislative Chambers lack civil servants dedicated to study scientific issues related to the environment.[27] On the other side, the internal regulation of the Chambers do not people allow to take part in the debates or propose alternatives.[28] Sometimes, political groups can decide to invite a NGO or experts on certain matters, but complete transparency fails. By conducting an administrative procedure, however, everyone can submit observations, alternatives and can know early the basis of the project.[29] Do the Member States comply with the Aarhus Convention and European Directives if they do not pass regulations providing guarantees for participation on the environmental impact assessment? Additionally, a legislative act overrides an administrative action or measure. Therefore, if there is a conflict between the organisms with competences on environmental issues and the legislative power, which is in charge of authorising the project, it does not matter what reasons the parliament has given, because it imposes its own will. As public administration has technical means and human resources in order to enforce and apply the new regulations related to transparency and information access on the environmental issues, the EIA administrative procedures tend to be more effective.

---

24 *C. Rodgers*, Environmental impact assessment: mapping the interface between agriculture, development and the natural environment?, ELR, 2011 (13), p. 90.

25 *N. Hartley & C. Wood*, *supra* note 3, p. 322.

26 *A.N. Glucke, O. Driesen, A. Kolhoff & H.A.C. Runhaar*, Public participation in environmental impact assesment: why, who and haw?, EIAR, 2013 (43), p. 107.

27 *C. Hatton, P. Castle & M. Day*, *supra* note 23, p. 245.

28 *J.J. Pernás García*, Integración y coordinación procedimental de la evaluación de impacto ambiental y de la autorización ambiental integrada, in A. Nogueira López (dir.), Evaluación de impacto ambiental. Evolución normativo-jurisprudencial, cuestiones procedimentales y aplicación sectorial, 2009, p. 96.

29 *Salomons & Hoberg*, *supra* note 2, p. 70.

3.2. ADEQUATE PROCEDURE TO PARTICIPATE AND COORDINATE PUBLIC AUTHORITIES

Directive 85/337/EEC could not be invoked in case the projects were authorised by a legislative act, as long as they were sufficiently specifics and they contained all necessary information to assess the project.[30] Therefore, Parliament should dispose all information before making a decision, but the problem has not been solved, because the Legislative Chamber lacks resources and skills that legislator needs to deal with the environmental problems, especially the environmental impact assessment.[31] Data and information need to be interpreted and analysed from a technical and scientific perspective. As commented above, Directive 2014/52/EU has given to the Member States a wide discretionary power to determine whether a project can be accepted by an administrative act or by a legislative one. The Directive required the States to provide necessary and precise information, but according to the reform of that, those requests have been removed and the final decision corresponds to the Member States, not to the European Commission.[32] The States must only give reasons on how the participatory process has been carried out, in case the European Commission asks them a report.

3.2.1. The European Union Case Law's Approach

The CJEU has solved some controversies about the EIA of projects passed by a legislative act. According to the jurisprudence, the EIA Directive must not be applied in case the assessed projects are detailed and adopted by a specific legislative act, because the goals pursued must be achieved by means the legislative procedure. The legislative act should contain the permit and it should supplement all the pertinent data in order to show that an adequate assessment of the effects for the environment has been made.[33] Giving the permit involves granting the promoter all the rights to carry out the draft. The Parliament must dispose all information on the emplacement of the infrastructure or installation, its design and size, measures provided to avoid, reduce and, if possible, compensate the relevant consequences on the environment.[34] The legislative power could raise

30 Council Directive 85/337/EEC of 27 June 1985 on the assessment of the effects of certain public and private projects on the environment, OJ L175/40.

31 *M. Verdú Amorós*, Ámbito de aplicación y procedimiento de la Evaluación ambiental estratégica, 2008, pp. 80–81.

32 *J. Petts & C. Brooks*, Expert conceptualisations of the role of lay knowledge in environmental decision-making: challenges for deliberative democracy, Environmental and Planning (E&P), 2006 (38), p. 1047.

33 *X. Ezeizabarrena Saénz*, El principio constitucional de participación ante la evaluación de impacto ambiental de las grandes infraestructuras, 2006, pp. 259–261.

34 Cases C-128/09 to C-131/09, C-134/09 and C-135/09, *Boxus* [2011] ECR I-9711, paras. 36–38. See *V. Edwards*, Significant EU environmental cases: 2011, Journal of Environmental Law, 2012 (24), p. 162.

all data during the previous administrative process.[35] If the legislative act involves the permission, it is necessary to fulfil all the guarantees provided by the administrative process, included supplying all information corresponding to the project's EIA from an environmental perspective.[36] The procedure's guarantees must be accomplished and internal courts must verify if they are enforced.[37]

That solution does not look very convincing, although the procedure has a previous assessment. The question is whether the legislative power disposes sufficient resources to analyse the measures adopted by promoter and the administrative authority.[38] In Spain those technical issues are considered by specialised civil servants integrated into the public administration, not to the Parliaments. It seems that the Parliament adopts technical measures, which are not real. The jurisprudence forces authorities to collect all information but the previous stages of the procedure are omitted. For example, it is unknown where public participation is, which would not be in accordance with the Aarhus Convention.[39] Furthermore, other administrations, like municipalities or regional authorities must be consulted, and the legislative power, integrated by political parties with their interests, has a wide margin to decide to invite other administrations for the procedure.[40]

Recently, the CJEU has established some criteria related to the projects passed by a legislative act. The Walloon Parliament authorised the works linked to the airport of Liège, Brussels and a railway infrastructure, which were based on the general interest. The European Court declared that permitting the projects by means of two acts derived from a national Law is not banned. However, the judgment considered it indispensable not to omit the guarantees of the procedure, both the EIA and the stages of participation, even though the authorisation was granted by a legislative act. The CJEU ordered internal jurisdictional authorities to verify whether the legislator disposed all detailed information to analyse the impacts and thereby the act did not have to comply with the EIA Directive.[41] In another lawsuit, about the authorisation of transferring part of a river, the administrative decision related to the EIA was appended to the Law permitting the transfer. That decision was made following the administrative procedure in accordance with the requirements on participation provided by the Aarhus Convention and the EIA Directive.[42]

35 *Boxus, supra* note 34, para. 44.

36 Cases C-287/98, *Linster* [2000] ECR I-6917, para. 56 and C-435/97, *WWF & other* [1999] ECR 1999 I-5613, para. 59.

37 C-508/03, *Commission v. United Kingdom* [2006] ECR I-3969, para. 102.

38 *E. Zaccai, L. Frendo & T. Bauler, supra* note 5, p. 277.

39 *J.F. Alenza García*, La evaluación de impacto ambiental a la luz de la jurisprudencia comunitaria, in A. Nogueira López (dir.), *supra* note 28, p. 49.

40 *A. García Ureta*, Convenio de Aarhus y convalidaciones legislativas: ¿recurso directo contra leyes en vía contenciosa?, La Ley, 2011 (7763), www.laleydigital.es.

41 Case C-182/10, *Marie-Nöelle Solvay & other* [2012], para. 41.

42 Case C-43/10, *Aftodioikisi Aitoloakarnanias* [2012], paras. 90 and 91.

As a conclusion, the legislative power must fulfil all the obligations related to the participatory process, including when the administrative decision has been annulled by the jurisdictional authorities. Public authorities should not only supply all information to the legislator, but also all the guarantees on participation must be implemented, so that people can allege what is relevant to their interests. Authorising a draft by a legislative act does not mean neglecting the procedure and, moreover, it cannot hamper public participation.[43]

3.2.2. Objections to the CJEU's Case Law: the Right to Participate in the EIA and the Strategic Environmental Assessment

If the EIA procedure was incorporated into the legislative procedure, in Spain the internal rules of Parliaments should be reformed. They should lay down the necessary stages and obligations in order to achieve effective participation, as the Aarhus Convention provides. Currently, Parliament cannot be forced to convene specialised NGOs bringing their allegations or advice. The people concerned by the project could not express their observations or opinions directly before the legislator. The European Union does not have any competence on this matter, because only States are entitled to organise their respective institutions.[44] However, public participation ensures greater acceptance of a final decision, even if participating citizens believe differently, because their observations have been taken into account by public authorities promoting the project.[45]

The new internal rules, applicable to the legislative power, should state all the guarantees established by the Aarhus Convention. If not, they would not adjust to an international legislation, as the CJEU has reminded. The modified Directive 2014/52/EU, on the contrary, allows the States a great power not to be subjected to the EIA Directive and, by the way, the Aarhus Convention. Participation on the procedures related to the environment must be effective, and that would be impossible in case some stages of those procedures were removed.[46] The only solution implies recognising the right to take part, imposing the legislator constraints to make it effective and adjust it to the Parliaments' internal rules. Member States should comply with this Directive by 16 May 2017.

The public consultation or a period of allegations can be materialised before the project is presented to the Parliament. In that case, public administration could take measures directed to provide information about the procedure and the assessed project.[47] Nevertheless, the legislator could change the conditions of

---

43 *C. Rodgers*, *supra* note 24, p. 91.

44 *S. Eden & C. Bear*, The good, the bad, and the hands-on: constructs of public participation, anglers and lay management of water environments, E&P, 2012 (44), p. 1202.

45 *V. Leitch*, Securing planning permission for onshore wind farms: the imperativeness of public participation, ELR, 2010 (12), p. 184.

46 *M. Hourdequin et al.*, *supra* note 3, p. 38.

47 *C. O'Faircheallaigh*, Public participation and environmental impact assessment: purposes, implications and lessons for public policy making, EIAR, 2010 (30), p. 20.

the project or adopt new measures tending to reduce the environmental impact. The problem is how the NGOs or the concerned people can refute or contradict the new approaches. If the procedure of public participation is ignored during the legislative procedure, it is difficult to implement the effective participation principle. Furthermore, the legislative act overrides administrative rules, guidelines or decisions.[48] It is very difficult to guarantee that the submitted allegations will have a real influence on the final decision,[49] but citizens can exercise a democratic control over politicians and they can deny the necessary support for the next elections.

Regarding the reasons to subject the project to an EIA, the CJEU judgments are very uncertain. The European Court stated that the public authority must not expose the motivation why the environmental impact assessment is not considered necessary.[50] However, citizens could appeal that decision before jurisdiction, if the request is rejected.[51] As will be explained below, the Spanish Constitution has contemplated bounds to overrule a legislative act, so this provision could breach the right to a due process of law or access to the jurisdiction. This point has been ignored by the CJEU, although it is very common in many Member States. The Constitutional Court in Spain even could not require the legislator to bring material conditions or measures in a Law authorising a project, because that Court in Spain exercises a negative control, which means that it only annuls the Law violating the Constitution, but it cannot propose a different regulation, decision or measure. This is a common problem for the legislative power when it passes a Law containing a detailed regulation or decision, instead of establishing general requirements. This kind of Law is named a 'single legislative act' and it requires a deeper approach in accordance with the Spanish legislation and jurisprudence.

3.3. SINGLE LEGISLATIVE ACTS AND EIA LEGISLATION

3.3.1. Single Legislative Acts: Concept and Characteristics

The legislator could not exempt a rule for specific cases, because it would be contrary to the equality and non-discrimination principles. The exemption could happen if it was based on justified and proportionate reasons, which has to be explained case by case according to the objective and subjective circumstances. The EIA requires an analysis of the impacts on the physical elements in a limited extent and a specific situation. Making an assessment of a coastal area is very different from studying the environment close to the mountains. The characteristics and conditions in both cases cannot be examined with the same criteria, because the

48 *A. García Ureta*, *supra* note 40.

49 *V. Leitch*, *supra* note 45, p. 192.

50 Case C-182/10, *Marie-Nöelle Solvay & other*, *supra* note 40, para. 56.

51 Case C-75/08, *Mellor* [2009] ECR I-3799, para. 58.

needs, lacks and problems cannot be transferred from one place to the other. Passing plans implies the same difficulty, as they fix determinations and regulate limits referred to a particular extent and they affect every legal issue, recognising rights or imposing obligations. Passing general rules competes to the legislator, because a single regulation could introduce non justified differences and breach the equality principle.[52]

The power to decide case by case belongs to public administrations or authorities, because they interpret the general legislation requirements and adjust to the particular scenario with effects on it.[53] The Spanish Constitutional Court has regarded single legislative acts as those referring to a single and particular case and finishing their efficacy and content if the measure is adopted by means that legislative act on that particular case.[54] In some specific controversies, the Spanish Constitutional Court accepted the single legislative acts, but exceptionally, and considered that some requirements, restrictively examined, should be fulfilled.[55] The reasons of those rigid safeguards are based on the limits to appeal the legislative act, which is laid down by the Constitution. In fact, many authors have considered they can be admitted, but they should have been examined under the right to appeal or a due process of Law.[56] The European Court of Human Rights (ECtHR) had forced the Spanish State to recognise the right to appeal in case the legislative acts are passed.[57] Thus, the Spanish legislation provided a step consisting in an audience before the Constitutional Court, if a legislative act was questioned by common courts when they had to apply that Law to give judgment. Additionally, the legislative procedure must include the proceedings provided by the administrative legislation in relation with the compulsory deprivation (or taking).[58]

It does not matter what rule or act has been adopted to take the compulsory measures. The relevant issue is that the requirements linked to the procedure have been accomplished, in order to acknowledge the right to access to the jurisdiction or participate in the decision-making process. The legislative act depends not only on the instrument used (a Law or a regulation), but also on the objectives established for the procedure. This is the functional or teleological sense of the Law, further than the formal considerations on it. The ECHR itself sentenced

52 *I. Lasagabaster Herrarte*, Fuentes del Derecho, 2007, p. 91; *R. Galán Vioque*, RUMASA: expropiaciones legislativas y leyes singulares (comentario en torno a las sentencias constitucionales y del Tribunal Europeo de Derechos Humanos recaídas en este asunto), Revista Andaluza de Administración Pública, 1997 (29), p. 126.

53 *J.A. Montilla Martos*, Las leyes singulares en el ordenamiento constitucional español, 1994, p. 112.

54 Spanish Constitutional Court (SCC) 166/1986 Judgment, para. 13.

55 SCC 48/2005 Judgment, para 6.

56 *G. Ariño Ortiz*, Leyes singulares, leyes de caso único, Revista de Administración Pública (RAP), 1989 (118), p. 57.

57 *F. Rubio Llorente*, Función legislativa, poder legislativo y garantía del procedimiento, in El Procedimiento legislativo. V Jornadas de Derecho Parlamentario, 1997, p. 30.

58 Article 37.2 of Constitutional Court Organic Law 2/1979.

that the property right can be violated if the damages are not compensated by the State, prompting an unfair inequality.[59] At this point, the proportionality principle must be invoked to justify discrimination and inequality. The legislator should explain case by case why the adopted alternatives are the most adequate and the least harmful for the people concerned.[60]

3.3.2. *The Recent Jurisprudence of the Spanish Constitutional Court*

In Castilla y León the Regional Parliament passed a Law consisting in authorising a project called 'La Ciudad del Medio Ambiente'. The legislative act was overruled by 50 congressmen that alleged the single Law breached the equality principle. The project included precise determinations about urbanised and non urbanised areas, so that the private partners and the public authorities could manage the lands' uses. Part of the soil was classified as residential and other sides were considered green protected areas. According to the Constitutional Court, that is not a single legislative act, because it fixes determinations to regulate land use. Even then, the exceptionality of the Law requires a case by case justification, which turns that Law into a single one.[61]

It looks a paradox that the legislator establishes provisions for a particular case, due to the fact those provisions can only be changed by another Law, taking into account the difficulties and obstacles derived from the legislative procedure, where achieving majorities is a complex task. Actually, the projects passed by a legislative act could be named 'armoured projects', because of the limits to appeal and control that act and the barriers to search sufficient consensus at reforming the provisions.[62] The main question refers to the delimitation of the respective competencies both of the legislative and executive authorities. The separation of powers implies that each one has different competences and functions, so that the other ones know how to act and in what extent. The Constitutional Court does not solve this controversy since it accepted the single legislative acts. In other words, the limits between the powers corresponding to the executive are confusing with those ones attributed to the legislative.[63] All of this requires a detailed interpretation of the Spanish Constitution.

The Spanish Constitution recognises that the Government can direct the domestic and foreign policy, and exercise the regulation power.[64] These

---

59 ECHR Judgment of 23 September 1982, *Sporrong and Lönroth v. Sweden*, paras. 66–69, and 5 November 2002, *Pincova v. Czech Republic*, para. 52.

60 ECC 48/2005 Judgment, para. 7.

61 SCC 203/2013 Judgment, para. 2.

62 *F. Rubio Llorente*, El procedimiento legislativo en España. El lugar de la Ley entre las fuentes del Derecho, Revista Española de Derecho Constitucional (REDC), 1986 (16), pp. 93 and 94. See also *F. Rey Martínez*, A vueltas con el concepto de Ley singular (análisis de la STC 203/2013, de 5 de diciembre), La Ley, 2014 (8288), www.laleydigital.es.

63 *J.A. Montilla Martos*, *supra* note 53, p. 185.

64 Article 97.1.

expressions look as general as the legislator wants to consider, because the majority of the doctrine understand that the executive power is subject to the legislator and it depends on what obligations are imposed by it. Thus, there might not be an exclusive power attributed to the government, because the Parliament, as the institution representing the popular sovereignty, places the limits of administrative or government's action. However, the Spanish Constitutional Court has declared that the regional governments have the competency to pass regulations and plans on urban and territorial issues. Exceptionally, the legislator could authorise these plans or regulations by a legislative act, but it does not specify which cases conform to this theory.[65] The legislative power itself could impose limits, but the powers attributed to the government by the Constitution cannot be neglected.[66]

Finally, the proportionality principle must be applied case by case and the legislator must explain why the regulations or measures have to be passed by a legislative act. In order to control them, the Constitutional Court should accomplish a balance test and justify the means used (a Law) are necessary to achieve the goals recognised by the Constitution. Furthermore, it should prove that those regulations do not prompt more damages than benefits, looking for a balanced decision. Passing single laws supposes that there is no more means that the public authorities can achieve the objectives, because of the complexity or relevance of the project. The facts and reasonability of the decision can be the mechanisms to analyse whether a single legislative act can be passed and enforced.[67] Sometimes, the Constitutional Court has alleged that political representatives have a wide discretionary power to make choices in accordance with their political ideologies.[68] So, the justification can be as broad as the constitutional provisions can admit.[69] Nevertheless, the necessity and proportionality require arguments and powerful reasons with their corresponding motivation. Regarding the project passed by the Regional Parliament of Castilla y León, it lacked the explanations related to why a legislative act was necessary or whether using another mean or rule was impossible to obtain the expecting results. In order to prevent from defencelessness, the legislator must act according to the proportionality principle.[70]

---

65 SCC 129/2013, Judgment, para. 8.

66 *J. Ortega Bernardo,* Límites constitucionales en la adopción por Ley de medidas concretas de carácter administrativo. Comentario a la STC 48/2005, sobre la Ley de expropiación para la ampliación de la sede del Parlamento de Canarias, RAP, 2007 (172), pp. 295–297.

67 SCC 203/2013, Judgment, para. 6.

68 SCC 48/2005, Judgment, para. 6.

69 *F. López Ramón,* La problemática de las leyes singulares y las reservas de ley para la declaración de parques nacionales y otros espacios naturales protegidos, in F. López Menudo (dir.), Derechos y garantías del ciudadano: estudios en homenaje al profesor Alfonso Pérez Moreno, 2011, pp. 770–773.

70 *R.J. Santamaría Arinas,* Leyes singulares, tutela judicial efectiva y recepción de la doctrina boxus por el Tribunal Constitucional español, RAP, 2014 (193), p. 174.

A similar case has been solved by the Spanish Constitutional Court recently. The regional Parliament of Castilla y León passed a Law modifying a plan for the regulation of natural resources in a protected area (Fuente Carriona, Palencia). A previous judgement, given by an ordinary court, had overruled a part of the plan, which involved banning to establish and build a ski resort. The Parliament ignored that resolution and approved the plan authorising that infrastructure. Some NGOs submitted a demand before the ordinary court – it had annulled the part of the plan – in which they asked that court to execute the resolution and alleged that it was impossible because the Law had permitted what the judgment had prohibited. Thus, the ordinary court referred the matter to the Constitutional Court in order to decide if the Law fulfilled the Constitution. According to the judgment, even though the Constitution does not provide a scope reserved to the administrative regulations, that plan did not require a Law. In that sense, the Court assessed whether the Law was adequate and proportional for the aims of a singular Law, such as some judgments did. The Regional Parliament had justified the Law on the grounds related to the economic growth, production of more employments, and the benefits of the tourism. However, the Constitutional Court held that those goals could have achieved by passing an administrative regulation and they were not sufficient to use an exceptional mechanism like a singular Law. Furthermore, as the Law had annulled a judicial resolution implicitly, the effective judicial protection had been violated, and it implied breaching a fundamental right recognised by the Constitution.[71]

3.3.3. *Some Critical Observations Related to Participation and the Procedure*

It is surprising that the main argument to justify a single legislative act is the possible violation of the right to access to jurisdiction or appeal a Law. What happens with the citizens' participation and the procedure on issues like EIA? It must be considered that sometimes the administrative procedures hamper long and expensive processes before jurisdiction, which, moreover, is not specialised on environmental issues.[72] In case an administrative procedure was the most adequate mechanism to take measures or make a decision, there cannot be any doubt on following it. The Spanish Constitutional Court confirmed that, if such regulations can be passed by the government, the legislator's intervention does not get any sense. On the other side, international legislative texts have pointed out the principle of early participation and obligations to provide information and exchange views.

The debate introduces some issues related to constitutional law, like the separation of powers. In the United Kingdom, for instance, passing projects by law

---

71 SCC 50/2015 Judgment, paras. 6, 7 and 8.

72 *R. Mcrory*, Regulation, enforcement and governance in environmental law, 2nd ed., 2014, pp. 201–203.

requires a certain connection with a previous administrative procedure, where the environmental impact assessment is guaranteed from a technical point of view, not so political.[73] The Supreme Court also verified in that case if the congressmen had sufficient information to make a decision adequately, in accordance with the EIA Directive. These hybrid procedures, between the Parliament and the Administration, prove that the legislative act cannot be understood in a formal sense, but it should be funded on technical or substantial basis. All of them allow the legislator to pass a project according to justified and proportioned conditions. Political parties deal with the pressure and influence exercised by big companies or economic interests that put the environmental effects off.

The Spanish Constitutional Court do not make any approach or interpretation about the European Union Law and the thesis exposed by the CJEU related to the EIA procedures. Modifying plans involves a strategic environmental assessment, which is regulated by Directive 2001/42/EC. This does not establish any exception concerning the legislative acts. The useful effect of the Directives supposes the respect to the aims deduced from its provisions, which means that a procedure that fulfils the principles and rights recognised by the Directive should be carried out in case the plans or their modifications are passed.[74] The Spanish Constitutional Court's jurisprudence has not taken into account the commented sentences emitted by the CJEU, in order to compel a previous procedure and supply sufficient information to make a decision to permit or not the installation, infrastructure or pass the plan.

Lastly, the Spanish Constitutional Court must reconsider the relevance of participation and coordination with other public authorities in the EIA procedures. In relation with a controversy on a project authorising an installation aimed to recycle wastes, the Law passed by the Regional Parliament had exempted the promoters from obtaining the compulsory licences and authorisations to settle the infrastructure. The legislator in this case did not ask the local authorities concerned any advice or allegation, although they have the competency to grant that permissions, for example to control impacts like the foreseeable noise, the occupied area relating to urban issues or the effects on people's health.[75] These issues are a matter for the concerned municipalities or the regional public authorities of the government or the executive power. This point was also omitted by the judgments commented, which neglected the influence that the previous procedure could have on the legislative procedures.[76] Although the Constitutional Court cannot instruct the legislator how to regulate the issues, it can give it

[73] *D. Edwards*, HS2. The first spike. HS2 action Alliance Ltd. vs. Secretary of State for Transport, Journal of Environmental Law (JEL), 2014 (26), pp. 324–326.

[74] *C. Poncelet*, Access to justice in environmental matters – does the European Union comply with its obligations?, JEL, 2012 (24), p. 292.

[75] SCC 129/2013, Judgment, para. 4.

[76] *R.J. Santamaría Arinas*, *supra* note 70, p. 174.

advices or recommendations not to breach the rules about participation and coordination, in accordance with the exposed legislation and jurisprudence.[77]

4. ACCESS TO JUSTICE ON ENVIRONMENTAL MATTERS

4.1. THE RIGHT TO APPEAL

In virtue of the Aarhus Convention, people with rights to participate can appeal the decision adopted by public authorities before an independent and impartial court, in case it affects the environment.[78] In Spain the drafts passed by law show, as a main failure, the barriers to go to courts. It must be reminded that the right to impugn a legislative act is very restrictive. Fifty congressmen or senators, the President of the Government, the Ombudsman and the majority of the Regional Parliaments are only entitled to appeal a legislative act. In the last case (the regional legislator) they can appeal when they believe that the State has impinged their competency on a certain matter.[79]

On the other side, the Spanish legislation provides bounds to appeal administrative decisions, regulations or plans (not legislative acts). Citizens affected by administrative regulations or decisions and some NGOs have been authorised to challenge those acts. NGOs have to fulfil the following requirements: according to their statutes, they must have been promoting activities for the environmental protection for, at least, two years; all of these have had to be exercised in the area of the installation, infrastructure or plan; and, finally, their articles of association must have included the environmental protection as their main aim.[80] Some regional legislations, like the Basque Environmental Law, have established the public action, so that everyone can appeal before courts every act, decision or plan passed by public authorities.[81]

This apparent contradiction between State and regional legislation is due to the regional authorities' competency to execute the regulations regarding the environment. That power is exercised by conducting the administrative procedure that finishes with a final appealable decision before courts. Moreover, during the administrative procedure people could present observations and the public authority must give a response to them.[82] If they want to oppose or refute that response or reasons, they always can impugn them. According to the European

77 *B. Lombaert*, Questions d'actualité relatives au contentieux des enquêtes publiques, in B. Jadot, *supra* note 4, p. 228.

78 *C. Hatton, P. Castle & M. Day*, *supra* note 23, p. 245.

79 Spanish Constitution, Article 162.1.

80 Law 27/2006, Article 23.1.

81 Law of the Basque Country 1998/3, Article 3.4.

82 *C. Nadal*, *supra* note 11, p. 35.

Court the conditions that may be required in order for a NGO to have a right of appeal must ensure a wide access to justice and render effective the provisions of the EIA Directive. Restrictions to guarantee the access must be proportional and adequate to the objectives provided by the Directive and the Aarhus Convention.[83]

The continental administrative law systems are based on reviewing the act or decision, so it is necessary to exhaust administrative review procedures in order to appeal that act or decision before courts.[84] The link between both procedures (administrative and judicial review) is focused on the last decision (exhausting administrative remedies), regulation or plan.[85] If administrative acts have prompted damages or violated individual rights, parties can request the compensation or ask judicial institutions to recover looses or resettle the previous situation. But, firstly judicial review consists in declaring that an act has breached the law.[86] The consequences of breaching will be examined if the litigators lodge the corresponding application.

The CJEU has not resolved the question related to the right to appeal a legislative act. It has declared that the judicial authority has the competency to exercise the control of decision, even though the controversy refers to a Law or legislative act, as long as such authority is empowered by law to pronounce a sentence on a certain matter.[87] The Spanish Constitutional Court intervenes on the issues provided by the Constitution and the Organic Law regulating its functions. However, it can be inferred from the jurisprudence emitted by the CJEU that judges and courts could not apply a domestic law, by considering contrary to the Constitution or the European law.[88] At this point, the domestic courts could make a preliminary reference to the CJEU or send the doubt to the Constitutional Court according to the domestic rules.

Even so, that does not involve that the right to appeal a legislative act extends to everyone or the concerned people. Formulating the preliminary reference only corresponds to the common court, and it could considerer that there is no breach of the EU law or the Constitution because it makes a different interpretation of the applying legislation.[89] The primacy of the EU law and its useful effect force the Spanish authorities to make a reform in its legislation related to participation and access to justice on the environmental issues.[90] At least, the people and recognised

83 *B. Müller*, Access to the Courts of the member states for NGOs in Environmental Matters un European Union Law, JEL, 2011 (23), p. 509. He cites Case C-263/08, *Djurgaarden*, para. 15. Even so, he is sceptic about the advances on this matter by CJEU, because the jurisprudence is variable. In favour of this outstanding see *C. Poncelet*, *supra* note 74, p. 293.

84 *A. Michelot*, A la recherche de la justice climatique – Perspectives á partir du principe de responsabilités communes mais différenciées, in C. Cournil & C. Colard-Fabregoule (dirs.), Changements climatiques et défis du droit, 2010, p. 192.

85 *N. Pérez Sola*, *supra* note 9, pp. 324–326.

86 *J.A. Razquin & A. Ruiz de Apodaca*, *supra* note 2, p. 391.

87 Case C-182/10, *Marie-Nöelle Solvay*, *supra* note 40, para. 52.

88 Case C-130/95, *Giloy* [1997] ECR I-4291, para. 28.

89 *J. Ortega Bernardo*, *supra* note 66, p. 299.

90 Case C-240/09, *Lesoochranárske* [2011] ECR I-1255, paras. 51 and 52.

NGOs concerned should have the right to appeal the legislative acts concerning the environment. These issues may have a strong impact on issues like climate change.[91] The intensive exploitation of existing natural resources affects biological survival and life conditions of many communities beyond the economic policies proposed by some states.[92]

4.2. THE SINGLE LEGISLATIVE ACTS AND THE RIGHT TO ACCESS TO JUSTICE ON ENVIRONMENTAL ISSUES

The Spanish Constitutional Court argued that this kind of laws does not break the right to give an access to jurisdiction or prompt defencelessness, because the Constitutional Court can examine if that right has been violated. It stated two non-accumulative requirements to consider that the breach has been made. The first one is that the rights holders have to be eligible to appeal legislative acts; regarding the second one, the control exercised by the Constitutional Court, has to be sufficient to provide an equivalent protection to the common jurisdiction's one when an administrative decision is impugned and examined.[93] With a view to verifying if that equivalence happens, the Court should make the balance applying the proportionality and reasonability principles. In that sense, the legislator must justify why the Law have been passed and whether other means could be used to achieve the same result and prove that they could to prompt the least bad or the least risks.[94]

Concerning the first requirement, it is tough to fulfil it because the right to impugn the legislative acts is very limited and the ordinary jurisdiction can only deliver the question or doubt about the constitutionality of the Law to the Constitutional Court, as it has been explained in the previous paragraph.[95] Regarding the second one, the legislator has a broad decision-making power on different matters, as their ideological and political tendencies express. Public administration, to the contrary, has a reduced and very limited discretionary power, because it is subject strictly to the legislation, both to exercise the power and make the decisions according to it. This principle is called the positive linking to the law.[96]

---

91 *B. Müller, supra* note 83, p. 511.

92 *F. Gemenne*, De l'équité dans l'adaptation aux impacts du changement climatique, in C. Cournil & C. Colard Fabregoule, *supra* note 84, p. 223.

93 *O.W. Pedersen*, Environmental principles and environmental justice, ELR, 2010 (12), p. 34. Although the risks are seen as a scientific matter, it has been opened to individual and subjective interpretation, but some problems require specific expertise and substantial resources and these are not often available to communities pursuing an environmental justice claim.

94 SCC 129/2013 Judgment, para. 6.

95 *I. Lasagabaster Herrarte, supra* note 52, p. 92.

96 *J.A. Montilla Martos, supra* note 53, p. 233.

The Spanish Constitutional Court should determine if other interests exist, for example the local authorities', in order to give them the opportunity to take part during the legislative or administrative procedures; it should also verify if the administrative procedure has been conducted, applying the requirements for the EIA; it should ensure that the regulations on territorial management have been accomplished; and, finally, it should examine if the project is adapted to the environmental legislation.[97] However, the Constitutional Court has declared that it does not have any power on these matters, because these issues are related to the current legality, and they do not refer to the Constitution implementation and enforcement. Common jurisdiction, and not the Constitutional Court, must resolve disputes linking to the current legality, so that the concerned or entitled people and the NGOs can appeal the decision authorising the project.[98] For that, a regulation, plan or the decision must be enacted by Administration or the Government, not the legislator. In other countries, like France, the *Conseil Constitutionelle* has analysed the environmental issues and resolved litigations concerning rights and obligations both for citizens and public authorities, because the legislator passed a Law developing the Constitution (the French Charter for the Environment), according to which powers have been attributed to the Conseil to protect rights linked to the environmental issues.[99]

Even so, the next question should be outlined: if the single legislative act passes the proportionality and reasonability test, does not it breach the right to access to jurisdiction? The right to appeal the Law would not change, because the legislative act would have to be challenged before the Constitutional Court; the common judges and courts must apply that Law, and the right to appeal is very limited. Moreover, EIA decisions include a cost-benefit analysis and that requires a deeper and technical assessment, which involves a qualification and specialisation.[100] According to the CJEU, a mechanism to appeal the EIA decision must be provided and the Aarhus Convention establishes the judicial review as a compulsory requirement.[101] Furthermore, the projects could produce impacts on elements not approached or analysed by the EIA, although other administrative interventions aim to assess them by means of different procedures. For example, noise or human health is examined by the authorities with competency on those matters.[102] Passing a legislative act prevents the people concerned, who live

97 SCC 129/2013 Judgment, para. 6.

98 *G. Valencia Martín*, Evaluación de impacto ambiental y autorización ambiental integrada, in A. Nogueira López, *supra* note 28, pp. 71 and 72.

99 *D. Marrani*, The intersection between Constitution, Human Rights and the environment: the French Charter for the environment and the new ex post constitutional control in France, ELR, 2014 (16), p. 112.

100 *O.W. Pedersen*, *supra* note 93, p. 38.

101 *L.A. Malone & S. Pasternack*, Defending the environment: civil society strategies to enforce International Environmental Law, 2004, pp. 15 and 16.

102 *A. Waite*, The quest for environmental law equilibrium, ELR, 2005 (34), p. 57.

near the installations or infrastructures, from directly appealing the decision authorising the project.

5. CONCLUSIONS

Firstly, the European and domestic authorities agreed that the guarantees provided by the Aarhus Convention should be implemented, but in Spain the legislator has tried to dodge fraudulently the goals and effects derived from it. The Spanish legislative authorities could authorise a project, an infrastructure or a plan concerning a certain area by a law. The rules of the procedure, aimed at elaborating and approving the act, do not give the rights and guarantees established by the Convention regarding the public participation. However, those guarantees and rights would be extended if the administrative procedure was followed.

Secondly, one of the administrative procedures is the EIA, whose steps and stages cannot be adapted to the legislative procedure. The EIA Directive has excluded the application of its rules when a legislative act is passed, and in that case, it has granted the Member States discretionary powers to justify that the guarantees on participation and access to justice, related to the EIA procedure, are enforced. The CJEU has declared that, if the legislator has sufficient information, it is not necessary to follow the EIA procedure. Nevertheless, what happens with the participation and the consultations to other public administrations concerned (municipalities or regional authorities)? In that extent, the Spanish legislation shows some contradictions and failures that could prompt confusion and lack of security.

Thirdly, the Spanish Constitutional Court has developed an ambiguous jurisprudence related to the single legislative acts. On one side, it accepts that laws are in accordance with the Constitution if they fulfil some requirements; on the other side, by the contrary, it considers that the Government or Administration have powers on some matters, which means that a single legislative act would be banned if the Parliament passed a Law about the issues corresponding to the executive power. The most surprising argument is that the Constitutional Court itself could not resolve issues related to the current legality. So, who solves them? It seems that common jurisdiction does it. Well then, in order to access to justice, an administrative decision must be made, and for that, previously an administrative procedure must be carried out, and it must accomplish the guarantees provided by the Aarhus Convention and the EIA Directive, if this was applicable.

Fourthly, although participation during the administrative procedure is undoubted, the final administrative decision allows the promoter to settle the activity. Therefore, if the legislative act cannot be appealed, the reasons and the responses to the allegations given by the legislator could not be controlled and impugned. So, participation would not make any sense and be ineffective. The legislative act could become a political one, which means that its control should be related to the ruled requirements, based on formal considerations, but not on the substantive or material ones. A breach of the European Union's law is not clear at all, taking into account the CJEU has delivered the litigation to the internal courts, so that they can verify whether the requirements on sufficient information and the adequate procedure have been accomplished. Moreover, the wide powers granted to the States not to apply the EIA Directive have been noted.

Finally, access to justice and participation on environmental matters cannot be conditioned by categories whose jurisprudential interpretation and development are very dubious. Single legislative acts cannot escape from an effective jurisdictional control, only because the Spanish Constitutional Court has created the concept of single law and has subjected it to some requirements. All of that brings suspicions regarding the legislator's powers and its progressive tendency to exclude authorising projects from the citizen's participation and turn technical or juridical decisions into political ones, which is not compliance with a democratic state under the rule of law.

CHAPTER 7

THE IMPLEMENTATION OF THE SECOND PILLAR OF THE AARHUS CONVENTION IN ITALY:

The Need for Reform and for Introduction of the So-Called 'Deliberative Arenas'

Viviana Molaschi

1. PRELIMINARY REMARKS ON THE SCOPE OF THE ARTICLE: PUBLIC PARTICIPATION IN THE ENVIRONMENTAL FIELD

This chapter aims at giving an overview of the level of public participation in environmental decision-making in Italy, with particular regard to the procedures concerning major works.

The role of public participation in improving the environmental 'performance' of contemporary democracies has been the subject of several studies.[1] When faced with environmental problems traditional democratic institutions and public administrations get into a crisis. Let us think, for instance, of the difficulties in managing the issues relating to the 'risk society':[2] complexity, uncertainty, 'man-made' risks and changes in the public perception of scientific and technological evolution, nowadays often perceived – rightly or wrongly – as a threat to environment and health. Emblematic is the matter of genetically

1 For an overview of the debate on environmental democracy see *G. Manfredi & S. Nespor*, Ambiente e democrazia: un dibattito, Rivista giuridica dell'ambiente 2010, p. 293 et seq.

2 See *U. Beck*, Risikogesellschaft. Auf dem Weg in eine andere Moderne, 1986 (in English: Risk Society. Towards a New Modernity). See also *A. Giddens*, The consequences of modernity, 1990. In Italy the impact of the 'risk society' in the environmental sector has been researched deeply by *R. Ferrara*, Etica, ambiente e diritto: il punto di vista del giurista, in R. Ferrara & C.E. Gallo (eds.), Le politiche ambientali, lo sviluppo sostenibile e il danno, 2014, p. 19 et seq., in R. Ferrara & M.A. Sandulli, Trattato di Diritto dell'Ambiente, 2014.

modified organisms,[3] one of the most debated technological innovations of the last few decades, which raises questions of a scientific, ethical, environmental, health, economic and social character. In tackling this issue neither science nor politics have been able to give exhaustive and conclusive answers.

Moreover, the environmental field is characterised by 'tragic choices'[4] concerning the allocation and consumption of resources that are limited and sometimes not replaceable. As underlined by scholars, the real 'tragedy' of the commons (water, forests, and so on) seems to be their scarcity and perishability.[5]

The incapability of contemporary democracies to face these challenges is at the basis of ever increasing distance and conflicts between public institutions and citizens, regarding the political decisions made in their name. In particular, during the last few decades quite often the realisation of infrastructure, industrial plants, waste disposal facilities and other types of works, potentially dangerous for the environment or health, or suspected of being so, has raised strong protests from the communities directly involved.[6] These phenomena of public opposition are generally known as the NIMBY (Not in My Back Yard) syndrome, the extreme expression of which is generally indicated as the BANANA syndrome (where BANANA stands for Build Absolutely Nothing Anywhere Near Anything).

Italy is experiencing a growing spread of 'proximity conflicts': public and private actors have antagonistic views on the meaning and on the pursuance of the public interest. On one hand, if we think of infrastructure and industrial plants, the realisation of these works corresponds to a precise public interest, related to needs for development of the country, through economic revival and the promotion of employment, especially in periods of economic crisis and depression; on the other hand, there are concerns among the population about their impact on the environment and health. And, in any case, the choices themselves on 'how' to create economic development and use public money can be the subject of animated diatribes.

These conflicts are frequently the effect of the DAD approach (Decide, Announce, Defend), which shows a lack of public participation in the decision-making process. One of the most well known examples in Italy is given by the construction of the high speed railway line (known as TAV), to connect Turin and Lyon, which has aroused tough opposition, initially only of the communities of the Val di Susa and later at a national level.[7] Without entering into the details

---

3 On this sensitive topic see, *ex multis*, *R. Ferrara & I.M. Marino* (eds.), Gli organismi geneticamente modificati. Sicurezza alimentare e tutela dell'ambiente, 2004.

4 The reference is to *G. Calabresi & P. Bobbit*, Tragic choices, 1978.

5 For this observation see *R. Ferrara*, *supra* note 2, pp. 20–21. The reference is to the article written by *G. Hardin*, The tragedy of the commons, Science 1968, p. 1243 et seq.

6 On these issues see, *ex multis*, *A. Macchiati & G. Napolitano* (eds.), È possibile realizzare infrastrutture in Italia?, 2010; *L. Bobbio & A. Zeppetella* (eds.), Perchè proprio qui? Grandi opere e opposizioni locali, 1999.

7 On the democratic *deficit* that has characterised the TAV construction process see *L. Bobbio*, Discutibile e indiscussa. L'Alta Velocità alla prova della democrazia, Il Mulino 2006, 1, p. 124

of this complex matter, and without expressing any value judgement on it,[8] it must be borne in mind that after protests, occupations of construction sites and interruptions of works were a political table – the Tavolo Istituzionale di Palazzo Chigi[9] – and a technical Observatory – the Osservatorio della Val di Susa[10] – set up. However, these institutions, aimed at finding shared solutions, were formal places of discussion mainly at an institutional level,[11] which did not promote public participation of citizens through dialogue and confrontation. Therefore, these interventions were insufficient, and the resistance to the high speed railway line is still ongoing and accompanying all the steps of its construction.

The underlined need for more social engagement leads to an examination of the participatory tools provided by the Italian legal system, in order to evaluate their adequacy. This is the focus of this contribution.

Reflections on participatory guarantees in the environmental field will require the analysis of the implementation in Italy of the Aarhus Convention on access to information, public participation in decision-making and access to justice in environmental matters, adopted by the UN Economic Commission for Europe (UNECE) in Denmark on 25 June 1998 and ratified in Italy by Law n. 108 of 16 March 2001. This Convention, a turning point in the evolution of environmental democracy,[12] links substantive environmental protection to

---

et seq.; *A. Algostino*, Democrazia, rappresentanza, partecipazione. Il caso del movimento No Tav, 2011. The bibliography on the construction of the TAV is incredibly wide: see also, *ex multis*, *L. Bobbio & E. Dansero*, La Tav e la Valle di Susa. Geografie in competizione, 2008. In general, on public participation in procedures of siting and realization of major works in Italy see *G. Pizzanelli*, La partecipazione dei privati alle decisioni pubbliche. Politiche ambientali e realizzazione delle grandi opere infrastrutturali, 2010.

8 The construction of the TAV is at the centre of a heated ideological and political debate in Italy.

9 The Tavolo Istituzionale di Palazzo Chigi is presided by the President of the Council of Ministers (or by the Undersecretary to the Presidency), and is constituted by the Ministers concerned, the representatives of the areas involved (Region, Province, Municipalities), the promoters of the project (the binational enterprise LTF-Lyon-Turin Ferroviaire), the representatives of the Italian-French Intergovernmental Commission (in Italian: CIG-Commissione intergovernativa italo-francese) and the Italian State Railways (RFI-Rete Ferroviaria Italiana and Trenitalia).

10 The Observatory has been instituted with the aim of analysing the environmental, social and economic aspects of the project. It is presided by the extraordinary commissioner appointed by the Government, and comprises representatives, with specific technical competence, of the institutions at a national, regional and local level, together with a representative of the Italian delegation of the CIG and experts appointed by the entrepreneurial subjects involved (RFI and LTF). This experience has also seen the intervention of subjects like the regional environmental protection agency (in Italian: ARPA-Agenzia regionale per la protezione dell'ambiente) and the metropolitan mobility agency (in Italian: Agenzia per la Mobilità Metropolitana), and experts as well as significant stakeholders. On the constitution and the activity of the Observatory see the critical analysis by *A. Algostino*, L'Osservatorio per il collegamento ferroviario Torino-Lione come case-study sulla democrazia e sul dissenso, Costituzionalismo.it, 2009 (2), p. 1 et seq.

11 For this observation see *A. Algostino*, *supra* note 7, p. 196.

12 The Convention has been welcomed by scholars as a universal instrument of environmental democracy: see *M. Prieur*, La Convention d'Aarhus, instrument universel de la démocratie environnementale, Revue juridique de l'environnement, numéro special, 1999, p. 1 et seq.

procedural rights, in order to involve the public in the environmental decision-making. Its implementation in Italy will be investigated as to the Environmental Impact Assessment (EIA), and the Strategic Environmental Assessment (SEA), regulated by Legislative Decree n. 152 of 3 April 2006, that is the Italian Environmental Code.[13] Particular attention will be paid to the so called 'special' EIA, regarding major works (infrastructure and industrial plants identified by the Government as strategic or of national interest), whose regulation is in Legislative Decree n. 163 of 12 April 2006, that is the Code of Public Contracts.

1.1. THE INTEREST IN STUDYING 'DELIBERATIVE ARENAS'

After having considered the level of public participation in the aforementioned procedures, pointing out gaps and criticalities, this chapter will investigate some possibilities of reform. In particular, in dealing with the issue of granting major public involvement, some preliminary evaluations will be formulated on the spread in the environmental (and planning) field of the so called 'deliberative arenas' (in Italian: *arene deliberative*), a new frontier of public participation in decision-making.[14]

By deliberative arenas are meant new forms of participation in public decision-making, like, for instance, participatory budgeting, citizens' juries, Planungszellen or planning cells, consensus conferences, deliberative opinion polls, the French *débats publics*, town meetings, and so on. They can be set in the theoretical and conceptual context of deliberative democracy,[15] within the framework of participatory democracy.[16] In fact, they are forms of public

On its role in granting environmental democracy see also, *ex multis*, *J. Wates*, The Aarhus Convention: A Driving Force for Environmental Democracy, JEEPL 2005 (2), p. 2 et seq.

13 An updated version of the Italian legislation mentioned in this chapter can be found at www.normattiva.it.

14 The reference is to the important work of *L. Bobbio*, Le arene deliberative, Rivista Italiana di Politiche Pubbliche, 2002 (3), p. 5 et seq.

15 The literature on deliberative democracy is very wide: among the Italian authors who have studied this topic see, *ex multis*, *L. Bobbio*, *supra* note 14; *R. Bifulco*, Democrazia deliberativa, in Enciclopedia del Diritto-Annali IV, 2011, p. 271 et seq.; *G. Bosetti & S. Maffettone* (eds.), Democrazia deliberativa: cosa è, 2004; *L. Pellizzoni* (ed.), La deliberazione pubblica, 2005.

16 On participatory democracy see, among the most important Italian works, *U. Allegretti*, Democrazia partecipativa, in Enciclopedia del Diritto-Annali IV, 2011, p. 295 et seq.; *Id.* (ed.), Democrazia partecipativa. Esperienze e prospettive in Italia e in Europa, 2010. This chapter adheres to the idea that deliberative democracy is a form of participatory democracy, having more circumscribed and defined borders: see *L. Bobbio*, Dilemmi della democrazia partecipativa, 2006 (1), p. 11, 14. However, the theoretical difference between deliberative democracy and participatory democracy, distinct conceptual frameworks to which deliberative arenas can be ascribed, is very controversial. On this complex point see also *U. Allegretti*, Democrazia partecipativa: un contributo alla democratizzazione della democrazia, in U. Allegretti (ed.), Democrazia partecipativa. Esperienze e prospettive in Italia e in Europa, 2010, p. 5, 16–17; *R. Bifulco*, Democrazia deliberativa, *supra* note 15, in particular at p. 275 et

participation inspired by two principles: inclusion and deliberation. As to the former, the democratic character of participation should require the involvement of everyone who can be affected by the decision-making. As to the latter, by deliberation is meant a process in which participants exchange arguments and counterarguments, become informed of the others' views and transform theirs in the search of the common interest.

Although the implementation of these two principles varies a lot in practice,[17] what matters is that deliberative arenas go beyond both the traditional participatory scheme of notice and comment and other participatory tools like consultations and public inquiries. They aim at meeting the need for creating new spaces and ways of public–private interaction, empowering citizen engagement, and, thanks to their 'discursive' character,[18] improve the decision-making process, leading to better more informed decisions, in the search for the general interest.[19] For these reasons they can play a significant role in the environmental (and planning) sector, characterised, as seen, by a high level of conflict, where they can contribute to making decisions marked by more 'ecological rationality'.[20]

A noteworthy example of application of these participatory instruments in this context is given by the already mentioned *débat public*, which is the most important French institute as to siting of major works, whose introduction into the Italian legal system is a key issue of the infrastructural debate in the country and will be discussed in this chapter.

The analysis on deliberative arenas that will be conducted will concern only institutionalised examples of these participatory means, embodied in pieces of legislation. Given this framework, the focus will be on experiences regulated at a regional level, where in Italy there are some avant garde examples.

---

seq. and *Id.*, Democrazia deliberativa, rappresentativa e partecipativa. Tre diverse forme di democrazia, in U. Allegretti (ed.), Democrazia partecipativa. Esperienze e prospettive in Italia e in Europa, 2010, p. 65 et seq.

17 On the differences between the theoretical model of deliberative democracy and the practical experiences that take inspiration from it see *L. Bobbio*, La democrazia deliberativa nella pratica, Stato e Mercato, 2005 (73), p. 67 et seq.

18 See *J.S. Dryzek*, Discursive Democracy, Politics, Policy and Political Science, 1990.

19 The search for 'generalisable interests' is also due to the fact that in deliberative processes each participant puts forward 'proposals under the rubric of general principles or policy considerations that others could accept': *D. Miller*, Deliberative Democracy and Social Choice, special issue of Political Studies, 1992 (40), p. 54, 55.

20 The reference is to the fundamental work of *J.S. Dryzek*, Rational Ecology: Environment and Political Economy, 1987. On the role of deliberative democracy in the environmental field see more recently, *ex multis*, *J.S. Dryzek & H. Stevenson*, Democratizing Global Climate Governance, 2014; *G. Smith*, Deliberative democracy and the environment, 2003. For an analysis from a juridical point of view see also *C. Fraenkel Haeberle*, Participatory Democracy and the Global Approach in Environmental Legislation, in E. Lohse & M. Poto (eds.), Participatory Rights in the Environmental Decision-Making Process and the Implementation of the Aarhus Convention: a Comparative Perspective, 2015, pp. 33 et seq.

2. THE AARHUS CONVENTION: A BRIEF OUTLINE

As anticipated in the introductory considerations to this work, the evaluation of the level of public participation in Italy entails an examination of the Aarhus Convention and of its implementation in the country.

The Convention recognises 'the right of every person of present and future generations to live in an environment adequate to his or her health and well-being'[21] and 'the duty, both individually and in association with others, to protect and improve the environment for the benefit of present and future generations'.[22]

These important statements can be set in a specific conceptual and axiological framework. The Aarhus Convention 'links environmental rights and human rights':[23] it is based on the awareness that 'adequate protection of the environment is essential to human well being and the enjoyment of basic human rights, including the right to life itself'. To this end, it 'acknowledges that we owe an obligation to future generations',[24] according to the principle of sustainable development, which founds a duty of environmental protection in the responsibility of everyone.[25]

The Convention represents a landmark in the evolution of environmental legislation because it links environmental safeguard to the level of democracy granted in the decision-making process.[26] In fact, as is underlined in the Introduction to the Convention given by the UNECE, it 'establishes that sustainable development can be achieved only through the involvement of all stakeholders'; 'links government accountability and environmental protection'; 'focuses on interactions between the public and public authorities in a democratic context'.

---

21 See Article 1 and the Preamble of the AC.

22 See the Preamble of the AC.

23 See the Introduction to the Convention given on the website of the UNECE: www.unece.org/env/pp/introduction.html.

24 See the Introduction to the AC.

25 The role of the principle of responsibility in the technological society has been highlighted by *H. Jonas*, Il principio di responsabilità, 2002 (Italian translation). The idea that environmental safeguarding is not only the object of a right but also of a duty has been studied and developed by some Italian authors: see, in particular, *F. Fracchia*, Introduzione allo studio del diritto dell'ambiente. Principi, concetti e istituti, 2013, p. 93 et seq.; *Id.*, La tutela dell'ambiente come dovere di solidarietà, Il Diritto dell'Economia, 2009 (3/4), p. 491 et seq.; *Id.*, The Legal Definition of Environment: from Rights to Duties (17 November 2005), Bocconi Legal Studies Research Paper No. 06-09, http://papers.ssrn.com/sol3/papers.cfm?abstract_id=850488; *Id.*, Sulla configurazione giuridica unitaria dell'ambiente: art. 2 Cost. e doveri di solidarietà ambientale, Il Diritto dell'Economia, 2002 (2), p. 215 et seq. The author has investigated the link between environment and duty in his works on sustainable development: see *Id.*, Lo sviluppo sostenibile. La voce flebile dell'altro tra protezione dell'ambiente e tutela della specie umana, 2010.

26 In these terms *D. Siclari*, La democrazia ambientale nel quadro dei diritti partecipativi e dell'accesso all'informazione ambientale, in S. Grassi & M.A. Sandulli (eds.), I procedimenti amministrativi per la tutela dell'ambiente, 2014, p. 471, 476, in R. Ferrara & M.A. Sandulli, *supra* note 2.

The pursuit of environmental democracy is grounded on the so-called three 'pillars' of the Convention: access to environmental information, participation in environmental decision-making, access to justice in environmental matters.

In this chapter, as clarified, the attention will be focused on participatory rights, and, specifically, on the second pillar, with particular regard to Article 6, dedicated to 'Public participation in decisions on specific activities', and Article 7, on 'Public participation concerning plans, programmes and policies relating to the environment'.

For what concerns Article 6, its implementation in Italy will be investigated as to the Environmental Impact Assessment (EIA), especially when major works come into consideration; for what regards Article 7, the Strategic Environmental Assessment (SEA) will come into consideration.[27]

3. THE IMPLEMENTATION OF THE SECOND PILLAR OF THE AARHUS CONVENTION IN THE ITALIAN ENVIRONMENTAL CODE: THE REGULATION OF THE 'ORDINARY' EIA AND THE SEA

Before analysing the participatory tools provided by the Italian Environmental Code for the EIA and SEA procedures,[28] as a preliminary remark, it is interesting to verify which role this piece of legislation gives to participation in the introductory part regarding 'Common Provisions and General Principles' of the regulation. Here, in fact, are the main principles that inspire the environmental protection

[27] The reason why the analysis will not cover also Article 8, which regards '[p]ublic participation during the preparation of executive regulations and/or generally applicable legally binding normative instruments', is due to the fact that in Italy an institutional procedure for public participation in preparing national legislation (i.e. laws adopted by Parliament or legislative decrees adopted by the Government within a delegation law) currently does not exist, even though there are some mechanisms for public involvement in legislative activities, like parliamentary hearings. However, according to Article 1(14) of Law n. 308 of 15 December 2004, which delegated the Government the power to reorganise the regulation on environmental matters, resulting in the Environmental Code, the Ministry of the Environment was obliged to establish through a specific act forms of consultation with Trade Unions, Business organisations and Environmental NGOs for the preparation of the decrees of implementation (see Decree 7 June 2005).

[28] For a general idea of the various environmental impact assessment procedures in Italy see, *ex multis*, *A. Milone*, Le valutazioni ambientali, in S. Grassi & M.A. Sandulli (eds.), *supra* note 26, p. 135 et seq.; *A. Police*, La valutazione di impatto ambientale, in P. Dell'Anno & E. Picozza (eds.), Trattato di diritto dell'ambiente, vol. II, Discipline ambientali di settore, 2013, p. 527 et seq.

regulation in the country, implementing the Italian Constitution, in respect of EU Treaties',[29] according to Article 3 *bis* (1).

Among the articles of the Constitutional Charter that are recalled by the latter, it is important to remember, as to the topic of this chapter, Article 3,[30] which, in its second paragraph, devoted to the principle of substantive equality,[31] states the duty of the Republic to act in order to guarantee 'effective participation … in the political, economic and social organization of the country'.[32]

Returning to the Environmental Code, from the title of Article 3 *sexies*, 'Right of access to environmental information and to participation for collaborative purposes', it is possible to observe that participation is meant only in a collaborative sense,[33] as an instrument useful for the public administration itself, which gives it the possibility to acquire a better knowledge of the facts and interests relevant to the decision. The other dimensions of public participation are not taken into consideration: neither participation as defence, that is giving the private individual the possibility to assert his/her own rights in the preparatory phase of the public decision;[34] nor, which is more remarkable, participation as an expression of democracy, that is as an essential tool to involve civil society in the decision-making process.

---

29 On the principles that concur in environmental protection derived from EU Treaties see, *ex multis*, *O. Porchia*, Le politiche dell'Unione Europea in materia ambientale, in R. Ferrara & C.E. Gallo (eds.), *supra* note 2, p. 153 et seq.; *R. Ferrara*, I principi comunitari della tutela dell'ambiente, Diritto amministrativo, 2005 (3), p. 509 et seq.

30 The other articles mentioned by the provision are Articles 2, 9, 32, 41, 42, 44 and 117(1) and (3). For an English version of the Italian Constitutional Charter see: www.senato.it/documenti/repository/istituzione/costituzione_inglese.pdf.

31 According to Article 3 of the Italian Constitution the principle of equality has two dimensions: formal equality (paragraph 1) and substantive equality (paragraph 2).

32 Article 3(2) of the Italian Constitutional Charter establishes: 'It is the duty of the Republic to remove those obstacles of an economic or social nature that constrain the freedom and equality of citizens, thereby impeding the full development of the human person and the effective participation of all workers in the political, economic and social organization of the country'. The importance of linking the principle of participation to substantive equality is highlighted by *U. Allegretti*, Democrazia partecipativa, *supra* note 16, p. 317, whose work analyses the constitutional grounds for public participation in Italy.

33 On the meanings of public participation in public decision-making see, *ex multis*, *S. Cassese*, La partecipazione dei privati alle decisioni pubbliche, Rivista trimestrale di diritto pubblico, 2007 (1), p. 13 et seq. Structural and functional aspects of public participation are also analysed in the volume by *E. Casetta*, Manuale di diritto amministrativo (Fabrizio Fracchia, ed.), 2013, in particular p. 514 et seq.

34 The concept of defence is generally used in the context of judicial controversies. However, Italian scholars have used it also to express the role of public participation in administrative procedures, whose articulation has been inspired by the structure of judicial proceedings. The possibility of the individual to introduce his/her point of view in the preliminary phase of the public decision-making is seen as a sort of 'anticipated' defence against the public action. From this point of view, participation also aims at preventing the confrontation with the public administration from becoming an irretrievable contrast that can lead to a judicial controversy. Some authors have underlined that, according to this perspective, thanks to public participation the public action is subject to the rules of justice and is fairer: see *S. Cassese*, *supra* note 33, p. 14.

Moreover, what raises perplexity is that, despite the mention of the principle of participation in the title, the content of the article is dedicated only to right of access to environmental information, and there is no statement on public participation.

Entering more in detail into the contents of the Environmental Code, the main sector for the application of Article 6 of the Aarhus Convention, on participation in decisions on specific activities, is, as anticipated, the EIA. This section will focus on the 'ordinary' EIA, while the 'special' EIA concerning major works, which has a different regulation with respect to the former, will be investigated in the following one.

The Italian EIA regulation is the outcome of the implementation of various EC and EU Directives: at the outset, the fundamental EIA Directive 85/337/EEC, which has been modified three times by Directive 97/11/EC, Directive 2003/35/EC and Directive 2009/31/EC. The initial Directive of 1985 and its three amendments have been codified by Directive 2011/92/EU. The latter has been modified in 2014 by Directive 2014/52/EU, which has not been transposed by Italy yet.

As to public participation, two of the listed Directives are in particular relevant: first, Directive 2003/35/EC, 'providing for public participation in respect of the drawing up of certain plans and programmes relating to the environment and amending with regard to public participation and access to justice Council Directives 85/337/EEC and 96/61/EC', which has sought to align the latter with the Aarhus Convention; secondly, the recent Directive 2014/52/EU, which also pays attention to transparency and participation.

The EIA is defined by the Italian Environmental Code as the procedure through which the effects of a project on the environment are preventively assessed (Article 5(1)(b)), with the goal of 'protecting human health, contributing with a better environment to the quality of life, maintaining the species, conserving the reproductive capacity of the ecosystem as an essential resource for life' (Article 4(4)(b)). The 'competent authority' in charge of the procedure is, at a national level, the Ministry of the Environment, Land Protection and Sea.[35]

Public participation is regulated by Article 24, entitled 'Consultation',[36] which contains, in first place, some provisions aimed at informing the public of the proposed project. The public is informed by publication of a notice both on the website of the 'competent authority' and in a national or regional/local

---

35 By 'competent authority', according to Article 5(1)(p), of the Environmental Code, is meant: 'the public administration that is responsible for the screening, the reasoned opinion, in case of assessment of plans and programs, and the final decisions on the EIA in case of projects'. As to the EIA provided at a national level, this authority is represented by the Ministry of the Environment, Land Protection and Sea (Article 7(5)). As for the EIA at a regional level, the competent authority is the public administration, having duties of environmental protection and valorisation, identified by regional laws (Article 7(6)).

36 For an analysis of Article 24 of Legislative Decree n. 152 of 2006 see *V. Molaschi*, Comment on Article 24, in R. Ferrara & G.F. Ferrari (eds.), Commentario breve alle leggi in materia di urbanistica ed edilizia, 2015, pp. 822 et seq.

newspaper, depending on the level of the authority competent to carry out the procedure. The contents of the notice regarding the project and its possible main environmental impacts have been recently specified by Law Decree n. 91 of 24 June 2014, converted into law by Law n. 116 of 11 August 2014, which has modified Article 24. In particular, it must indicate where and how the relevant documentation will be available and the time (60 days) within which it is possible to submit observations.

'Strengthening public access to information and transparency' is one of the goals of the new Directive 2014/52/EU, which amends Directive 2011/92/EU:[37] in order to 'allow the public to access that information easily and effectively', it provides that 'Member States shall take the necessary measures to ensure that the relevant information is electronically accessible to the public, through at least a central portal or easily accessible points of access, at the appropriate administrative level'. Moreover, a reasonable time-frame shall be provided for allowing sufficient time for informing the public (Article 1, which amends Article 6 of the previous Directive).

Once the duties of publicity and transparency are fulfilled, *ex* Article 24 of the Italian Environmental Code, anyone who might be concerned can submit observations: even though their written character is not explicitly indicated, the provision is commonly interpreted in the sense that they are written.

The decision as to the EIA, taken by the Ministry of the Environment, Land Protection and Sea, must take into account, *inter alia*, the comments provided, examining them 'concomitantly, singly or by groups'. According to the administrative judge, detailed reasons do not have to be given if they are rejected. It is sufficient that from the acts of the procedure it emerges that they have been considered; a concise motivation of the negative evaluation, which does not necessarily have to regard every single argument of the proposer, is deemed adequate.[38]

The Environmental Code regulation is characterised by some participatory tools that go beyond merely documental participation, as established by the Italian general law on administrative procedures, Law n. 241 of 7 August 1990,[39] and guarantee a deeper citizen involvement. However, there are some limits, which will be pointed out.

Article 24 provides the possibility to call a public inquiry for the examination of the impact assessment study, of the opinions of the public administrations involved in the proceeding and of the citizens' comments. The inquiry concludes

[37] See the Preamble of Directive 2014/52/EU.

[38] See, for instance, Cons. Stato, section IV, 1049/2009; Tar Lazio, section II, 5481/2005.

[39] Law n. 241 of 1990, *ex* Article 29(2-*bis*), establishes the 'essential levels', according to Article 117(2)(m) of the Constitution, of public participation granted in the Italian legal order. These levels can be derogated *in melius*, providing more advanced participatory means, but not *in peius*, diminishing the participatory guarantees.

with a report on the works and on the findings, which are taken into consideration for the final decision.

However, the call for the hearing depends on the willingness of the 'competent authority'. Moreover, the completion of the public inquiry entails neither interruption nor suspension of the terms provided for the fulfilment of the preliminary activity of the procedure.[40] This aspect puts time restraints on the inquiry.

It is possible to predict some changes regarding the time limits when the new Directive 2014/52/EU is implemented in Italy. The new Directive, in fact, requires the provision of 'reasonable time-frames for the different phases, allowing sufficient time for', in particular, 'the public concerned to prepare and participate effectively in the environmental decision-making'. To this aim, it establishes that 'the time-frames for consulting the public concerned on the environmental impact report referred in Article 5(1) [of the Directive] shall not be shorter than 30 days' (Article 1, which modifies Article 6 of the previous Directive).

Finally, according to the Environmental Code, if the public inquiry has not taken place, the 'proponent'[41] of the project can be called, also at his/her own request, to a 'synthetic cross-examination' with the subjects who have submitted opinions and comments. The cross-examination, like the public inquiry, is not the effect of a request by the public concerned.

In order to appraise the level of participation granted in Italian environmental legislation, it is necessary to consider also the implementation of Article 7 of the Aarhus Convention, which regards public participation concerning plans, programmes and policies relating to the environment.

The main field where this implementation can be verified is the SEA, which is also regulated by the Environmental Code, which has transposed Directive 2001/42/EC, on the assessment of the effects of certain plans and programmes on the environment. According to the Italian Environmental Code, the SEA has the goal of granting a high environmental protection level and of contributing to the integration of environmental considerations when those plans and programmes are elaborated, adopted and approved, ensuring that they are consistent and help conditions for a sustainable development (Article 4(4)(a)).

The authority in charge of the procedure at a national level is, like in the case of the EIA, the Ministry of the Environment, Land Protection and Sea,[42] which,

---

40 According to Article 26 of the Environmental Code, the decision on the EIA must be issued within 150 days from the submission of the project and the relevant documents by the proponent.

41 By 'proponent', according to the Italian terminology (literally, in Italian, '*proponente*'), or 'developer', the expression used in the Directives that have regulated the EIA over the years, is meant, according to Article 5(1)(r), of the Environmental Code: 'the public or private subject who elaborates the plan, programme or project that falls under the regulation of the Code itself'. The Legislative Decree gives a definition that refers both to the Environmental Impact Assessment and to the Strategic Environmental Assessment.

42 See *supra* note 35.

in this case, is responsible for issuing a reasoned opinion 'before the approval of the plan or programme, or at the starting of the procedure or, in any case, during the preparation phase of it' (Article 11(3)).

It is interesting to observe that the Italian general law on administrative procedures, Law n. 241 of 1990, does not guarantee participation in planning acts and procedures: Article 13 excludes the latter from the application of participatory tools,[43] even though it preserves particular rules which regulate their adoption in specific sectors. This means that the level of participation provided in the environmental field and, more specifically, for the SEA is more extensive than in other sectors. From this point of view, it must be highlighted that, according to the Italian administrative judge, violation of the regulation regarding public participation in the SEA implies the illegitimacy of the plans or programmes themselves.[44]

These provisions are similar to those concerning the EIA as to the notice of the procedure and the prescriptions aimed at ensuring that the documentation – in particular the plan or programme proposal and the environmental report – is at the disposal of the public. However, there are differences regarding the participatory instruments. According to Article 14 of the Environmental Code,[45] participation consists only of 'written comments'. In this case, the law establishes explicitly the written character of the observations, thanks to a clarification in Legislative Decree n. 128 of 29 June 2010. No possibility of public inquiry is provided, differently from what Article 24 of Legislative Decree n. 152 of 2006 establishes for the EIA.

4. PUBLIC PARTICIPATION IN THE 'SPECIAL' EIA CONCERNING MAJOR WORKS.

Participation encounters limits also in the special procedure of the EIA regarding major works: infrastructure and industrial plants identified by the Government as strategic or of national interest.

Law n. 443 of 21 December 2001, known as 'Target Law' (in Italian: *Legge Obiettivo*), aimed at speeding up administrative procedures related to such major works, delegated the Government the power enact a legislative decree that, *inter alia*, simplified the EIA in this kind of procedures (Article 1(2)).

The Government issued Legislative Decree n. 190 of 20 August 2002, whose provisions have been afterward embodied in Legislative Decree n. 163 of 2006,

---

43 According to Article 13 of Law n. 241 of 1990, the provisions on participation in the administrative procedure do not apply to activity of the public administration directed at issuing normative, administrative general, planning and programming acts.

44 Tar Lombardia-Brescia, Section 1, 668/2013.

45 For an updated analysis of this article see *M.L. Schiavano*, Comment on Article 14, in R. Ferrara & G.F. Ferrari (eds.), *supra* note 36.

that is the Code of Public Contracts, which now regulates the procedure of planning, approval and realisation of strategic works and also the 'special' EIA provided for them, derogating the provisions of the Environmental Code.

In the EIA for strategic infrastructure and industrial plants the environmental impact assessment is integrated in the procedure of approval of the related preliminary projects: *ex* Article 183(6) of the Code of Public Contracts, the decision on the environmental compatibility is adopted by the Interministerial Committee on Economic Planning (in Italian: CIPE, *Comitato Interministeriale per la Programmazione Economica*), 'concomitantly with the approval of the preliminary project'. According to Article 165(3), in fact, when an environmental impact assessment is prescribed by legislation, the preliminary project to be approved by the CIPE is submitted together with the environmental impact assessment report drawn up by the developer. The composite character of the evaluation conducted by the CIPE emerges from Article 165(7) of the Code, which establishes that the approval of the preliminary project by the CIPE 'entails the assessment of the environmental compatibility'.

The fact that in the 'special' EIA the ascertainment of the environmental compatibility is not an act of the Minister of the Environment, Land Protection and Sea, but of the CIPE, is one of the main differences with respect to the 'ordinary EIA'. However, the Minister of the Environmental intervenes in the procedure, which is characterised by the involvement also of other Ministers. *Ex* Article 183(5) of Legislative Decree n. 163 of 2006, the CIPE approves the preliminary project on the proposal of the Minister of Infrastructure and Transport (and, in some cases, of the Minister of Economic Development), which is formulated, *inter alia*, on the basis of the evaluation of environmental compatibility given by the Minister of the Environment, Land Protection and Sea. Therefore, in short, the Minister of the Environment, Land Protection and Sea does not issue the act of environmental compatibility, but gives his/her evaluation on it within the proceeding.

As to public participation, it must be preliminarily observed that, according to the Code of Public Contracts, private subjects, even those more directly concerned, are involved neither in the phase in which the works are identified, the phase that implies their preliminary siting, nor in the phase of the preliminary approval of the project, which establishes the exact siting of the works,[46] and still less in that of the approval of the final project, which allows the beginning of its realisation.[47] This makes the special procedure of EIA for strategic infrastructure and plants, which, as seen, is a sub-phase which precedes the approval of the preliminary project by the CIPE, particularly important in order to assure some

46 Article 165 simply establishes that in the cases in which the EIA is not provided, the preliminary project is deposited in the competent office for consultation by the public and notice of the deposit is given on the website of the region and of the contracting subject.

47 In this case participation is granted only to the individuals affected by expropriation procedures, according to Article 166(2) of the Code of Public Contracts.

kind of participation.[48] Even though the EIA does not regard specifically the siting, it is indubitable that some aspects of siting are taken into consideration in the assessment: in fact, the environmental impact assessment study, according to Article 183(2), must contain a description of the project with the information regarding its location, as well as a brief description of the principal alternatives examined, with indications of the main reasons of the choice from the environmental impact point of view.

As to public participation, Article 183(4) establishes that the Ministry of the Environment, in elaborating its evaluation, takes into account possible observations of public and private subjects interested, submitted within 30 days from the production of the documents by the contracting subject or by the proponent authority. Even though it is not specified in the regulation, it is clear that the provision refers again to written comments. Moreover, the time-frame seems rather restrictive: in the 'ordinary' EIA it is 60 days.

Finally, according to judicial decisions, the Ministry has no obligation to state precisely whether or not the comments have been considered.[49]

No public inquiry is provided, differently, again, from the regulation of the 'ordinary' EIA.

5. THE EXAMPLE OF THE LAW OF TUSCANY N. 46 OF 2013 ON REGIONAL PUBLIC DEBATE AND PROMOTION OF PARTICIPATION IN THE ELABORATION OF REGIONAL AND LOCAL POLICIES

Public participation seems to be the object of major attention at a regional level, where it is possible to notice some significant experiences of implementation of deliberative or, more in general, participatory democracy instruments.[50] Let us think, for instance, of Law of Emilia Romagna n. 3 of 9 February 2010, containing rules for the definition, reorganisation and promotion of procedures of consultation and participation in the elaboration of regional and local policies,[51] and, in particular, of Law of Tuscany n. 46 of 2 August 2013 on regional public

48 This aspect is underlined by *A. Tonetti*, La procedura di localizzazione di opere pubbliche. Il caso italiano, in *A. Macchiati & G. Napolitano* (eds.), *supra* note 6, p. 163, 179.

49 This aspect is highlighted by *R. Ferrara & A. Milone*, La valutazione di impatto ambientale delle opere strategiche, in M.A. Sandulli, R. De Nictolis & R. Garofoli (eds.), Trattato sui contratti pubblici, vol. IV – Le tipologie contrattuali, 2008, p. 2906.

50 On the distinction between the two forms of democracy see the works cited, *supra* at note 16.

51 On Law of Emilia Romagna n. 3 of 2010 see *M. Ciancaglini*, Tra democrazia partecipativa e concertazione. La legge regionale 3/2010 dell'Emilia Romagna, Istituzioni del Federalismo, 2011 (2), p. 215 et seq.

debate and promotion of participation in the elaboration of regional and local policies.[52]

The focus of this chapter will be the latter, relevant to this work because of the introduction in Italy of the French *débat public*, although only at a regional level.

It must be clarified that Law of Tuscany n. 46 of 2013 has replaced the previous pioneering Law n. 69 of 27 December 2007,[53] which was a source of inspiration for the Emilia Romagna legislation,[54] introducing some correctives to the participatory procedures provided in it. Law 69/2007 itself was the outcome of a deliberative method, used to discuss and decide its contents, by means of a large-scale 21st century town meeting, which took place in Carrara in November 2006.

The legislation of Tuscany has two scopes: first of all, as anticipated, it brings to Italy, along the lines of the French *débat public*, the regional public debate; secondly, it provides regional support for local participatory processes.

According to Article 2, the following are entitled to intervene in the participatory procedures provided by the Law: resident citizens and foreigners and stateless persons lawfully resident in the area concerned by the participatory processes; as to the public debate, persons who work, study or live in the area, who are interested in the area itself or in the object of the participatory process, whose intervention is considered useful by the person responsible for the debate.

As to the specific kinds of participatory tools, it must be clarified that the *débat public*[55] was introduced in France, following the Quebec model, by Law n. 95–101 of 2 February 1995, the so-called '*Loi Barnier*', as a consequence of the strong protests against the construction of the high speed railway line between Lyon and Marseilles. It regards infrastructure projects of national importance, and occurs at an early stage of the administrative process, before the developer of the project has prepared a final plan. Since 1997 it has been organised and managed by the *Commission nationale du débat public* (CNDP).

---

52 On Law n. 46 of 2013 see *V. De Santis*, La nuova legge della Regione Toscana in materia di dibattito pubblico regionale e promozione della partecipazione, AIC – Osservatorio 2013, p. 1 et seq., www.osservatorioaic.it/.

53 For an analysis of Law n. 69 of 2007 see *R. Lewansky*, Institutionalizing Deliberative Democracy: The 'Tuscany Laboratory', Journal of Public Deliberation, 2013 (9:1), Article 10; *F. Bortolotti & C. Corsi* (eds.), La partecipazione politica e sociale tra crisi e innovazione. Il caso della Toscana, 2012; *M. Ciancaglini*, La democrazia partecipativa in Toscana. Note a margine della legge regionale n. 69/2007, Osservatorio sulle fonti, 2008 (3), p. 1 et seq.; *A. Floridia*, La democrazia deliberativa, dalla teoria alle procedure. Il caso della legge regionale toscana sulla partecipazione, Le Istituzioni del Federalismo, 2007 (5), p. 603 et seq.

54 For a comparison between the two pieces of legislation see *A. Mengozzi*, Idee democratiche e spazi politici della governance partecipativa. Un modello e due leggi regionali a confronto, Istituzioni del Federalismo, 2011 (2), p. 255 et seq.

55 On the *débat public* see, *ex multis*, *L. Casini*, La partecipazione nelle procedure di localizzazione delle opera pubbliche. Esperienze di diritto comparato, in A. Macchiati & G. Napolitano (eds.), *supra* note 6, p. 139, 150 et seq.; *Y. Mansillon*, L'esperienza del débat public in Francia, Democrazia e diritto, 2006 (3), p. 101 et seq.; *B. Delaunay*, La réforme de la procédure du débat public entre en vigueur, Actualité Juridique – Droit Administratif, 2002, p. 1447 et seq.

It is interesting to underline that the French regulation was improved, as a consequence of the Aarhus Convention,[56] by Law n. 2002–276 of 27 February 2002 on the '*démocratie de proximité*', which made recourse to the public debate mandatory for certain types of works, and transformed the CNDP, the national commission entrusted with it, into an independent administrative authority, widening its competences.[57] Today the *débat public* is regulated in France by the *Code de l'environnement,* at Articles 121 et seq.

The public debate is defined by Article 7 of Law of Tuscany n. 46 of 2003 as a 'process of information, public confrontation and participation on works, projects and interventions that have a particular importance for the regional community, in environmental, territorial, landscape, social, cultural and economic matters'. The Law establishes that the public debate as a rule takes place in the preliminary phases of elaboration of a project, work or intervention, when all the diverse options are still possible. It can also take place in subsequent phases, but, in any case, not after the start of the final planning stage.

A qualifying point of the Tuscany legislation is, following the example of the *Commission nationale du débat public*, the establishment of an independent authority, the regional Authority for the guarantee and the promotion of participation (from now on simply Authority), which, according to Article 5, activates or evaluates the activation, in the provided cases, of the public debate.

More in detail, the public debate, regulated by Article 7 et seq., which, under the preceding regional regulation of 2007, was facultative, with the new Law has become mandatory for works of public initiative that involve total investments of more than €50,000,000 and for provisions of siting contained in regional plans, concerning national public works, which also involve total investments of more than €50,000,000.

The introduction of the public debate by Law n. 69 of 2007 led to some significant successes, like the well-known case of the municipality of Castelfalfi;[58]

---

56 On the implementation of the Aarhus Convention in France see *P. Patrito*, La Convenzione di Aarhus in Francia, in A. Angeletti (ed.), Partecipazione, Accesso e Giustizia nel Diritto Ambientale, 2011, p. 133 et seq. The Convention, as underlined, has been considered as a universal instrument of environmental democracy: see *M. Prieur, supra* note 12. However, there is some criticism: see, for instance, *J. Bétaille*, The direct effect of the Aarhus Convention as seen by the French 'Conseil d'Etat', Environmental Law Network International, 2009 (2), p. 63 et seq., who thinks that the impact of the Convention has been relative, because French judges remain 'shy' about it.

57 See, subsequently, also Law 2010-7880 of 12 July 2010, the so-called '*Loi Grenelle II*', which has enlarged its composition.

58 Castelfalfi is a mediaeval village, in the municipality of Montaione. The village was bought by the Touristik Union International (TUI), a German multinational enterprise in the field of tour operators and tourist resorts, with the aim of restructuring it and realising new tourism infrastructure. The municipality, after an initial rejection of the project, started a public debate, involving the population. The outcome of the process was a report, pointing out criticalities and proposing corrective measures. The document was acknowledged by the municipality during the discussion and approval of the project. Castelfalfi is now an important point of reference for tourism in Tuscany. On this significant example of application of the

however, this instrument, because of its facultative character, was underutilised. Establishing in the following piece of legislation cases in which the public debate is compulsory aims at remedying the previous scarce recourse to it, due to the wide discretionary power in evaluating its admissibility. Also in this choice of the regional legislator of 2013 it is possible to see a clear influence of the French Law of 2002 on *débat public*, which has prescribed its mandatory nature for some kinds of infrastructural and development projects.

For private works that exceed the above financial threshold, the public debate is activated by previous evaluation of the Authority.

The public debate also takes place on some types of national works on which the region is called to express its voice, according to times and modes compatible with the regulation at a national level: road and railway infrastructure, power lines, plants for waste transport and storage, ports and airports, water catchment areas for hydroelectric plants, radio communication networks.

For minor (public or private) works, whose investment value is between €10,000,000 and €50,000,000, for which the public debate is not compulsory, the latter can be activated by the Authority on its own initiative or by the motivated request of some subjects: the regional government, the regional assembly, local authorities, subjects who contribute in various ways to realising the works and also by at least 0.1% of residents (Italian citizens, foreigners or stateless persons) above the age of 16, who may be organised in associations or committees. This latter kind of initiative is particularly significant because it follows a bottom-up model.

As to the procedure, according to Article 10, the public debate is convened by the Authority through a motivated act. The latter establishes modalities and instruments, with the goal of ensuring the maximum information, promoting participation and granting an impartial chairing, equality and inclusion of all the points of views. The phases and length of the debate are also established. The debate must not last more than 90 days (from the completion of the technical preliminary phase), although a motivated extension of one month, based on objective reasons, is possible. The person responsible for the public debate is appointed by the same act. He/she is chosen among experts on participatory methodologies and practices, through a public competition. The debate can be also managed by the Authority itself.

Ex Article 12, once the public debate is concluded, the Authority receives the final report drawn up by the person responsible for the debate: the report refers contents and outcomes, pointing out the arguments upheld and the conclusive proposals. The report is published and sent to the regional government, to the regional assembly and to the developer or to the subject responsible for the work. The latter, within three months, communicates the intention to give up the project

public debate see *A. Floridia*, La democrazia deliberativa: teorie, processi e sistemi, 2012, p. 85 et seq.

or intervention or to submit alternative solutions, to propose modifications or to confirm the work.

The regional Law coordinates the public debate with the (regional or provincial) EIA, whose regulation – Law of Tuscany n. 10 of 12 February 2010 – recalls the one at a national level as far as public participation is concerned (see Article 53 of Law n. 10 of 2010, regarding public inquiry and cross examination).

First of all, Article 8(7) establishes that in those cases in which the public debate is provided for and the work is subject to the (regional or provincial) EIA, the carrying out of the former is a mandatory condition for the starting of the assessment procedure. More specifically, according to Article 9, in the cases of 'above threshold' works[59] the public debate must be carried out before the start of the EIA, within which what has emerged from the public debate is taken into consideration. This statement aims at avoiding procedural overlapping and those very cases in which, despite a positive EIA, some works are stopped because of the opposition of the communities concerned.

The Tuscany Law also provides at Article 13 et seq. forms of regional support for local participatory processes that are different from the public debate. The regional support can consist of financial, methodological and logistic and organisational assistance, the last one with particular reference to information and communication technologies. These provisions are a key content of the Law, because they can allow the entry of other deliberative arenas into the public scene.

It is a task of the Authority to evaluate and approve or reject for regional support the participatory projects that are submitted to its attention. In particular, it gives priority to the projects on plans, works or interventions that have a considerable potential impact on the landscape or environment, in accordance with the criteria given by Article 17.

Besides the local authorities and enterprises (on their own projects and interventions that have a significant impact of an environmental, social and economic nature), the following can apply for regional support: associations and committees, with the support of the residents who sign the application; the residents in the areas of the provinces[60] and municipalities and town districts involved by the proposed participatory project, accompanying their application with a certain number of signatures.[61] Again this kind of initiative follows again a bottom-up scheme.

The provisions of the Tuscany Law relating to the support for local participatory processes have had a positive response: from 2008 to November

[59] See Article 8(1)(a) and (b), which refers to works whose value is more than €50,000,000 or to siting provisions contained in regional plans relating to national works which require as a whole investments superior to the same amount of money, and Article 8(2), regarding works of private initiative above the same threshold.

[60] It must be borne in mind that at present a process of revision of the Italian Constitution is in underway which aims, *inter alia*, at abolishing the provinces.

[61] The Article also provides a possibility of application by educational institutions, according to the modalities established in Article 19.

2012, 220 applications were submitted, and 116 of them were financed,[62] and the recourse to this opportunity of civic engagement is increasing.[63]

6. CONCLUSIONS: PARTICIPATORY GAPS AND CRITICALITIES OF ITALIAN ENVIRONMENTAL LEGISLATION: THE NEED FOR REFORM AND FOR INTRODUCTION OF DELIBERATIVE ARENAS

The developed analysis shows that in the Italian environmental legislation the level of implementation of the second pillar of the Aarhus Convention is still inadequate. There are many participatory gaps that distance it from the principle of environmental democracy enshrined in the Convention, giving the Italian system only a weak 'voice' to the public.[64]

First of all, as seen, participation in environmental proceedings is the object of insufficient attention in the introductory part of the Environmental Code, dedicated to the main principles that guide environmental legislation. It would have been expected that it should play a key role as a consequence of the Aarhus Convention.

From this point of view, it is interesting to highlight that in France the Convention has led to a constitutional reform: in 2005 Constitutional Law 205–2005 of 1 March 2005 has included among the Constitutional documents the *Charte de l'environnement* of 2004, which, at Article 7, provides the right of every person, within the conditions and the limits defined by law, to access to information related to the environment in possession of the public authorities and, what is more noteworthy, to participate in the elaboration of public decisions having an incidence on the environment.[65]

---

62 See the 2012–2013 annual report of the regional Authority for participation, www.regione.toscana.it/-/legge-69-2007-testi-e-documenti-di-approfondimento.

63 For an updated list of the financed projects see: www.consiglio.regione.toscana.it/oi/processi.aspx?idc=47.

64 The weak 'voice' of public participation in the environmental field is highlighted by *M. Occhiena*, Forza, debolezza e specialità della partecipazione ambientale, in G. Arena & F. Cortese (eds.), Per governare insieme: il federalismo come metodo. Verso nuove forme della democrazia, 2011, p. 315, 322, who observes the inconsistency with respect to the implementation of the first pillar, devoted to access to environmental information, where legislation is more advanced. See also *V. Molaschi*, The implementation of the Aarhus Convention in Italy: a strong 'vision' and a weak 'voice', in E. Lohse & M. Poto (eds.), *supra* note 20.

65 Article 7 of the *Charte de l'environnement* literally establishes: '*Toute personne a le droit, dans les conditions et les limites définies par la loi, d'accéder aux informations relatives à l'environnement détenues par les autorités publiques et de participer à l'élaboration des décisions publiques ayant une incidence sur l'environnement*'.

As to the modalities, the participation designed by the Italian Environmental Code is mostly limited to documents and written observations, like in the Italian law on administrative procedures, Law n. 241 of 1990. However, written comments are the antitheses of dialogue, of the logic of rational confrontation, able to transform for the common interest the preferences of the participants, implied by deliberative arenas. This probably explains why in Italy there are frequent cases in which projects, even of modest dimensions, despite a previous positive environmental impact statement, are blocked or abandoned because of the protests aroused.

Moreover, neither legislation nor interpretation given by judicial decisions impose on the public authority any obligation of complete and precise motivation on how the participatory contributions offered by the public are evaluated, an aspect that weakens the effectiveness of public participation and environmental protection itself. In fact, environmental safeguards can be achieved if the environmental point of view is represented in decision-making procedures and the public authorities have the duty to consider it, as a 'rule of the procedure', it being understood that the power to decide belongs to the public administration.[66]

When more advanced participatory means are provided, like, in the 'ordinary' EIA, public inquiry and cross examination, their regulation follows a top-down layout: there is no obligation to heed a request 'from below', i.e. following bottom-up logic.

Participation encounters limits also in the case of the SEA, an instrument capable of orienting administrative decisions from the planning phase, when plural options are still possible, including those regarding the siting of projects.

The fact that participatory tools are more limited in the SEA than in the 'ordinary' EIA, because of the lack of the possibility of public inquiry or of other forms of public consultations, has been strongly criticised by authors, who have maintained that this regulation is a violation of the Aarhus Convention and of Directive 2001/42/EC itself.[67]

This diminishment of participatory guarantees is even more striking if we think of what has been defined the 'epistemological' difference between the EIA and the SEA,[68] which not only have diverse objects, but correspond to two distinct levels of knowability of environmental conditions.

In short, the EIA tackles problems regarding how to realise a certain work: it implies a cognitive and predictive framework that is relatively defined, according to the 'cause-effect' scheme. In contrast, in the case of the SEA, where the

---

66 In these terms see *R. Ferrara*, Politiche ambientali e sistema delle semplificazioni amministrative: verso quali scenari?, Il Piemonte delle Autonomie, 2014 (2), p. 1, 9, http://piemonteautonomie.cr.piemonte.it/cms/index.php/politiche-ambientali-e-sistema-delle-semplificazioni-amministrative-verso-quali-scenari.

67 See *A. Milone, supra* note 28, p. 179.

68 For this observation see *E. Boscolo*, Vas e Via riformate: limiti e potenzialità degli strumenti applicativi del principio di precauzione, Urbanistica e appalti, 2008 (5), p. 542, to whom is due the analysis of the two instruments that follows.

assessment concerns plans and programmes, data and information are never all available, because of the variability of exogenous factors: the possible scenarios are dynamic and complex, and elude the forecasting capability of the authority responsible for the planning activity. As to the latter, this statement of fact makes the provision of public participation means even more important, given their function in overcoming the so called 'information asymmetries' of the public decision-maker.[69]

Surprisingly, the choice of the Italian legislator has been towards another direction, while, according to scholars, it would have been possible to provide instruments that were more incisive than written observations, like consultations and facilitated group listening, focus groups, community visioning, deliberative opinion polls. Moreover – they suggest – it would have been possible to take into account the French experience of the *débat public*.[70]

Participatory guarantees are more debased in the case of EIA regarding major works (infrastructure, industrial plants), which generally raise tougher opposition and protests by the communities involved.

Traditionally, environmental interests have 'an enhanced consideration within administrative proceedings',[71] which implies a burdening of the procedures, given the need for a deeper preliminary phase and for guaranteeing transparency and public participation. For this reason, some authors speak of a 'special environmental administrative law',[72] in which the urge for simplification that can be observed in the recent evolutions in administrative proceedings finds a limit in the necessity of a careful consideration of the interests at stake, first and foremost the environmental one.

Within this framework, the 'ordinary' EIA has been shaped as an instrument aimed at ensuring the supremacy of environmental protection needs, and, as seen, it is characterised by more participatory guarantees than the ones provided in Law n. 241 of 1990, despite the limits that have been highlighted.

Therefore, it was predictable that this procedure would have been considered a source of delays and, consequently, one of the obstacles to the process of building up Italy's infrastructure.[73] From this point of view, it is significant that the regulation of the 'special' EIA is not contained in the Environmental Code,

---

69 On public participation as an essential tool for the public decision-maker for taking decisions in situations of incomplete and uncertain information see *R. Ferrara*, Introduzione al Diritto amministrativo, 2011, p. 132 et seq., who recalls the studies of *H. Simon*, Administrative behavior. A study of decision-making processes in administrative organisations, 1947.

70 See *E. Boscolo*, *supra* note 68, p. 545 and *Id.*, Introduzione alla valutazione ambientale strategica, in Bottino et al., Codice dell'ambiente. Commento al d.lgs. 3 aprile 2006, n. 152, 2008, p. 247, 251.

71 See *M. Gola*, L'amministrazione degli interessi ambientali, 1995, in particular p. 225 et seq.

72 For this definition see *G. Morbidelli*, Il regime amministrativo speciale dell'ambiente, in Scritti in onore di Alberto Predieri, II, 1996, p. 1122 et seq.

73 On the EIA as an element of 'complication' in the process of 'infrastructuring' of Italy see *E. Boscolo*, La VIA 'accelerata' per le grandi opere: l'interesse ambientale quale limite alla semplificazione, Urbanistica e appalti, 2003 (2), p. 129 et seq.

but in the Code of Public Contracts: this collocation can be indicative of a lesser importance given to environmental values, which are outweighed by the needs for simplification and acceleration of the procedures, an underestimation to which weaker participatory tools follow.[74] This regulatory choice is even in contrast with the structure of Law n. 241 of 1990 itself, according to which the significance of environmental interests makes some of the measures of simplification of administrative procedures inapplicable.[75]

Aside from any kind of political consideration, that is beyond the scope of this paper, the experience of the high speed railway line between Lyon and Turin is mostly the consequence of the depicted regulatory framework. It shows the limits of a weak participation, not sufficiently defined and structured into the proceedings, which has led the administration to create *ad hoc* institutions (the Tavolo Istituzionale di Palazzo Chigi and the Osservatorio della Val di Susa), to duplicate segments of the preliminary activity, following extempore procedures, which do not give any guarantee regarding the outcome, costs and times of the activity to be carried out.[76]

It is interesting to highlight that the Osservatorio della Val di Susa itself has pointed out to the Government 'the opportunity to insert in the Italian legal order appropriate procedures to ensure as to the realization of the most important infrastructure the confrontation *ex ante* with the local communities and with the multiple articulations of society, instead of *ex post*', as it occurred in the case of the high speed railway line.[77]

From the developed analysis it emerges that the Aarhus Convention represents a missed opportunity in Italy. The need for reform of the provisions regarding public participation in the analysed procedures has been underlined by many: scholars, stakeholders, practitioners, politicians, and so on.

The Commission of Sages – Working group on institutional reforms, appointed by the previous Italian President of the Republic on 30 March 2013 – in its final report of 12 April 2013 (before the present Government came into office) proposed the introduction of public debate on major infrastructure interventions, 'as required by the Aarhus Convention of 1998 and what has been a long-established reality in France, with Law 276 of 2002, dedicated to '*démocratie de proximité*'. In France, in fact, the procedure of the *débat public* has contributed significantly to decreasing the conflict rate regarding these kinds of works.

---

74 The degradation of participatory guarantees in the 'special' EIA is underlined by *G. Pizzanelli*, *supra* note 7, p. 360.

75 Law n. 241 of 1990 contains some provisions aimed at slimming down administrative activities and simplifying the relative procedures. However, when the environmental interest comes into consideration, the need for a complete preliminary activity, in order to make well pondered decisions, prevails and limit the scope of simplification measures.

76 For these observations see *A. Tonetti*, *supra* note 48, pp. 172–173.

77 See the so called 'Pracatinat Agreement', in Italian 'Punti di accordo per la progettazione della nuova linea e per le nuove politiche di trasporto per il territorio', Pracatinat, 28 June 2008, www.governo.it/Presidenza/osservatorio_torino_lione/PDF/Pracatinat_accordo_2008.pdf.

While the Italian national legislator has been 'lazy', the regional legislator, as seen, is more 'willing'. It is to be hoped that the example represented by Law n. 46 of 2013 of Tuscany is followed in future reforms to be realised at a national level, in order to grant 'effective' public participation as required by the Italian Constitution. The recent bill, which delegates to the Government the task of implementing Directives 2014/23/EU and 2014/24/EU, the so-called new public procurement directives, contains, among the various criteria and guiding principles, the provision of forms of public debate of local communities residing in territories interested by the realisation of major works impacting the environment.

PART III

ENVIRONMENTAL IMPACT ASSESSMENT

CHAPTER 8

TRANS-BOUNDARY ENVIRONMENTAL IMPACT ASSESSMENT IN CROSS-BORDER OIL AND GAS PIPELINES:

What Lessons Can Be Learned from the Espoo Convention and the EU EIA Directive

Mehdi Piri DAMAGH

1. INTRODUCTION

By now, most people are aware of the critical issue of supplying energy to sustain the daily life of contemporary societies. Economic Growth requires increasing amounts of energy. There are only few options available for transporting crude oil and natural gas over long distances. Pipelines are one of the most common means of transporting crude oil and natural gas. Cross-border oil and gas pipelines play an important role in the global energy trade, specifically in Europe. Over long distances, many pipelines traverse international borders to reach their final destinations. As a matter of fact, Europe imports natural gas mainly via pipelines (80%).[1] Crude oil, on the other hand, is mainly shipped by tankers and only 20% is imported through pipelines.[2] Hence, there are many pipelines transporting natural gas, oil, and other hazardous liquids across Europe.[3] The EU's dependency on the pipelines as an important means for transporting oil and gas cannot be under-estimated.

---

1 *M. Scotti & B. Vedres*, Supply Security in the European Natural Gas Pipeline Network, in B. Vedres & M. Scotti (eds.), Networks in Social Policy Problems, 2012, p. 237, 239 et seq.

2 *J.M. Pedraza*, Electrical Energy Generation in Europe: The Current and Future Role of Conventional Energy Sources in the Regional Generation of Electricity, 2014, p. 74.

3 See for more information, Directorate General for Internal Policies, An Assessment of the Gas and Oil Pipelines in Europe, 2009, www.europarl.europa.eu/RegData/etudes/note/join/2009/416239/IPOL-ITRE_NT(2009)416239_EN.pdf.

Pipelines carry gas and oil across long distances usually from processing facilities to distribution centres or storage facilities. Pipelines are often used to export gas and oil from supplier countries to consumer countries, thus becoming cross-border pipelines. Cross-border pipelines usually cross the borders of more than two countries. In spite of the economic prosperity of pipelines, substantial environmental risks are created as a result of the construction and operation of oil and gas pipelines. In addition, cross-border pipelines pose additional structuring challenges. This is mainly because some level of governmental intervention is often needed to make the project viable. Parties involved in such projects mostly seek to avoid political and economic turbulence in transporting oil and gas via pipelines. They usually try to prevent pipeline accidents and in the case of an accident, they try to minimise the harm, which has been caused, by the most appropriate means. Parties involved at both levels of government and private sponsors often conclude intergovernmental agreements as well as commercial contracts in order to address any issue that may arise during the operation and construction of a proposed pipeline.

The transportation of oil and gas via pipelines may result in trans-boundary damage to the neighbouring states. Indeed, trans-boundary damage may arise from the operation of the cross-country as well as cross-border pipelines.[4] Cross-country pipelines are laid within the jurisdiction of one state. Therefore, unless regional or international instruments require it, a cross-country pipeline will be regulated only by the state in whose territory such a pipeline has been laid. There is no one particular international law instrument, dealing exclusively with cross-border oil and gas pipelines. Therefore, most of the rules that will determine the applicable legal regime to a given cross-border pipeline can be found in the bilateral or multi-lateral agreements that have been concluded by the states concerned.[5] Bilateral or multilateral agreements between the states involved in the pipeline project often do not provide any rule in relation to the prevention of trans-boundary damage to third party countries. In addition, there is no international or regional convention specifically dealing either with safety

[4] There are several examples of pipeline incidents worldwide. For instance, as a result of the Kirkuk-Ceyhan Oil Pipeline accident in 2010 two people were killed and one injured. The Kirkuk-Ceyhan Oil Pipeline transfers crude oil from Kirkuk (Iraq) to Ceyhan (Turkey), see Energy News Update: Two Killed in Turkish Oil Pipeline Explosion, Iraq Energy Institute (11 August 2010), http://iraqenergy.org/news/?detailof=523&content=Two-Killed-in-Turkish-Oil-Pipeline-Explosion. The Unecha-Ventspils oil-products pipeline, which is a Russian oil pipeline, ruptured in Belarus in 2007. As a result, nearly 100 tons of diesel fuel spilled into a river flowing into Latvia. Some of the spilled diesel fuel polluted a 15 km stretch of the Ulla River in Latvia, see *T. Hellenberg and P. Visuri*, Analysis of civil security system in Europe, Country study, Latvia, 2014, p. 21, http://anvil-project.net/wp-content/uploads/2014/02/Latvia_v1.1.pdf.

[5] See e.g. Foreign and Commonwealth Affairs, Transmission of Natural Gas through a Pipeline between the United Kingdom of Great Britain and Northern Ireland and the Kingdom of the Netherlands, 2005, Cm. 6675; see e.g. Agreement Relating to the Transportation of Petroleum Via the Territories of the Azerbaijan Republic, Georgia and the Republic of Turkey through the Baku-Tbilisi-Ceyhan Main Export Pipeline, Art. 2, 18 November 1999.

standards for cross-border pipelines or with the compensation of harm that would result from an incident with a cross-border pipeline. Therefore, similar rules govern trans-boundary damage caused by cross-border and trans-boundary damage caused by cross-country pipelines.

Prevention of trans-boundary damage from hazardous activities has attracted the attention of both the public and governments. As authors rightly suggest, trans-boundary environmental impact assessment is one of the main instruments used to predict, evaluate and minimise such risks.[6] Indeed, in the absence of trans-boundary EIA, an affected state often suffers from a lack of information about the adverse impacts of such activities. Even when they are aware, affected states may have some obstacles for the establishment of litigation against polluters and eventually for the enforcement of the decision in the source state.[7] EIA is the main tool to ensure that the potential environmental impacts of proposed projects are fully assessed before granting the project. The goal of EIA is to force polluters in the source state to internalise the externality caused through their polluting activities. Hence, it is quite important to carefully analyse the legal regime applicable to trans-boundary environmental impact assessment in the case of the cross-border pipelines.

In many cases, the construction and operation of cross-border pipelines has led to trans-boundary damage.[8] As matter of fact, there is no international or regional convention specifically regulating cross-border pipeline projects. The Convention on Environmental Impact Assessment in a Trans-boundary Context (Espoo Convention) which is a regional convention under the auspices of the United Nations Economic Commission for Europe set up obligations of Contracting Parties to assess environmentally adverse impacts of certain hazardous activities and to consult affected states prior to decision-making.[9] Large diameter oil and gas pipelines are also included in the list of the hazardous

---

6 *N. Craik*, The International Law of Environmental Impact Assessment: Process, Substance and Integration, 2008, p. 12; *R. Warner*, Environmental Assessments in the Marine Areas of the Polar Regions, in E.J. Molenaar, A.G. Oude Elferink & D.R. Rothwell (eds.), The Law of the Sea and the Polar Regions (139–162) 2013, p. 142; *K. Bastmeijer & T. Koivurova*, Trans-boundary Environmental Impact Assessment: An Introduction, in K. Bastmeijer & T. Koivurova (eds.), Theory and Practice of Trans-boundary Environmental Impact Assessment, 2008, pp. 2–3.

7 See for instance *A. Nollkaemper*, Cluster-litigation in cases of trans-boundary environmental harm, in M. Faure and S. Ying (eds.), Trans-boundary Environmental Pollution: The Case of China, 2008, pp. 11–38.

8 For an overview of a few cases of trans-boundary damage which were caused by cross-border pipelines see *M. Piri Damagh & M. Faure*, The Effectiveness of Cross-Border Pipeline Safety and Environmental Regulations (under International Law), North Carolina Journal of International Law and Commercial Regulation, 2014 (40:1), pp. 55–134.

9 Before the adoption of the Espoo Convention, several steps had been taken to implement trans-boundary EIAs. These steps initiated in 1972 the United Nations Conference on the Human Environment in Stockholm and followed by the UNCLOS. For more discussion, see *W. Scharge*, The Convention on Environmental Impact Assessment in a Trans-boundary Context, in K. Bastmeijer & T. Koivurova (eds.), Theory and Practice of Trans-boundary Environmental Impact Assessment, 2008, pp. 29–30 et seq.

activities in Appendix I of the Espoo Convention.[10] Thus, the terms of the Espoo Convention are applicable to large diameter oil and gas pipelines as well. In the EU, Environmental Impact Assessment (EU EIA Directive) appeared for the first time in the EIA Directive (85/337/EEC) in 1985. In Article 7 of the EIA Directive (85/337/EEC) Member States were required to forward information gathered concerning significant effects of a project likely have trans-boundary impacts on the environment in another Member State. After the EU became a member of the Espoo Convention, in line with the provisions of Espoo Convention, the EU Directive (85/337/EEC) was amended in 1997. In the EU EIA Directive 97/11/EC, trans-boundary EIA expressly indicated in Article 7 and Member States were required to conduct a trans-boundary EIA for projects which were likely have significant trans-boundary impacts. The EU EIA Directive has been amended three times later in 2003, 2009 and 2014. In this chapter the Directive 2014/52/EU amending the EIA Directive 2011/92/EU will be taken into consideration.

The Environmental Impact Assessment Directive requires trans-boundary EIA for all projects listed in Annex I. Large diameter oil and gas pipelines are also included in the list of the projects coved by the EIA Directive. Therefore, the EIA Directive requires all Member States to formulate domestic methods for conducting environmental impact assessments for oil and gas pipelines. The EIA Directive does not specifically refer to cross-border pipelines as projects with a trans-boundary impact, which requires trans-boundary EIA. Rather, Article 7 of the EU EIA Directive requires a Member State to carry out trans-boundary EIA where a project is likely to have significant effects on the environment in another Member State or where a Member State, which is likely to be significantly affected, so requests. As a consequence, the course of the laying of large diameter oil and gas pipelines could be subject to Article 7 of the EU EIA Directive.

It is also important to note that the regulations on guidelines for trans-European energy infrastructure, Regulation 347/2013 (TEN-E Regulation) include provisions for the construction and operation of oil and gas pipelines.[11] In fact, the TEN-E Regulation aims to support the development of energy networks within Europe. According to Article 1, natural gas and oil pipelines expressly fall under energy infrastructure categories. The TEN-E Regulation targets various aspects of energy networks, including permit granting processes and public participation, regulatory treatments, investment and financing, which are of course not all relevant to this chapter. Although the cross-border projects such as pipelines are expressly included in the list of common interest projects, not many provisions with respect to conducting a trans-boundary EIA for such projects have been articulated in the TEN-E Regulation. In fact, the assessment of the environmental effects of the common interest projects within the permit granting procedure has been spelled out, but conducting an environmental

[10] See: www.unece.org/fileadmin/DAM/env/eia/documents/legaltexts/conventiontextenglish.pdf.
[11] See Article 2 of the TEN Regulation, see also Annex II, para. 2.

impact assessment is not required. Therefore, only a brief overview of the TEN-E Regulation will be discussed in this chapter.

The Convention on Environmental Impact Assessment in a Trans-Boundary Context 1991 and the EU EIA Directive 2011 contain some relevant rules concerning trans-boundary EIA and basically they encompass cross-border pipelines as large-scale projects, which require mandatory EIA. Nevertheless, as will be discussed in the chapter, the EU EIA Directive and Espoo Convention mainly deal with the projects with trans-boundary impacts, while cross-border pipelines are indeed trans-boundary projects, which may also have trans-boundary impacts. Keeping these issues in mind, the question arises of whether the provisions of the Espoo Convention and the EU EIA Directive concerning the conduct of a trans-boundary EIA can be effectively applied in the case of cross-border pipelines or not. In other words, this chapter aims to discuss the lessons which can be learned from the application of trans-boundary EIAs for cross-border pipelines under the Espoo Convention and the EU EIA Directive.

As a starting point of the discussion it should be taken into consideration that the cross-border nature of the cross-border pipeline increases the level of complexity of organising trans-boundary EIA procedure. Examples such as the Nord Stream gas pipeline (NSGP) clearly indicate that a proper application of trans-boundary environmental impact assessment under the Espoo Convention and the EU EIA Directive, may be faced with a few but important obstacles. This chapter aims to shed light on the current status of the application of trans-boundary EIA of cross-border pipelines in the EU specifically by examining trans-boundary EIA procedure adopted by the Espoo Convention and EU EIA Directive. For this purpose, a review of the relevant rules of the Espoo Convention, EU EIA Directive and also the TEN-E Regulation in relation to trans-boundary EIA in the case of the cross-border pipelines, will be provided. Second the trans-boundary EIA procedure in the case of cross-border pipelines will be analysed. In doing so, given the limited practical experience in applying the trans-boundary EIA procedure to cross-border pipelines, the trans-boundary EIA procedure which has been implemented to the NSGP will be analysed. Afterwards, by considering obstacles that have been observed in applying trans-boundary EIA procedure in the NSGP, the possibility of applying the Espoo Convention and EU Directive in addressing such challenges will be examined.

2. THE CURRENT LEGAL FRAMEWORK OF TRANS-BOUNDARY EIA FOR CROSS-BORDER PIPELINES IN THE EU

2.1. THE ESPOO CONVENTION

The Espoo Convention is exclusively aimed at preventing trans-boundary damage by mandating the environmental impact assessment of large-scale projects such as oil and gas pipelines.[12] In fact, in its broadest terms, the parties are obliged to take appropriate measures to prevent, reduce and control significant adverse trans-boundary environmental impacts from proposed activities. Article 1 of the Espoo Convention defines 'trans-boundary impact' as: 'any impact … within an area under the jurisdiction of a Party caused by a proposed activity the physical origin of which is situated wholly or in part within the area under the jurisdiction of another Party.' In accordance with Article 2 of the Espoo Convention, the states of origin are required to ensure that an environmental impact assessment has been undertaken before granting permission to proposed activities listed in Appendix I of the Convention, including large diameter pipelines. Therefore, the Espoo Convention is expressly aimed at the prevention and control of significant adverse impact by requiring trans-boundary environmental impact assessment for a proposed activity.

According to Article 3 of the Convention, for a project that is likely to cause a significant adverse trans-boundary impact a state of origin is obliged to submit required information about possible trans-boundary impacts to an affected state and to the public of the affected state in the area likely to be affected. According to Article 3(2), a trans-boundary EIA could be conducted only when the affected state is willing to participate in the assessment procedure. A state of origin, therefore, is obliged to inform the affected state but the affected state may withdraw from the trans-boundary EIA process. However, Article 3(6) highlights that when an affected party intends to participate, it should submit information which it has obtained relating to the possible adverse impacts of the proposed activity under its jurisdiction. Finally the state of origin will decide about granting the project or not by considering the outcomes of the trans-boundary EIA.

In this respect, Koivurova and Polonen argue that the Espoo Convention obliges Contracting Parties to conduct a national environmental impact assessment that also includes the observation and participation of the potential foreign affected actors for the project which may have trans-boundary impacts.[13] It is noteworthy to mention that cross-country oil and gas pipelines also have

---

12 See *M.L. Larsson*, The law of environmental damage: liability and reparation, 1999 (1), p. 140. Meanwhile, this Convention and particularly Article 2 does not pose any duty of prevention of trans-boundary harm. See *N. Craik*, *supra* note 6, p. 103.

13 *T. Koivurova & I. Polonen*, Trans-boundary Environmental Impact Assessment in the Case of the Baltic Sea Gas Pipeline, Int'l. J. Marine & Coastal Law (25), pp. 153 et seq.

the potential to cause trans-boundary damage.[14] One may argue that the Espoo Convention is basically drafted to require trans-boundary environmental impact assessment specifically for domestic oil and gas pipelines. On the other hand, pursuant to Article 2(1) of the Espoo Convention, a joint EIA could be conducted for joint projects which have impacts on both of two parties of origin, e.g. cross-border pipelines. Therefore, it is possible under the Espoo Convention that two parties of origin implement a trans-boundary EIA for a proposed cross-border pipeline.

As mentioned, according to the Espoo Convention Protocol, cross-border pipelines are listed as a complex large-scale project.[15] This Protocol mandates parties to run a strategic environmental assessment for complex activities. The Secretariat of the Espoo Convention underlined the strategic dimension of cross-border pipelines and the necessity of conducting a strategic environmental assessment for the NSGP.[16] However, as Koivurova and Polonen correctly state, focusing on the duty of the states of origin to conduct the SEA, the Member Parties of the Espoo Convention cannot mandate a developer to conduct a strategic environmental assessment.[17] Hence, it is in principle a duty of the states of origin to conduct the SEA. In this chapter, however, trans-boundary EIA is the focal point and the performance of SEA will not be discussed.

2.2. THE EU EIA DIRECTIVE

The first EU EIA directive and its further amendments have been codified by the EU Directive 2011. The EU Directive 2011 is also amended by the EU Directive 2014. In this chapter we will take into account the recent adoption of the revised Directive 2014. It is already mentioned that large-scale oil and gas pipelines are listed in Annex I of the EU EIA Directive which include projects for which the preparation of an EIA is compulsory. Article 7 of the EU EIA Directive requires Member states to conduct a trans-boundary EIA for the projects, which may have trans-boundary impacts. Article 7, however, does not contain any reference to

14 For example, on 31 May 2013 a landslide ruptured an oil pipeline in Ecuador, dumping some 11,000 barrels of crude oil into the Coca River, which in turn flows into the Napo River. The Napo River flows to Peru and then Brazil. As it flowed it contaminated water in downstream countries. For more information see: www.cbsnews.com/8301-202_162-57588758/ecuador-oil-spill-threatens-brazil-and-peru/.

15 Accessible at: www.unece.org/fileadmin/DAM/env/eia/documents/legaltexts/protocolenglish.pdf.

16 See Exchange of Good Practices, Large-scale Trans-boundary Projects, Application of the Espoo Convention to complex activities, Note by the Secretariat (ECE/MP.EIA/ WG.1/2009/4, 2 March 2009), Economic Commission for Europe Meeting of the Parties to the Convention on Environmental Impact Assessment in a Trans-boundary Context, Working Group on Environmental Impact Assessment, Twelfth meeting, Geneva, 11–13 May 2009, www.unece.org/env/documents/2009/eia/wg.1/ece.mp.eia.wg.1.2009.4.e.pdf.

17 *T. Koivurova & I. Polonen*, *supra* note 13, pp. 156–157 et seq.

the activities for which the preparation of a trans-boundary EIA is mandatory. Rather, Article 7 provides that if a Member State is mindful of significant effects of a proposed project on the environment of another Member state, or where a Member State, likely to be significantly affected, so requests, the former state shall conduct a trans-boundary EIA. According to Guidance on the Application of the Environmental Impact Assessment Procedure for Large-scale Trans-boundary Projects (Guidance on the Application of the EIA), which is prepared by the European Commission, the affected Member States are entitled to request notification for any project likely to have a significant effect on their environment. This means that, contrary to the Espoo Convention for which the scope of its application is limited to activities listed in Appendix I of the Convention, under the EU EIA Directive, the Member State can request notification for any projects likely have significant trans-boundary impacts.[18] It is noteworthy to mention that the EU EIA Directive mandates conducting a trans-boundary EIA only if the concerned parties, including the state of origin and the affected states are Members of the EU. Hence, the concerned states may exclude the implementation of trans-boundary EIA for the project which extends to the territory of an EU Member State and a non-Member State.

According to Article 7, the Member State in whose territory the project is intended to be carried out (hereafter the state of origin) must send adequate information in relation to the description of the project and any available information on its possible trans-boundary impact to the potentially affected Member State. The affected state should be given reasonable time in order to declare its will to participate in trans-boundary EIA procedures. If the affected state indicates its intent to participate in a trans-boundary EIA, the state of origin should forward the required documents to the relevant authorities and the public of the affected Member State. The public and authorities of the affected state should give their comments within a reasonable time and forward them to the state of origin. It is up to the affected state to decide how the information should be distributed to its public. Indeed, the national legislation of the affected state will determine these issues. Of course, practical problems such as translating the documents and presenting them to the public may emerge.[19]

Article 7 (4) introduces an obligation for the Member States concerned to enter into consultations regarding the potential trans-boundary effects of a proposed project and if applicable to take appropriate measures to reduce or eliminate such effects. It can be argued that the EU EIA Directive mainly requires Member States to take into account the trans-boundary impacts of the projects that are intended

---

18 European Union, Guidance on the Application of the Environmental Impact Assessment Procedure for Large-scale Trans-boundary Projects, 2013, http://ec.europa.eu/environment/eia/pdf/Transboundry%20EIA%20Guide.pdf.

19 See on that *A.E. Olufemi*, Environmental Impact Assessment, in M Fitzmaurice, D.M. Ong & P. Merkouris (eds.), Research handbook on international environmental law, 2010, pp. 227, 232 et seq.

to be carried out in their territories. Therefore, under the EU EIA Directive trans-boundary EIA is mandated only for the projects, which have the potential to cause trans-boundary damage. The application of trans-boundary EIA for cross-border projects, however, remains subject to general provisions of trans-boundary EIA.

In Article 8, the state of origin is required to take into account the results of consultations and the information gathered through the trans-boundary EIA procedure. Article 9 requires the state of origin to make available to the public a description of the measures that will be required to mitigate adverse environmental effects. In addition, Article 11 of the EU EIA Directive entitles members of the public concerned to have access to the review procedure before a court of law or another body established by law to challenge the substantive or procedural legality of decisions.

2.3. THE TEN-E REGULATION

In accordance with Article 7 of the TEN-E Regulation the permit granting processes for projects of common interest, including oil and gas pipelines, must be done in the manner that is required by national laws. Each Member State shall designate a national competent authority for co-ordinating the permit granting process for projects of common interest. Furthermore, the EU Commission issued a non-binding guidance 'Streamlining environmental assessment procedures for energy infrastructure "Projects of Common Interest" (PCIs)' in order to ensure a coherent application of environmental assessment procedures for such projects. According to Article 7(4) of the TEN-E Regulation, Member States are required to take into account the guidance, which is provided by the EU Commission in adapting measures for streamlining EIA for such projects.

Article 8(5) of the TEN-E Regulation considers projects, in which decisions for permit granting should be taken in two or more Member States. This of course could be the case for the cross-border pipelines, which are laid across different Member States. The TEN-E Regulation does not impose a specific obligation on a Member State to conduct a joint assessment but it requires it to take necessary steps for efficient and effective cooperation.[20] Member States are also requested to endeavour to provide for joint procedures, concerning the assessment of environmental impacts.

Public participation in the common interest projects under TEN-E Regulation should be carried out without prejudice to any requirements of the Espoo Convention and EU EIA Directive.[21] The public participation under the TEN-E Regulation is also applicable for projects with trans-boundary impacts

[20] Article 8(5).
[21] Article 9(2).

and cross-border projects.[22] But no specific procedure is envisaged for cross-border projects or projects with trans-boundary impacts. Only Article 10(4b) requires Member States to set a joint schedule in order to align their timetables. Therefore, the TEN-E Regulation forms part of a regulatory regime governing the construction and operation of cross-border pipelines. But it is not intended to require the conduct of a trans-boundary EIA for such projects. One may argue that non-binding guidance 'Streamlining environmental assessment procedures for energy infrastructure' recommends Member States to jointly or through a third body organise cross-border co-ordination for environmental assessment procedures. This suggestion of course seems practical for the co-ordination of environmental assessment procedures for cross-border pipelines. But it still needs the mutual agreement of all parties involved in the project. Furthermore, it cannot be considered as a direct recommendation for conducting a trans-boundary EIA. Therefore, in the rest of this chapter the TEN-E Regulation will not be the focal point.

3. AN ANALYSIS OF APPLYING TRANS-BOUNDARY EIA TO CROSS-BORDER PIPELINES

It is mentioned in the previous section that the provisions of the EU EIA Directive and Espoo Convention are applicable to cross-border pipelines. In fact, both of these instruments require a trans-boundary environmental impact assessment for projects with trans-boundary effects. The cross-border pipelines are projects, which are stretched across international borders. The cross-border nature of such projects creates extra challenges compared with the normal TEIA procedure for projects with trans-boundary effects. The question arises of whether the EU EIA Directive and Espoo Convention can be applied to such projects in a way that addresses these extra challenges, or not. For this purpose, we will analysis the application of the provisions of these two instruments to cross-border pipelines. Currently there is not much practical experience in applying the trans-boundary EIA procedure to cross-border pipelines. Indeed, the main example of applying trans-boundary EIA is the Nord Stream gas pipeline project. A trans-boundary EIA of the Nord Stream gas pipeline was implemented under the Espoo Convention. Therefore, we first describe the extra challenge of applying a trans-boundary EIA to cross-border pipelines by taking into account the experience, which has been learnt from conducting an environmental impact assessment of the Nord Stream gas pipeline. Second, we attempt to assess the compatibility of the provision of the Espoo Convention and the EIA Directive to address such challenges.

---

22 Article 9(5) and(6).

3.1. A CRITIQUE: CHALLENGES OF APPLYING TRANS-BOUNDARY EIA TO THE CROSS-BORDER PIPELINES, THE CASE STUDY OF THE NORD STREAM GAS PIPELINE

The Nord Stream gas pipeline (NSGP) is a 1,220 km long transmission offshore natural gas pipeline (two parallel lines). This pipeline crosses the exclusive economic zones of Russia,[23] Finland, Sweden, Denmark and Germany, as well as the territorial waters of Russia, Denmark, and Germany. The NSGP transfers Russian gas to Germany. Thus, the NSGP is a cross-border pipeline. Interestingly there is only a commercial agreement in relation to the construction and operation of the NSGP, which is signed between private parties.[24] Meantime, the competent authorities of Germany, Denmark, Sweden, Finland and Russia, as states of origin (since the NSGP passes through their jurisdictions), in a meeting on the 19 April 2006 unanimously concluded that the Nord Stream gas pipeline project falls under Article 3 of the Espoo Convention.[25] As a consequence, the operator of the pipeline, Nord Stream AG, was required to conduct a trans-boundary EIA in order to obtain permission for the construction and operation of the proposed pipeline. For analysing the application of the Espoo Convention to cross-border pipelines in practice, the EIA of the Nord Stream Gas Pipeline, which was done in accordance with the provisions of the Espoo Convention, is examined as a case study.

In order to obtain permission from the affected states, the Nord Stream Company, as an operator, was involved in extensive consultations with each of the countries concerned (as states of origin), to be certain that the NSGP complied fully with the respective national legislation. Therefore, a foreign company, which intended to lay a pipeline on the continental shelf of one of the contracting parties of the Espoo Convention, initiated the trans-boundary EIA procedure. In addition to those five nations, the NSGP may concern Estonia, Latvia, Lithuania and Poland as affected states; however, no segment of the NSGP falls under their jurisdictions. Therefore, these four states, as affected states, were also part of the consultation process. In conformity to the provisions of the Espoo Convention, each of the states of origin as well as the Russian Federation opened its EIA procedure to all the origin and affected states. The involvement of that many states and parties of course increased the level of complexity of the EIA of the project.[26]

---

23 The Russian Federation has signed but yet not ratified the Espoo Convention. But with regard to the Nord Stream Project, Russia is acting as a Party of Origin to the extent possible under its legislation. Hence, for the purpose of this Article the term 'Parties of Origin' as used herein shall include the Russian Federation.

24 *P. Högselius*, Red Gas: Russia and the Origins of European Energy Dependence, 2012, p. 215.

25 Espoo Report – Chapter 3 – Politics and Permits, www.nord-stream.com/press-info/library/?pk=238.

26 *Ibid.*

Various types of documents both at the national as well as at the international level were prepared by the Nord Stream Company and translated into all affected nations' languages in view of the public participation. The public in the origin and affected states, including governmental authorities and non-governmental actors, had provided documents and sent comments concerning the EIA of the project. Eventually, the final EIA report of the project was prepared and submitted to the states of origin for obtaining their permission. All permits, which were needed to formally begin construction of the Nord Stream pipeline, were received by July 2012 from the states of origin.[27]

The EIA of the NSGP has been considered by many authors as a model way of how a trans-boundary EIA may be applied under the Espoo Convention for these complex projects.[28] There are also a few critical issues concerning the trans-boundary EIA procedure in the NSGP. In this chapter, however, we only focus on the extra challenges arising out of conducting TEIA for a cross-border pipeline.

The first challenge is related to the route of the pipeline. This of course attracted criticism from different parties, including one of the state of origin (Finland), one of the affected states (Estonia), the European Parliament and finally for the Espoo Secretariat.[29] In fact, Article 5 of the Espoo Convention provides the possibility of consultations for the state of origin and affected state concerning possible alternatives to the proposed activity. It seems it is possible to suggest alternative routes only within the territory of the state(s) of origin. Basically such a ruling makes sense when a proposed activity is totally located within the territory of the state of origin. In the case of oil and gas pipeline, however, from an environmental point of view it does not make sense to limit alternative routes only within the territory of the state(s) of origin.

In the same line of reasoning, Finland as one the states of origin notified the Nord Stream Company about its concerns in relation to the lack of studying alternative routes of the NSGP near the Russian island of Gogland and the route in the South of the Gulf of Finland (Estonian Section).[30] But the Nord Stream Company informed Finland that after consultation with the Russian

---

27 According to the Nord Stream Pipeline official site: www.nord-stream.com/press-info/library/?pk=238. Of course it is necessary to note that in order to address Polish safety concerns, the German Federal Office for Shipping and Hydrography approved re-routing of a 12-kilometre section in the German EEZ on 26 February 2010. Danish Energy Agency also granted operations permit for Line 1 in June 2011 and line 2 in July 2012.

28 See generally *T. Koivurova & I. Polonen, supra* note 13; *S. Vinogradov*, Challenges of Nord Stream: Streamlining International Legal Frameworks and Regimes for Submarine Pipelines, in Universität Kiel, Institut für Internationales Recht (ed.), German Yearbook of International Law – Jahrbuch für internationales Recht, 2009, pp. 241, 248 et seq.

29 *T. Koivurova & I. Polonen, supra* note 13 p. 169; See also Exchange of Good Practices, Large-scale Trans-boundary Projects, Application of the Espoo Convention to the complex activities, note by the Secretariat, Economic Commission for Europe, Meeting of the parties to the Convention on Environmental Impact assessment in the Transboundary context, Working Group on Environmental Impact Assessment, Twelfth meeting, Geneva, 11–13 May 2009, www.unece.org/env/documents/2009/eia/wg.1/ece.mp.eia.wg.1.2009.4.e.pdf.

30 *Ibid.*

authorities, the Company did not intend to investigate a possible alternative route in the territorial waters of Russia.[31] Since Russia is not a member of the Espoo Convention, it could easily decline permitting a feasibility study in its own territorial water. In addition, the request of the Company to conduct seabed studies in Estonia's Exclusive Economic Zone (EEZ) was rejected by the Estonian authorities.[32] This issue of course falls under the scope of the application of the Law of the Sea Convention (UNCLOS).[33] As Articles 58 and 79 of the UNCLOS Convention spell out, the delineation of the course for the laying of offshore pipelines on the continental shelf and in the Exclusive Economic Zone will be subject to the permission of the coastal state. The coastal state, however, cannot impede the construction of offshore pipelines on its continental shelf and in the Exclusive Economic Zone. In this case, as a request of the Finnish authorities, the Nord Stream consortium requested permission from the Estonian authorities to perform a seabed survey in the Estonian EEZ. The Estonian authorities rejected the request of the Nord Stream consortium to conduct sub-sea surveys in its EEZ, by indicating that: 'because the results of drilling work on the continental shelf will give information about Estonia's natural resources and their possible use, the Estonian government has the right to reject the research application'.[34] The legality of the refusal of the Estonia in permitting a seabed survey under the UNCLOS Convention is a matter of discussion.[35] Discussion of this issue, of course, is beyond the scope of this chapter. Meanwhile, it is noteworthy to highlight that the Espoo Convention does not include provisions related to the alternative routes of a proposed pipeline in affected states.

The second contentious issue was raised by the European Parliament by publishing the European Parliament resolution on the environmental impact of the planned gas pipeline in the Baltic Sea to link up Russia and Germany.[36] The European Parliament resolution *inter alia* referred to a lack of adequate descriptions of possible alternative routes (not limited to the states of origin and, including onshore routes).[37]

As the cases of Estonia and Russia indicated, an alternative route in the affected parties or non-member parties might have been more environmentally sound rather than in the state of origin. Moreover, according to the European

---

[31] The NSGP Environmental Impact Assessment Report, p. 365, www.nord-stream.com/press-info/library/?q=&language=en&type=3&category=4&per_page=10.

[32] *A. Lott*, Marine Environmental Protection and Trans-boundary Pipeline Projects: A Case Study of the Nord Stream Pipeline, Merkourios-Utrecht J. Int'l & Eur. L., 2011 (27), pp. 55, 56.

[33] For more discussion about the rights and obligations of states involved in respect of the laying the Nord Stream pipeline in the Baltic Sea, see *A. Lott*, *supra* note 32.

[34] http://uk.reuters.com/article/2007/09/20/nordstream-estonia-idUKMAR13135420070920.

[35] See *ibid.*

[36] Accessible at: www.europarl.europa.eu/sides/getDoc.do?type=TA&reference=P6-TA-2008-0336&language=EN.

[37] The European Parliament Resolution on the environmental impact of the planned gas pipeline in the Baltic Sea to link up Russia and Germany 2008, paras. 26 and 31, www.europarl.europa.eu/sides/getDoc.do?type=TA&reference=P6-TA-2008-0336&language=EN.

Parliament resolution all possible alternative routes for the construction of such pipelines, in particular the terrestrial route, should also be taken into consideration by the decision-makers. However, these issues remained unresolved in the case of the NSGP.

The second challenge arises in the circumstances in which part of a cross-border pipeline has been laid or will be laid in the territory of countries that are not Parties to the Espoo Convention or EU Member States. In the case of the NSGP project, the states of origin, except Russia, and the affected states were members of the Espoo Convention and hence participated in the EIA process. As noted, in the case of the NSGP, Russia was not a member of the Espoo Convention. Therefore, Russia could simply reject the request for the assessment of alternative routes in its territory. Consequently, some of the affected states seriously criticised the effectiveness of the EIA of the project.[38] In this particular case the main problem was obviously the fact that a decision on the pipeline was finally taken in Russia, which is not a member to the Espoo Convention.

The third challenge in the case of the cross-border pipeline arose from the extra procedural requirements involved in the project. In other words, the developer prepared separate national EIA reports in accordance with the national requirements of each of the states of origin as well as an overall assessment of the whole project. This created additional procedural challenges for the developer as well as the states of origin and the affected states.[39] As the case of the Nord Stream gas pipeline has shown us, the fragmented trans-boundary EIA has been done simply because each of the states of origin evaluated the EIA reports only based on their own national regulations. Therefore, the developer of the pipeline should prepare trans-boundary EIA reports for each of the states of origin in accordance with its national EIA procedure. Even more complex, in cases such as the NSGP, for which the construction and operation of a proposed pipeline will have trans-boundary impacts on several affected states, the affected state may receive several trans-boundary EIA reports for the same project. This will increase the level of complexity and difficulty within a tight timeframe, and the affected state may face difficulties in responding correctly.

Moreover, among the various criticisms that were presented by the European Parliament, one of the most fundamental issues concerned a lack of overall assessment of the NSGP project, including a separate strategic study of various alternatives.[40] Meanwhile, not only did the developer prepare national EIAs but it

---

38 Estonian environmental groups complained to the European Commission about the EIA of the Nord Stream Gas Pipeline, www.elfond.ee/en/news/896-nord-stream-baltic-sea-pipeline-assessements-breach-eu-laws-estonian-environmental-groups-alert-european-commission. See also: www.neurope.eu/article/nord-stream-faces-more-obstacles.

39 *C. Redgwell*, Contractual and Treaty Arrangements Supporting Large European Trans-boundary Pipeline Projects: Can Adequate Human Rights and Environmental Protection Be Secured?, in M. Roggenkamp, L.B. Hernández, D.N. Zillman & I. del Guayo (eds.), Energy Networks and the Law: Innovative Solutions in Changing Markets, 2012, p. 103, 114 et seq.

40 European Parliament resolution, *supra* note 36, paras. 17 and 21.

also provided holistic descriptions of the project, including the overall assessment of the project in a very extensive and detailed manner. One may argue that the developer prepared EIA reports beyond the minimum requirements of the Espoo Convention. In fact, as Koivurova and Polonen argue, the states involved in the project put pressure on the developer to conduct an overall assessment of the project.[41] Therefore, although neither the Espoo Convention, nor the EU EIA directive requires an overall assessment of such large-scale projects, in the case of Nord Stream, the developer conducted a detailed and extensive EIA for the entire length of the pipeline. A cross-border pipeline may have partial and sectorial impacts on the environment of each of the concerned parties. But such a pipeline may also have overall effects on the entire length of the project. This issue of the necessity of overall assessment is confirmed by the EU Court of Justice in the case C-227/01, *Commission v. Spain* in 2004.[42] the Court pronounced: 'If the argument of the Spanish Government were upheld, the effectiveness of Directive 85/337 could be seriously compromised, since the national authorities concerned would need only to split up a long-distance project into successive shorter sections in order to exclude from the requirements of the Directive both the project as a whole and the sections resulting from that division.'[43] Similar arguments stressed by the Court in case C-2/07.[44]

In theory a lack of preparation of the holistic assessment of a cross-border project may give rise to an under-estimation of the overall impacts of the project on all the states involved. Moreover, according to the reports, which were published by the Nord Stream Company, the actual impacts of the project after the construction and during the operation are in general in line with the results of the assessments in the planning phase of the project.[45]

3.2. APPLYING THE ESPOO CONVENTION AND EU EIA DIRECTIVE IN THE CONTEXT OF SUCH CHALLENGES

Four general challenges were observed in applying trans-boundary EIA under the Espoo Convention to the Nord Stream gas pipeline. Of course, one may argue that the states of origin could have applied the EIA in a better way to address all the challenges raised under the Espoo Convention. In other words, the direction given by the European Commission in the Guidance on the Application of the

41 *T. Koivurova & I. Polonen, supra* note 13.

42 Case C-227/01, *Commission v Spain*, 16 September 2004.

43 *Ibid.*, para. 53.

44 Case C-2/07, *Paul Abraham and Others v Région Wallonne and Others* [2008] ECR I-01197, 28 February 2008, para. 42.

45 Environmental Impacts of Constructing the Nord Stream Pipelines Minor and Local, www.nord-stream.com/press-info/press-releases/environmental-impacts-of-constructing-the-nord-stream-pipelines-minor-and-local-442/.

Environmental Impact Assessment Procedure for Large-scale Trans-boundary Projects supports the idea that the Espoo Convention and EU EIA Directive are well drafted to address concerns arising out of the application of trans-boundary EIA for cross-border projects. The next step, therefore, is to evaluate whether such challenges have to be dealt with as matters governed by these instruments or as issues excluded from the scope of the application of these instruments. In the remainder of this section, we will discuss the application of the Espoo Convention and EU EIA Directive to each of these areas separately below.

3.2.1. The Assessment of Alternatives

As mentioned, one of the main criticisms voiced was that the EIA report failed to examine alternative routes of the NSGP project. In the case of the cross-border pipelines, alternatives can be assessed by taking into account various means of transporting energy or by examining the alternative routes of a proposed pipeline. Indeed, there are various ways for transporting natural gas and crude oil form source points to demand areas. In its broadest terms, the EIA report should include possible alternative solutions for meeting the aims of the proposed project. The developer should also examine the alternative locations for the proposed project.[46] Article 5(3) of the EU Directive and Article 5 of the Espoo Convention require the developer to provide an outline of the main alternatives to the project including, the no-action alternative. Nevertheless, both of these instruments only require an outline of the main alternatives in the territory of the one of the states of origin and not in the territory of the affected states.

In fact, in the EU EIA Directive, it is merely articulated that the information to be provided by the developer shall include an outline of the main alternatives studied by the developer.[47] Therefore, it seems that the choice of alternatives to a proposed pipeline can be outlined only in the state of origin territory. If we assume that the information will be transferred to the affected state and its public for public participation, the affected state and its public can only make comments in relation to alternative locations in the state of origin.

In the same way, the Espoo Convention requires the identification of the alternative locations in the EIA report. Similar to the EU EIA Directive, alternative routes for the proposed projects can only be suggested in the state of origin's territory. Article 5 of the Espoo Convention, requires the concerned states to enter into consultations in relation to possible alternatives to the proposed activity, including the no-action alternative. The possibility of assessing alternative routes in the territory of the affected states is not clearly indicated in the Espoo Convention. But it seems that the affected states can ask for the

46 *R.C. Das & D.K. Behera*, Environmental Science: Principles and Practice, 2008, p. 314.

47 Article 5(3) of the EU EIA Directive.

assessment of a proposed pipeline route in the territories of any of the states of origin.

It can be learned from the NSGP project that an alternative route in the affected parties may be more environmentally sound rather than in the state of origin. Nevertheless, in certain circumstances any request for the assessment of the alternative route of the pipeline in the territory of the affected states, by one of the states of origin, can be rejected by the request of an affected state.[48] Indeed, basically it is the state of origin that has planned to permit the construction of the pipeline in its territory and not the affected state. On the other hand, if one of the affected states suggests the assessment of the alternative route of the pipeline in the territory of another affected state, such an affected state can withdraw such request. Therefore, we argue that the possibility of the assessment of alternative routes of the pipeline in the territory of the affected states is restricted. This is also the case for non-Member States.

3.2.2. Trans-Boundary EIA in Cases Involving Non-EU Member States and Countries that are not Parties to the Espoo Convention

In those cases, where some of the states involved in implementing the cross-border pipeline project are not parties to the Espoo Convention or EU Member States, it is very likely that their national EIAs, if applicable, would differ from the requirements of the Espoo Convention and EU Directive. In the EU EIA Directive, it is expressly articulated that only if a Member State is aware that a project is likely to have significant effects on the environment in another Member State, the former Member state is required to conduct a trans-boundary EIA. Therefore, the scope of its application is limited to the European Union Member States. Under the Espoo Convention, the state of origin and the affected state are defined as parties to the Convention. Therefore, the provisions of the Espoo Convention may basically be applied only to the parties. Meanwhile, Article 2(9) stipulates that in any case of a bilateral or multilateral agreement, which provides more stringent measures than those of this Convention, the provisions of this Convention shall not be enforced. In addition, Article 8 of the Espoo Convention permits parties to the Convention to establish bilateral or multilateral agreements or other arrangements in order to implement their obligations under this Convention. Meanwhile, according to Appendix VI of the Convention, which provides elements for bilateral or multilateral agreements, such agreements are mainly limited to set agreements between parties to the Convention. Therefore, it seems the proper application of the effective trans-boundary EIA for the cross-border pipelines is expected only in such cases, which bilateral and multilateral agreements have been or will be concluded between the parties to the Convention, and states, which are involved in the project, but are not parties to the Convention.

---

[48] For instance the case of the refusal of Estonia to permit a sea-bed survey in its EEZ.

As a result in those cases where some states (or even just one state) are not members to the Convention, the states may externalise pollution costs to other states concerned and vice versa. As the case of the NGSP project shows, the second challenge is that, the Espoo Convention can only be correctly implemented in practice, if all states concerned, including the states of origin and the affected states, are parties to the Espoo Convention. Otherwise a proper application of the EIA to the proposed cross-border pipelines may not be achieved.

3.2.3. *Complying with National EIA Requirements*

For large-scale trans-boundary projects, the developer must comply with the requirements of the national EIA regulations of the country where the project will be implemented. Indeed, according to Article 7(5) of the EU EIA Directive, the state of origin should determine the detailed arrangements for implementing a trans-boundary EIA. Thus, the developer is required to comply with the requirements of the state in whose territory the project is intended to be carried out. Therefore, unless agreed otherwise, the developer is required to conduct a fragmented trans-boundary EIA for each section of a proposed pipeline. As indicated in the NSGP, the parties involved require the developer to conduct an overall assessment of the project. This was of course more than the minimum requirements of the Espoo Convention. Under the Espoo Convention, Parties may agree to prepare a joint EIA. The preparation of a joint EIA report can improve public participation and avoid conflicts in integrating different EIAs for the specific project.[49]

In the EU EIA Directive, there is no direct rule, requiring the preparation of a joint report to overcome these complexities and difficulties arising out of conducting fragmented trans-boundary EIAs. Meanwhile, Article 7(5) requires the Member States, including the state of origin and the affected states to enter into consultations regarding, inter alia, the potential trans-boundary effects of the project and the measures envisaged to reduce or eliminate such effects. One may argue that the requirements of Article 7(5) are not specifically limited to measures envisaged to reduce trans-boundary effects, but rather parties may also agree on the establishment of a joint body in order to prepare a joint EIA report.

On the other hand, under the Espoo Convention, the preparation of a joint environmental report for the whole project is intended. In accordance with Article 8 and Appendix VI, item (g) Parties can agree on the preparation of a joint EIA. The preparation of the joint EIA report is not mandatory under the Espoo Convention. In fact, the preparation of the joint EIA report can be applicable, if all the states concerned have agreed with the establishment of the joint EIA. Such issues should be determined through bilateral and multilateral

49 See *F.M. Hernández*, Analysis of the Espoo Convention as Applied to Mega Projects: The Case of Nord Stream 37, May 2008 (unpublished Master of Science thesis, Lunds Universitet, on file with author), p. 44.

agreements between parties concerned. The Espoo Convention does not give any further detail in relation to the preparation of the joint EIA. Nevertheless, the Guidance on the Application of the Environmental Impact Assessment first recommends developers to prepare a joint environmental report for the whole project and afterward prepare the individual national environmental reports. But as the Guidance on the Application of the Environmental Impact Assessment expressly notes, such measures are voluntary and hence left to the discretion of the states concerned.

3.2.4. *The Overall Assessment of the Project*

It has been mentioned that the overall assessment of the project was intended by the European Court of Justice to be an integral part of the EIA procedure. The European Parliament also criticised the lack of an overall assessment in the case of the NSGP Project. Meanwhile, in the EU EIA Directive, neither is the state of origin obliged to provide the overall assessment of the project to affected states, nor is the developer required to provide an overall assessment report to the state of origin. Of course, the state of origin may require the developer to assess the overall impact of the project through its national regulations.

The Espoo Convention only requires the assessment of a trans-boundary impact which might be caused by a proposed activity. Therefore, similar to the EU EIA Directive there is no clear obligation upon the state of origin to submit the overall assessment of the project to the affected state. It is possible, however, for the states concerned to establish a joint body and thereby they require the developer to provide the overall assessment of the project. Furthermore, if the parties agreed to implement a joint EIA for the entire length of the pipeline, they can require the developer to assess the overall effects of a proposed project. Meanwhile, as noted, the performance of a joint EIA requires bilateral and multilateral cooperation between all the states concerned, which of course is not easy to reach.

4. CONCLUSIONS

The Espoo Convention and EU EIA Directive are indeed established to oblige contracting parties to assess trans-boundary environmental impacts prior to granting the go-ahead for large-scale projects. As a result, contracting parties are expressly instructed to conduct a trans-boundary EIA as one of the main environmental regulations applicable to pipelines. However, projects such as the Nord Stream pipeline are trans-boundary projects, which may also have trans-boundary impacts. The trans-boundary EIA procedure under the Espoo Convention and EU EIA Directive is designed to reduce the trans-boundary impact of activities with trans-boundary risks. In the case of cross-border pipelines, although they are included in the list of activities subject to trans-boundary EIA, they still need to be assessed by taking into account their transboundary features. As recommended by the Guidance on the Application of the Environmental Impact Assessment, the Parties to the Espoo Convention may implement a joint EIA for the whole project. Meanwhile, undertaking a joint EIA requires further bilateral or multilateral agreements between the parties concerned. Overall, this chapter concludes that although it is possible to undertake a joint EIA for cross-border pipelines under the Espoo Convention, it is not mandatory for parties to do so. Therefore, if the parties would like to apply the minimum standards provided by the Espoo Convention and EU EIA Directive, they can simply ignore undertaking a joint EIA. As a consequence, the overall assessment of the project remains unattended to. Moreover, undertaking several national EIAs for a project, which stretches across national borders, complicates public participation and reduces its effectiveness. Thus, it is highly recommended to draft an instrument specifically dealing with EIA for cross-border projects, in which a joint EIA could be mandated. Undertaking a joint EIA facilitates the overall assessment of the project and provides alternatives to the project e.g. routes of the pipeline. This of course reduces the level of the complexity and extra administrative costs which are involved in undertaking fragmented national EIAs for cross-border projects.

CHAPTER 9

ENVIRONMENTAL IMPACT ASSESSMENT TO SUPPORT MARINE INNOVATION:

The 'Rochdale Envelope' and 'Deploy & Monitor' in the UK's Ocean Energy Industry

Glen WRIGHT*

A new industrial revolution is taking place in the oceans, as humankind increasing looks offshore to meet its needs for energy, resources and food.[1] This growing demand for marine space and resources is placing further pressure on an ocean whose health is already declining. This evolving situation is encapsulated by the emerging 'Blue Economy' discourse, which advocates sustainable development of the oceans to meet economic and social needs.[2] The European Union (EU), in its Blue Growth Agenda, highlights the potential to 'harness the untapped potential of Europe's oceans, seas and coasts for jobs and growth ... whilst safeguarding biodiversity and protecting the marine environment'.[3] Developing a blue economy is a major challenge that necessitates the evolution of existing regulatory frameworks.

Marine renewable energy (MRE) resources, such as offshore wind, wave, and tidal, have been identified by the EU as one of the five key 'value chains' that can contribute to a blue economy.[4] Offshore wind is growing rapidly,[5] with projects

* Research Fellow, International Maritime Policy, IDDRI.

1 *H.D. Smith*, The Industrialisation of the World Ocean, Ocean & Coastal Management, 2000 (43), p. 11; *T. Stojanovic & C.J.Q. Farmer*, The Development of World Oceans & Coasts and Concepts of Sustainability Marine Policy, 2013 (42), p. 157.

2 *A. Dom*, Limits to Blue Growth, *EP Intergroup CCBSD* (Seas at Risk, 2014); *N. Kathijotes*, Keynote: Blue Economy – Environmental and Behavioural Aspects Towards Sustainable Coastal Development, Procedia – Social and Behavioral Sciences, 2013 (101), p. 7; *J.C. Surís-Regueiro, M. Dolores Garza-Gil & M.M. Varela-Lafuente*, Marine Economy: A Proposal for Its Definition in the European Union, Marine Policy, 2013 (42), p. 111.

3 *European Commission Maritime Affairs*, Blue Growth: Opportunities for Marine and Maritime Sustainable Growth, 2012.

4 *Ibid.*

5 *Global Wind Energy Council*, Global Wind Report: Annual Market Update 2013, pp. 53–57.

moving into deeper waters, and new technologies being developed.[6] In the United Kingdom (UK) offshore wind currently meets around 3% of total electricity demand, but this figure is likely to rise substantially in pursuit of the UK's legally binding target[7] to source 20% of its total energy consumption from renewables by 2020.[8]

Ocean energy technologies,[9] which utilise waves and tides to generate electricity, are now attracting considerable interest and investment,[10] and bringing their own unique challenges to existing marine governance and project approval frameworks.[11] Indeed, ocean energy is not simply a technically challenging extension of onshore renewable energy technologies: 'the policy environment, governance, patterns of resource use, conservation values, and distribution of ownership rights are all substantively different'.[12] Interest in ocean energy is particularly high in Europe, where the European Commission has developed an action plan to support the sector.[13] The UK, and Scotland in particular, has emerged as the frontrunner in this new industry, with ocean energy enjoying political support, resources and technical expertise.[14]

1. ENVIRONMENTAL IMPACT ASSESSMENT FOR OCEAN ENERGY

Ensuring that the deployment of innovative new technologies does not negatively impact the marine environment is a defining challenge of the push towards a blue economy. This is particularly acute in relation to new renewable energy

6 e.g. floating turbines.

7 Under the EU Renewable Energy Directive (2009). See Department of Energy and Climate Change, The UK Renewable Energy Strategy (2009), www.decc.gov.uk/en/content/cms/what_we_do/uk_supply/energy_mix/renewable/res/res.aspx.

8 *G. Scarff, C. Fitzsimmons & T. Gray,* The New Mode of Marine Planning in the UK: Aspirations and Challenges, Marine Policy, 2015 (51), p. 96.

9 The term 'ocean energy' is used to denote wave and tidal technologies, whereas the broader term MRE incudes offshore wind. Ocean energy also encompasses ocean thermal energy technology (OTEC) and salinity gradient technology. These technologies have followed a different development pathway to wave and tidal. In this chapter, 'ocean energy' refers to the wave and tidal technologies currently approaching commercialisation in the UK.

10 For up-to-date investment figures, see the latest edition of the REN1 Global Status of Renewables report, www.ren21.net/.

11 *G. Wright,* Marine Governance in an Industrialised Ocean: A Case Study of the Emerging Marine Renewable Energy Industry, Marine Policy, 2015 (52), p. 77; *S. Kerr et al.,* Establishing an Agenda for Social Studies Research in Marine Renewable Energy, Energy Policy, 2014 (67), p. 694.

12 *S. Kerr et al., supra* note 11.

13 The EC has convened an Ocean Energy Forum with the potential to develop into a European Industrial Initiative between 2017–2020. See http://ec.europa.eu/maritimeaffairs/policy/ocean_energy/forum/index_en.htm.

14 *K. Johnson, S. Kerr & J. Side,* Marine Renewables and Coastal communities – Experiences from the Offshore Oil Industry in the 1970s and their Relevance to Marine Renewables in the 2010s, Marine Policy, 2013 (38), p. 491; *Kerr et al., supra* note 11.

technologies, where there is concern that damage will be caused to local and regional ecosystems in pursuit of broader climate mitigation goals ('paradoxical harm').[15] In this vein, a recent report of the United Nations (UN) Open-ended Informal Consultative Process on Oceans and the Law of the Sea notes that ocean energy

> 'could foster increased energy security, generate employment and play a role in mitigating the impacts of climate change. At the same time, the importance of assessing and studying the impacts of [ocean energy], including on the marine environment, was stressed ...'[16]

In most jurisdictions, existing EIA regulation is applied unaltered to ocean energy projects. This is partly because EIA is intended to be a generally applicable regulatory tool, however, new technologies generally develop within existing legal frameworks, but inevitably elicit new legal responses as commercialisation approaches.[17] It is in this context that some specific modifications of the EIA process for new offshore technologies are considered in this chapter, with particular reference to ocean energy.

The overall EIA process for ocean energy context is essentially the same as any other EIA process, though the European Marine Energy Centre (EMEC)[18] has helpfully developed a set of guidelines that provides an outline of the EIA process for ocean energy projects and highlights the scientific knowledge that will have to be generated.[19] As part of the screening and scoping stages, developers will have to identify available information regarding the proposed deployment site, followed by baseline studies to describe the nature of the site.[20] This data is then used to identify all possible impacts and assess worst-case scenarios and potential mitigation options before compiling the relevant documents for submission to the relevant regulatory authorities.

The EIA process in the ocean energy context is complicated by two factors: knowledge gaps and poorly developed regulatory processes. Ocean energy technologies suffer from a paucity of knowledge on two levels. Firstly, other

15 *R. White*, Climate Change and Paradoxical Harm, in S. Farrell, T. Ahmed & D. French (eds.), Legal and Criminological Consequences of Climate Change, 2012.

16 United Nations General Assembly, Report on the Work of the United Nations Open-Ended Informal Consultative Process on Oceans and the Law of the Sea at Its Thirteenth Meeting (A/67/120, 2012) vol 40091.

17 In the marine context see, e.g., J.D. Nyhart, The Interplay of Law and Technology in Deep Seabed Mining Issues, Virginia Journal of International Law, 1974 (15), pp. 827, 830.

18 An ocean energy testing and research centre based in Orkney in Scotland.

19 European Marine Energy Center, Environmental Impact Assessment (EIA) Guidance for Developers at the European Marine Energy Centre, 2005. The precise regulatory requirements vary by jurisdiction, and will change as legislation is developed and implemented. The guidelines nonetheless provide a useful starting point.

20 These baseline studies could relate to a range of issues, such as determining local fish and mammal populations. At EMEC, baseline data is already available for use in EIA.

renewable energy technologies are well established,[21] but practical experience with the deployment of ocean energy technologies is limited. While a spectrum of potential environmental interactions has now been mapped out,[22] research to date has generally studied small-scale deployments. A commercial-scale industry will likely have different interactions with the marine environment that will need to be explored and managed over time. Secondly, the marine environment is notoriously difficult to study, and scientific research is limited by high costs, inaccessibility, and relative lack of development compared to onshore. These difficulties make EIA in the marine environment unusually challenging.[23]

The scientific uncertainty caused by these information gaps is compounded by under-developed regulatory frameworks and EIA processes that are not yet adapted to better meet the needs of emerging technologies in the marine environment. While some aspects of the relevant regulatory frameworks are being improved to better fit the ocean energy context,[24] recent commentary confirms that ocean energy continues to bear a considerable regulatory burden, particularly in relation to EIA:

> 'marine energy attracts a depth of scrutiny from environmental regulators and statutory nature conservation bodies that more established marine industries such as fishing and shipping have managed to escape.'[25]

The resulting time and cost is a considerable barrier to the development of ocean energy projects, and encourages developers to be guarded about sharing their results, meaning that privately collected data is less likely to be publicly available to

---

21 For example, regulators can draw on over a century of experience with conventional hydropower technologies.

22 *G. Boehlert & A. Gill*, Environmental and Ecological Effects of Ocean Renewable Energy: A Current Synthesis, Oceanography, 2008 (23); *R. Inger et al.*, Marine Renewable Energy: Potential Benefits to Biodiversity? An Urgent Call for Research, Journal of Applied Ecology, 2009, p. 1; *M.P. Simmonds et al.*, Marine Renewable Energy Developments: Benefits versus Concerns (Paper SC/62/E8 presented to the IWC Scientific Committee, 2010 (unpublished)); *C. Frid et al.*, The Environmental Interactions of Tidal and Wave Energy Generation Devices, Environmental Impact Assessment Review, 2012 (32), p. 133; *A. Linley*, Environmental Interactions with Marine Renewable Energy, Marine Scientist, 2012, p. 22.

23 *A.K. Smith*, Impact Assessment in the Marine Environment – the Most Challenging of All, in Impact assessment in the marine environment (International Association of Impact Assessment annual conference), 2008.

24 *A.-M. O'Hagan*, A Review of International Consenting Regimes for Marine Renewables: Are We Moving towards Better Practice ?, in 4th International Conference on Ocean Energy, 2012; *G. Wright*, Regulating Marine Renewable Energy Development: A Preliminary Assessment of UK Permitting Processes, Underwater Technology: The International Journal of the Society for Underwater, 2014 (32), p. 1.

25 *S. Merry*, Marine Renewable Energy: Could Environmental Concerns Kill off an Environmentally Friendly Industry?, Underwater Technology, 2014 (32), p. 1.

benefit the industry as a whole.[26] This has a significant impact on the development and sustainability of the technology.[27]

1.1. CASE STUDY: MARINE CURRENT TURBINES, NORTHERN IRELAND

Marine Current Turbines (MCT), a private company now wholly-owned by Siemens, deployed its SeaGen device in Strangford Lough, Northern Ireland in April 2008. This was the first deployment of a commercial-scale tidal energy device and it has since generated over 3GWh of electricity to the grid. The experience of MCT has already been illuminating in a number of respects, and the final report of the environmental monitoring programme notes that it has informed policy development in the UK (though it not specify how exactly it has influenced policy).[28]

MCT proceeded through each stage of the EIA process over the course of several years producing, amongst other documents: a Scoping Report; an Environmental Impact Statement (EIS); an EIA report; an Environmental Action and Safety Management Plan; and an Environmental Monitoring Programme (EMP). MCT established a scientific working group to advise on the scientific and operational details of the EMP and mitigation measures, while a broader liaison group was established to engage stakeholders and place the scientific research in context.

The EMP is remarkable in its extent and depth, particularly the compliance and monitoring regime that was agreed with the regulator in order to obtain consent at a cost of £3 million to the developer over a period of three years.[29] This regime involves a range of pre- and post-deployment monitoring activities, including: surveillance and post-mortem evaluation of animal carcasses; a sonar marine mammal detection system enabling automatic precautionary shutdown; manual shutdown when a mammal is within 50m of the device; land-based visual surveys; and telemetry studies and acoustic data logging for harbour porpoise activity.[30] The implementation of MCT's EMP began in June 2005 and ended in 2011 with a final report concluding that no major impacts on marine mammals were detected in three years of post-installation monitoring.

This onerous process was partly due to the fact that the receiving environment was designated as both a Special Protection Area and a Special

[26] *J.K. Sterne et al.*, The Seven Principles of Ocean Renewable Energy: A Shared Vision and Call for Action, Roger Williams University Law Review, 2009 (4), pp. 600, 611. Nonetheless, some efforts to collaborate on data sharing are taking place. See e.g. Tethys (http://tethys.pnnl.gov/).

[27] *H. Jeffrey & J. Sedgwick*, ORECCA European Offshore Renewable Energy Roadmap, September 2011, p. 14.

[28] *G. Keenan et al.*, SeaGen Environmental Monitoring Programme, 2011, p. 10.

[29] *L. Riddoch*, Seal of Approval, The Nature of Scotland, 2009, p. 21.

[30] *G. Keenan et al., supra* note 28, pp. 13–18.

Area of Conservation,[31] and partly because it was the first deployment of its kind, necessitating extensive EIA to convince regulators that the project should be permitted. The final SeaGen EMP report echoes this sentiment, stating 'the SeaGen EMP provides an ambitious plan beyond what might be expected of future projects now that more knowledge is available'.[32]

Overall, MCT agrees that the process has proven the sustainability of their device, improving scientific knowledge and allowing the regulator to take an adaptive management approach and reducing the mitigation burden in subsequent variations of the licence.[33] However, such an intensive EIA process is burdensome and 'could prove too much for future projects'.[34]

2. ISSUES WITH EIA FOR OCEAN ENERGY PROJECTS

Given the foregoing, the main issues can be summarised briefly as follows:

- *Lack of scientific certainty regarding impacts.* This causes the EIA process to be particularly costly and time consuming as compared to EIA processes for well-established technologies in well-understood environments.
- *Lack of available date on the receiving environment.* Low availability of suitable scientific data regarding the marine environment means that developers must invest substantial time, cost, and effort in establishing of baseline data.
- *Utilisation of scientific knowledge.* The EIA process and regulators must ensure that existing data is identified and utilised in order to minimise the knowledge gaps and reduce the regulatory burden.
- *Data-sharing.* Developers that invest substantially in the generation of new scientific knowledge are unlikely to be willing for this to be used to assist the consenting of other projects,[35] potentially resulting in the inefficient duplication of data. The EIA process would ideally facilitate the diffusion and utilisation of new scientific knowledge generated in the course of permitting.
- *Regulator capacity.* Regulators need to be equipped with tools to acquire scientific data relevant to policy and consenting decisions, rather than require it solely from the proponent. Regulators need relevant data in order to set standards, monitor the receiving environment, and enforce compliance with

[31] Under the EC Wild Birds Directive (79/409/ EEC) and the EC Habitats Directive (92/043/EEC) respectively.

[32] *Keenan et al., supra* note 28, p. 10.

[33] *Ibid.*, p. i.

[34] *L. Riddoch, supra* note 29.

[35] In at least one case, that of Crest Energy in New Zealand, the developer specifically argued that the data generated in the EIA process should not be available for utilisation by other developers. See *G. Wright,* A Tidal Power Project, New Zealand Law Journal, 2011, p. 260.

permits and licences. Without the appropriate resources and capabilities, this task falls to developers.

- *Innovation.* Placing too great a burden on the proponent of an innovative project will slow the development of new industries. An equitable balance needs to be found that allows for innovation without imperilling the marine environment.

3. INTRODUCING RISK INTO THE REGULATORY FRAMEWORK

The precautionary principle, which is essentially the legal implementation of the adage 'better safe than sorry', is a well-entrenched tenet of environmental law.[36] The principle can be stated as a call to action for environmental measures, as in the Principle 15 of the Rio Declaration:[37]

> 'Where there are threats of serious or irreversible damage, lack of full scientific certainty shall not be used as a reason for postponing cost-effective measures to prevent environmental degradation.'

The principle can also be framed as a failsafe, ensuring that potentially harmful activities do not go ahead until there is full scientific certainty as to its impacts. In this context, the UN's *World Charter for Nature* states that when 'potential adverse effects are not fully understood, the activities should not proceed.'[38]

Within the EU, the precautionary principle is enshrined in Article 191 of the Lisbon Treaty (Treaty on the Functioning of the European Union), which states: 'Union policy on the environment shall aim at a high level of protection ... It shall be based on the precautionary principle and on the principles that preventive action should be taken.'[39]

Where an action risks causing harm to the environment, in the absence of scientific consensus or certainty that the action is not harmful, the precautionary principle places the burden on the proponent of the action to provide this

---

36 See e.g. *J. Cameron & J. Abouchar,* The Precautionary Principle: A Fundamental Principle of Law and Policy for the Protection of the Global Environment, BC Int'l & Comp. L. Rev., 1991 (14), p. 1; *D. Freestone & E. Hey,* The precautionary principle and international law: the challenge of implementation, 1996.

37 Rio Declaration on Environment and Development Report of the United Nations Conference on the Human Environment, Stockholm, 5–16 June 1972, UN Doc. E.73.II.A.14 and corrigendum, chapter I.

38 World Charter for Nature, GA Res. 37/7, U.N. GAOR, 37th Sess., Supp. No. 51, at section (ll)(11)(b), UN Doc. A/Res/37/7 (1992).

39 Consolidated versions of the Treaty on European Union and the Treaty on the Functioning of the European Union, OJ 2012 C326/1.

certainty.[40] Regulators have traditionally taken a cautious approach to novel applications, including towards renewable energy projects, strictly following the precautionary principle even where the risk of environmental impact is comparatively low and placing the burden of attaining scientific certainty on project proponents.[41] The nature of the marine environment, coupled with the emerging consensus the ocean energy is relatively benign, leaves developers with the very difficult task of detecting small changes in an environment that is naturally highly variable.

By not allowing for the introduction of some risk into decision-making, the regulatory framework can lead decision makers to perceive a potential environmental harm as being more likely than it truly is. Sunstein argues that such a cautious approach 'threatens to be paralyzing'.[42] There is therefore a need, in certain circumstances, for an element of risk to be introduced into regulatory frameworks, yet this proposition directly contradicts one of the most fundamental principles of environmental law.

The extent to which uncertainty can be accommodated within existing legal frameworks and how adaptive and risk-based management strategies interact with the precautionary principle is an overarching problem for policymakers. The extent to which the introduction of risk is legally permissible remains largely unknown in many legal systems, while in others, such as the EU, such strategies appear to directly contravene environmental directives. This context must be borne in mind when considering how risk-based management might be introduced into regulatory frameworks. Indeed, a project funded by the EU's Horizon 2020 research and innovation programme aims to explore this issue.[43]

The choice between a strictly precautionary approach and a risk-based approach has the potential to shape regulation and facilitate or hinder industry development, and as such it is a heated issue. For example, a 'fiercely contested' debate took place in the UK over which approach was more appropriate in the consenting of offshore wind farms.[44]

A risk-based approach aims to shift the focus of decision-making toward the assessment and management of risk. Risk-based regulation provides a systematic framework that prioritises regulatory activities, and the scientific studies required to meet regulatory requirements, according to an evidence-based assessment of

---

40 *F.B. Cross,* Paradoxical Perils of the Precautionary Principle, Washington and Lee Law Review, 1996 (53).

41 *RenewableUK,* Consenting Lessons Learned: An Offshore Wind Industry Review of Past Concerns, Lessons Learned and Future Challenges, 2011, p. 18.

42 *C.R. Sunstein,* Beyond the Precautionary Principle, Chicago Public Law and Legal Theory Working Paper, 2003 (38), p. 1.

43 See RiCORE, http://ricore-project.eu/.

44 *RenewableUK, supra* note 41, p. 18.

risk.[45] This enables existing research to be more fully integrated into consenting processes by not requiring the developer to prove complete certainty as to all the details of its specific case. In being more permissive, a risk-based approach can also drive additional scientific study into impacts.

There are a number of ways that this approach can be operationalised and both approaches discussed below take a step towards risk-based management. Regardless of the mechanism, the flexibility and risk introduced by such approaches must be carefully managed to protect regulators, but also to be useful for developers. Too much flexibility could threaten the permanence of a licence and create an unstable investment environment, while too little could hamper development. Balancing certainty and flexibility is therefore crucial, though few, if any, jurisdictions currently take a structured and holistic approach to this. At the very least, the legal framework needs to be predictable in the way it adapts regulatory processes to new information.

4. CASE STUDY: THE UK

Two modifications of the EIA process have emerged in the UK as a response to the issues discussed above: the 'Rochdale Envelope', which allows a project description to be broadly defined in a consent application to allow for technological change over the life of a project;[46] and the 'Deploy and Monitor' approach (D&M), which permits deployment before complete certainty as to impacts.[47]

Despite being widely discussed and increasingly utilised within the industry, neither approach has received much attention in the academic literature. The following sections therefore aim to introduce these concepts to the literature, provide an overview for further discussion, and offer some critical commentary on the use of these approaches, potential stumbling blocks, and the future of such reforms to traditional EIA processes.

---

45 *D. Peterson & S. Fensling,* Risk-Based Regulation: Good Practice and Lessons for the Victorian Context, in Victorian Competition and Efficiency Commission Regulatory Conference, 2011, p. 1.

46 *S. Freeman,* Pushing the 'Envelope', Offshore Wind Engineering, 2013 (Summer), p. 6; *B. Walker,* Managing Uncertainty; *G. Wright,* Strengthening the Role of Science in Marine Governance through Environmental Impact Assessment: A Case Study of the Marine Renewable Energy Industry; *The Crown Estate.*

47 *Marine Scotland,* Survey, Deploy and Monitor Licensing Policy Guidance; *G. Wright, supra* note 46.

4.1. ROCHDALE ENVELOPE

The 'Rochdale Envelope' approach to EIA derives from a UK planning law case[48] and has been reinvigorated by the MRE industry. In this new context, the approach has 'very quickly become popular'.[49] The Rochdale Envelope allows a developer to describe its project within a number of agreed parameters for the purposes of an EIA (this forms the 'envelope') and provide its EIS based on the maximum extents of the parameters, i.e. a 'worst-case scenario'. For example, where a developer is considering a range of rotor diameters, they could elaborate the EIS on the basis of the maximum diameter under consideration, rather than deciding on a smaller diameter at the time of consent. This provides the developer with a level of flexibility and allows for the evolution of the technology and the project in the years between consenting and deployment.

The eponymous cases concerned a planning application for a business park in Rochdale, which was initially approved by the local authority. The planning application was an 'outline application', i.e. it provided basic information regarding the size and scale of the development and formed the first step towards the construction of the business park, with detailed matters (such as siting, design, external appearance, means of access and landscaping) reserved for further consideration at a later time. The consent allowed a period of 10 years within which the reserved matters had to be detailed and a full application made. The consent was subject to numerous conditions, including that further detail be provided in relation to mitigating environmental impacts. In particular, one condition required the preparation of a framework document that would show the design and layout of the proposed development and set out the phases of construction.

The complainants sought to challenge the approval on a number of grounds, primarily that there was: (i) a failure to adequately describe the project as required by the relevant planning laws; and (ii) a failure to give the relevant information required environmental effects regulations (which themselves implement an EU Directive).[50]

The court held that the nature of an outline application meant that many of the particulars of a development would not be available at the early stages of an application, and that this lack of detail was therefore not necessarily problematic in itself. However, it was held that the submission of a merely illustrative master plan and indicative schedule of uses was tacit acknowledgement that the description of the development was inadequate for the purposes of supplying

48 *R. v. Rochdale MBC ex parte Milne (No. 1)* and *R. v. Rochdale MBC ex parte Tew* [1999] and *R. v. Rochdale MBC ex parte Milne (No. 2)* [2000].

49 *S.J. Dolman & M.P. Simmonds*, Ensuring Adequate Consideration of Cetaceans in Scotland's Ambitious Marine Renewable Energy Plans, 2012.

50 EC Directive No. 85/377 on the assessment of the effects of certain public and private projects on the environment.

relevant information for environmental effects regulations. That is, as the application did not contain any information as to the design, size, or scale of the development, it was not possible to evaluate the environmental impacts, thereby precluding the ability to grant planning permission within the law.

Despite the failure of this particular application, the Rochdale Envelope principle was elucidated by Justice Sullivan, who colourfully observed that projects had been confined 'in a legal straitjacket by the assessment regulations ... drawn so tightly as to suffocate such projects'. He states:

> 'If a particular kind of project ... is, by its very nature, not fixed at the outset, but is expected to evolve over a number of years depending on market demand, there is no reason why [planning regulations] should not recognise that reality. What is important is that the environmental assessment process should then take full account at the outset of the implications for the environment of this need for an element of flexibility ... the difficulty of assessing projects which do require a degree of flexibility is not a reason for frustrating their implementation.'

Justice Sullivan noted the clear wording of the relevant EU Directive, that planning applications must be approved in 'full knowledge of the project's likely significant impact on the environment.' However, he stated that this

> 'should not be regarded as imposing some abstract state or threshold of knowledge which must be attained in respect of all projects, but should be applied to the particular project in question. For some projects it will be possible to obtain a much fuller knowledge than for others. The directive seeks to ensure that as much knowledge as can reasonably be obtained, given the nature of the project, about its likely significant effect on the environment is available to the decision taker.'

The Rochdale cases thereby establish the basic idea that a project description can be broadly defined, within a number of agreed parameters, for the purposes of an environmental assessment and planning application.

Table 1. Selected examples of use of the Rochdale Envelope for ocean energy projects

Project	Report	Size (MW)	Use/parameters of Rochdale Envelope	Comments/regulator response
Wave			Wave	
Brough Head[51]	Scoping	200	• BHWF plans to use the Rochdale Envelope approach • Sets out parameters in scoping report • Following site selection BHWF will adjust the extents and magnitudes defined in its scoping document accordingly	Marine Scotland (MS) notes:[52] • Purpose of scoping report is to broadly identify/assess the most important issues; • Rochdale envelope 'is not a substitute for accurate project details and in this instance appears to undermine the purpose of the scoping phase since so little is actually known about the project'; • 'downgrading of the scoping phase could result in information overload when the EIA is finally submitted which is time consuming for the developer and the regulatory process'; and • Rochdale Envelope is 'usually applied to unknowns such as exact device dimensions and numbers'.
Costa Head	Scoping	200	SSE states that it plans to use the Rochdale Envelope approach during the EIA process.	MS notes that the eventual EIS must:[53] • Contain a rationale for requiring such flexibility; • Define ranges (size, shape, tonnages etc.) or alternatives (e.g. for cable routes); • Contain justification of what constitutes the 'worst-case'; and • Discuss how the worst-case impacts different receptors.
Tidal			Tidal	
Inner Sound[54]	Scoping	400	• Project still in the early stages of design • Rochdale Envelope will be used • Two turbine models to be used – both will undergo planned testing and assessment which will feed into EIA • Various options available for all other elements of project	MS, in its response:[55] • Notes interaction of Rochdale Envelope with EU Habitats Directive (proposal can only be consented 'if it can be ascertained beyond reasonable scientific doubt that it will not adversely affect the integrity of a Natura site'); • States that the Rochdale Envelope must apply to both offshore and onshore elements together: 'i.e. what is the maximum extent of onshore/associated development that is required to support the maximum number of tidal turbines'; and • Explicitly recommends use of the Rochdale Envelope for turbine siting.

Westray South[56]	Scoping	200	• The project developer has not yet chosen a technology, meaning that substantial uncertainty exists as to final environmental interactions • The scoping document narrows the choice to non-surface piercing horizontal axis turbines with rotor diameter of up to 20m and a generating capacity of at least 1MW. • Up to 200 devices may be deployed, with a limit of 45 in the first phase of deployment.	MS notes the technology-neutral nature of the project, but nonetheless requires that the proponent must justify the need for flexibility and take responsibility for determining whether changes made later are material to the EIA process: 'The EIA will reduce the degree of design flexibility required and that [the EIS] provided for consent will be further refined as a condition of consent'.[57]
Test site			**Test site**	
Falmouth Bay Short Term Test Site (FabTest)	Description of proposed facility	-	• Description of the range and extent of potential devices and mooring systems to be tested.	FabTest is a preconsented testing site intended to be used by a range of devices.

51 Brough Head Wave Farm Limited, Brough Head Wave Farm Scoping Report, 2011.
52 Marine Scotland, Brough Head Wave Farm, West Orkney Scoping Opinion, 2011.
53 Marine Scotland, Costa Head Wave Farm Orkney Scoping Opinion, 2012.
54 MeyGen Phase 1 EIA Scoping Document, 2011.
55 Marine Scotland, Meygen, Phase 1, Tidal Turbine Array, Inner Sound, Pentland Firth: Scoping Opinion, 2011.
56 SSE Renewables, Environmental Scoping Report: Westray South Tidal Array, 2011.
57 Marine Scotland, SSER Westray South Tidal Array, Westray Firth Orkney: Scoping Opinion, 2012.

The UK's Overarching National Policy Statement for Energy subsequently alluded to the Rochdale Envelope approach,[58] and the Infrastructure Planning Commission (IPC) has published a guidance note on using the Rochdale Envelope.[59] The Scottish Government has committed to developing a guidance document on application of the approach[60] and has endorsed use of the Rochdale Envelope in a letter to heads of planning,[61] while the Crown Estate led a dedicated workshop to discuss issues relating to the use of the approach for ocean energy projects.[62]

The Rochdale cases, and subsequent IPC Guidance Note, set out a few principles applicable to use of this approach:

- An application seeking to make use of the Rochdale Envelope should acknowledge the need for details to evolve over a number of years. In practice this has meant that proponents have explicitly signposted the fact that they will use the Rochdale Envelope.
- As to the definition of impacts themselves, the level of detail of the proposal must be sufficiently clear and adequately described and tested in order for an EIA to be able to properly consider the range of likely environmental effects and necessary mitigation measures. While the assessment may conclude that a particular environmental impact could fall within a fairly wide range, it is consistent with EU regulations to adopt the worst-case scenario.[63]
- Mitigation measures should be developed that could deal with this worst-case so as to ensure that the development is environmentally benign, even if the worst case eventuates.
- The EIS must specify the upper and lower limits of a range of parameters, such as height, width and length of each building in the context of a business park development. Without such details, it is very difficult to assess likely environmental impacts, and any permission granted without such detail will be highly vulnerable to legal challenge.
- The flexibility provided by the Rochdale Envelope is not to be abused and does not excuse developers from their obligation to provide adequate descriptions of their projects.

---

58 *Department of Energy and Climate Change*, Overarching National Policy Statement for Energy (EN-1), p. 47.

59 *Infrastructure Planning Commission*, Using the 'Rochdale Envelope', pp. 2–3.

60 *Marine Scotland*, Marine Scotland Policy Development for Marine Renewables and Offshore Wind Covering Marine Planning and Licensing; *Scottish Government*, Simplified Marine Licensing, 2012, www.scotland.gov.uk/Topics/marine/marineenergy/background/licensing. 'Work is underway, in consultation with the marine offshore renewables industry and other stakeholders, to produce Scottish Government licensing policy guidance on the application of the "Rochdale Envelope" approach.' This had not yet been completed at the time of writing.

61 *C. Davidson*, Environmental Impact Assessment Directive: Questions and Answers. Letter from Planning Directorate to Heads of Planning.

62 The Crown Estate.

63 Specifically the objectives of European Council Directive 85/337/EEC.

- The planning authority determines what degree of flexibility can be permitted in each case, having regard to the particularities of an application. Any consent awarded by an authority based on the Rochdale Envelope approach must create 'clearly defined parameters' for the developer to work with.
- The authority can impose conditions to ensure that the project evolves within these parameters. It will clearly be prudent for developers and authorities to ensure they have assessed the range of possible effects implicit in the flexibility provided by the permission.

4.2. DEPLOY & MONITOR

The Deploy and Monitor (D&M) approach allows for a consent to be granted for a project before there is complete certainty as to the potential environmental impacts, enabling the developer to conduct monitoring, data collection, and scientific research. Generally the approach is advocated as a means to facilitate the development of small-scale projects or test deployments.

The D&M approach again introduces an element of risk, allowing the regulator to assess the likely risk of a project and consent it appropriately. The approach therefore directly violates the precautionary principle, but does allow for existing scientific knowledge to be better accounted for: where good baseline exists data for an area and a technology poses little risk, a deployment could be made with little regulatory oversight. As will be discussed below, a survey component can be incorporated to preliminarily rule out particularly sensitive sites before proceeding with deployment.[64]

At its most permissive, D&M would relieve developers of much of the onerous requirements of the usual EIA process, on the basis that the weight of evidence suggests that ocean energy technologies are environmentally benign. This approach would allow for deployment of an ocean energy device with relatively few initial restrictions, but with subsequently monitor the deployment to confirm that this is the case in practice. If the monitoring showed the device not to be benign, the consent could be terminated.

Such an unbridled implementation of D&M is not strongly advocated in the literature, or by developers. This is likely because the environmental impacts of such a lax approach could be much greater and developers are likely to support whichever framework can best prove the sustainability of their devices. A framework that allows deployment under few conditions may prove less burdensome to developers in the short-term, but one impactful deployment could be a setback to the entire industry.

64 *D. Leary & M. Esteban,* Renewable Energy from the Ocean and Tides: A Viable Renewable Energy Resource in Search of a Suitable Regulatory Framework, Carbon & Climate Law Review, 2009, p. 417; *House of Commons Energy and Climate Change Committee,* The Future of Marine Renewables in the UK, 2012.

Nonetheless some stakeholders are clearly concerned that such an approach could eventuate. For example, the Head of Climate Change at the Royal Society for the Protection of Birds (RSPB) states:[65]

> 'in a perfect world where we already had a thorough understanding of marine biodiversity in our waters, then we would be feeling a lot more relaxed about deploy and monitor because you would be able to filter out all the most sensitive sites; but, given that we have an imperfect and partial understanding of where wildlife is in the seas, I do not think deploy and monitor is appropriate for now …
>
> There are instances where deploy and monitor might be appropriate [i.e.] there is good baseline data for that area and we know that that area does not have areas of significant biodiversity interest. For now, because we have imperfect knowledge of biodiversity, deploy and monitor is not appropriate as a general rule, but it might be in certain instances.'

The addition of a 'survey' component, alluded to in the above passage, would enable particularly sensitive sites to be excluded completely.[66] Thus this is at the stronger end of the D&M spectrum. With the addition of the extra component, this approach has come to be called 'Survey, Deploy and Monitor' (SDM). Leary and Esteban eluded to such an approach early on in the development of the legal literature relating to ocean energy, stating:

> 'Available evidence suggests that the environmental burdens of offshore energy schemes are likely to be low, provided developers show sensitivity with appropriate site selection and *planning authorities controlling development in sensitive locations*.'[67]

This approach therefore exercises a certain level of precaution by utilising existing scientific knowledge to exclude certain sites, while also allowing deployment in other areas, thereby enabling additional studies to be undertaken. This will then provide both scientific data in relation to the technology and the receiving environment.

Scotland is apparently the only jurisdiction actively applying D&M,[68] which it has started to formalise through the development of a *Survey, Deploy and Monitor Licensing Policy Guidance* (SDM Guidance).[69] The Guidance is an attempt to turn the broad proposition of D&M into something concrete that can be used by

65 *House of Commons Energy and Climate Change Committee, supra* note 64, Ev 26.

66 This could be achieved by zoning, declaration of a strict marine protected area, or simply through regulatory practice.

67 *D. Leary & M. Esteban, supra* note 64 (emphasis added).

68 *A.-M. O'Hagan, supra* note 24.

69 *Marine Scotland*, Survey, Deploy and Monitor Licensing Policy Guidance, 2012.

regulators to ensure sustainable deployment of devices and the generation of new scientific knowledge.

Under the SDM Guidance, a proposal undergoes a formal risk-assessment. Where there is already sufficient scientific knowledge to provide a suitable EIA, the decision-maker can fast-track the approval. The proposal will be assessed as low, medium or high risk based on the level of certainty regarding impacts, and this will be used to guide the requirements for site characterisation and EIA. A fast-tracked development is one for which there are sufficient grounds to request consent based on a minimum of one year of survey effort and analysis to understand the characteristics of the receiving environment prior to the application, based on the overall picture given by assessment of the three factors described below.

The classification of a MRE proposal for the purposes of the SDM Guidance depends on three factors: (i) the sensitivity of the receiving environment; (ii) the scale of the proposed deployment; and (iii) the risk posed by the particular technology.[70] Each is graded low, medium, or high based on the available scientific evidence provided by the proponent. The three individual assessments are combined into an overall risk assessment by Marine Scotland Licensing Operations Team (MS-LOT); the final overall assessment is assigned by Marine Scotland based on MS-LOT's recommendations.

Figure 1. Relevant factors for determining risk classification under Scotland's SDM Guidance

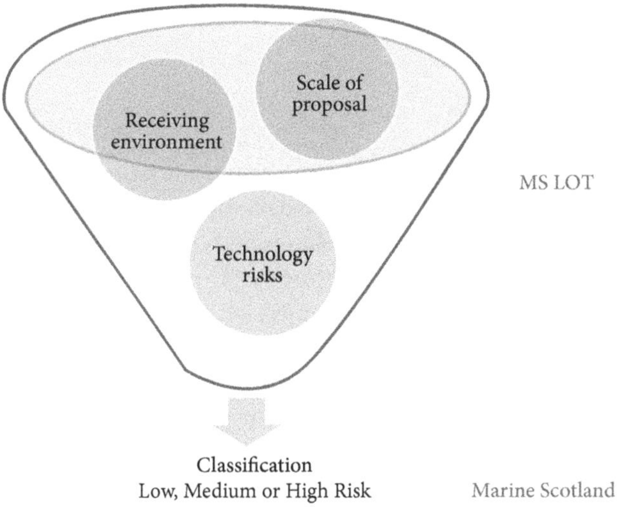

The scale of a development is based on the proposed total installed generating capacity. A small-scale proposal assessed as low risk can be up to 10MW, medium

[70] *Ibid.*

between 10–50MW, and large-scale, and therefore high-risk, developments are those over 50MW.

Regarding the sensitivity of the receiving environment, the regulator undertakes an assessment of the environmental sensitivity of the proposed deployment location based on maps, one each for wave and tidal, which combine data from 19 different datasets. This enables areas of differing sensitivity to be distinguished. These maps are indicative only, are not considered 'complete',[71] and are subject to revision as more data becomes available.

Figure 2. Environmental risk map for wave energy projects in Scotland, showing areas of low, medium and high environmental risk

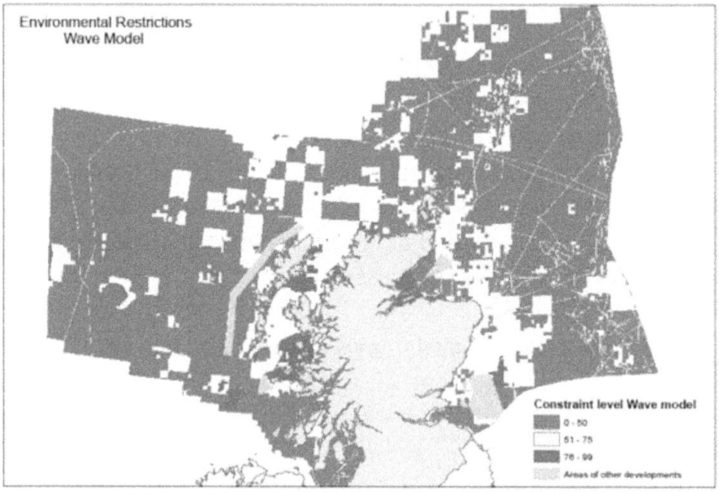

Source: Marine Scotland (2012)[72]

The classification of device risk is based on the potential environmental impacts identified. It is 'an expression of how the device or technology (including moorings or support) is installed, moves, behaves and interacts with the surrounding environment', providing a 'broad assessment of the potential effects of the device on marine life.[73] The SDM Guidance provides a table of impacts that will be considered,[74] but building an exhaustive list would likely prove impossible.

At the low end of the risk scale will be small developments of well-understood technology, in an area of low environmental sensitivity. In this case, the regulator *might* consider fast tracking the application, if the available information is

[71] In that they do not provide an overall assessment of a site's environmental richness, biodiversity, or sensitivity to other forms of development.

[72] *Marine Scotland*, Survey, Deploy and Monitor Licensing Policy Guidance, 2012, p. 8.

[73] *Ibid.*, p. 2.

[74] See *Marine Scotland*, A Review of the Potential Impacts of Wave and Tidal Renewable Energy Developments on Scotland's Marine Environment.

'considered robust or underpinned by strategic survey information'.[75] This will require one year of site characterisation data to inform an EIA and licence application.

At the high end of the scale are large developments utilising a high-risk device, to be deployed in an environmentally sensitive area. Such a proposal would not be suited to a fast-tracking approach. Instead the regulator would require a minimum of two years of site characterisation data in support of the application. The developer would also usually be expected to undertake testing and monitoring of a test device or demonstration array in a different location elsewhere in order to reduce the uncertainty surrounding the interactions of the device with wildlife.[76]

In between the two is a medium-risk deployment, for which it is initially presumed that two years of site characterisation data would be required. However, if the regulator considers that the environmental risk is lower than anticipated, or that the data gathered is adequate to inform the EIA process after one year, it would be 'prepared to discuss relaxation of the requirements for further site characterisation, on receptor-specific or hazard-specific bases'.[77] Marine Scotland call this the '2–1 approach': it envisages that the second year's studies will not be automatically suspended, but continued as the project develops during the second year. The application for a medium risk deployment will normally be supported by data from a relevant demonstration device or devices.

In the event that environmental data generated in the monitoring phase alerts the regulator to the need for further information regarding a particular aspect of the receiving environment or project, the SDM Guidance allows the EIA process to continue in parallel with the additional research, rather than halting the entire consenting process. While the outcome of the consent application will not be determined until all additional data requirements have been met, this flexibility ensures that a lack of data will not significantly slow the approval process for a relatively low risk project where there are only some discrete uncertainties remaining.

This risk assessment should allow more rapid deployment and therefore provide developers with the opportunity to generate new scientific information regarding impacts, without having to study every potential impact in advance to a high level of certainty.

---

75 *Marine Scotland*, Survey, Deploy and Monitor Licensing Policy Guidance, 2012, p. 6.

76 This is based on size: a proposal for a large (>50MW) array should be informed by studies of a smaller 'demonstration array', while in turn a proposal for a demonstration array should be informed by studies of a single demonstration device (and/or relatively smaller demonstration array).

77 *Marine Scotland*, Survey, Deploy and Monitor Licensing Policy Guidance, 2012, pp. 5–6.

5. CHALLENGES

As new innovative industries emerge, project developers are likely to press for a risk-based approach to planning and increasing flexibility. At the same time, regulators may become more reluctant to take risks, stifling development of important innovations. In this context, the Rochdale Envelope and D&M approaches will likely face a number of challenges as their use becomes more widespread and ocean industrialisation advances.

Flexibility will be a key issue. Despite encouraging developments, the level of flexibility provided in the EIA process is often limited. The 'worst-case scenario' developed under the Rochdale Envelope places the perceived potential risks at the extreme end of the scale, while the level of flexibility is assumed to be low and there may be limited opportunity to alter the project outside the envelope.[78] Similarly, the D&M process remain cautious, with only the lowest level of risk allowing for a fast-tracked consent; obtaining this classification will still require considerable investment in research and monitoring on the part of the developer.[79] It also remains to be seen whether the SDM guidance is capable of reliably integrating accumulated scientific knowledge into the process in order to adapt the regulatory approach accordingly.

This reflects a broader tension between precaution and risk. These regulatory tools are most useful to developers when they provide the greatest amount of flexibility, while regulators will generally be most satisfied where the flexibility is constrained and the project, and resultant environmental interactions, can be precisely defined. If a developer is required to submit a rigid project description or to conduct extensive baseline environmental studies, this could result sub-optimal projects being developed, slower development of the technology, and delays in construction.

With this tension in mind, there are a number of potential pitfalls that developers may fall into. An EIS based on a Rochdale Envelope approach may fail to cover all material effects, or an application may be assessed under the SDM Guidance to be high risk where only a relatively small amount of additional scientific knowledge would reduce this classification. Evidently it is easier to ensure that regulations are adhered to if more information is provided, but this translates to greater time and cost, and potentially less flexibility, at the expense of faster development of a renewable energy technology.

A major issue, not immediately apparent from the analysis above, is the relationship between the Rochdale Envelope and cumulative impact assessment. Where a number of project developers each submit an EIS based on the worst-case scenario, the theoretical cumulative impacts of those projects may exceed

---

[78] Walker notes that regulators tend to assume that only minor variations will occur between consenting and construction of the final project. *B. Walker, supra* note 46.

[79] *Marine Scotland*, Survey, Deploy and Monitor Licensing Policy Guidance, 2012, p. 5.

regulatory thresholds for certain environmental receptors. This could cause the regulator to refuse consent, thereby precluding any further consideration of other aspects of the project. This has already happened in the UK in the offshore wind context, where a proposed 540MW offshore wind farm in the North Sea failed to obtain consent.[80]

Figure 3. Graphical representation of cumulative impacts under three hypothetical deployment scenarios

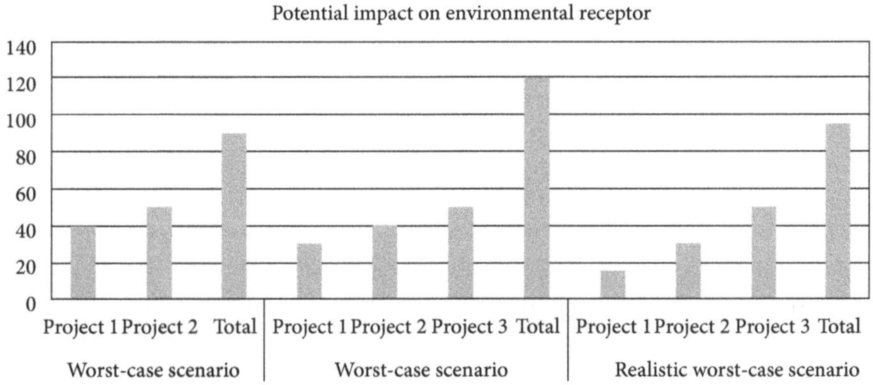

There may be an issue regarding public and stakeholder perception of risk-based approaches function. It is likely that perceptions of unfettered flexibility are likely to cause community opposition. The success of approaches to planning flexibility may therefore depend to some extent on how effectively it can be communicated to stakeholders that environmental effects of the eventual project are fully assessed during the consenting process.

Another stakeholder issue is that increased flexibility can make it more complicated for stakeholders, especially those with limited resources, to engage with the planning process. Where the EIA process is reasonably static, it is much easier to engage; increased flexibility means that stakeholders will likely have more changes, documentation and data to deal with. Stakeholders have already commented on this in relation to the Rochdale Envelope. The Whale and Dolphin Conservation Society stated that it understood the need for the Rochdale envelope approach, but 'without understanding the detailed design of the wave farm it is very difficult ... to comment to a great level of detail'.[81] Likewise, responding to a proposed extension to an offshore wind farm, the Maritime and Coastguard Agency (MCA) noted that 'the vast number of variables suggest that an accurate

80 Centrica's Docking Shoal project. For background, see *K. Shearer*, Assessment of Cumulative Impacts in Offshore Wind Developments, 2013.

81 *Marine Scotland*, Costa Head Wave Farm Orkney, Scoping Opinion, 2012.

worst case scenario cannot be developed'.[82] The MCA agreed in principal to the development, but required further consultation later.

Perhaps one of the most important and overarching issues is the relationship of such approaches to the legal framework within which they are operated. The Rochdale Envelope, for example, has a strong legal foundation in case law, establishing a legally-binding precedent. However D&M, as implemented by the SDM Guidance, is currently only a policy approach put forward by the regulator. As such, there are no legislated underpinnings: the approach is open to challenge by other levels of government and other actors and stakeholders, and even to change or disregard by the regulator itself. As such, the approach cannot be fully relied upon by a developer. The interaction between such policies and the formal legislative arrangements will become clearer over time, but for now it is sufficient to note that there is some concern that the nature of the legislative framework could limit the extent to which purely policy interventions can manage a transition to a more flexible and effective EIA framework.

Even more crucially, the lack of any legal mandate to introduce risk into environmental decision-making is likely to hamper efforts to more rapidly deploy innovative technologies. As a regulator is accountable for the decisions they make within the existing legal framework, they are understandably unlikely to be willing to implement policies that, while striking a sensible balance between ocean energy and concerns regarding potential environmental risks, are contrary to the precautionary principle and the regulatory frameworks based on the principle.

6. FUTURE DEVELOPMENT

It is clear that the Rochdale Envelope and D&M approaches to the EIA process will play a key role in authorising ocean energy projects in UK waters. Depending on how successfully these approaches balance the various competing concerns and interests, it is likely that they will become an important part of regulatory change in the context of the blue economy more generally.

However, it is equally clear that such approaches are not without significant challenges. They must be developed, implemented, and supported by a range of other complementary reforms in planning processes, such as Strategic Environmental Assessment[83] and Marine Spatial Planning.[84] This chapter aimed

82 Statement of Common Ground between DONG Energy Walney Extionsion (UK) Limited and Maritime and Coastguard Agency in Relation to the Proposed Walney Extension Offshore Wind Farm.

83 See *M. Doelle*, The Role of Strategic Environmental Assessments (SEAs) in Energy Governance: A Case Study of Tidal Energy in Nova Scotia, Journal of Energy & Natural Resources Law, 2009, p. 111; *G. Wright, supra* note 46.

84 See *C.A. Thoroughfood,* Marine Spatial Planning: A Call for Action, Oceanography, 2010, (23), p. 9; *A.-M. O'Hagan,* Marine Spatial Planning (MSP) in the European Union and Its

to provide an introduction to the Rochdale Envelope and D&M, as well as a starting point for further discussion and research. In this regard, a number of avenues for research could usefully be pursued.

Firstly, it would be interesting to better understand how developers have used these tools in practice, whether any widespread good practices have emerged, both for regulators and developers, and how their implementation can be improved. In particular it would be helpful to identify and analyse cases where a project was refused planning permission based on an erroneous or overly broad use of the Rochdale Envelope or where a project utilising the SDM Guidance was classified more or less strictly than envisaged. A comparative study with similar approaches in other jurisdictions would be of great interest, if such approaches exist elsewhere.

Secondly, there is an urgent need to better understand how to assess cumulative impacts based on realistic scenarios in the context of the Rochdale Envelope. A principled basis for introducing an element of risk to the existing precautionary approach is needed, though this will not be easy. Any such approach must ensure that projects are facilitated, without compromising the process, the environment, or even the perception of the effectiveness of the process.

Thirdly, there needs to be a much better understanding of how such 'soft' and bottom-up approaches to altering the EIA framework fit in with existing legal mandates and obligations. Without a solid legal foundation, it is unlikely that existing efforts will reach their full potential, or that substantial modifications will ever come to fruition.

Fourth, the relationship between the Rochdale Envelope and D&M and other aspects of planning policy should be explored with the aim of setting out a more comprehensive framework for the balancing of the various interests within EIA processes. The two approaches discussed, as relatively simple and narrowly applicable concepts, can serve only the limited purpose for which they were intended. This is not enough, alone, to ensure that regulators and policymakers are making principled, risk-based decisions in EIA processes that balance both local and global environmental considerations.

Finally, there may be an opportunity for these nuanced approaches to EIA, and similar regulatory developments, to develop into some framework for broader collaborative governance between developers and regulators. This is certainly occurring in Scotland, with Marine Scotland working closely with developers to offer assistance and discuss the developers' approach to the consenting process.

Application to Marine Renewable Energy, International Energy Agency Ocean Energy Systems Implementing Agreement, 2012, www.ocean-energy-systems.org/ocean_energy/in_depth_articles/msp_in_the_european_union/.

7. CONCLUSION

The experience of the MRE industry with existing EIA frameworks suggest that substantial reform is required if the push towards a blue economy agenda is to advance. It is essential that innovative new marine technologies are supported by complementary regulatory frameworks and strong scientific evidence as to their environmental interactions. EIA can play a part in providing both.

A risk-based approach is clearly needed in order to make the best use of existing scientific knowledge and to permit deployment of devices that can generate new knowledge. The Rochdale Envelope and Deploy and Monitor approaches pioneered in the UK provide a starting point for factoring in a certain level of risk in project-level decision-making.

There will, no doubt, be further challenges to the legitimacy and parameters of such approaches as further industrialisation of the marine environment takes place. However, with further research and reform, EIA could become a significant part of efforts in all jurisdictions to better balance precaution with risk, ensure sustainability of innovative new marine activities, and ultimately help progress the blue economy.

PART IV
WATER

CHAPTER 10

THE CASE FOR SMART GOVERNANCE IN EUROPEAN WATER LAW

David SALM*

1. INTRODUCTION

The European Water Framework Directive prohibits deteriorating bodies of surface water and states that it is the common responsibility of all EU Member States to improve the water quality.

Since the Water Framework Directive (WFD)[1] became EU law in 2000, national policy makers and government agencies have struggled to comprehend and properly implement its regulatory reach. Article 4(1)(a)(i) WFD provides that member states need to prohibit deteriorating the status of all bodies of surface water. I will elaborate on this further in section 2.4.

On top of that, Article 4(1)(a)(ii) and (iii) WFD demand the Member States to not just passively prohibit deteriorations, but to take pro-active measures to protect, enhance and restore bodies of surface water in order to gradually reach a good status.[2] I will expand on this provision in section 2.5.

---

* David Salm, c/o Institut für Umwelt- und Planungsrecht, Universitätsstraße 14–16, D-48143 Münster, Germany, +49 251 83 29 795, david.salm@uni-muenster.de. I would like to thank the *Deutsche Bundesstiftung Umwelt* (German Federal Environmental Foundation) for their support in financing my PhD studies and the submission of this chapter through their scholarship programme.

1 Directive 2000/60/EC of the European Parliament and of the Council of 23 October 2000 establishing a framework for Community action in the field of water policy, OJ L327, 22.12.2000, p. 1; most recently amended by Council Directive 2013/64/EU of 17 December 2013 amending Council Directives 91/271/EEC and 1999/74/EC, and Directives 2000/60/EC, 2006/7/EC, 2006/25/EC and 2011/24/EU of the European Parliament and of the Council, following the amendment of the status of Mayotte with regard to the European Union, OJ L353, 28.12.2013, pp. 8–12. I will abbreviate this as 'WFD'. All citations of the WFD refer to its most current version as cited above. Whenever no specific version of the WFD is explicitly cited, I refer to the most current English text version of the law as cited in this footnote.

2 Subparagraph (iii) applies a more lenient standard to artificial and heavily modified bodies of water. For those bodies of water it shall suffice to achieve good ecological potential and good surface water chemical status.

The timeframe of fifteen years granted to accomplish the aforementioned 'good status' is approaching its end. Hardly surprisingly, Member States are nonetheless far from achieving the WFD's ambitious objectives.[3] National authorities increasingly require higher standards before permitting new pollution sources such as coal-fired power plants. Furthermore, national courts are facing the WFD's legal requirements when hearing lawsuits brought before them by citizens and NGOs seeking to repeal the permit of certain activities that might deteriorate the status of water bodies.

In May and July of 2013, respectively, the District Court (*Tingsrätt*) of Östersund (Sweden)[4] and the German Federal Administrative Court (*Bundesverwaltungsgericht*)[5] filed motions with the European Court of Justice (ECJ) requesting a preliminary ruling.[6] The filing courts point out that the WFD's provisions might not only prohibit deteriorations which lead to the assignment of a new – worse – status class in accordance with Article 2 No. 21–23, Annex V (e.g. from 'good' to 'moderate' ecological status), as it is prominently vindicated by operators of polluting enterprises, government agencies and certain EU executives[7] ('status class approach'). Instead, the *Östersunds Tingsrätt* and the *Bundesverwaltungsgericht* suggest that deteriorations which remain below the threshold of assigning a new status class shall also be covered by the prohibition.

The submitting courts proposed a stricter approach which would essentially prohibit any activity that might have a negative impact on the status of bodies of surface water. This so-called 'status quo theory' has gotten quite a bit of traction within the German legal discourse.

On 23 October 2014, Advocate General *Jääskinen* delivered his opinion on the *Weservertiefung*[8] case.[9] *Jääskinen* essentially followed the status quo approach and accordingly recommended the ECJ an answer to the *Bundesverwaltungsgericht*

3 Cf. section 2.5 for further detail.

4 Östersunds Tingsrätt (Sweden), Request for preliminary ruling of 6 May 2013 – M-3173-09, M-10108-11, M 312–13. This motion was dismissed on 20 August 2013 (ECJ, ruling C-251/13 of 20 August 2013) because the plaintiff at the Swedish court withdrew his action.

5 Federal Administrative Court, Request for preliminary ruling of 11 July 2013 – 7 A 20.11, filed under number C-461/13 at the ECJ.

6 As the Swedish motion has been dismissed (cf. *supra* note 4), I will solely refer to the *Bundesverwaltungsgericht's* ECJ case C-461/13 (cf. *supra* note 5) – '*Weservertiefung*' (Dredging of the river Weser).

7 Cf. *K. Faßbender*, Zur aktuellen Diskussion um das Verschlechterungsverbot der Wasserrahmenrichtlinie, Zeitschrift für Europäisches Umwelt- und Planungsrecht (EurUP), 2013 (2), p. 70, 79 et seq. with further references; Advocate General *Jääskinen*, Opinion C-461/13, recitals 22, 34 et seq. (not published in English as of 14 January 2015. Throughout this chapter, I used the German version of *Jääskinen's* opinion as reference).

8 Cf. *supra* note 6.

9 Advocate General *Jääskinen*, Opinion C-461/13.

in the same line.[10] On 1 July 2015, the ECJ gave a judgment affirming this understanding of the law.[11]

I believe that neither the status class nor the status quo approach fully consider the legal provisions of the WFD.

With the ECJ's decision being recently delivered, I aim to outline the upcoming issues and their possible solution for national authorities in implementing the ECJ's judgment.

Disagreeing with crucial aspects of the judgment, I will draft an alternative interpretation of the law. I will focus especially on the matter's implications for the regulation and admission of large-scale projects within the European Union. I will deliver a new interpretation of the WFD's provisions which takes the planning and regulatory leitmotif as much into account as it considers the directive's aim for ambitious environmental protection. In other words, I aim to make a case for smart governance in the application of European water law.

2. THE WATER FRAMEWORK DIRECTIVE'S REGIME

2.1. HISTORICAL OVERVIEW

Before 2000, there was no specific sectorial common approach to regulate the water law within the European Union.[12] Transnational water protection was only ensured when other provisions of European[13] or international[14] law were affected.

Then, whereas 'the conclusions of the Community Water Policy Ministerial Seminar … highlighted the need for Community legislation covering ecological quality'[15] it was deemed 'necessary to develop an integrated Community policy on water'.[16, 17]

---

10 Advocate General *Jääskinen*, Opinion C-461/13, recital 100 et seq. I will expand on *Jääskinen's* opinion in greater detail in section 3.2.

11 ECJ, judgment C-461/13 of 1 July 2015, recital 71.

12 *F. Ekardt & R. Weyland*, Neues vom wasserrechtlichen Verschlechterungsverbot und Verbesserungsgebot, Natur und Recht (NuR) 2014 (36), p. 12.

13 e.g. the former Council Directive No 96/61/EC of 24 September 1996 concerning integrated pollution prevention and control, OJ L257, p. 26 (now succeeded by Directive 2010/75/EU of the European Parliament and of the Council of 24 November 2010 on industrial emissions (integrated pollution prevention and control), OJ L334/17 – IED).

14 e.g. the Convention on Environmental Impact Assessment in a Transboundary Context – Espoo Convention.

15 WFD, recital 2.

16 WFD, recital 9.

17 For a systematic exposition of the WFD's environmental objectives, cf. *H.E. Oldendorp*, Europese waterkwaliteitsnormering in de Kaderrichtlijn water, Tijdschrift voor Omgevingsrecht en Omgevingsbeleid (TOO), 2014 (2), pp. 25–70, recital 8.2.

According to Art. 4(2)(e) TFEU, the competence for legislature in water law (which falls under Art. 191 et seqq. TFEU)[18] is shared between the Union and the Member States. Consequently, according to Article 5(3) TEU, EU regulation may only be applied 'if and in so far as the objectives of the proposed action cannot be sufficiently achieved by the Member States, either at central level or at regional and local level, but can rather, by reason of the scale or effects of the proposed action, be better achieved at Union level'.

To assume that the Water Framework Directive complies with this subsidiarity principle[19] seems particularly compelling when taking into account the transnational effects of water pollution. Rivers are only every so often stand-alone national bodies of waters. Instead, most of them are integrated into a widespread grid starting at the various sources and mostly emptying into the North, Baltic or Mediterranean Sea. From an environmental perspective, it is obvious that as little pollution as possible should be tolerated in total. But on top of that, the limited amount of pollution (in other words: the tolerable total pollution level) should be fairly distributed amongst the riparian states of a certain river grid. From a law and economics perspective, tolerable pollution is a scarce resource,[20] for the distribution of which a property rights approach may seem fit.[21] Thus, if in every Member State polluters would merely have to comply with national pollution thresholds, the polluters in member states that lay closer to the river's source would use up most or all of the pollution level that is deemed tolerable in total.[22] This economic finding has been adopted by the WFD in recital 23.[23]

---

[18] Cf. the commencement clause of the WFD. Note that the WFD was passed into law before the Lisbon Treaty applied, so the Directive originally refers to Art. 175(1) TEC. Furthermore, cf. *C. Calliess*, AEUV Art. 191, in C. Calliess & M. Ruffert (eds.), EUV/AEUV Kommentar, 4th ed., 2011, p. 1918, 1920.

[19] *P. Craig & G. de Búrca*, EU Law – Text, Cases and Materials, 5th ed., 2011, pp. 95–100.

[20] Cf. *R. Perman et al.*, Natural Resource and Environmental Economics, 3rd ed., 2003, p. 4.

[21] *H.-B. Schäfer & C. Ott*, Lehrbuch der ökonomischen Analyse des Zivilrechts, 4th ed., 2005, pp. 549–551, 554–559; *R.N. Stavins*, Economic Incentives for Environmental Regulation, in P. Newman (ed.), The New Palgrave Dictionary of Economics and the Law, 2nd vol., 1998, pp. 6, 9.

[22] In economics, this scenario is known as the tragedy of the commons, cf. *G. Hardin*, The Tragedy of the Commons, Science, 1968 (3859), p. 1243, 1245.

[23] The wording in the WFD's first recital ('water is *not a commercial product* like any other *but, rather, a heritage* which must be protected, defended and treated as such'; emphasis added) might, at superficial glance, lead to the conclusion that the WFD does not deem water or its pollution a commodity or economic resource. However, even if the recital were to be interpreted in this way, this would not contradict the application of economic theory to the legal framework as such. Law and economics does not seek to monetize or commoditize every aspect of life, as some critics (cf. *K.-H. Fezer*, Aspekte einer Rechtskritik an der economic analysis of law und am property rights approach, Juristenzeitung (JZ) 1986, pp. 563–588) suggest (this argument is compellingly refuted by *F. Laudenklos*, Methode und Zivilrecht in der ökonomischen Analyse des Rechts, in J. Rückert & R. Seinecke (eds.), Methodik des Zivilrechts – von Savigny bis Teubner, 2nd ed., 2012, p. 431, 443 et seq.). Rather, the economic analysis of law is a consequentialist social theory (cf. *A. Sen & B. Williams*, Utilitarianism and Beyond, in id. (eds.), Utilitarianism and Beyond, 1982, pp. 1–22) whose proponents such as myself simply

To deter the aforementioned urge for early pollution, a supranational regulatory approach was reasonable.

The WFD implements a bundle of legal tools, a full overview of which exceeds the scope of this chapter.

2.2. RIVER BASIN DISTRICTS

To mark the WFD's holistic regulatory aspiration, Article 3 stipulates that the entire land area (and the rivers it comprises) of the European Union shall be divided into river basin districts.[24] In principle, these districts are to be managed as a whole, rather than just within state borders as before (while the polluted water still flowed downstream and did not stop at the border). However, the management of the river basin districts still remains in the national competences of the Member States, since the European Union does not have the power to execute its directives.[25] In fact, executional competence might even be delegated to state or local level according to national constitutional law.[26] Thus, while the original idea of zoning river basin districts over the entirety of the EU was to ensure a comprehensive environmental approach, the actual achievement of the WFD seems to be merely (but also at least) an intensified level of cooperation among the various Member States.[27]

2.3. RIVER BASIN MANAGEMENT PLANS AND PROGRAMMES OF MEASURES

Based on the river basin districts, the WFD obliges Member States to develop river basin management plans[28] and programmes of measures.[29] The management plans provide a general overview of a river basin district's status. The programmes of measures define efforts which the competent authorities have to undertake in order to comply with the WFD's provisions on water quality. In summary, the

aim to explain legal phenomena with economic tools. Thus, when I use economic arguments to describe legal challenges, I pursue to test and justify a legal answer to a factual problem.

24 A map showing all river basin districts in the European Union and the corresponding GIS data can be found on the European Environmental Agency's website: www.eea.europa.eu/data-and-maps/data/wise-river-basin-districts-rbds-1.

25 Cf. *P. Craig & G. de Búrca*, *supra* note 19, pp. 218 et seq.

26 For a detailed overview of the situation in the EU cf. Report from the Commission to the European Parliament and the Council on the Implementation of the Water Framework Directive (2000/60/EC) – River Basin Management Plans of 14 November 2012, COM(2012) 670 final, p. 35 et seq.

27 In fact, Article 3 WFD states quite trenchantly that it merely governs the *coordination* of administrative arrangements within river basin districts. Cf. also Art. 13(2) WFD.

28 Art. 13 WFD.

29 Art. 11 WFD.

river basin management plans have a descriptive function, while the programmes of measures aspire to set normative requirements to subsequent executive action.

2.4. THE PROHIBITION OF DETERIORATION

As I mentioned earlier,[30] one of the key elements of the WFD's legal regime is the prohibition to deteriorate the status of bodies of surface water. Article 4(1)(a)(i) WFD provides that:

> 'In making operational the programmes of measures specified in the river basin management plans for surface waters, Member States shall implement the necessary measures to prevent deterioration of the status of all bodies of surface water ...'.

This provision effectively establishes a ban on certain activities that deteriorate the water quality.[31] In order to measure the water quality, the WFD and its fifth Annex provide a wide range of indicators. The respective data concerning those indicators for all rivers and other bodies of water are regularly measured and gathered. These data are then assessed and compared to a status that is assumed as normal.[32] Consequently, one of five ecological and two chemical status classes is assigned to all river segments, ranging for ecological status from 'high' via 'good', 'moderate' and 'poor' through to 'bad'. Chemical status is marked as 'good' or 'not good'.[33]

As indicated in the introduction, one major issue with the execution of the WFD is the question what requirements a polluting activity must meet to come

---

[30] Cf. section 1.

[31] *T. Elgeti, S. Fries & R. Hurck*, Der Begriff der Zustands- und Potenzialverschlechterung nach der Wasserrahmenrichtlinie, NuR, 2006 (12), p. 745, 747.

[32] Neither the WFD nor other laws define this 'normal status', which cannot but be seen as a major flaw. It is not even obvious how this normal status shall be defined since almost all bodies of water have been modified and polluted by civilisation for hundreds of years. Art. 4(1)(a)(iii) WFD which governs 'heavily modified' bodies of water only provides little remedy since it is clearly designed to be the exception, not the standard. *M. Reinhardt* powerfully elaborates on this subject in his paper Inventur der Wasserrahmenrichtlinie, NuR, 2013 (35), pp. 765–773. This problem is worsened by the fact that the EU has not even passed common methodological standards, cf. *Bundesverwaltungsgericht* (Federal Administrative Court of Germany), Beschluss (court order) of 2 October 2014, Case 7 A 14.12, ZUR, 2015 (1), pp. 43–45. For a more in-depth analysis from a science (i.e. biological) perspective, cf. *D. Hering et al.*, The European Water Framework Directive at the Age of 10: A Critical Review of the Achievements With Recommendations for the Future, Sci Total Environ, 2010 (19), pp. 4007–4019; *S. Birk et al.*, Three Hundred Ways to Assess Europe's Surface Waters: An Almost Complete Overview of Biological Methods to Implement the Water Framework Directive, Ecological Indicators, 7/2012 (18), pp. 31–41. Unfortunately, Advocate General *Jääskinen* does not recognise the scope of this problem in his opinion, C-461/13, recitals 92 et seq.

[33] Table 1.2 Annex V WFD.

under the deterioration prohibition. I will discuss this immediately in connection with the *Weservertiefung* case in section 3 of my chapter.

However, before I provide a more detailed account, I would like to point out yet another problem with Art. 4(1)(a)(i) WFD. The wording ('In making operational the programmes of measures specified in the river basin management plans') shows that Art. 4 WFD and its prohibition of deterioration cannot be comprehended without recognising the regime of river basin management plans and programmes of measures. The relationship between planning devices such as plans and programmes on the one hand and a self-executing prohibitional provision ('prevent deterioration') on the other hand will turn out to be the crossroads that determine the legal impact of the entire Water Framework Directive. This is not only the case in the *Weservertiefung* action,[34] but also concerning the permission of large-scale projects in the European Union in general. I will elaborate on that in section 4.

2.5. THE IMPERATIVE OF IMPROVING

The Water Framework Directive not only demands Member States to inhibit deteriorating (i.e. polluting) behaviour. Article 4(1)(a)(ii) et seq. states that:

> 'In making operational the programmes of measures specified in the river basin management plan for surface waters, Member States shall *protect, enhance and restore* all bodies of surface water, subject to the application of subparagraph (iii) for artificial and heavily modified bodies of water, *with the aim of achieving good surface water status* at the latest 15 years after the date of entry into force of this Directive ...'.[35]

Subparagraph (iii) applies a more lenient standard to artificial and heavily modified bodies of water.[36]

On 22 December 2015, the deadline[37] for achieving this 'good status' will expire. I would like to emphasise that this deadline is not the usual transposition period that all EU Directives require since they have to be adopted by the member states in order to come into effect.[38] Rather, the deadline is a novel

34 Federal Administrative Court, Request for preliminary ruling of 11 July 2013 – 7 A 20.11, filed under number C-461/13 at the ECJ; cf. section 3.1 for further detail.

35 Emphasis added.

36 For those bodies of water it shall suffice to achieve good ecological potential and good surface water chemical status.

37 *H.E. Woldendorp* provides a comprehensive overview about all relevant implementation time schemes in his paper *supra* note 17, pp. 25–70, recital 4.1.

38 Art. 288(3) TFEU; cf. also *M. Ruffert*, Art. 288 AEUV, in *C. Calliess & M. Ruffert*, EUV/AEUV – Das Verfassungsrecht der Europäischen Union mit europäischer Grundrechtecharta, 2011,

regulatory approach in European governance:[39] It stipulates the timeframe for the achievement of material objectives.[40] This means that Member States must strive to comply with the good surface water status until this date. However, the provision does not command strict liability for the achievement of the objective (i.e. good surface water status throughout the whole of Europe) as such.[41]

The deadline ends less than a year from now. It is virtually undisputed that the improvement imperative will not be met at all. The European Commission published a comprehensive report on the issue stating that as of 2012, only around 44 percent of rivers met the criteria for good or high ecological status.[42] Furthermore, regional studies and publications of Member States' governments on the situation in Germany and England suggest that in these highly industrialised regions, only about 15–30% of rivers and other surface waters will presumably meet the WFD's requirements, i.e. be of 'good' or even 'high' ecological status.[43] Moreover, the data not even suggests that substantial improvement is to be expected any time soon.[44] *M. Reinhardt* has therefore called the improvement imperative a 'normative utopia'.[45] On the bright side, it seems to be at least possible to achieve a good chemical status on a broad scale.[46]

---

recital 51. I will not further elaborate on the ECJ's jurisdiction on direct effect. For reference cf. *P. Craig & G. de Búrca*, *supra* note 19, pp. 191–200.

39 *M. Reinhardt*, *supra* note 32, p. 765, 767.

40 Cf. *A. Epiney*, Umweltrecht in der Europäischen Union, 3rd ed., 2013, pp. 409 et seq. for further detail. She outlines the binding character of this deadline and expands on the wording and history of Art. 4 WFD.

41 Cf. *A. Epiney*, *ibid.*; *J. Albrecht*, Umweltqualitätsziele im Gewässerschutzrecht, 2007, p. 380.

42 Report from the Commission to the European Parliament and the Council on the Implementation of the Water Framework Directive (2000/60/EC) – River Basin Management Plans of 14 November 2012, COM(2012) 670 final, p. 20.

43 Cf. the comprehensive overview on the country of England in *Her Majesty's Government of the United Kingdom of Great Britain and Northern Ireland*, Trends in Pressures on Biodiversity – Surface Water Status, 2014, www.gov.uk/government/uploads/system/uploads/attachment_data/file/382514/21._Surface_Water_Status_2014_final.pdf and the comprehensive overview for the Federal Republic of Germany in *Bundesministerium für Umwelt, Naturschutz, Bau und Reaktorsicherheit* (Federal Ministry for the Environment, Nature Conservation, Building and Nuclear Safety), Die Wasserrahmenrichtlinie – Auf dem Weg zu guten Gewässern, 2010, pp. 21–30; see also *R. Breuer*, Praxisprobleme des deutschen Wasserrechts nach der Umsetzung der Wasserrahmenrichtlinie, NuR, 2007 (29), p. 503, 503 et seq. For a mapped overview on the regional split of surface water status cf. Report from the Commission to the European Parliament and the Council on the Implementation of the Water Framework Directive (2000/60/EC) – River Basin Management Plans of 14 November 2012, COM(2012) 670 final, p. 21.

44 Cf. *Her Majesty's Government of the United Kingdom of Great Britain and Northern Ireland*, Trends in Pressures on Biodiversity – Surface Water Status, 2014, www.gov.uk/government/uploads/system/uploads/attachment_data/file/382514/21._Surface_Water_Status_2014_final.pdf, figure 21.1.

45 *M. Reinhardt*, *supra* note 32, p. 765, 765 et seq. Cf. also *R. Breuer*, *supra* note 43, pp. 503–513.

46 Report from the Commission to the European Parliament and the Council on the Implementation of the Water Framework Directive (2000/60/EC) – River Basin Management Plans of 14 November 2012, COM(2012) 670 final, p. 21 et seq.; *Bundesministerium für Umwelt, Naturschutz, Bau und Reaktorsicherheit*, Die Wasserrahmenrichtlinie – Auf dem Weg zu guten Gewässern, 2010, pp. 27–30.

Considering this, most scholars predict the European water regime to 'switch into a state of exception'[47] with regard to Member States presumably widely making use of the exemption rules under Art. 4(7) WFD from Article 4(1)(a)(ii)'s provisions by 22 December 2015.[48] In light of the fact that this exemption was not designed for extensive application[49] and therefore does not include a notification procedure,[50] theoretically, a three- or four-figure number of legal conflicts might arise between the European Commission and Member States in 2016.[51] Therefore, the subtly perceivable enforcement deficit of the WFD impends to burst out in several infringement proceedings at the ECJ.

2.6 INTERIM FINDINGS

The WFD provides a variety of legal tools to conserve and improve the water quality of rivers in the European Union. The key notion is the requirement to comprehensively assess and plan the management of river basin districts. The ecological or chemical status of said districts is not to be deteriorated. On top of that, member states must take action to actively improve the water quality. In summary, there are three major issues to be resolved:

- First, it is unclear how the regulatory planning approach concerning the programmes of measures interacts with the prohibition of deteriorating behaviour. On a methodological level, this is a systematic conflict between a modern regulatory instrument[52] and a classic top-down ban (classified by some legal scholars as an instrument of direct behavioural control).[53] In particular, it is uncertain whether precedent planning is an essential prerequisite for Art. 4(1)(a)(i).

---

47 *M. Reinhardt, supra* note 32, p. 765, 773.

48 *W.F. Spieth & N.C. Ipsen*, Die Wasserrahmenrichtlinie als neues Damoklesschwert für Genehmigungsprojekte?, Neue Zeitschrift für Verwaltungsrecht (NVwZ), 2013, p. 391, 393 et seq.; *M. Reinhardt, supra* note 32, p. 765, 773.

49 *F. Ekardt & R. Weyland* critically elaborate on this issue in their paper *supra* note 12, p. 12, 18.

50 Art. 108(3) TFEU could have been a model for such a clause, but a chance to implement this in the WFD with the necessary member states' consent in the counsel seems to be very unlikely now that national governments increasingly start to realise the economic implications of the WFD's provisions.

51 Cf. *R. Breuer, supra* note 43, p. 503, 513.

52 *R. Breuer, supra* note 43, p. 503, 505 et seq.; Report from the Commission to the European Parliament and the Council on the Implementation of the Water Framework Directive (2000/60/EC) – River Basin Management Plans of 14 November 2012, COM(2012) 670 final, p. 30; with regard to the general notion of regulatory instruments in environmental law cf. *W. Erbguth & S. Schlacke*, Umweltrecht, 5th ed., 2014, pp. 78–83.

53 *W. Erbguth & S. Schlacke, supra* note 52, pp. 83–86.

- In addition, the word 'deterioration' needs to be interpreted.[54] In particular, it shall be examined how intense a polluting activity has to be in order to amount to a deterioration.
- Last but not least, the systematic connection between items (i) and (ii)as well as (iii) within Art. 4(1)(a) WFD proves to be relevant for answering both the first and the second question.

3. THE *WESERVERTIEFUNG* CASE

As indicated in the introduction, the German Federal Administrative Court (*Bundesverwaltungsgericht*) filed a motion for preliminary ruling with the European Court of Justice in order to resolve certain questions, particularly concerning the provisions set by Art. 4 WFD.[55] In the case pending at the *Bundesverwaltungsgericht*, an environmental protection NGO (the Bund für Umwelt und Naturschutz Deutschland – BUND) challenged the legality of a planned dredging of the River Weser.[56] BUND argues that dredging the Weser will most likely result in a deterioration of its ecological status. They claim that among other things, several tidal effects will be amplified.[57] Since the *Bundesverwaltungsgericht* doubted the conformity of the Weser dredging with EU law, it tabled the decision after oral argument and filed the aforementioned motion with the ECJ. Meanwhile, the dredging project remains suspended until a decision is delivered.

3.1. THE *BUNDESVERWALTUNGSGERICHT*'S QUESTIONS TO THE ECJ

Compliant with ECJ preliminary ruling procedure,[58] the *Bundesverwaltungsgericht* asked the Court the following questions concerning the interpretation and application of EU law:[59]

1. Is Art. 4(1)(a)(i) WFD to be interpreted as meaning that Member States must – unless a derogation is granted – refuse to authorise a project if it may cause

[54] On a methodological level, this question is a classic legal exegesis, as opposed to the first issue. However, systematic comparisons remain of course a tool of legal analysis, cf. *J. Rückert & R. Seinecke*, Zwölf Methodenregeln für den Ernstfall, in *ibid.* (eds.), Methodik des Zivilrechts – von Savigny bis Teubner, 2nd ed., 2012, p. 23, 28 et seq.

[55] ECJ case C-461/13 – '*Weservertiefung*'.

[56] Bundesverwaltungsgericht – BVerwG, court order of 11 July 2013, 7 A 20.11 – Deutsche Verwaltungsblätter – DVBl. 2013, pp. 1450–1453.

[57] Cf. Bundesverwaltungsgericht – BVerwG, court order of 11 July 2013, 7 A 20.11, recital 8.

[58] Cf. *P. Craig & G. de Búrca*, *supra* note 19, pp. 449 et seq.

[59] ECJ, judgment C-461/13 of 1 July 2015, recital 28.

a deterioration in the status of a body of surface water, or is that provision merely a statement of an objective for management planning?
2. Is the term 'deterioration of the status' in Art. 4(1)(a)(i) WFD to be interpreted as covering only detrimental changes which lead to classification in a lower class in accordance with Annex V of the WFD?
3. If the second question is to be answered in the negative: under what circumstances does a 'deterioration of the status' within the meaning of Art. 4(1)(a)(i) WFD arise?
4. Are the provisions of Art. 4(1)(a)(ii) and (iii) WFD to be interpreted as meaning that the Member States must – unless a derogation is granted – refuse to authorise a project if it jeopardises the attainment of good surface water status or of good ecological potential and good surface water chemical status by the date laid down by the directive, or are those provisions merely a statement of an objective for management planning?

The ECJ heard this case on 8 July 2014. Consequently, Advocate General *Jääskinen* delivered his opinion on the case on 23 October 2014. The ECJ decided the case on 1 July 2015.[60]

Thus, I will focus on two aspects. I will discuss what consequences arise from the judgment for project planners and national authorities. Secondly, I will provide my own interpretation of the legal issues at stake that in some respects differs from the ECJ's.

3.2. ADVOCATE GENERAL *JÄÄSKINEN*'S OPINION

Advocate General *Jääskinen* questioned the logical consistency of the *Bundesverwaltungsgericht*'s question in his opinion.[61] Instead of simply answering them, he starts with arguing that it might be preferable to sum them up into two blocks:[62]

According to *Jääskinen*, questions one and four of the request concern the notion whether Art. 4 WFD was merely a general objective for river basin management planning or whether it prohibits – except when an exemption applies – the realisation of water deteriorating projects.[63]

Respectively, questions two and three of the request concern the interpretation of the term 'deterioration of the status'.[64]

60 ECJ, judgment C-461/13 of 1 July 2015.
61 Advocate General *Jääskinen*, Opinion C-461/13, recitals 28, 85.
62 Such a summary has already been proposed by *F. Ekardt* and *R. Weyland* in their paper *supra* note 12, p. 12, 14, though Advocate General *Jääskinen* does not refer to it in his opinion.
63 Advocate General *Jääskinen*, Opinion C-461/13, recital 29.
64 Advocate General *Jääskinen*, Opinion C-461/13, recital 30.

I would like to point out that *Jääskinen*'s – and the ECJ's[65] – technique of summing up and altering the submitting court's motion is quite questionable. It is not the ECJ's[66] duty to answer its own questions – *nemo iudex sine actore* – but rather to answer precisely those questions that the submitting court brought up. If the ECJ considers the submitting court's questions so ill-framed that it deems itself entirely unfit to properly answer them, it remains at liberty to dismiss the submitting court's motion on grounds of estoppel.[67] However, if the court decides to answer the questions raised, it may not exceed their wording without infringing *ne ultra petita*. Neither the Advocate General nor the ECJ even revisit the initial questions in their concluding arguments.[68] *Jääskinen's* entire opinion is based on his own reinterpretation of the questions. This technique has prominently been used by the German *Bundesverfassungsgericht* (Federal Constitutional Court) in its disputed *Nassauskiesungsbeschluss*[69] – a decision on a very similar matter as pending with the ECJ in the *Weservertiefung* case. With this approach, poignancy is lost.[70] This becomes obvious in *Jääskinen*'s opinion because his summary of the second and third question brought up by the *Bundesverwaltungsgericht* ignores the improvement imperative and solely focuses on the deterioration prohibition.[71] This judicial activism style of freely reframing carefully shaped questions of Member States' courts is even more dangerous in an EU context considering the diverse cultures of legal systems within the European Union and the European Court of Justice's task to interpret European law while respecting national legal heritage – even more so if this technique is nonchalantly used apodictically stating 'it [were] appropriate to deal with [the questions raised by the national court] together'.[72]

3.2.1. Article 4 WFD as a Self-Executing Norm

The first part of *Jääskinen*'s opinion sets the course for his line of thought. He argues that while the WFD does not fully harmonise European water law, it also does not stop at providing a programmatic approach that is sought to be

65 ECJ, judgment C-461/13 of 1 July 2015, recitals 29, 52.

66 The Advocate General is a full member of the ECJ under Art. 19(2)(2) TEU, cf. *P. Craig & G. de Búrca*, *supra* note 19, p. 62, thus this notion equally applies to him or her.

67 Cf. Art. 21(1) Statute of the Court of Justice.

68 Advocate General *Jääskinen*, Opinion C-461/13, recital 110; ECJ, judgment C-461/13 of 1 July 2015, recital 71.

69 Entscheidungen des Bundesverfassungsgerichts, volume 58, pp. 300 et seq.

70 For example, the *Bundesverwaltungsgericht* has raised questions two, three and four under the condition that question one is answered affirmatively, cf. Bundesverwaltungsgericht – BVerwG, court order of 11 July 2013, 7 A 20.11 – Deutsche Verwaltungsblätter – DVBl 2013, p. 1450, 1451. Therefore, combining questions one and four, *Jääskinen* already chose the path for the answer to the first question to necessarily be 'yes'.

71 He does, however, come back to this problem in recital 39. From a logical standpoint, this means that he answered a question which he neglected to exist in the first place.

72 ECJ, judgment C-461/13 of 1 July 2015, recitals 29, 52. This statement falls short of an intelligible reasoning as to why 'it is appropriate'. Moreover, it withholds the important fact that the questions at hand are not simply merged, but also altered.

implemented in river basin management plans and programmes of measures.[73] In their statement to the court, the Dutch government particularly propagated the latter.[74] *Jääskinen* rather proposes that Art. 4 WFD is directly applicable to the approval regime for projects, making this provision a self-executing norm. *Jääskinen* acknowledges, however, that the textual link for this interpretation in the WFD is somewhat uncertain.[75] He does not explicitly mention dissenting opinions from EU executives on this matter, but still references them in footnote 34. That said, his statement that a self-executing interpretation of Art. 4 WFD is 'the only one that meets its wording as well as its purpose' seems rather bold. I will come back to this issue in section 4. In summary, *Jääskinen* argues that all provisions of Art. 4 WFD are directly applicable without the need for transposition through administrative or governmental second-order measures.

3.2.2. The Interpretation of 'Deterioration' and 'Good Status'

The scope of Advocate General *Jääskinen*'s answer to the *Bundesverwaltungsgericht*'s first and fourth question can only be grasped when also taking into account his proposition for the second and third question which concern the deterioration prohibition and the imperative of improving.

As I already indicated in the introduction, there are two major ways in which the word 'deterioration' is understood.[76]

Some legal scholars have proposed that a 'deterioration' of the surface water body's status occurs when it has to be reassigned to a new – worse – status class according to Annex V WFD – hence it's description as status *class* approach.[77] For obvious reasons, this interpretation was and is popular with governments of heavily industrialised member states.[78]

As I have outlined, five status classes are defined into which all bodies of surface water (or sections thereof) are assessed under Article 2 No. 21–23, Annex V WFD. This assessment process and especially the applied indicators are neither coherent nor transparent throughout all Member States of the European Union.[79]

---

73 Advocate General *Jääskinen*, Opinion C-461/13, recital 54.

74 Advocate General *Jääskinen*, Opinion C-461/13, recital 34; consenting *H.E. Oldendorp*, *supra* note 19, pp. 25–70, recital 12.3. Cf. also *B. Stüer & E.-M. Stüer*, Anmerkung zu BVerwG, Vorlagebeschluss und Hinweisbeschluss vom 11.07.2013 – 7 A 20.11 – Weservertiefung, Deutsche Verwaltungsblätter – DVBl. 2013, p. 1457, 1458.

75 Advocate General *Jääskinen*, Opinion C-461/13, recital 58.

76 Cf. Advocate General *Jääskinen*, Opinion C-461/13, recitals 90 et seqq.

77 This approach is proposed by *W. Köck*, Die Implementation der Wasserrahmenrichtlinie, ZUR, 2009 (5), p. 227, 229 et seq.; *T. Elgeti, S. Fries & R. Hurck*, *supra* note 31, p. 745, 747 et seq.; *J. Albrecht*, *supra* note 42, p. 346 et seq.; *R. Breuer*, *supra* note 43, p. 503, 507; *W.F. Spieth & N.C. Ipsen*, *supra* note 48, p. 391, 392 et seq. The notion of a status class versus a status quo approach/theory is so prevelant in legal literature that the ECJ referred to this terminology in its judgment.

78 Advocate General *Jääskinen*, Opinion C-461/13, recitals 22, 34 et seq., 89.

79 Cf. section 2.4 for further detail.

However, once level indicators have been checked, the next step is not immediately to assign an overall status class to a body of surface water (or sections thereof). Rather, there are several subcategories, all of which are valued with the five status classes. The lowest score throughout the different subcategories (not their average value) then determines the final status class of a body of surface water. Therefore, in Figure 1 the body of surface water would be assigned a 'poor' overall rating.

Figure 1. The lowest-scoring subcategory determines a surface water body's overall ecological status

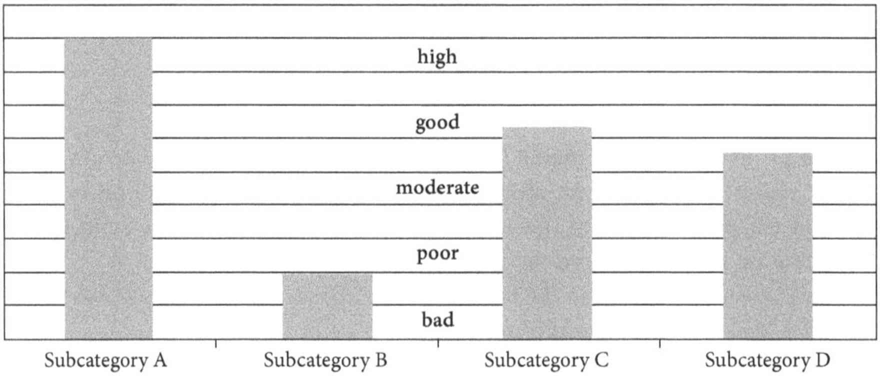

It can easily be understood what troubles could arise within this 'one out, all out' method.[80] A new project typically does not affect all subcategories in the same way. For example, the discharge of hot water into a river might affect fish habitats but have no influence at all on the river's velocity or salinity. Due to the 'one out, all out' rule, such impacts are handled differently according to the (in principle unrelated) *ex ante* status of other subcategories. Only if the worst subcategory is negatively influenced and only if this happens in such a way that this subcategory has to be reassigned a worse status, the status class approach acknowledges the impact as 'deteriorating' within the meaning of Art. 4 WFD. Due to this, the example in Figure 2 would not qualify as deterioration while the example in Figure 3 would.

80 Cf. Advocate General *Jääskinen*, Opinion C-461/13, recital 102.

Figure 2. The significant deterioration of subcategory A has no effect on the overall status rating

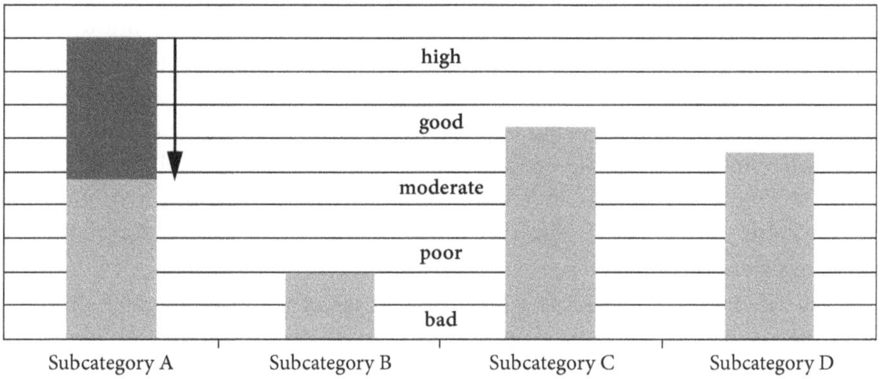

Figure 3. The slight deterioration of the lowest-scoring subcategory leads to an overall demotion into a lower status class

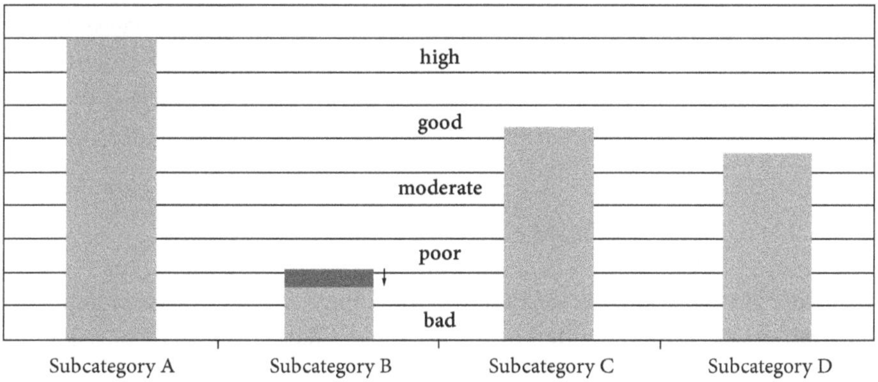

This could lead to adverse effects: new pollutions might be permitted again and again until the water quality is diminished to a low threshold throughout all subcategories without infringing the deterioration prohibition. This contradicts the environmental reasoning of the WFD.

Therefore, most legal scholars as well as the *Bundesverwaltungsgericht*, prefer another approach: the so-called status quo theory.[81] Its proponents point out that the status classes have a mere descriptive function that should not be

[81] This approach is represented by *A. Epiney, supra* note 40, p. 400; *M. Gellermann*, Gewässerausbau im Lichte des neuen wasserwirtschaftlichen Ordnungsrahmens, Deutsche Verwaltungsblätter – DVBl 2007, p. 1517, 1519 et seq.; *F. Ekardt & R. Weyland, supra* note 12, p. 12, 17; *B. Söhnlein*, Das Verschlechterungsverbot der §§ 25a I Nr. 1, 25b I Nr. 1 WHG in der Planfeststellung, Neue Zeitschrift für Verwaltungsrecht – NVwZ 2006, p. 1139, 1140; *S.R. Laskowski*, Kohlekraftwerke im Lichte der EU-Wasserrahmenrichtline, ZUR, 2013, p. 131, 132 et seq.

utilised to interpret the term 'deterioration'. Moreover, the question of the systematic connection between the deterioration prohibition and the imperative of improvement[82] proves to be relevant in this context. Even if the Water Framework Directive actually intended to prohibit only those deteriorations that also lead to the reassignment of a worse status class for the surface water body, the deterioration prohibition still has to promote the good status objective to be achieved. Moreover, comparing this approach to the former, in its constriction on the classification processes result, the status class approach fails to regard the issues arising from the classification process itself. I agree with the proponents of the status quo approach that this unintentionally incentivises deterioration-inducing measures.

The advocates of the status quo theory, on the other hand, might exceed the wording of the law when they propose that every single negative influence on surface waters should be considered deterioration. In section 4, I will sketch out the regulatory approach of the WFD which commands a high level of government planning and which is not as concerned with prohibiting new polluting activities as the proponents of the status quo theory suggest.

In essence, Advocate General *Jääskinen* follows the status quo theory,[83] which seems reasonable considering the aforementioned arguments when viewed as an isolated legal question. However, in combination with his view on the question of self-execution of Art. 4 WFD[84] and certain *obiter dicta* in his opinion, this could hinder a smart governance approach.[85]

3.3. THE ECJ'S JUDGMENT

On 1 July 2015, the ECJ decided the matter.[86] Judge *Berger* of Austria delivered the opinion as Rapporteur in which the Grand Chamber of the Court joined. In essence, the court followed *Jääskinen*'s reasoning, thus my commentary in section 3.2 applies.[87]

The differences between the Advocate General's opinion and the ECJ's ruling lay not so much in the line of argument, but rather in minor changes concerning the legal consequences. The court does not deviate from *Jääskinen's* general recommendations, but it specifies them. While *Jääskinen* provided a variety of

---

82 Cf. section 2.6.

83 Advocate General *Jääskinen*, Opinion C-461/13, recital 109.

84 Cf. section 3.2.1.

85 I will elaborate on this in section 4.

86 ECJ, judgment C-461/13 of 1 July 2015. Since the proceedings were initiated by a request for preliminary ruling, the German *Bundesverwaltungsgericht* (federal administrative court) will now eventually have to decide about the legality of the dredging of the river Weser.

87 This chapter was essentially written based upon *Jääskinen*'s opinion. However, as is shown here, it applies to the ECJ's judgment since the Court basically followed the Advocate General's recommendations as it most frequently does, cf. *P. Craig & G. de Búrca*, *supra* note 19, p. 62.

possible interpretations for the prohibition of deterioration, the ECJ narrowed this down. Consequently, it ruled that the deterioration of one of the quality elements for determining the overall status class of a body of surface water suffices for a 'deterioration' to apply.[88] It also concludes that Member States' authorities are obliged to refuse authorisation for an individual project if the project impeded the status class in the described manner.[89]

3.4. CONSEQUENCES FOR LARGE-SCALE INDUSTRIAL PROJECTS

Recapitulating *Jääskinen*'s recommendations and the ECJ's judgment, the situation for projects with the potential of water pollution seems to be quite difficult.

On the one hand, every single polluting activity shall qualify as deterioration as soon as it deters the quality of one element of the overall surface water body score. And while most scholars who proposed the status quo approach still remained certain that at least a de minimis threshold shall apply, Advocate General *Jääskinen* bluntly reviews this problem in only one recital of his opinion, 'anyway wanting to indicate that neither the wording nor the objective of the WFD … could acknowledge the existence of a de minimis threshold'.[90] However, the ECJ neither adopted nor rejected this notion.

On the other hand, the ECJ interprets Art. 4(1) to not primarily be a programmatic norm addressed to the planning administration but as a self-executing prohibition that directly applies to project approval.[91]

These notions merge into the ECJ's answer to the submitting court's question that 'Member States are required … to refuse authorisation for an individual project where it may cause a deterioration of the status of a body of surface water'.[92]

I cannot stress enough how sweepingly severe the consequences of this interpretation of the law are. Every water-related industrial project – particularly if of large scale – inevitably has an ever so slight negative impact on certain qualities of the respective body of surface water. If every single one of these impacts shall constitute deterioration within the meaning of the law as soon as one quality indicator is impaired (explicitly without granting the option to

88 ECJ, judgment C-461/13 of 1 July 2015, recital 69.

89 ECJ, judgment C-461/13 of 1 July 2015, recital 71. However, the Court's reasoning does not lead to this conclusion systematically, cf. recital 50. Premise and conclusions do not match up.

90 Advocate General *Jääskinen*, Opinion C-461/13, recital 108. This finding is not compromised by *Jääskinen*'s reassurance that there was a threshold which is 'that one, which derives from applicable Union law as laid down in the 51st recital of the Directive in conjunction with Art. 4(8) and (9) as well as Art. 11(3)(a) WFD'. These norms don't include any thresholds whatsoever.

91 ECJ, judgment C-461/13 of 1 July 2015, recital 43.

92 ECJ, judgment C-461/13 of 1 July 2015, recital 71.

weigh up the consequences!),[93] such projects are simply no longer approvable. My colleague *L. Löffler* points out in her submission to this book how a different part of the WFD might prohibit coal-fired power plants[94] – that is *de lege lata*, not future tense and most certainly not just *de lege ferenda*.[95]

It was therefore not panic or exaggeration but mere hindsight when *W.F. Spieth and N.C. Ipsen* asked whether the Water Framework Directive was 'industrial projects' new sword of Damocles' in their eponymous paper.[96]

That said, it seems unlikely that the WFD will actually be enforced in the exact same way that is technically pre-set by the ECJ's judgment. Member States will not simply seize to permit large-scale industrial projects and from an institutional economics standpoint it will be the rational thing for them not to do so. The ECJ's questionable[97] technique of summing up the submitting court's questions into new ones that don't fully add up to the originally raised ones provides the Member States with a loophole of discretion that they will gratefully use.

As I have delineated above, Art. 4 WFD and its timetable have been described as a 'normative utopia'.[98] The European Commission will hardly initiate infringement proceedings for every project that is admitted from 23 December 2015 onwards and it has not done so yet although, as I pointed out above, the deterioration prohibition has been applicable law as of the early 2000s.[99]

Member States will most likely claim exemptions under Art. 4(7) WFD for all projects they regard politically and economically desirable – a way explicitly opened by the ECJ's judgment.[100] As I indicated, this exemption rule does not provide a mandatory notification procedure,[101] which further decreases the chance of infringement proceedings to be initiated. Then again, this also increases legal uncertainty as the Commission might find out about the admission anyway by chance after some time would have passed and would then initiate proceedings. This leads to follow-up problems concerning *effet utile* since admissions might have gained legal finality under national administrative law.

NGOs will probably continue to intensify their legal actions against admissions on ground of an alleged infringement of Art. 4(1) WFD, particularly concerning large-scale projects. If Member States' administrations and courts had not been aware of the issue before the *Weservertiefung* case,[102] they certainly

---

93 ECJ, judgment C-461/13 of 1 July 2015, recital 69.

94 Cf. also *S.R. Laskowski*, *supra* note 81, pp. 131–143; *W.F. Spieth & N.C. Ipsen*, *supra* note 48, p. 391, 395.

95 See *L. Löffler* in this volume.

96 *W.F. Spieth & N.C. Ipsen*, *supra* note 48, pp. 391–395.

97 Cf. section 3.2.

98 Cf. section 2.5.

99 Cf. section 2.5.

100 ECJ, judgment C-461/13 of 1 July 2015, recital 71.

101 Cf. section 2.5.

102 And, shortly before that, the *Östersunds Tingsrätt* case, cf. *supra* note 6.

are now. This might lead to longer average admission procedures and less legal certainty for investors.

The admission of otherwise (i.e. apart from water law aspects) not objectionable projects will either fall under a narrow exemption rule or not be legally possible after all. This might lead to a subtle shift within admission practice that prefers politically desirable projects, as administrations might be more willing to invest the political capital to risk legal contest of their decisions than they would be with other businesses. In particular, it seems possible that private investors may be left unconsidered as opposed to public infrastructure planning. This problem is escalated even further by the wording of Art. 4(7) WFD[103] which, among other things, provides that 'the reasons for those modifications or alterations are of overriding public interest'. Under the aspects of rule of law, due process and legal equality, this situation is substantially undesirable.

4. THE CASE FOR SMART GOVERNANCE

Member States' secretaries hardly intended the WFD to be the end of virtually all industrial project admissions by the end of 2015.[104] And though a contradictory intention of the lawmaker is already a strong argument in itself, I would also like to alert to some hermeneutical aspects of the WFD in order to reinforce my line of thought. These aspects help raise doubts whether the Advocate General's concluding arguments and the ECJ's judgment really hit the spot concerning the WFD's *ratio legis*.

Art. 4(1) WFD does provide that deteriorations are prohibited. And indeed, I concur with the ECJ that the narrow status class interpretation does not satisfy the environmental ambition of the law. However, the Court's judgment fails to acknowledge the full wording of Art. 4 WFD which reads: 'In making operational the programmes of measures specified in the river basin management plans Member States shall ...'. In fact, on a systematic level, this provision applies to all legal aspects discussed above.

Thus, a normative planning approach is the starting point for all legal considerations concerning Art. 4 WFD.[105] It is crucial to keep this in mind when applying the deterioration prohibition or discussing the self-executing character of said norm. And while it is clear that the starting point of a thought process does not necessarily constitute its ending,[106] it is evenly problematic to forget about it altogether. If Art. 4 WFD really was – as *Jääskinen* argues – primarily if not entirely self-executing, the first sentence would be of no semantic relevance

103 As I indicated in section 2.5, this provision will most likely come into use on a wide scale from 23 December 2015 on.
104 Cf. *W.F. Spieth & N.C. Ipsen*, *supra* note 48, p. 391, 395.
105 Cf. *W. Köck*, *supra* note 77, p. 227, 229.
106 As *Jääskinen* correctly points out in his opinion, recital 67.

whatsoever. In fact, that sentence would be exclusively programmatic itself, although *Jääskinen* and the ECJ explicitly refused the notion of a programmatic legal wording. Therefore, their argument becomes circular and disbands.

If Art. 4 WFD was indeed entirely self-executing and if Member States retained no discretion, planning new projects would come to a halt. The result would not only impair the economic development of the European Union. It would also have adverse effects on the environment in the long run. If no new and efficient coal-fired power plants could be built, old and less efficient ones will become more profitable and would stay on the grid for years to come. Alternatively, factories, power plants and other large-scale projects would be externalised to countries bordering the European Union, hence increasing overall pollution levels while formally complying with the WFD as interpreted by the ECJ.

Even the European Commission has stated that the Water Framework Directive's approach is explicitly governmental and that it employs new techniques rather than just remaining in the old prohibition scheme of grandfathered law.[107] A smart way for Member States to apply this would be to assess which deteriorations are economically viable and which are not. These considerations would enhance the normative vigour of river basin management plans and programmes of measures. This is especially compelling in pollution-intensive sectors like energy production. Over the past years, detailed data of large-scale projects' contribution to water pollution has been aggregated under the WFD's regime. The pollution values could be compared to the effective output of single large-scale projects (e.g. produced megawatts of electric energy). This provides Member States' authorities with comparison data which could be used in determining which large-scale projects shall be entitled to pollution rights through building and water law permits.

I would like to stress that I do not want to condone centrally planned economic policy. In the unfortunate absence of market economy tools – like a pollution property rights market governed by a cap-and-trade policy – certain government interventions are needed in order to balance out inefficiencies caused by primary market interventions such as environmental policy.[108]

My argument is that Member States are merely obliged to think beyond the specific projects at hand when deciding about their approval under the WFD.[109] Otherwise, economically and environmentally inefficient projects would engage in a race to claim the scarce resource of acceptable deterioration.[110] Soon, no new

---

107 Cf. Report from the Commission to the European Parliament and the Council on the Implementation of the Water Framework Directive (2000/60/EC) – River Basin Management Plans of 14 November 2012, COM(2012) 670 final, pp. 30 et seqq.

108 This basic notion of the 'intervention spiral' has been described by *L. v. Mises*, Kritik des Interventionismus, 1929.

109 Unfortunately, the Advocate General *Jääskinen* refutes this notion without providing insight as to why, cf. Advocate General *Jääskinen*, Opinion C-461/13, recital 69. The same holds true for the ECJ's judgment, recital 68.

110 Cf. section 2.1.

projects could be admitted for a long time. This approach directly derives from Article 4(1) WFD: what other objective could the commandment to 'mak[e] operational the programmes of measures specified in the river basin management' have indeed if not to hurdle the national acquis of mere *ex-post* regulation? This crucial aspect is what the ECJ's judgment essentially remains short on.

The smart governance approach would effectively lead to the shutdown of old, inefficient and relatively heavily polluting projects in exchange for new, more efficient ones, thereby gradually improving water quality in pursuit of the 'good status' in implementing river basin management plans and programmes of measures through the legal tool of project approval. My proposal combines the governance notion of Art. 4 WFD with its improvement imperative. At the same time, Member States' discretion remains respected and the door for economic innovation through competitive federalism is left open.

Of course, this raises issues of potential expropriation claims. These must be answered according to applicable Member States' law – albeit compliant to the European legal principles of adequacy and effectiveness.

A dynamic economy in which progress has room to breathe is preferable to the impending stagnancy and legal uncertainty that arises from the incautious ECJ judgment.

CHAPTER 11

COAL-FIRED POWER PLANTS UNDER EU WATER LAW:

The Phasing-Out Requirement of Priority Hazardous Substances – An Obstacle to the Permission of Coal-Fired Power Plants?

Lisa LÖFFLER*

1. INTRODUCTION

Despite technological progress and the use of the latest filtering systems coal-fired plants still unavoidably discharge mercury into the environment.[1] Mercury is a heavy metal that is considered highly toxic to human health and the ecosystems.[2] In order to avert the particular hazard of mercury it has been added to the list of priority hazardous substances under Annex X of the Water Framework Directive[3] in 2001. Annex X[4] includes all priority substances, the emission, discharge, and loss into the environment of which need to be stopped or gradually ended. This provision is usually referred to as the phasing-out requirement which demands an

* The author is a PhD candidate and research fellow at the Institute of Environmental and Planning Law, Münster University, Germany. Her PhD studies are promoted by a scholarship of the German Federal Environmental Foundation (DBU).

1 *K. Sundseth et al.*, Substance Flow Analysis of Mercury Affecting Water Quality in the European Union, Water, Air, & Soil Pollution, 2012 (223), p. 429, 432 et seq.

2 Communication from the European Commission to the European Parliament and the Council: COM (2005) 20 final, Community Strategy Concerning Mercury, p. 1, 2 et seq.; *UNEP*, Mercury – Time to Act, p. 1, 23 et seq., www.unep.org/PDF/PressReleases/Mercury_TimeToAct_hires.pdf; EEB & zero mercury working group, Opportunities to reduce mercury emissions through the Thematic Strategy on Air Pollution (TSAP) review and the revision of the National Emission Ceilings (NEC) Directive, p. 1, www.eeb.org/?LinkServID=AD428325-5056-B741-DBD38576E1DD11C9&showMeta=0&aa.

3 European Parliament and Council Directive 2000/60/EC establishing a framework in the field of water policy, OJ 2000 L327/1.

4 Last amendment of Annex X by European Parliament and Council Directive 2013/39/EU on priority substances in the field of water policy, OJ 2013 L226/1.

end to emissions of the listed substances. It is one of the key goals of the Directive, as it is expressly mentioned in the purpose of the WFD (Art. 1(c)) WFD).

Acknowledging the impact of mercury on human health and ecosystems, this contribution considers the legal implications of the phasing-out requirement for the permission of coal-fired power plants. The chapter is structured in three sections. The first part deals with facts and figures concerning coal-fired power plants and its impact on human health and the environment. The second part analyses the different legal interpretations of the phasing-out requirement. The article ends with a conclusion focusing on the significance of the phasing-out requirement for the permission of coal-fired power plants.

So far, the effect of the phasing-out requirement on the permission of coal-fired power plants was especially subject of a German driven discussion in legal literature and jurisdiction.[5] This contribution wants to provide this issue to an English-speaking audience with the aim to encourage an EU-wide debate.

2. FACTS AND FIGURES CONCERNING COAL-FIRED POWER PLANTS

Apart from their problematic 'carbon footprint',[6] coal-fired power plants raise concerns because of their significant emission of mercury.[7] In 2012, the primary production of electricity generated by coal-fired power plants had a proportion of 20.7% of the EU-wide energy mix.[8] The share of coal-fired power plants with regard to the total amount of mercury emissions is surprisingly high. A study of the German Federal Environment Agency reveals that in 2012 a total amount of 10.37 tons of mercury was emitted in Germany. Large power stations of the energy industry emitted by far the largest share of 6.94 tons.[9] Nevertheless, there are plans for the construction of 50 additional power stations in the European Union, including four plants in Germany and eight plants in Poland.[10]

---

5 See section 3.

6 See German Federal Environmental Agency (UBA): www.umweltbundesamt.de/daten/energie bereitstellung-verbrauch/stromerzeugung.

7 UNEP, Global Mercury Assessment, 2013, p. 1, 6 et seq., www.unep.org/PDF/PressReleases/GlobalMercuryAssessment2013.pdf; European Commission, *supra* note 2, p. 1, 4 et seq.

8 European Commission: EU energy in figures, Statistical Pocketbook 2014, p. 1, 36 et seq., http://ec.europa.eu/energy/publications/doc/2014_pocketbook.pdf.

9 German Federal Environmental Agency (UBA): Emission development of heavy metals in Germany 1990–2012, www.umweltbundesamt.de/themen/luft/emissionen-von-luftschadstoffen.

10 *P. Kremer*, The Prohibition of Mercury Discharges from Coal-Fired Power Stations under European Law, JEEPL, 2013 (2), p. 132, 133 et seq.; see also the list (elaborated by Deutsche Umwelthilfe e.V.) of German coal-fired power stations in planning: www.duh.de/fileadmin/user_upload/download/Projektinformation/Kohlekraftwerke/New_coal_plants_Germany_2012_DUH.pdf.

Via air, water, and soil pathways, mercury finds its way into the environment, where living organisms absorb it. Once ingested, mercury effects the central nervous system and it can cause a more frequent chronic poisoning, if the organism suffers a continuing exposure.[11] These organisms are particular at risk at early development stages, e.g. unborn life and infants.[12]

3. THE PHASING-OUT REQUIREMENT OF MERCURY AND ITS DIFFERENT INTERPRETATION

Due to the threat of mercury the European Union took concrete and binding measures through European water law with the aim to reduce the input of mercury into the environment:

On 22 December 2000 the WFD entered into force. Its environmental goals are contained in Art. 4 (1) WFD. Besides the concept of non-deterioration (Art. 4(1)(a), 1st indent WFD) and the duty to provide for a good chemical water status within 15 years – exceptions of this timeframe might be possible (Art. 4(1)(a) 2nd and 3rd indent WFD) – the Phasing-Out requirement of priority hazardous substances (Art. 4(1)(a), 4th indent WFD) is part of the main environmental goals of the WFD.

Since 2001 the WFD thus includes a list of priority hazardous substances in Annex X,[13] also including mercury, the emission of which shall be phased out. These substances were considered toxic, persistent, and are liable to bioaccumulation (see recital 29 WFD) via a scientifically based methodology introduced in Art. 16(2) WFD. This methodology consists of a simplified risk assessment procedure, which is based on standardised scientific principles.[14] In 2005 the Community Strategy Concerning Mercury[15] followed. This was considered a clear demonstration by the Union to acknowledge the danger of mercury and its potential to cause damages. In that strategy, the European Commission proposes a large number of measures to reduce the emissions of mercury and to prevent

---

11 In most cases the chronic poisoning is caused by a constant consumption of fish or seafood; see also UNEP, *supra* note 2, p. 1, 14 et seq.; UNEP, *supra* note 7, p. 1, 3 et seq.; as a minor interpellation from the German Green Party, Fraktion Bündnis 90/Die Grünen showed, the consumption of fish more than three times a month by an infant can lead to a dangerous mercury concentration. The consumption of fish several times a week by an adult can have similar effects, see: *German Bundestag*, Bundestags-Drucksache 17/8776, p. 1, 2 et seq., http://dipbt.bundestag.de/doc/btd/17/087/1708776.pdf.

12 *M. Karagas et al.*, Evidence on the human health effects of low level methyl mercury exposure, Environmental Health Perspectives, 2012 (6), p. 799, 804 et seq.

13 Decision of the European Parliament and the Council, No 2455/2001/EC, establishing the list of priority hazardous substances in the field of water policy, OJ 2001 L 331/1.

14 See 5th and 6th recital, Decision, *supra* note 13.

15 European Commission, *supra* note 2.

exposure.[16] In 2008, the daughter directive of the WFD on environmental quality standards in the field of water policy[17] (hereafter EQD) entered into force.[18] With respect to mercury, Annex I part A no. 21 EQD standardises the water-related annual average concentration, which serves the protection against long-term and irreversible consequences, as well as the maximum concentration to protect against short-term and acute ecotoxic effects.

The review of the Community Strategy Concerning Mercury[19] of 2010 determined that an assessment of the European Environmental Law will examine whether limits restricting the emission of mercury are necessary.[20] However, until today, there has not been another area of law – apart from EU water law – which directly limits mercury emissions into the environment.[21] The REACh Regulation[22] and also the IE Directive,[23] which both deal with mercury, do not assign specific emission limits for the substance.

These measures and the implementation of the WFD and its daughter directive led to a debate whether the operation and the permission of coal-fired power plants were compatible with EU water law,[24] in particular with the phasing-out requirement. The question arose whether the phasing-out requirement needed to be implemented in domestic law and which level of obligation this provision should have if the Member States did not meet their obligations to transpose the requirement into national law. A point of discussion has also been the question what the consequences should be for the permission of coal-fired power plants, which are some of the heaviest emitters of mercury.

---

16 European Commission, *supra* note 2, pp. 4–12.

17 Directive of the European Parliament and of the Council, *supra* note 4.

18 Dealing the latest legal developments concerning Chemical Quality of Water in Europe, *K. Kern*, New Standards for the Chemical Quality of Water in Europe under the New Directive 2013/39/EU, JEEPL, 2014 (1), p. 31.

19 Communication from the Commission to the European Parliament and the Council: COM (2010) 723 final on the review of the Community Strategy Concerning Mercury.

20 *Ibid.*, p. 1, 12 et seq.

21 *P. Kremer, supra* note 10, p. 132, 136 et seq.

22 Regulation of the European Parliament and the Council (EC) No 1907/2006 concerning the Registration, Evaluation, Authorisation and Restriction of Chemicals (REACH), OJ 2006 L396/1.

23 Directive of the European Parliament and the Council 2010/75/EU on industrial emissions (integrated pollution prevention and control), OJ 2010 L334/17.

24 i.a. *S.R. Laskowski*, Kohlekraftwerke im Lichte der EU-Wasserrahmenrichtlinie, ZUR 2013 (3), p. 131; *P. Kremer, supra* note 10; *M. Gellermann*, Europäisches Wasserrecht und Kohlenutzung in der Perspektive des Primärrechts, NVwZ, 2012 (14), p. 850; *B. & E.-M. Stüer*, Vorbescheid und erste Teilgenehmigung für das Trianel-Kraftwerk in Lünen aufgehoben, DVBl, 2012 (4), p. 245, 250 et seq.; *O. Reidt & G. Schiller*, Quecksilbereinträge in oberirdische Gewässer durch Kohlekraftwerke, NuR, 2011 (33), p. 624; *W. Spieth & N.C. Ipsen*, Verbietet die Wasserrahmenrichtlinie den Bau von Kohlkraftwerken?, NVwZ, 2011 (9), p. 536; *W. Durner & N. Trillmich*, Ausstieg aus der Kohlenutzung kraft europäischen Wasserrechts, DVBl, 2011 (9), p. 517; *F. Ekardt & L. Steffenhagen*, Kohlekraftwerkbau, wasserrechtliche Bewirtschaftungsziele und das Klimaschutzrecht, NuR, 2010 (32), p. 705.

3.1. THE PHASING-OUT REQUIREMENT UNDER EU WATER LAW

Art. 4(1)(a) 4th indent WFD contains the phasing-out requirement. It determines that 'Member States shall implement the necessary measures in accordance with Article 16(1) and (8), with the aim of progressively reducing pollution from priority substances and ceasing or phasing out emissions, discharges and losses of priority hazardous substances'. The phasing-out requirement does apply both on specific emissions and discharges as well as on diffuse sources. Therefore, priority hazardous substances, which are listed in Annex X of the WFD, should be reduced progressively 'with the ultimate aim of achieving concentrations in the marine environment near background values for naturally occurring substances and close to zero for man-made synthetic substances' (Art. 1 last indent).[25] With the aim to achieve this environmental standard in all surface waters, the phasing-out requirement is to be considered as an environmental quality standard. At the same time, it is classified as an emission limit with values near background concentration for naturally occurring substances and zero concentration for synthetic substances.[26] The conceptual meaning of this environmental goal is therefore unequivocal. However, the time frame for the implementation and enforcement of the phasing-out requirement in the EU Member States is still fiercely disputed. Furthermore, the specific legal effect of this provision is unclear considering that EU Member States still did not comply with their obligation to implement Art. 4(1)(a) 4th indent WFD into national law.[27] Finally, the consequences of a potential enforcement are also unclear. Thus, it has not been determined whether the requirement should affect the refusal or the permission of a coal-fired power plant by the national authorities.

3.2. THE TIME FRAME FOR THE IMPLEMENTATION OF THE PHASING-OUT REQUIREMENT

The WFD neither sets a specific time frame for the implementation of the phasing-out requirement, nor determines a period within which the emissions of substances contained in Annex X of the WFD have to be ended. The implementation of the concept of non deterioration (Art. 4(1)(a) 1st indent WFD) and the duty to provide for a good chemical water status (Art. 4(1)(a) 2nd, 3rd indent

---

25 See also 4th recital, Decision, *supra* note 13.

26 *W. Köck & S. Möckel,* Quecksilberbelastungen von Gewässern durch Kohlekraftwerke – Auswirkungen auf die Genehmigungsfähigkeit, Legal Opinion on behalf of German Environmental Aid, 2010, p. 1, 22 et seq.; *H. Ginzky,* Die Pflicht zur Minderung von Schadstoffeinträgen in Oberflächengewässern, ZUR, 2009 (5), p. 242, 244 et seq.

27 At least Germany, France, Spain and the United Kingdom did not implement the phasing-out requirement in their national water regime.

WFD) within 15 years can be extended or diluted if the EU Member States meet the conditions in Art. 4(4) to (7) WFD.[28] These provisions do, however, not apply to the phasing-out requirement and its implementation in national law. Art. 4(1)(a) 4th indent WFD does not refer to these facilitations. Due to the missing reference to Art. 4(4) to (7) WFD, the timeframe for implementing the phasing-out requirement, applies without exception.[29]

Art. 16(6) WFD contains the duty of the European Commission to submit concrete proposals for 'the cessation or phasing-out of discharges, emissions and losses of the (priority) substances ..., including an appropriate timetable for doing so. The timetable shall not exceed 20 years after the adoption of these proposals by the European Parliament and the Council'. Art. 16(8) 1st sentence WFD requires the Commission proposal within two years after the inclusion of the substance concerned on the first list of priority substances, which in the case of mercury means by 16 December 2003.[30] In such a case, in absence of an agreement at Community level, Art. 16(8) 2nd sentence WFD would restore the subsidiary duty of the Member States to take implementing measures concerning the phasing-out requirement six years after the entry into force of the WFD. Art. 16(8) 2nd sentence WFD reads: 'For substances included in the first list of priority substances, in absence of agreement at Community level six years after the date of entry into force of this Directive, Member States shall establish environmental quality standards for these substances for all surface waters affected by discharges of those substances'. As the WFD entered into force on 22 December 2000, the obligation of the Member States to draw up and implement phasing-out measures would have therefore been effective by 22 December 2006.[31] If there were no agreements at Community level, the legal consequence would be the obligatory and EU-wide reduction of priority hazardous substances in all surface waters to the natural background loads for naturally occurring substances and close to zero emissions for synthetic substances until 22 December 2026.

It is, however, very much debated whether there has been such a proposal at Community level yet. Some voices in legal literature argue that until now there has not been a European proposal. Furthermore the formation of a subsidiary duty of the Member States (Art. 16(8) 2nd sentence WFD) to implement national measures in accordance with Art. 4(1)(a) 4th indent WFD would require a proposal

[28] *P. Kremer, supra* note 10, p. 132, 142; *W. Köck & S. Möckel, supra* note 26, p. 1, 21 et seq.; *H. Ginzky, supra* note 26, p. 242, 245 et seq.

[29] *P. Kremer, supra* note 10, p. 132, 141 et seq.; *S.R. Laskowski, supra* note 24, p. 131, 140 et seq.; *W. Köck & S. Möckel, supra* note 26, p. 1, 22 et seq.; *H. Ginzky, supra* note 26, p. 242, 245 et seq.

[30] Decision, *supra* note 13, entered into force on 16 December 2001.

[31] Different view, *H. Jekel & H.-H. Munk*, Phasing-out für prioritäre gefährliche Stoffe – Was regelt die EG-Wasserrahmenrichtlinie wirklich?, ZUR, 2013 (7/8), p. 403, 406 et seq., who do not – against the wording of Art. 16(8) sentence 2 WFD – recognise any duty of the EU Member States to take measures for the phasing-out of the substances listed in Annex X WFD.

on European level and the absence of an agreement.[32] Considering the actions of the Commission in 2006 and 2008 it can, however, be established that these conditions have been met.

On 17 July 2006 the European Commission published a proposal for a Directive of the European Parliament and the Council on environmental quality standards in the field of water policy.[33] With this proposal, the European Commission itself explicitly implemented its obligations laid down in Art. 16(6) to (8) WFD, 'with the exception of introducing additional emission controls'.[34] Nevertheless, the Commission proposed a timetable for the cessation of priority hazardous substances. According to this proposal, emissions and losses of these substances should end in 2025.[35] As Art. 4(1)(a) 4th indent WFD provides that the Phasing-out requirement is concretised by the establishment of a precise timeframe for the cessation of priority hazardous substances the Commission complied with its obligation to present a proposal at Community level (Art. 16(8) 1st sentence WFD).

There has, however, not been an agreement at Community level. The implementation of the Commission's proposal led to the adoption of the EQD on 16 December 2008.[36] In contrast to the proposal of the Commission, the Directive does not consider any timeframe for the cessation of priority hazardous substances. The adoption of the EQD therefore confirms the absence of an agreement concerning the phasing-out requirement at Community level. Hence, the absence of an agreement on Community level can be proved. As a result, Art. 16(8) 2nd WFD transfers the duty to enact the necessary measures from the Commission to the EU Member States 'six years after the date of entry into force of this Directive'.[37] Entering in the Commission's obligation of Art. 16(6) WFD, the Member States also need to comply with the timetable set in the provision. The Member States have to implement and enforce the necessary measures within 20 years. As a consequence, the emissions and loss of priority hazardous substances, such as mercury, have to be ended by 16 December 2028.[38]

---

32 *H. Jekel & H.-H. Munk, supra* note 31, p. 403, 406; *O. Reidt & G. Schiller, supra* note 24, p. 624, 630 et seq.; *W. Spieth & N.C. Ipsen, supra* note 24, p. 536, 539 et seq.; *W. Durner & N. Trillmich, supra* note 24, p. 517, 523.

33 Commission proposal COM(2006) 397 final for a Directive of the European Parliament and of the Council on environmental quality standards in the field of water policy and amending Directive 2000/60/EC, COD 2006/0129.

34 *Ibid.*, p. 2.

35 Commission proposal, *supra* note 33, p. 8, 16.

36 Directive, *supra* note 4.

37 *K. Kern, supra* note 18, p. 31, 32 et seq. footnote 3.

38 *S.R. Laskowski, supra* note 24, p. 131, 136 et seq.; *W. Köck & S. Möckel, supra* note 26, p. 1, 22 et seq.

3.3. THE LEGAL EFFECT OF THE PHASING-OUT REQUIREMENT

The phasing-out requirement has, until now, not been concretised by European legislation or by the EQD. In addition to that, EU Member States also did not follow up the obligation of Art. 16(8) 2nd sentence WFD to take further action in case a European agreement concerning the phasing-out of priority hazardous substances failed. The wording of Art. 4(1)(a) 4th indent WFD is clearly directed towards the EU Member States. Moreover, the EQD waives a European concretisation of the phasing-out requirement and contains an explicit recommendation to transfer this duty to the EU Member States (see recital 8 EQD).[39] This leads to the question whether the phasing-out requirement has direct effects within EU Member States.

3.3.1. *Arguments Against Direct Legal Effect*

Three arguments speak against a direct legal effect of the phasing-out requirement. First of all scholars argue that the requirement is far too vague in order to result into a direct effect.[40] Furthermore, direct applicability of the requirement would be contrary to the prohibition of a third party effect[41] as a rule of EU law.[42] The consequence of a direct legal effect would be a proximate ban of coal-fired power stations, affecting the plant operators as third parties. Lastly, assuming a direct effect of the phasing-out requirement the WFD would not have been enacted following the right procedures, since its enforcement, the cessation of mercury emissions, would result in a de facto prohibition of coal-fired plants. In such a case, the WFD would have had to be enacted following the procedures of Art. 192(2)(c) of the Treaty on the Functioning of the European Union (TFEU), as these 'measures [would] significantly affect ... a Member State's choice between different energy sources and the general structure of its energy supply' (Art. 192(2)(c) TFEU). This procedure requires unanimity in the EU Council. The WFD was enacted following the procedures of the former Art. 175(1) Treaty of the European Community, now Art. 192(1) TFEU, which is the basis of environmental legislation. Legal acts based on Art. 192(1) TFEU can be adopted within the ordinary legislative procedures, which do not require unanimity in the

39 *W. Köck & S. Möckel, supra* note 26, p. 1, 21 et seq.

40 *H. Jekel & H.-H. Munk, supra* note 31, p. 403, 405 et seq.; *W. Spieth & N.C. Ipsen, supra* note 24 p. 536, 540 et seq.; *W. Durner & N. Trillmich, supra* note 24, p. 517, 521 et seq.; *O. Reidt & G. Schiller, supra* note 24, p. 624, 629 et seq.

41 CJEU Judgment: inter alia Case C-152/84, *Marshall I* [1986] ECR 723, para. 48; Case C-14/86, *Pretore di Salò/X* [1987] ECR 2545, para. 19; Case C-221/88, *Busseni* [1990] ECR I-495, para. 23; Case C-168/95, *Arcaro* [1996] ECR I-4705, para. 36 et seq.; Case C-201/02 *Delena Wells* [2004] ECR I-723, para. 56.

42 *W. Durner & N. Trillmich, supra* note 24, p. 517, 525 et seq.

EU Council. Assuming a legal effect, the WFD would have been enacted following the wrong procedures, resulting therefore in nullity of the provision.[43]

Based on these considerations, the Phasing-out requirement would not have a direct legal effect for EU Member States. In consequence, this provision would have no impact on the permission practice of coal-fired power plants, pending further concretisation.

3.3.2. *Arguments in Favour of a Direct Legal Effect*

The case law of the Court of Justice of the European Union (CJEU) speaks, however, in favour of a direct legal effect of the phasing-out requirement. Since the phasing-out requirement has not been concretised by any European legal act, it is necessary to consult the case law concerning direct effects of Directives and the prohibition of the frustration of European secondary law.

The CJEU's current case law and its developed criteria for a binding effect can be summarised as follows: directives are directly effective in case the transposition period has run out,[44] if there is a lack of implementation of the directive or the provision in question,[45] and if it is unconditional and sufficiently precise.[46]

As the obligation to implement the phasing-out requirement was transferred to the EU Member States (see Art. 16(8) 2nd sentence WFD), they should have established the necessary measures since 2006. So far, there has been no implementation of the phasing-out requirement in the EU Member States examined.[47] A provision is unconditional if it is not subject, to the taking of any measures either by the Union institutions or by the Member States.[48] The provision is sufficiently precise to be relied on, when the obligation, which it imposes, is set out in unequivocal terms.[49] The explicit goal of Art. 4(1)(a) 4th indent WFD is to progressively reduce pollution of priority hazardous substances and to cease or to phase out emissions, discharges, or losses of priority hazardous substances listed in Annex X. Thus, the objective is both unconditional and unequivocal: a continuous reduction of these substances to, at least, the natural background loads by 16 December 2028.

This reasoning goes hand in hand with the prohibition of frustrating the objectives of a directive and serves thereby an effective implementation of

[43] *Ibid.*, p. 517, 522 et seq.; *W. Spieth & N.C. Ipsen, supra* note 24, p. 536, 538 et seq.
[44] CJEU Judgment: Case C-148/78, *Ratti* [1979] ECR-1629, paras. 43–47; Opinion of Advocate General Jacobs, Case C-156/91, *Hansa Fleisch Ernst Mundt* [1992| ECR I-5567, para. 18.
[45] CJEU Judgment: inter alia Case C-126/82, *Smit* [1983] ECR 73, para. 10; Case C-152/84, *Marshall I* [1986] ECR 723, para. 46; Case C-190/87, *Moormann* [1988] ECR 4689, para. 23.
[46] CJEU Judgment: inter alia Case C-148/78, *Ratti* [1979] ECR 1629, para. 23; Case C-80/86, *Kolpinghuis Nijmegen* [1987] ECR 3969, para. 7; Case C-194/94, *CIA Security International* [1996] ECR I-2201, paras. 42, 44.
[47] *Supra* note 27.
[48] *J.H. Jans & H.H.B. Vedder*, European Environmental Law, 4th ed., 2012, p. 184; *A. Epiney*, Umweltrecht der Europäischen Union, 3th ed., 2013, p. 175.
[49] *J.H. Jans & H.H.B. Vedder, supra* note 48, p. 184.

European secondary law: the CJEU in this respect ruled that EU Member States may not take actions which could defeat the goals of a directive even during its transposition period. The Court based this ruling on Art. 288(3) TFEU in conjunction with Art. 4(3) Treaty of the European Union (TEU) and the legal principle of '*effet utile*'.[50] Thus, 'during the period prescribed for transposition of a directive, the Member States to which it is addressed must refrain from taking any measures liable seriously to compromise the attainment of the result prescribed by that directive ... Such an obligation to refrain owed by all the national authorities ... must be understood as referring to the adoption of any measure, general or specific, liable to produce such a compromising effect'.[51]

Following this case-law, all government bodies are directly bound to the requirement to phase-out the substances listed in Annex X WFD. They must refrain from taking any measures to compromise this provision. Moreover, they are required to implement and enforce Art. 4(1)(a) 4th indent WFD into national law by 16 December 2028. As the EU Member States have not yet transposed and operationalised the provision in national law[52] and national authorities continue to grant new permissions to coal-fired power stations, these rules are undermined.

The prohibition of a third party effect[53] as a rule of EU law does not protect against 'mere adverse repercussions on the right of third parties, even if the repercussions are certain'.[54] The phasing-out requirement, in the case of mercury, obviously harms the property law of the person operating a coal-fired power station. However, the prohibition of third party effects only includes the case of a direct effect of public measures. The phasing-out requirement targets the cessation of priority hazardous substances. The effect on the property law is a 'mere adverse repercussion'. Finally, the question of the legislative power is determined by content, aim and in particular the key aspect of the provision.[55] The unequivocal purpose of the phasing-out requirement is the prevention of water pollution, as part of environmental policy. The consequence of this provision has *de facto* effect on the energy production, but does not focus on a specific energy source.[56] The EU Member States still determine their specific energy mix, even though they withdraw from mercury polluting energy industries.

---

50 CJEU Judgment: inter alia Case C-129/96, *Inter-Envrionnement Wallonie* [1997] ECR I-7411, para. 45; Case C-165/09 to Case C-167/09 (Joined Cases), *Stichting Natuur en Milieu* [2011] ECR I-4599, para. 78; Opinion of Advocate General Kokott, Case C-43/10, *Aachelos* [2012] ECR I-651, paras. 99–101 et seq.

51 CJEU Judgment: Case C-165/09 to Case C-167/09 (Joined Cases), *Stichting Natuur en Milieu* [2011] ECR I-4599, para. 78.

52 *Supra* note 27.

53 CJEU Judgment, *supra* note 39.

54 CJEU Judgment: Case C-201/02, *Delena Wells* [2002] ECR I-723, para. 57.

55 CJEU Judgment: inter alia Case C-2/00, *Cartagena* [2001] ECR I-9713, para. 22; Case C-336/00, *Huber* [2002] ECR I-7699, para. 30; Case C-491/01, *British American Tobacco* [2002] ECR I-11 453, para. 93.

56 *S.R. Laskowski, supra* note 24, p. 131, 139 et seq.

This conclusion leads to the following results concerning the permission of coal-fired power plants.

First Scenario – Existing and Operating Coal-Fired Power Stations

In case of an existing power plant it would not be necessary to take back the water permit due to the phasing-out requirement. The case-law of the Court of Justice does not demand such far-reaching measures. Furthermore, phasing-out implies a process rather than an immediate end to the emission of mercury.

However, the extension of a water permit can be joined with the obligatory collateral clause to phase out mercury emissions by 16 December 2028. The affected operator of the coal-fired power plant can make dispositions to meet with the clause.

If a coal-fired power plant is still operating and emitting mercury after that date, the national authorities have to take back the water permit to comply with EU law.

Second Scenario – Coal-Fired Power Station in Planning

In the case of a power plant in planning status, the phasing-out requirement makes it necessary for the authorities to enforce the phasing-out of mercury emissions until 16 December 2028. This has to be achieved by demanding the creation of a scientifically approved action plan, for reducing the emissions of mercury to a natural background load.

4. SUMMARY

There is an obligation of EU Member States to adhere to the phasing-out requirement (Art. 4(1)(a) 4th indent WFD) and to refrain from taking any measures to compromise the aims of the provision. EU Member States have to implement and to enforce the phasing-out requirement by 16 December 2028. Thus, the emissions, discharges and losses of priority hazardous substances into the environment have to be ended by this date. By 16 December 2028 coal-fired power stations, emitting mercury are no longer licensable. Existing coal-fired power plants have to phase-out mercury emissions by 16 December 2028. Operators of coal-fired power plants in planning have to meet the zero-mercury emissions requirement by that date. Otherwise, the national authorities have to deny the application of the required water permit.

CHAPTER 12

THE PERMISSIBILITY OF PROJECTS FOR INTERBASIN WATER TRANSFER UNDER THE PRISM OF THE EU WATER AND ENVIRONMENTAL LEGISLATION

Vasiliki (Vicky) Karageorgou*

1. INTRODUCTION

One of the overriding problems of the 21st century is that of the protection and the sustainable use of the scarce water resources,[1] which is intensified due to the climate-induced changes on water ecosystems.[2] Population growth, economic activities, such as industry and agriculture that presuppose an increased use of water, and increasing urbanisation are, among others, significant drivers for an over-exploitation of the water resources in many regions, which often results in shortages of water availability.[3]

In such circumstances, demand-oriented measures are not entirely sufficient. Supply-oriented measures are also considered to be possible solutions to increasing water demand in areas which are not able to live within their ecological limits.[4] Interbasin water transfers (IBTs) are regarded as one of the most prominent supply oriented solutions for coping with the above-described situations.[5] For the purposes of this chapter, the term of 'interbasin water transfer' refers to the transfer of water from one river basin to another through the development of

* Assistant Professor, Panteion University, Athens.

1 *J. Gupta & J.W. Dellapenna*, The Challenge for the Twenty-First Century: A Critical Approach, in J.W. Dellapenna & J. Gupta (eds.), The Evolution of the Law and Politics of Water, 2009, p. 391, 405 et seq.

2 *Intergovernmental Panel on Climate Change (IPPC)*, Climate Change and Water, Technical Paper, June 2008.

3 *D. Getsches*, Spain's Ebro River Transfers: Test Case for Water Policy in the European Union, International Journal of Water Resources Development, 2003 (19), p. 501, 504.

4 *J. Jupta & P. van der Zaag*, Interbasin Water Transfers and Integrated Water Resources Management: Where Engineering, Science and Politics Interlock, Physics and Chemistry of the Earth Part, 2008 (33), p. 28, 29.

5 The desalination of sea water or the reuse of treated water constitute significant options in this direction.

the necessary infrastructure, that includes, *inter alia*, the construction of dams, pipelines and reservoirs.[6] Since the implementation of such projects presupposes large-scale and significant interventions, the consequences arising from their realisation can be far-reaching not only from an environmental but also from a social and an economic point of view.[7]

The main aim of the chapter is to answer the central question of whether EU water law and EU environmental law in general provide either concrete rules or at least certain clear-cut criteria and other relevant instruments for assessing the permissibility of the IBTs as a possible solution for satisfying water demand in water-stressed regions. In this context, it should be clarified that although EU water law can be predominantly viewed as a specific field of the EU environmental law, it has a certain level of autonomy in relation to the latter for reasons relating mainly to the specificity of its content, its strong transboundary dimensions and its interdependencies with international water law.[8] On the basis of this remark, in the framework of this chapter the provisions of the EU water law are analysed separately from those of the EU environmental law. Moreover, it is worth noting that the chapter is inspired by the '*Acheloos* case', namely a long-term and controversial case, which relates to the plans for the diversion of the relevant river through a composite project.

To this end, the second section of the chapter analyses the experience gained through the implementation of certain relevant projects worldwide with a view to demonstrating the various issues triggered by their realisation. The third section first analyses briefly how the 'paradigm shift' underpinning the quite recent water governance regimes and the environmental law in general can exert certain influence on the way that large-scale infrastructural projects, such as IBTs can be assessed. The emphasis is then shifted on the relevant provisions and the principles of the EU water law primarily, which are critical for assessing the compatibility of IBTs with the established concepts, taking into consideration that the fundamental legal instrument in this field, namely the Water Framework Directive, is a prominent example of a Governance Mode Directive.[9] Moreover, the relevant instruments or principles of the EU environmental law are also considered. In the fourth section, the *Acheloos* case will be examined in detail with a view to demonstrating not only its interesting legal perspectives but also the attendant governance issues. Finally, certain conclusions will be drawn

---

6 *Davies et al.*, The Ecological Impacts of Inter-Basin Water Transfers and their Threats to River Basin Integrity and Conservation, Aquatic Conservation: Marine and Freshwater Ecosystems, 1992 (2), p. 325, including in their definition also the intra-basin transfers.

7 *J. Jupta & P. van der Zaag, supra* note 4, p. 31; *D. Getsches, supra* note 3, p. 504.

8 *H.F.M.W. van Rijswick & J.M. Havekes*, European and Dutch Water Law, 2012, p. 79 et seq., 121 et seq.

9 *S. van Holten & H.F.M.W. van Rijswick*, The Governance Approach in European Union Environmental Directives and its Consequences for Flexibility, Effectiveness and Legitimacy, in M. Peeters and R. Uylenburg (eds.), EU Environmental Legislation: Legal Perspectives on Regulatory Strategies, 2014, p. 13, 29 et. seq.

concerning the issue of the compatibility of the IBTs with the EU water and environmental law.

2. LESSONS LEARNED BY THE IMPLEMENTATION OF THE IBTs WORLDWIDE

The implementation of the IBTs all over the world[10] demonstrates that they seem to be a quite common strategy for addressing the water needs in water-scarce regions. For the purposes of the analysis three already implemented IBT schemes, namely the Tagus Segura Transfer Scheme, the Lesotho Highlands Water Project and the Snowy River Scheme, were taken into consideration with a view to reaching certain conclusions as regards their various implications. It should be clarified that the reason for which the first and the third example of interbasin water transfer schemes are chosen for a brief analysis relates mainly to the fact that their design and implementation was driven mostly by the need to boost agricultural production in the recipient regions. In this context, they do not only have similarities with the chosen case-study of Acheloos in terms of the purposes served by their implementation, but they are also critical to demonstrating in more general terms that the water volumes required by the model of extensive agriculture can result in the choice of supply-oriented measures, such as the IBTs. Moreover, the Snowy River Scheme was also chosen because of its scale and the dependence of its viability on the climate change impact on water resources. Finally, the reason for which the second example was chosen lies primarily in its transboundary dimension and in the relevant perception that it constitutes a 'win-win' project in terms of providing sufficient benefits also to the donor area.[11]

2.1. BRIEF ANALYSIS OF THE SCHEMES

The first example is, as already mentioned, the Tagus Segura Transfer Scheme in Spain, which consists of five dams and a long pipeline, in order to channel water from the Taju Basin to the Segura Basin. The main aim of the project, which was approved by Law 21/1971 and became operational in the late seventies, was to provide sufficient water volumes to be used primarily for irrigation in the recipient area of Alicante, Marcia and Almeria provinces and secondarily

10 *F. Gischuki & P.G. McCornick*, International Experiences of Water Transfers: Relevance to India, in U. Amarasinghe & B.R. Sharma (eds.), Strategic Analysis of the National River Linking Project of India (NRLP), 2008, p. 345, 347 et seq.

11 *D. Gray & C.W. Sadoff*, Beyond the River: The Benefits of Cooperation on International Rivers, Water Policy, 2002 (4), p. 389 et. seq.

for urban water supply.[12] From an economic and distributional point of view it is significant that the relevant legislative framework (Law 21/1971 and Law 52/1980) provided that the beneficiaries in the recipient area had to pay for the infrastructure and the operational costs of the transferred water and moreover that a part of the revenues collected through the introduction of water fees in the recipient area had to be given in the donor areas as a form of compensation. The latter, though, received in fact lower compensation than those provided due to the reduction of the fees in certain cases.[13] It is also critical from an environmental point of view that the project design was based on the estimated water surplus in the donor area.[14] Finally, the relevant legal regime especially at the time of the approval of the scheme was neither underpinned by the adoption of integrated water management approaches, nor included the necessary legal instruments for assessing the impacts of such projects (EIA), but instead it focused mainly on the utilisation of water resources for the satisfaction of human needs. Subsequently, it could hardly provide clear-cut criteria or even guidelines concerning the acceptability of IBTs as a supply-oriented measure in water-stressed regions.[15]

The second example of an IBT, which is implemented by two states, is the Lesotho Highlands Water Project. The development of the scheme was based on a Treaty signed between the governments of Lesotho and South Africa in 1986, which defined the responsibilities of the two states, the strategies for settling disputes and the direct and indirect benefits associated with the project implementation.[16] The project comprises several dams to be constructed in four phases and the associated water infrastructure, which is necessary for transferring water from the Senqu River in Lesotho to the Vaal River in South Africa. Both rivers form the headquarters of the Orange River Basin.[17] The main aim of the project was to supply sufficient water volumes to the Gauteng's Region in South Africa, which comprises the cities of Johannesburg and Pretoria as well as their surroundings and is the industrial heartland of the country and simultaneously to provide Lesotho with the necessary hydropower.[18] As regards

---

12 *F. Gischuki & P.G. McCornick, supra* note 10, p. 353; *WWF Discussion Paper*, Interbasin Water Transfers and Water Scarcity in a Changing World? A Solution or a Pipedream?, 2nd edition, 2009, p. 12, http://assets.panda.org/downloads/pipedreams/18.08.2009.pdf.

13 *WWF Discussion Paper, supra* note 12, p. 11.

14 The governance arrangements were also rather weak, as the scheme was approved without any public consultation procedures due to the nature of the political regime at that time (dictatorship).

15 It is also worth noting that the National Hydrological Plan which was approved by the Spanish Government in 2001 with the purpose of ensuring harmonisation with the requirements of the WFD, authorised another inter-basin transfer scheme for channelling water from the Ebro River to other basins. This project which was massively opposed by the local communities of the donor area, was later revoked by the Spanish Government (*D. Getsches, supra* note 3, p. 508 et seq.).

16 *F. Gischuki & P.G. McCornick, supra* note 10, p. 357; *L.J.M. Haas, L. Mazzei & D.T. O' Leary,* Lesotho Highlands Water Project: Communication Practises for Governance and Sustainability Improvement, World Bank Working Paper no. 200, 2010, p. 3 et seq.

17 *J. Jupta & P. van der Zaag, supra* note 4, p. 30.

18 *L.J.M. Haas, L. Mazzei & D. O' Leary,* supra note 16, p. 3.

the economic viability of the project it is of particular importance that the costs for the completion of the Phase I and II of the project were considerably higher than those predicted.[19] Furthermore, certain distributional issues have been raised, as the arrangements between States concerning the benefits provided to the donor country (e.g. the royalties paid to Lesotho) did not prove sufficient to ensure that all the communities affected by the project received full compensation[20] and moreover were empowered to re-establish a stable development path. From an environmental standpoint, the consideration of the environmental impacts of the scheme can be regarded as insufficient especially at the initial phase, as the project started without an EIA study. A composite EIA study with a proper environmental flow analysis was carried out in the second phase, but at this stage only limited design changes could be made.[21] Finally, the relevant legal regimes for water management and environmental protection in the critical States were not developed at such a level, in order to contain specific criteria or even guidelines concerning the acceptability of such kinds of projects, which could exert substantial influence on the relevant Treaty. Subsequently, only general requirements for ensuring the existing quality of the environment were included in the Treaty, while the environmental flow policies, which were later adopted, have, despite the deficiencies in their implementation, contributed to the mitigation of the environmental impacts.[22]

Finally, the third project that is considered is the Snowy Mountains Scheme in Australia which constitutes an integrated water and hydropower scheme and consists of sixteen (16) dams, seven power stations, 225km of tunnels and one pump station. The development of the scheme which was constructed several decades ago was based on an Intergovernmental Agreement concluded by the national and two state governments (New South Wales and Victoria) in 1958.[23] The main purpose of the project was to channel and transfer water from the Snowy River to the Murray and Murrumbidgee Rivers, to be used for hydropower and irrigation, as the Murray-Darling Basin is Australia's food bowl.[24] From an economic point of view, the implementation of the scheme has yielded substantial

19 The cost escalation can be attributed, at least to some extent, to the corruption discovered in the realisation of the Lesotho Highlands Water Project (*F. Gischuki & P. G. McCornick, supra* note 10, p. 357; *International Rivers*, Lesotho Highlands Water Project Corruption, www.internationalrivers.org/resources/lesotho-water-project-corruption-3662.

20 Certain communities displaced by the dam projects still struggle before the Courts to get the compensation owed to them (*International Rivers*, Khabang Lejone Community in Lesotho takes the Lesotho Highlands Development Authority to court for delayed payment of compensation, www.internationalrivers.org/resources/9047.

21 *F. Gischuki & P.G. McCornick, supra* note 10, p. 358.

22 *WWF Discussion Paper, supra* note 12, p.18.

23 *A. Sennet et al.*, Challenges and Responses in the Murray-Darling Basin, Water Policy 2014 (16), p. 117, 134. The scheme is operated and maintained by the Snowy Hydro Limited after its corporatisation in 1997 (*Snowy Hydro Limited*, Sydney, www.snowyhydro.com.au.

24 *J. Gray*, Dollars and Dreams-Legal Aspirations and Report Cards in the Murray-Darling Basin of Australia, in L. Westra, P. Taylor & A. Michelot (eds.), Confronting Ecological and Economic Collapse: Ecological Integrity for Law, Policy and Human Rights, 2013, p. 156, 157.

benefits for certain sectors of the economy (agriculture, tourism) especially in the recipient area.[25] The cost of the scheme was estimated at 800 million dollars and it therefore incurred some criticism as regards whether the project would pass the economic viability test on strict cost-benefit terms.[26] From an environmental point of view, the impacts of the scheme on the environment were not considered at the planning and construction stage, as emphasis was solely placed on the diversion and transfer of waters and the relevant legislative framework was not underpinned by the incorporation of environmental considerations. Subsequently, the implementation of a scheme of such a considerable magnitude without comprehensive planning and assessment procedures has had far-reaching consequences for the landscape of both the donor and the recipient area and for the biophysical condition of the river itself.[27] In response to the increasing environmental concerns, certain legislative and policy measures have been adopted quite recently, which aim at mitigating the impact of the scheme on the environmental flows and at restoring the aquatic habitat of the Snowy River, while also the relevant developments in water law and policy in Australia exerted influence on the management practices of the scheme.[28] Finally, the future viability of the scheme is also, to some extent, dependent on the climate change impact on water resources.

2.2. REMARKS CONCERNING THE IMPLICATIONS OF IBTs

The comparative examination of the above projects leads to certain observations as regards the different issues triggered by the implementation of IBTs (environmental, social, economic) and the importance of the existence of legal regimes which set criteria for their design and implementation. A first category of remarks relates to the impacts on the natural environment that are caused by the design and implementation of the IBTs. In particular, the donor basins have experienced serious environmental degradation that can be attributed, *inter alia*, to the overestimation of the available water quantities and to the non-compliance with the minimum stream flow requirements,[29] while the implementation of

25 *WWF Discussion Paper, supra* note 12, p. 15.

26 *J. Pigram*, Australia's Water Resources – From Use to Management, 2007, p. 119.

27 *J. Pigram, supra* note 26, p. 119 et seq.; *WWF Discussion Paper, supra* note 12, p. 15.

28 For the environmental flow policies see *State of New South Wales, State of Victoria and Commonwealth*, Snowy Water Inquiry Outcomes Implementation Deed, Document No. NWEWG 21 (Conformed Executive Version), 3 June 2002, which is the principal document governing the interstate agreements for sharing the flows of the Snowy River. For the developments in Water Law see *J. McKay & S. Marsden*, Australia: The Problem of Sustainability in Water, in J.W. Dellapenna & J. Gupta (eds.), The Evolution of the Law and Politics of Water, 2009, p. 175, 176 et seq.

29 The above-mentioned factors were decisive in the case of the Tagus-Segura Transfer Scheme as regards the significant environmental degradation that the donor area has experienced (*WWF*

the schemes has not always been beneficial for the natural environment of the recipient areas.[30] Moreover, the already significant environmental impacts are expected to be intensified due to the climate-induced changes on water availability and quality.[31]

Several observations can be made from the review of the three cases from an economic point of view. In particular, it can be persuasively argued that the implementation of IBTs can foster unsustainable production models, such as extensive irrigated agriculture, in the recipient areas (the Segura Basin in Spain and the Murray Basin in Australia respectively), underlining the linkage between unsustainable patterns of water use and the relevant development models. The economic efficiency of IBTs can also be questioned due to the fact that in certain cases, the total costs for the construction of IBTs have exceeded the relevant estimations.[32] Furthermore, the complex distributional decisions relating to the costs and benefits of the schemes between affected regions and interest groups can lead to situations where the significant economic benefits gained by the regions near the recipient basin are at the expense of the communities in the donor area that do not receive adequate compensation.[33] Finally, the conclusion which is drawn by reviewing the three cases under the prism of the good governance principles is that the governance arrangements between the donor and the recipient areas were rather weak and insufficient for avoiding social conflicts.[34] This can also be attributed to the fact that the project implementation started at a time at which the principles and the mechanisms of the participatory environmental governance were not well established. Moreover, the relevant environmental and water legislation applied at the initial stages of the implementation of the schemes

---

Discussion Paper, supra note 12, p. 12). Moreover, significant threats to the endangered species in the donor region of Lesotho can be attributed to the inconsistent implementation of the flow requirements (*WWF Discussion Paper, supra* note 12, p. 18). Finally, the reduced flows in the Snowy River Basin resulted in significant losses of floodplain wetland habitats, salt water intrusions in the estuary and losses of migratory fish populations. See *G. Wright,* Interbasin Water Transfer: the Australian Experience with the Snowy Mountains Scheme, Proceedings of the International Workshop (UNESCO, Paris, 25–27 April 1999). IHP-V | Technical Documents in Hydrology I No. 28, 1999, pp. 101–106; *J. Pigram, supra* note 26, p. 119.

30 From one point of view, the expansion of the irrigated agriculture in the Segura Basin resulted in an over-exploitation of the groundwater aquifers (*F. Gischuki & P. G. McCornick, supra* note 10, p. 353). From the other point of view, the water transferred to the Murray Basin in the case of the Snowy Mountains Scheme has contributed to the maintenance of wetlands protected under the Ramsar Convention and to the aquatic habitat of the recipient area in general (*WWF Discussion Paper, supra* note 12, p. 16).

31 *R. Garnaut,* The Garnaut Climate Change Review: Final Report, 2008, p. 477 as regards the impact of climate change on the future of the Snowy Mountains Scheme.

32 *F. Gischuki & P.G. McCornick, supra* note 10, pp. 357–358 as regards the Lesotho Highlands Water Project.

33 See *WWF Discussion Paper, supra* note 12, p. 12 as regards compensation within the framework of the implementation of the Tagus-Segura Transfer Scheme; *J. Jupta & P. van der Zaag, supra* note 4, p. 30 as regards the distributional issues triggered by the implementation of the Lesotho Highlands Water Project.

34 *WWF Discussion Paper, supra* note 12, p. 21.

was not developed at such a level, as to provide the necessary instruments for the assessment of the relevant impacts and to contain rules underpinned by an integrated approach as regards water management. The main observation which arises from the above analysis is that the choice of IBTs as an option for satisfying increasing water demand presupposes the extensive examination and the reasoned exclusion of all the other less complicated and more environmentally friendly alternatives. Moreover, there is an increased need for their justification both from the legal and the scientific perspective and the arrangement of adequate compensation for those affected by the project implementation as an integral part of the application of the good governance requirements.

3. ASSESSING THE IBTs UNDER THE PRISM OF THE NEW REGULATORY CONCEPTS IN WATER AND ENVIRONMENTAL LAW, WITH EMPHASIS ON THE DEVELOPMENTS AT EU LEVEL

3.1. THE 'PARADIGM SHIFT' IN WATER LAW AND ITS RELEVANCE FOR ASSESSING IBTs

Water law, which constitutes the cornerstone for an effective, fair and sustainable management and the protection of the scarce water resources at the various levels of governance, has been subject to a partial 'paradigm shift'.[35] In particular, water law regimes, despite the significant divergences to be observed in different parts of the world, cover quite similar issues and their current regulative concepts reflect, more or less, the changing notions of ownership and water rights, the struggle between the perception of water as a public good and the emerging trend for the privatisation of water services, the discussion about the appropriate scale for water management and the incorporation of environmental concerns in water management.[36] This gradual but continuing change of the relevant regulatory approaches can be regarded as a response to the need of copying with certain significant economic, social and environmental changes, such as population growth, increasing urbanisation, climate induced changes on water resources and increased water demand as well as with the situations arising thereof (e.g. accessibility and affordability of water services).[37] Moreover, these developments

35 *J.W. Dellapennna*, The Berlin Rules on Water Resources: The new Paradigm for International Water Law, www.ualg.pt.

36 *J. Gupta & J.W. Dellapenna*, *supra* note 1, p. 396 pointing out that Water Law Regimes are characterised by coherence in the North and pluralism in the South.

37 *M. Ambrus, H.K. Gilissen & J.J.H. van Kempen*, Public Values in Water Law: A Case of Substantive Fragmentation?, Utrecht Law Review 2014 (10), p. 8, 10 et seq. analysing how the three aspects of water (economic, social and environmental) are addressed in water law

in water law have to be viewed in conjunction with the partial change of 'paradigm' in environmental law. Such a change of 'approach' is underpinned by the adoption of presumably more flexible environmental regulations and instruments, the introduction of monitoring mechanisms as well as the increased input of science in decision-making processes, in order to cope with the inherent uncertainties associated with the non-linear functions of the ecosystems (non-equilibrium paradigm), the 'risks' associated with the technological development, and more recently the uncertainties related to climate change.[38]

In this context, the new regulatory paradigm in water law is, *inter alia*, characterised by the adoption of an integrated regulatory approach in managing and protecting freshwater that pays attention not only to the satisfaction of the human needs but at least to some extent to the intrinsic value and the 'needs' of the water ecosystems.[39] Moreover, a central element of the new 'paradigm' in water law, although not yet fully implemented, relates to the introduction of mechanisms of adaptive management, such as transparent and flexible water licensing regimes, efficient demand-side management and monitoring mechanisms, as a means to increase resilience to the effects of the climate change.[40] This, at least, partial re-orientation of water law regimes is thus significant in terms of defining the regulatory concepts and the direct or indirect criteria under which the permissibility of each specific IBT will be assessed. This does not mean, though, that such a re-orientation can be in any case sufficient to ensure the existence of relevant rules and criteria for such an assessment, as this depends, to a significant extent, on the art by which the critical norms are formulated in terms of vagueness and flexibility and on the subsequent margin of discretion which is left to the competent authorities.[41]

regimes and how certain core public values in Water Law are reflected in the rules of conduct at the various level of governance.

38 *D. Tarlok*, The 'Non Equilibrium Paradigm' in Ecology and the Partial Unraveling of Environmental Law, Loyola Law Review, 1994 (27), p. 1121, 1139 et seq. For the transformation of the Environmental Law attributed to its endeavor concerning the regulation of risks see *A. Scherzberg*, Risikosteurung durch Verwaltungsrecht: Ermöglichung oder Begrenzung von Innovationen?, VVDStRL, 2003 (63), p. 214, 222 et seq. See also *J. Ebbesson*, The Rule of Law in Governance of Complex Socio-Ecological Changes, Global Environmental Change, 2010 (20), p. 412 et seq. analysing how the mechanisms of adaptive governance could be compatible with the requirements of the rule of law.

39 The recent Water Law Reforms reflecting the above described paradigm shift were influenced to a significant extent by two regulative concepts, the so-called Integrated Water Resources Management and the adoption of the human-rights approach to water management (*A. Iza & R. Stein* (eds.), RULE-Reforming Water Governance, 2009, p. 20 et seq.).

40 *C. Bruch*, Adaptive Water Management: Strengthening Laws to Cope with Uncertainty, in A.K. Biswas, C. Tortajada & R. Izquiero (eds.), Water Management Beyond 2020, 2009, p. 89, 92 et seq.; *A. Keessen & H.F.M.W. van Rijswick*, Adaptation to Climate Change in European Water Law and Policy, Utrecht Law Review, 2012 (8), p. 38 et seq.

41 *S. van Holten* & *H.F.M.W. van Rijswick, supra* note 9, pp. 44–45 analysing the risk of decreasing the effectiveness of EU environmental law in cases where the provisions of the so-called Governance-Mode Directives offer more policy discretion to the Member States concerning policies and standard setting.

Furthermore, it is of relevance that although two of the most significant legal instruments dealing with transboundary water management, namely the UN Convention on the Law of the Non-Navigational Uses of International Watercourses[42] (UN Watercourses Convention) and the Convention on the Protection and Use of Transboundary Watercourses and International Lakes[43] (Water Convention) do not address specifically the issue of IBTs, they can provide certain directions for planned IBTs with transboundary dimensions. This can be attributed to the fact that both the principle of equitable and reasonable utilisation of the shared water sources and the 'no harm' rule which are established in the UN Watercourses Convention,[44] as well as the principle of sustainable water use and the precautionary principle established in the Water Convention, are critical for extracting certain criteria relating to the assessment of planned IBTs. These standards relate to the satisfaction of basic human needs as a justifying reason for large water infrastructure projects, the obligation to examine alternatives,[45] the preservation of water sources in a long-term perspective and the obligation to take proactive action to avoid adverse effects on water ecosystems also under circumstances of high uncertainty. Finally, the relevant concept adopted by the Water Convention which is based on the obligation of the riparian states to establish a cooperative framework for transboundary water management including joint institutional arrangements, quality objectives and monitoring mechanisms, constitutes a concrete framework under which IBTs with transboundary dimensions should be assessed.[46]

---

42 The Convention has entered into force on August 2014 and has 35 Contracting Parties so far.

43 The Convention which was negotiated as a Regional Instrument, entered into force on October 1996. In February 2013, the relevant amendments, which allow accession by all UN Members, entered into force (Guide to Implementing the Water Convention, UN Doc. ECE/MP.WAT/39, 2013). See also *A. Rieu-Clarke & R. Kinna*, Can Two Global UN Water Conventions Effectively Co-exist? Making the Case for a Package Approach to Support Institutional Coordination, RECIEL, 2014 (23), p. 13, 20 et seq.

44 *J.W. Dellapena*, The Customary International Law of Transboundary Fresh Waters, Int. J. Global Environmental Issues, 2001 (1), p. 264, 284 et seq.

45 *J. Jupta & P. van der Zaag, supra* note 4, p. 33.

46 *Guide to Implementing the Water Convention, supra* note 43, p. 9 et seq. See also *A. Keessen, J.J.H. van Kempen & H.F.M.W. van Rijswick*, Transboundary River Basin Management in Europe-Legal Instruments to Comply with European Water Management Obligations in Case of Transboundary Water Pollution and Floods, Utrecht Law Review, 2008 (4), p. 35, 37 et seq. analysing the framework of transboundary cooperation established by other Regional Agreements and its relevance for the achievement of the environmental quality objectives of the EU Water Law.

3.2. THE RELEVANT PRINCIPLES, CRITERIA AND INSTRUMENTS FOR ASSESSING IBTS UNDER THE EU WATER AND ENVIRONMENTAL LAW

3.2.1. *The Critical Principles and Rules in EU Water Law*

The above-described 'paradigm shift' in water law is reflected to a significant extent in the Water Framework Directive[47] (WFD), which constitutes a significant and innovative piece of environmental legislation that aims to make a fundamental shift in the way that Europe's water are protected and managed for a variety of reasons. The first reason relates to the comprehensive way, by which it addresses the relevant issues relating to surface waters and groundwater, in order to surpass the fragmentation that characterised the previous legislative framework,[48] while it constitutes, as already mentioned, a clear example of the new governance approach in the EU environmental law.[49] The second and most significant reason relates to the adoption of a holistic approach as regards water management and protection.[50] This is reflected in a very characteristic way in the recognition of the principle of sustainable water use as the guiding principle that should underpin the water governance regimes (Art. 1(b)), which requires that the watercourses are managed and protected in such a way that safeguards their re-generation capacity, so that the sustainability of the possibility to use water as the core element of the principle can be ensured and moreover the preconditions for a fair water share in an intergenerational perspective can be satisfied.[51] For the purposes of the present chapter it is worth mentioning that although the Directive does not contain any specific rule concerning either the permissibility of IBTs as water infrastructure projects or the specific conditions under which they should be implemented, certain provisions in conjunction with the principle of sustainable water use are critical for assessing the compatibility of such kinds of projects with its regulative concept. Furthermore, a clear position on this issue,

---

47 Directive 2000/60/EC of the European Parliament and of the Council of 23 October 2000 establishing a Framework for Community Action in the Field of Water Policy, OJ L327.

48 *J. Jans & H.H.B. Vedder*, European Environmental Law – After Lisbon, 4th ed., 2012, p. 392; *A. Epiney*, Umweltrecht der Europäischen Union, 3rd ed., 2013, p. 393.

49 *S. van Holten & H.F.M.W. van Rijswick, supra* note 9, p. 23.

50 *P. Canelas de Castro*, European Community Water Policy, in J. W. Dellapenna & J.Gupta (eds.), The Evolution of the Law and Politics of Water, 2009, p. 227, 233 et seq.; *O. Green et al.*, EU Water Governance: Striking the Right Balance between Regulatory Flexibility and Enforcement?, Ecology and Society, 2013 (18), www.ecologyandsociety.org/vol18/iss2/art10/.

51 The principle is also established in the Water Convention (Art. 2(2)(b)), and in certain national water laws, such as the German Federal Water Act (Art. 1). For a constructive analysis of the principle see *P. Lindhout*, Cost Recovery as a Policy Instrument to Achieve Sustainable and Equitable Water Use in Europe and the Netherlands, Dissertation, Utrecht University, March 2015, p. 12 et seq. analysing also the linkage with the normative goal of equitable water use; *P. Lindhout*, A Wider Notion of the Scope of Water Services in EU Water Law: Boosting Payment for Water-Related Ecosystem Services to Ensure Sustainable Water Management?, Utrecht Law Review, 2012 (8), p. 86, 87, 96.

is adopted, as it will be analysed later, in the EU Strategy on Water Scarcity and Droughts,[52] which is a soft-law document presenting several policy options to address these issues at EU level and its implementation is dependent on the full implementation of the WFD.

In this context, two significant criteria which are relevant for judging the permissibility of IBTs from a general point of view could be extracted from the principle of sustainable water use inextricably linked with the normative goal of equitable water use (Art. 1(e) of WFD). The first one lies in the recognition of the carrying and the re-generational capacity of the aquatic ecosystems as the central measure for assessing the acceptable rate of the various water uses and of the infrastructural projects, while the second relates to the preservation of watercourses from both a qualitative and a quantitative perspective to such an extent that they can satisfy the water needs of the future generations.[53]

Furthermore, a central provision of the Directive lies in Article 4, which establishes demanding environmental quality objectives that have to be achieved within a prescribed time-frame.[54] These ambitious objectives are 'watered' to some extent both by their inherent flexibility, as lower standards ('good ecological potential') are foreseen for waters that are classified as 'heavily modified or artificial' and by the provided derogations (Article 4(4) to (8)). Moreover, although the application of such derogations is subject to strict conditions, they still leave enough room for escaping from the achievement of the environmental quality standards, as they were drafted in a vague manner.[55] Subsequently, the objective of 'good surface water status' and the specific goal of 'good ecological status' which is defined also in relation to the extent of the anthropogenic alteration to the water bodies,[56] set, besides the difficulties for setting the specific quality standards and the doubts concerning their achievability,[57] quite precise standards

---

52 *Communication from the Commission to the European Parliament and the Council*, Addressing the Challenge of Water Scarcity and Droughts in the European Union, COM (2007), 414 final.

53 *P. Lindhout, supra* note, 51, p. 12 et seq; *M. Ambrus, H.K. Gilissen & J.J.H. van Kempen, supra* note 37, p. 24, 26; *A. Epiney, supra* note 48, p. 394; *V. Karageorgou*, Interbasin Water Transfers and Sustainable Water Use: A Relationship of Contradiction or Compatibility?, in L. Westra, K. Bösselmann & C. Soskolne (eds.), Globalization and Ecological Integrity in Science and International Law, 2011, pp. 328, 330–332.

54 *A. Epiney, supra* note 48, p. 398 et seq.; *W. Köck*, Die Implementation der EG Wasserrahmenrichtlinie, ZUR, 2009, p. 227, 228 ff as regards the non-deterioration principle; *J.J.H. van Kempen,* Countering the Obscurity of Obligations in European Environmental Law: An Analysis of Article 4 of the European Water Framework Directive, Journal of Environmental Law, 2012 (24), p. 499, 520 et seq.

55 *A. Epiney, supra* note 48, pp. 408–409; *A. Keessen & H.F.M.W. van Rijswick, supra* note 40, p. 45; *S. van Holten* & *H.F.M.W. van Rijswick, supra* note 9, p. 36.

56 *W. Howarth,* The Progression Towards Ecological Quality Standards, Journal of Environmental Law, 2006 (18), pp. 3, 19–21; *S. van Holten* & *H.F.M.W. van Rijswick, supra* note 9, p. 31.

57 *W. Howarth, supra* note 56, p. 22 et seq.; Moreover, another central issue relates to the qualification of the objectives either as obligations of best efforts or as obligations of result. See *A. Keessen et al.*, European River Basin Districts: Are they Swimming in the Same Implementation Pool?, Journal of Environmental Law, 2010 (22), p. 197, 206 et seq.; *J.J.H. van Kempen, supra* note 54, pp. 499–533 proposing a method based on the CJEU jurisprudence for

for the assessment of major infrastructural water projects, such as IBTs that may have adverse effects on the aquatic ecosystems.[58]

Moreover, also relevant in this context are the provisions of the WFD that introduce an integrated ecosystem-oriented management and planning model. A central element of this system lies in Article 3, which defines the river basin district as the organising unit for the river basin management, so that water management should take place on the basis of hydrological instead of administrative boundaries.[59] Furthermore, another significant element of the adopted model relates to the crucial role of planning for achieving the environmental objectives, as the River Basin Management Plan (RBMP), which is established in Article 13 and is based on systematic assessment and monitoring (Articles 5 and 8 of the WFD respectively), constitutes a detailed account of how the specific objectives set for each concrete river basin can be achieved within a concrete time-frame.[60] The RBMP can be regarded as an effective instrument for applying the integrated water management approach established by the Directive, because it constitutes the appropriate framework not only for a comprehensive analysis of the actual situation of the river basin and the factors that can affect it, but also for balancing the often conflicting needs of the water users mainly by defining priorities.[61] Furthermore, a key component of the RBMP is the Programme of Measures (Article 11), which includes both the mandatory measures appropriate for meeting the requirements of other pieces of the EU water legislation as well the licensing for water abstraction and discharges in line with the WFD, and the voluntary measures, in the case that they are necessary to achieve the environmental objectives.[62] Subsequently, the systematic interpretation of Articles 13 and 11 in conjunction with Article 4 leads to the conclusion that the implementation of water infrastructure projects such as IBTs can be authorised only when it is extensively documented primarily in the RBMP of the donor area that their implementation will not jeopardise the achievement of the environmental objectives.

In this context, it is also of relevance that although the Directive does not include any specific obligation for facilitating equitable and consistent adaptation to climate-induced changes in water sector, it provides the framework to address such kind of impacts in the context of the planning process for the elaboration of the RBMPs.[63] A significant reason thereof lies in the fact that the analysis under

the legal qualification of the objectives set in Article 4 and reaching a conclusion, according to which the vast majority of the objectives constitute obligations of result.

58 *W. Köck, supra* note 54, p. 229, n. 26; *W. Howarth, supra* note 56, p. 21.

59 *P. Canelas de Castro, supra* note 50, p. 234; *A. Epiney, supra* note 48, p. 396.

60 *P. Canelas de Castro, supra* note 50, p. 236.

61 *L. Krämer*, Dimensionen Integrierter Gewässerpolitik, in H.J. Koch & Th. Bruha (eds.), Integrierte Gewässerpolitik in Europa, 2001, pp. 41, 47–48.

62 *O. Green et al., supra* note 50; *A. Epiney, supra* note 48, p. 411 et seq.

63 *Common Implementation Strategy for the Water Framework Directive*, River Basin Management in a Changing Climate, Guidance Document No 24, 2009, p. 39; *A. Keessen & H.F.M.W. van Rijswick, supra* note 40, p. 46.

Article 5 should also include the direct and indirect climate-induced changes, while monitoring mechanisms can provide relevant data, in order to identify change as it happens. On the basis of this analysis RBMPs should, thus, be 'climate-proof',[64] although this is not always an easy case first, because it presupposes that the Programmes of Measures facilitate adaptation by including measures already assessed against their effectiveness to cope with the changing climate conditions and by giving emphasis to the adoption of 'non-regret' measures.[65] Moreover, it should also be ensured that a change in the course of action is legally provided even during the planning period, when this is proven necessary by the monitoring results for the achievement of the environmental quality objectives.[66] Under this prism, also the decisions relating to water infrastructure, which involve long-term investments and have to be in line with the Programmes of Measures, have to be checked against their effectiveness to cope with changing climate conditions.[67]

Finally, two key elements of the WFD, which are more or less relevant for the purposes of the present chapter, are established in Articles 9 and 14 respectively. In particular, the former Article establishes the requirement for full cost recovery for water services, which presupposes the internalisation of the environmental and resource cost in the relevant prices.[68] The context of this provision can be of relevance when the financial cost and the economic viability in general of a planned IBT is examined, in the sense it has to be estimated how the cost of the project, including the environmental and resource cost, caused by its implementation can be recovered mainly by the water users concerned.[69] Furthermore, Article 14 establishes mandatory requirements for the disclosure of

---

64 *J. Veraart & M. Bakker*, Climate Proofing, in F. Ludwig, H. van Schaik & M. van der Valk (eds.), Climate Change Adaptation in the Water Sector, 2009, p. 109.

65 *Common Implementation Strategy for the Water Framework Directive, supra* note 63, p. 63 et seq.; *Ecologic*, Climate Change and the EU Water Policy – Inducing Climate Change in River Basin Planning, November 2007, http://ecologic.eu/download/projekte/1850-99/1877/1877_climate_change_and_eu_water_policy.pdf, as regards the definition of the 'non-regret' measures.

66 In this direction *A. Keessen & H.F.M.W. van Rijswick, supra* note 40, pp. 46–47.

67 *European Environment Agency*, Climate Change and Water Adaptation Issues, Technical Report No 2, 2007, p. 31; *Common Implementation Strategy for the Water Framework Directive, supra* note 63, p. 63 et seq.

68 *P. Lindhout, supra* note 51, p. 66 et seq. and 77 et seq. providing an in-depth analysis concerning the legal nature of the provision (rule or principle) and its essential elements. For the relationship with the polluter pays see *P. Lindhout & B. van den Broek*, The Polluter Pays Principle: Guidelines for Cost Recovery and Burden Sharing in the Case Law of the European Court of Justice, Utrecht Law Review, 2014 (10), pp. 46–59. For the application of the relevant provision in Netherlands and in Germany see *P. Lindhout*, Application of the Cost Recovery Principle on Water Services in the Netherlands, JEEPL, 2013 (10), pp. 309–332; *M. Reese*, Cost Recovery and Water Pricing in Water Services and Water Uses in Germany, JEEPL, 2013 (10), pp. 355–377 supporting a rather narrow interpretation of water services and placing emphasis on the margin of discretion left to MS for the application of the provision.

69 *European Environment Agency*, Assessment of cost-recovery through water pricing, Technical Report 16/2013, p. 89; *P. Lindhout, supra* note 51, p. 151 et seq. arguing persuasively that the application of the cost recovery obligation to several categories of water projects depends significantly on the definition of water services; *M. Reese, supra* note 68, p. 370 et seq.

information and the participation of the public in the elaboration of the RBMPs. These procedural arrangements aim to increase the transparency as regards the content of the most significant decisions of water management as well as their acceptability and legitimacy mainly by enabling the consideration of the often conflicting interests of the water users and facilitating the adoption of more balanced and rational decisions.[70] Subsequently, the design of any planned IBT should be subject to an extensive public consultation procedure both in the donor and the recipient region.

In conclusion, EU water law provides certain, more or less direct and indirect, criteria for assessing the compatibility of the designed large-scale water infrastructure projects, such as IBTs, with the established concept of an integrated and ecosystem-oriented management of the scarce water sources and the river basin as a whole. These criteria can be regarded as quite advanced in relation to those established in other legal systems. Furthermore, it is of significance that on the basis of the regulatory concept of the WFD, a clear-cut position on this issue is adopted, as already mentioned, in the EU Strategy on Water Scarcity and Droughts. In particular, the Strategy establishes a clear hierarchy as regards the policy options for satisfying increased water demand by proposing that water-saving and efficiency measures should be the most preferential policy response and the effective water pricing policies and alternative solutions, such as desalination, should be regarded as second best solution. Finally, additional water supply infrastructure, such as IBTs should be examined only when all other options are exhausted and demand still exceeds water availability.[71] Such a thesis is not without regulatory implications mainly due to the interconnectedness of the Strategy with the regulatory concept of the WFD.

3.2.2. The Critical Principles and Instruments in EU Environmental Law

EU environmental law provides certain legal instruments which are crucial for the in advance consideration of the environmental impacts of the various options of water infrastructure, including IBTs and for the assessment of the relevant plans and programmes which provide the framework for the authorisation of such kinds of projects. In particular, the Environmental Impact Assessment (EIA) constitutes a very significant legal instrument in terms of providing a systematic methodology for the assessment of the possible environmental consequences of the designed water infrastructure projects, also in relation to other alternatives that have to be considered before choosing the proposed option.[72] Furthermore,

70 *O. Green et al., supra* note 50; *A. Keessen & H.F.M.W. van Risjiwick, supra* note 40, pp. 42–43.

71 *Communication from the Commission to the European Parliament and the Council,* Addressing the Challenge of Water Scarcity and Droughts in the European Union, *supra* note 52, pp. 7, 10.

72 The Directive 2011/92/EU, which constitutes the codified version of the initial EIA Directive (85/337/EEC) and its subsequent amendments, was recently amended by the Directive 2014/52. See *A. Epiney, supra* note 48, pp. 300, 306 concerning the examination of alternatives.

the Strategic Impact Assessment (SEA)[73] constitutes also a crucial legal instrument for ensuring the compatibility of water infrastructure projects with the Water and Environmental Legislation in general, given the fact that RBMPs, which set the basic directions for examining supply-oriented solutions, are subject to a Strategic Assessment as regards their environmental impacts.[74] Finally, taking into consideration the uncertainties associated with the implementation of the water infrastructure projects and the possible harm that can be caused to the aquatic and the natural environment of the donor area, it is of crucial importance to apply the standards arising from the precautionary principle[75] within the framework of the above-mentioned assessment procedures, in order to come to conclusions which ensure a sufficient level of protection also under complex and uncertain situations.

4. THE CASE OF ACHELOOS UNDER THE PRISM OF ITS LEGAL AND GOVERNANCE PERSPECTIVES

4.1. BACKGROUND INFORMATION FOR THE ACHELOOS DIVERSION SCHEME

The 220km-long Acheloos River is one of the longest rivers in Greece. It flows from north to south through to the humid western part of the country. The diversion plans date back in the twenties, but their realisation was not discussed intensively because of the lack of the technical means and the necessary funds for the implementation of such an ambitious project. The relevant discussion revived in the seventies and the project was defined technically in the early 1980s.[76] The initial version of the project which included the construction of several dams and other interventions provided the diversion of 1.5 billion m^3 water from the Upper Acheloos River to the Plain of Thessaly on an annual basis.[77] The economic viability of the project was not, though, carefully examined.[78] Its main purpose

[73] Directive 2001/42/EC of the European Parliament and of the Council of 27 June 2001 on the Assessment of the Effects of Certain Plans and Programmes on the Environment [2001] OJ L197. See *J. Jans & H.H.B. Vedder, supra* note 48, p. 354 et seq.

[74] *N. de Sadeleer*, The Appropriate Impact Assessment and Authorization Requirements of Plans and Programmes likely to have Significant Impacts on Natura 2000 Sites, elni Review, 1+2/2013, p. 7 et seq. analysing the specific procedural mechanism ('Appropriate Impact Assessment') established in Article 6(3) of the Habitats Directive (92/43/EEC).

[75] *N. de Sadeleer*, The Effect of Uncertainty on the Threshold Levels to which the Precautionary Principle Appears to be Subject, Environmental Risk, Vol. II, 2004, p. 453, 464 et seq.

[76] *K. Hadjibiros*, The River Acheloos Diversion Scheme, www.hydrodinosaurs.fr.st.

[77] Several construction works, such as the Dams in Mesohora and Sykia and a part of the diversion tunnel were included in the 'Integrated Mediterranean Programmes' and received EU funding. In spite of receiving EU financing, only the dam in Mesohora and certain auxiliary works were partially constructed (*K. Hadjibiros, supra* note 76).

[78] The first economic analysis carried out in 1988 came to the conclusion that the scheme's economic viability was marginal, although it did not consider the environmental cost of the water transfer (*K. Hadjibiros, supra* note 76).

was primarily to boost agricultural production in the main agricultural region of Greece, Thessaly and secondary to provide water services in the urban areas. Even at its initial phase the project sparked a long and intense debate between its proponents and the opponents, which resulted, at least to some extent, in a quasi-social conflict between the future beneficiaries from the recipient region and those affected by the implementation.[79] The critique against the project, the failure to present it as an energy-only project with the aim to receive EU funding and the issues raised as regards the 'real' diversion potential led to the re-definition of the project,[80] which was characterised by the significant reduction of the diverted water (600m^3). The insufficient consideration of the environmental impacts of the project and the lack of any form of compensation to those affected gave rise to a long judicial battle before the Greek Council of State and the CJEU, as will be presented below.

4.2. THE JURISPRUDENCE OF THE COUNCIL OF STATE BEFORE THE REQUEST FOR A PRELIMINARY RULING

The Rulings of the Council of State (Supreme Administrative Court) in the *Acheloos* case constitute a characteristic example of the Court's environmental-related jurisprudence, which is underpinned by the sufficient consideration of the relevant legal developments at international and EU level, the deployment of methods of dynamic interpretation and the recognition of broad criteria concerning the entitlement of citizens and NGOs to take legal action.[81] In this context, the Council of State annulled the relevant environmental licences granted for specific components of the diversion project on the grounds of the violation of the EIA legislation.[82] The reasoning of the Court, which was identical in the two rulings, was based on the assumption that the EIA studies, on which the licences were based, did not satisfy the requirement of the EIA legislation

[79] *K. Hadjibiros, supra* note 76. For the environmental issues triggered by the project implementation also in the light of the concept of sustainable water use see *K. Sakellaropoulou & N. Sekeroglou*, The Sustainable Management of Water Resources, Nomos and Physis (e-journal), November 2006, www. nomosphysis.org.gr.

[80] *V. Danilakis,* The Controversial Project for the Diversion of the River Acheloos: Pros and Cons in Anticipation of the CJEU Ruling?, Nomos and Physis (e-journal), December 2009, www. nomosphysis.org.gr.

[81] The Court developed broad legal standing criteria by recognising the right to take legal action not only to a wide circle of persons, but also to NGOs, legal entities and even groups of persons not possessing legal personality who are interested in the protection of the environment (*K. Menoudakos*, The Protection of the Environment in Greek Public Law – The Contribution of the Jurisprudence of the Council of State, Nomos and Physis (e-journal), February 1997, www.nomosphysis.org.gr.

[82] Decision 2759/1994 held invalid the Joint Ministerial Decision granting environmental licence for the dams and reservoirs in Pyli and Mousaki and Decision 2760/1994 annulled the relevant Decision granting environmental licence for the dams and reservoirs in Sykia and Mesohora. Both petitions for annulment were submitted by a group of national NGOs.

for a comprehensive assessment of the impacts of the composite project, because each of them referred only to some of its specific components. In this context, the Court stressed the need for a composite and comprehensive EIA study of the highest scientific standard as a prerequisite for the environmental authorisation of this large-scale and technically complex project (Decision 2759/1994, paras. 14, 15; Decision 2760/1994, paras. 11–15).

The Council annulled also the environmental licence granted for the composite project in its 'soft' redefined version and the relevant approval of the Minister of Culture on the grounds that the comprehensive EIA study did not examine extensively certain alternatives concerning the structure, the art of construction and the capacity of the designed dams, so that the realisation of the diversion project could not cause significant harm to the cultural monuments protected under the Granada Convention (Plenary Decision 3478/2000, paras. 17–21). From a general point of view, the decision signalises the adoption of a more balanced approach concerning the formulation of the principle of sustainable development, as, although the Court did not shed enough light on the specification of its content, the principle was perceived in its dominant three-pillar version.[83] On the basis of this assumption and in accordance with the self-restricting approach concerning the scope of the judicial control, the Court rejected the argument of the petitioners that the composite project contradicts the principle of sustainable development, as it did not come to the conclusion that either the EIA was based on inaccurate data or that the expected harm to the environment could be of such scale as to violate this principle.

In an effort to align with the standards set in the previous ruling, the administration carried out a supplementary EIA Study which examined extensively all possible alternative options for the realisation of the diversion project and its impact on certain cultural monuments protected under the Granada Convention, on which the new environmental permit granted in 2003 was based. The Court annulled this time the relevant permit for reasons relating to the violation of the water legislation (Plenary Decision 1688/2005). In particular, the Court's reasoning was based on the assumption that the authorisation of a water infrastructure project could be compatible with the then existing water legislation (Law 1739/1987) only when it was examined and positively assessed within the framework of the Regional Programmes for Water Utilization. On the basis of this premise, the Court ruled that due to the absence of such Water Programmes for the Critical Basins, which could set the conditions for

83 *G. Dellis*, From the Shipyard of Pylos to the Mining Sites of Kassandra: The Sustainable Development Between the Law Making Powers of the Judge and the Myth-Evocations of the Legal Theory, in Council of State (ed.), Collective works celebrating the 75 years of the Greek Council of State, 2004, p. 1057, 1062 et seq. criticising the relevant jurisprudence of the Council of State in the late eighties and in the nineties relating to the recognition of an *a priori* prerogative to the protection of the environment in comparison to other state goals or individual rights, which was not based on a balancing procedure with specific methods and clear criteria.

the implementation of such a complex water infrastructure project and on which the environmental permit could be based, the latter was invalid. The Court came to this conclusion by interpreting the relevant provisions of the existing water legislation also in the light of the principle of sustainable water use, as established in the WFD, although at this time the Directive was not yet transposed into the national law[84] (paras. 14–16).

In response to the Decision 1688/2005, the then Ministry of Environment authorised a RBMP for the critical basins of Acheloos and Pineios by a formal Law (Articles 9 and 13 of Law 3481/2006, Hellenic Government Gazette Issue A/162/2.08.2006). A new environmental permit that was based on the EIA Study, which was included in the environmental permit annulled by the latest Court Decision, was also granted by the same Law. Certain environmental NGOs and citizens of the affected region submitted three petitions for annulment either of the RBMP and the environmental permit included in the form of a formal Law or of the administrative acts, which provided for the continuation of certain construction works by virtue of Article 13(4) of Law 3481/2006. The Council of State, which decided to join the cases due to their contextual relevance, requested the CJEU to give answers to 14 complex questions concerning the interpretation of four EU Directives, which related to several aspects of the diversion project (Decision 3053/2009). It is worth noting that although the Court took the view that only the act by which an instruction was given to the company awarded the relevant contract to continue the works for the construction of a certain dam is an administrative act, against which a petition for annulment can be admissibly exercised, it came to the conclusion that the issuance of this act makes possible the continuation of the whole composite project. On the basis of this assumption, the Court assumed responsibility for reviewing the legality of the whole project, a position which was criticised on the grounds that it raises issues of judicial activism, as the linkage of the critical administrative act with the composite project enabled the review of the formal laws on which the project was based in terms of their compatibility mainly with the EU law.[85] Despite such a critique, the Court justified the relevant position, to a significant extent, persuasively, by stressing the need for ensuring the effective exercise of the right to judicial protection. Moreover, the relevant decision can be regarded as a characteristic example of the influence which both the principle of the effective legal protection as a general principle of the EU Law and the right to a fair trial established in ECHR (Article 6) exerted on the jurisprudence of the Council of State, which is reflected even on the wider definition of critical terms of administrative law,

---

[84] *Gl. Siouti*, The Diversion of the Acheloos River in the Jurisprudence of the Council of State, in A. Marangopoulou-Giotopoulou, A. Bredimas & L. Sisilianos (eds.), The Protection of the Environment in Law and in Praxis, 2008, p. 72, 79.

[85] *E. Trova*, Comments on the Decision 26/2014 of the Council of State, Environment and Law 4/2013, p. 672.

such as the administrative act, as a prerequisite for accepting the admissibility of petitions for annulment and ensuring thereby effective legal protection.[86]

4.3. THE CJEU RULING IN THE *ACHELOOS* CASE

The CJEU ruling[87] dealt with significant definitional issues mainly in the field of EU water and environmental law. The first four questions related mainly to whether the formal law, by which the diversion project was authorised before the expiry of the deadline for the notification of RBMPs, was in conformity with the WFD. Departing from the thesis that Article 13(6) of the WFD only sets an ultimate time-limit for the production of RBMPs and not a special time-limit for the transposition of the provisions which relate to the RBMPs, such as Article 4 (para. 47), the Court took the view that in absence of a specific provision concerning inter-basin water transfer, the central provision against which the permissibility of the diversion project should be assessed is Article 4(1), as the project implementation can endanger the achievement of the environmental objectives set in this provision[88] (para. 49). Moreover, the Court clearly recognised the linkage between the achievement of the environmental objectives and the elaboration of RBMPs in the sense that their realisation is dependent on the adoption of certain conservation measures within the framework of the Programmes of Measures as an integral part of RBMPs (paras. 51–52). On the basis of these assumptions and the fact that the diversion project was authorised at a time at which the time-limit for the notification of RBMPs had not expired, the Court came to an initial conclusion, according to which Article 4(1) is not applied to the concrete RBMP adopted by law and water transfer between river basins is in principle allowed before the notification of the RBMPs (paras. 53–56). By recalling, though, its settled case law concerning the advance effects of the Directives,[89] the Court indirectly applied Article 4(1). The indirect application of the above provision is, though, limited, because it constitutes the basis for the application by analogy of the derogation provision set in Article 4(7). The Court's thesis was based on the assumption that the obligations of the Greek Authorities under the advance effect doctrine could not go further than those established by the derogation provision (paras. 64, 65). Subsequently, the Court came to conclusion that the project can be permissible only if it satisfies the conditions set Article 4(7), a fact which is up to the national court to decide (para. 68).

86 *E. Prevedourou*, The Influence of the European Law on the Judicial Proceedings before the Council of State, 2012, p. 56 et seq.

87 CEJU Judgment, Case C-43/10, *Nomarchiaki Aftodioikisi Aitoloakarnanias and Others*, 2012, OJ C 355/2.

88 Opinion of the Advocate General Kokott in Case C-43/10, *Nomarchiaki Aftodioikisi Aitoloakarnanias and Others*, delivered on 13 October 2011, para. 66.

89 CJEU Judgment, Case C-129/96, *Inter-Environment Wallonie* [1997] ECR I-7411, para. 45.

The Court's reasoning concerning the application by analogy of Article 4(7) of the WFD does not seem, though, to be sufficiently persuasive, first because it does not take sufficiently into consideration the exceptional character of this provision, which speaks for its restrictive application.[90] Furthermore, such a thesis circumvents Article 4(7)(b), which aims to ensure that the design of such projects is justified within the framework of the RBMPs,[91] a justification which also includes the consideration of their impacts under the changing climate conditions. Subsequently, this position practically results in the 'relaxation' of the relevant conditions for the implementation of the water infrastructure project, a consequence which seems to be in contradiction with the main Court's argument for the application by analogy of the above provision.[92]

Furthermore, the Court answered the question about a possible violation of Article 14 of the WFD because of the approval of the RBMP within the framework of a legislative procedure, which it did not provide for a public consultation procedure, by ruling that this Article does not apply to this case, as the critical RBMP cannot be regarded as such within the meaning of Articles 13 and 15 of the WFD (paras. 73–74). The thesis of the Court does not seem to be persuasive, because it was based on a merely 'formal' argument,[93] without placing sufficient emphasis on the content of the critical RBMP and on the fact that it would continue to be in force after the elapse of the relevant deadline for the elaboration of the other RBMPs, as it was rightly pointed out by the AG[94] (paras. 122–123).

---

90 *P. de Smedt & H.F.M.W. van Rijswick*, Nature Conservation and Water Management-One battle?, in C.H.Born et al. (eds.), The Habitats Directive in its EU Environmental Law Context, European Nature' s Best Hope?, 2015, p. 417, 424 et seq. analysing the scope and the conditions for the application of the derogation provisions of Article 4, relating also to the requirement to ensure the same level of protection as in the existing EU Legislation.

91 The Court did not shed enough light on the application of this vague formulated provision as, in contrast to the AG (paras. 85–91), it did not analyse in-depth which objectives of a diversion project could constitute either a reason of an overriding public interest or a sustainable development measure and how the benefits of the project can be balanced against the benefits of achieving the environmental objectives. In this context see also *P. de Smedt & H.F.M.W. van Rijswick, supra* note 90, p. 427 et seq. analysing what could be classified as a 'sustainable development measure' and arguing that the explanation of the reasons for the application of the Article 4(7) in the RBMPs is a reporting obligation, a position which can be accepted under the framework in which it is developed for ensuring a level of flexibility concerning the development of major infrastructure projects (e.g. it is presupposed that precise and updated scientific information on the current water status and the risks associated with the project implementation is available and taken into consideration, the conditions for the application of the derogation provision are extensively discussed in public consultation procedures and are meticulously assessed within the framework of the decision-making procedures).

92 *G. Balias*, The Judgments of the CJEU and the Council of State concerning the diversion of the Acheloos River: A Critical Assessment, Nomiko Bima 2012, pp. 2231, 2232–2233.

93 The Court based its position on the fact that in the course of the judicial proceedings which were initiated by the Commission against Greece for not producing RBMPs within the set deadline, Greece did not claim that it had produced an RBMP within the meaning of the WFD (CJEU Judgment, Case 297/11, *European Commission v. Greece, et al.* [2012]).

94 The AG came to the conclusion that the approval of a RBMP by Law violates Article 14 of the WFD, as the Directive does not provide any derogation from the specific conditions for the approval of RBMPs, such as those provided in Article 1(5) of the EIA Directive.

The CJEU also had to deal with the issue of the compatibility of the adopted course of action with the EIA Directive, as the environmental permit for the diversion project granted by Law 3841/2006, was based on the EIA study which was carried out as part of the administrative process that resulted in the issuance of the previous environmental licence, which was annulled. Furthermore, the relevant public participation procedures were limited to the publication of the critical study. The Court based its position on the relevant jurisprudence concerning the application of the exception from the EIA procedure established in Article 1(5) of the EIA Directive[95] (Article 1(4) of Directive 2011/92) and ruled that the critical issue, which is up to the national court to determine, is whether the conditions for the application of this exception are satisfied. Moreover, the Court held that the fact that the EIA study, on which the specific legislative act was based, had served as the basis for an annulled environmental permit is irrelevant provided that the relevant information was not outdated[96] (paras. 86, 87, 91).

The other issue which was raised by the Council of State related to whether Law 3841/2006, which authorised the diversion project, satisfied the requirements of the SEA Directive. Departing from the fact that the plan to divert a river cannot be conceived as a plan within the meaning of the Article 2(a) of the Directive, because it is not required by legislative or regulatory provisions, the Court, in line also with the Opinion of the AG (para. 149), came to the conclusion that it falls outside its scope of application[97] (para. 96).

Finally, the Court had to deal with several questions relating to the compatibility of the authorisation of the diversion project with the EU Nature Conservation Law.[98] In this context, the Court answered positively the relevant question concerning the applicability of the provisions of Article 6 of the Habitats Directive to the national habitats and habitats of species, which were proposed to be included in the relevant list for Sites of Community Importance (SICs) and could be affected by the project implementation, because in accordance with Article 254 TEEC the relevant Commission Decision was in effect, as it was notified

95 ECJ Judgment, Case C-437/97, *WWF and Others* [1999] ECR I-5613; ECJ Judgment, Case C-287/98, *Linster* [2000] ECR I-5613; CJEU Judgment, Joined Cases C-128/09 to C-131/09, C-134/09 and C-135/09, *Boxus and Others* [2011] ECR I-9711; CJEU Judgment, Case C-182/10, *Solvay and Others*, 2012, OJ C98.

96 The AG placed specific emphasis on the need that the national court examines whether the information was still sufficient by the time of the adoption of the legislative act, in order to determine whether the objectives of the EIA Directive are achieved (paras. 143–144).

97 It is worth noting that the relatively 'problematic' formulation of the relevant question of the Council of State, which was limited to the possible application of the SEA Directive to the diversion plan, did not hinder the AG from examining the core issue of the applicability of the Directive to the RBMP authorised by Law 3841/2006. On the basis of her well-founded thesis that this Plan is a RBMP in the meaning of the WFD, the AG came to the subsequent and persuasive conclusion that it is also subject to the provisions of the SEA Directive (para. 152).

98 *P. de Smedt & H.F.M.W. van Rijswick, supra* note 90, p. 426 et seq. analysing the issues triggered in cases of cumulative application of the WFD and the Habitats Directive.

to Greece before the enactment of the Law 3841/2006[99] (para. 105). Furthermore, the Court dealt with the question of the Council of State, which related to the existence of reliable data as a precondition for granting development consent and was formulated in a way that it did not take sufficiently into consideration the scope of application and the specific functions of the 'Appropriate Impact Assessment'[100] (AIA) as a distinct assessment instrument in relation to the EIA Instrument. In this context, the Court referred to its relevant jurisprudence for the content and the type of the above-mentioned instrument.[101] On the basis of this assumption, the Court ruled that Article 6(3) of the Habitats Directive does not allow the authorisation of a diversion project, which is likely to have a significant effect on the integrity of a Special Protected Area for birds in the absence of updated and reliable data concerning birds in this area, because such a lack hinders the competent authorities from carrying out an AIA based on the best scientific knowledge (paras. 112–113 and 115). Furthermore, another issue which was raised related to whether the supply of drinking water and the irrigation could be classified as reasons of overriding public interest capable of justifying the diversion project under Article 6(4) of the Habitats Directive. In line with its relevant jurisprudence, according to which the relevant reasons must be both public and overriding (CJEU Judgment, *Solvay and Others*, para. 75), the Court ruled, in line also with the Opinion of AG (para. 222), that both the supply of drinking water and the irrigation can be, in principle, regarded as such reasons (para. 122). Moreover, it ruled that where the diversion project can adversely affect the integrity of a SCI hosting a priority natural habitat or a priority species, its implementation can be justified mainly by the reasons linked to the supply of drinking water (para. 126), as in accordance with its relevant jurisprudence health considerations prevail over nature protection. It can be argued that the Court's position concerning the classification of irrigation as a reason of overriding public interest does not take sufficiently into account both the restrictive language of the derogation provision and the severity of its impact on the environment.[102]

In this context, the Court also dealt with issues relating to compensatory measures provided in Article 6(4) of the Habitats Directive.[103] In particular, it

---

99 The AG expressed a differentiated opinion concerning the applicability of Article 6 para. 3, which was based on the assumption that the authorisation procedure had been in progress for a long time, giving thus priority to the administrative efficiency and legal certainty instead of the dynamic environmental protection (para. 190).

100 *N. de Sadeleer, supra* note 74, p. 12 et seq.

101 In line with the regulative context of Article 6(3) of the Habitats Directive and the relevant jurisprudence of the CJEU, the Council of State should have examined in the course of the main judicial proceedings whether the critical EIA Study incorporated also a form of Assessment which fulfils the requirements of the AIA or not (*G. Balias, supra* note 92, pp. 2234, 2235).

102 *N. de Sadeleer, supra* note 74, pp. 19, 20; *G. van Hoorick*, Compensatory Measures in European Nature Conservation Law, Utrecht Law Review, 2014 (10), pp. 161, 168–169.

103 *G. van Hoorick, supra* note 102, pp. 163 et seq. The questions concerning the reasons of overriding public interest and the criteria for determining the sufficiency of the compensatory measures could not have been raised, if the Council of State would have focused on the central

ruled that both the extent of the diversion project and the scale of works are factors that have be taken into account, in order to identify precisely the adverse impact on the site concerned and to determine the necessary compensatory measures, in order to ensure the overall coherence of the Natura 2000 network (para. 132). Furthermore, the Court ruled that the nature conservation regime of the Habitats Directive, interpreted in the light of the principle of sustainable development enshrined in Article 6 EC, allows the conversion of a natural fluvial ecosystem into a man-made fluvial lacustrine ecosystem provided that the conditions of Article 6(4) of the Directive are satisfied (paras. 134–139). It is worth noting that both the Court and the AG did not shed enough light on the specification of the content of the sustainable development principle, which was perceived in its dominant three pillar version, as it is demonstrated by the adoption of a conciliatory approach as regards its content and the relationship between the three pillars (economic, social and environmental). Furthermore, the Court's position, according to which the obligation of Article 6(4) for compensatory measures allows the conversion of a natural ecosystem into a man-made system, provided that the conditions to ensure the overall coherence of the Natura 2000 network are satisfied, does not seem to be compatible with the *ratio* of the introduction of such measures as condition for the application of the derogation provision and with the relevant criteria for ensuring biological integrity and ecological functionality of the protected sites in question, as they are determined in the relevant Guidance Document.[104] From a general point of view, despite certain doubts concerning the foundation of some positions mainly under the prism of a teleological interpretation of the relevant legislative regimes, the Court's ruling is significant in terms of determining the critical rules for judging the permissibility of water transfer schemes especially under the prism of the EU water law. Moreover, the fact that the authorisation procedure started before the entry into force of several important pieces of the EU water and environmental legislation and lasted several years, played a significant role when the Court ruled on the applicability of certain EU rules.

issue of whether an AIA had been carried out or not, because the application of the derogation provision of Article 6(4) presupposes the existence of an AIA (CJEU Judgment, Case C-521/12, *T.C. Briels and Others*, 2014, paras. 35, 36). See also *P. de Smedt & H.F.M.W. van Rijswick, supra* note 90, p. 426.

104 *G. van Hoorick, supra* note 102, p. 169 with an extensive analysis of the relevant Guidance Document (European Commission, Guidance document on Article 6(4) of the 'Habitats Directive' 92/43/EEC, 2007).

4.4. THE DECISION OF THE COUNCIL OF STATE AFTER THE CJEU RULING

The final act of this long judicial battle was the Decision of the Council of State (26/2014, Plenary Session), which reviewed the legality of the composite project in the light of the findings of the CJEU Ruling. In particular, the Court ruled that the project does not satisfy the requirements of Article 4(7) of the WFD for certain reasons. The first one relates to the fact that it is not justified in the RBMP authorised by law why the pursued objectives of irrigation and supply of drinking water in the region of Thessaly can outweigh the benefits arising from the achievement of the environmental objectives, while the second relates to the insufficient documentation in the RBMP as regards to whether other more environmental friendly alternatives were examined and excluded for reasons relating to their technical feasibility or their disproportionately high cost. Finally, another reason related to the fact that it had not been demonstrated that all the technically practical measures for the mitigation of the adverse effects of the diversion project have been taken (paras. 12, 13, 14). Subsequently, the Court's Ruling at this point took sufficiently into consideration the relevant position of the CJEU.

The Court's position concerning the permissibility of the diversion project with the EIA Directive can, though, raise issues of partial incompatibility with the relevant position of the CJEU. In particular, the Court ruled that the environmental licence for the project granted by a specific legislative act does not satisfy the relevant provisions of the EIA Directive and the national legislation as regards public information and consultation first because in accordance with the relevant Rules of Procedure, the parliamentary discussion did not provide the opportunity for the public to get informed and to participate in any form of dialogue concerning the EIA study. Furthermore, the relevant requirements were not satisfied, because the Members of the Parliament did not have either sufficient time or the necessary scientific support, in order to elaborate the relevant material and assess adequately the consequences of the project (para. 17). Subsequently, the Court's position is partially not in line with the relevant CJEU finding, because the scrutinisation of the relevant parliamentary procedure is relevant only to the extent necessary for the Court to review whether the second condition of the exception established in Article 1(5) of the EIA Directive, namely the achievement of its objectives through the legislative process, is satisfied. Moreover, the review of the observation of the public participation provisions within the framework of the parliamentary procedure did not serve any purpose in the sense that, as the judicial review should focus on the examination of the fulfilment of the conditions for the application of the exception (Article 1(5)), in the case of such an application, deviations from the ordinary administrative procedure are acceptable and in the case of the non-application, the EIA Directive as a whole is violated.[105]

Furthermore, the Court ruled that the authorisation of the relevant project violates the provisions of Article 6(3) and (4) of the Habitats Directive. In particular, it held that, although an AIA had to be carried out in this case due to the likely effects of the project on the protected sites, the lack of updated and reliable data concerning birds made it impossible, so that the authorisation of the diversion project violates the critical provision (Article 6(3)). Moreover, the Court ruled that the derogation provision of Article 6(4) cannot be applied to this case, because the conditions for its application (exclusion of alternatives and adoption of compensatory measures) were not met (para. 21). Subsequently, the Court' s ruling at this point is quite ambiguous in the sense that it was not sufficiently clarified that the derogation provision can be applied only if an AIA had been conducted.

The Court dealt also with the issue of the compatibility of the authorisation of the diversion project with the relevant provisions for the protection of the cultural heritage. After an extensive review of the relevant Studies, the Court ruled that the authorisation of the diversion project was invalid, because both the relevant constitutional provision for the protection of the cultural environment (Article 24(6)) and the provisions of the Granada Convention were violated due to the insufficient protection of certain cultural monuments in the donor area (para. 27).

Finally, although the Court did not specify the regulative contours of the complex principle of sustainable development either by adopting its third pillar version or by giving an *a priori* priority to the environmental pillar, it ruled that the diversion project as a whole contradicts this principle, as it is established in the EU primary law and in the Constitution. The Court's reasoning was based on the assumption that the diversion project violates a series of rules of the EU and national environmental legislation (para. 29), thereby indirectly prioritising the environmental protection. Moreover, the Court justified quite persuasively the change of its position in relation to that in a previous ruling (Decision 3478/2000) by the fact that the recent legal developments (entry into force of the WFD, revised CAP) which took place, created a new framework. The Court's thesis, according to which the review of the compatibility of the composite project with this principle on the basis of the file material and the common experience does not exceed the limits of the judicial control, can be, though, regarded as partially questionable, because, as it was argued by the minority opinion, it remains doubtful whether the judge on the basis of the above can directly assess the consequences of the project. The strong technical and scientific background of the case can also support such an approach.

---

105 *E. Trova*, *supra* note 85, p. 672 et seq.

From a general point of view, the Court's ruling is, by and large, in line with the relevant finding of the CJEU and is also significant in terms of recognising that even in times of an economic crisis, major infrastructure projects justified by socio-economic reasons cannot be permitted and implemented without the observance of strict environmental standards.

5. CONCLUDING REMARKS

The analysis of the normative aspects concerning IBT schemes as a response to the emerged water crisis leads to certain conclusions that can provide guidance for answering the central question of the chapter. The first conclusion is that although EU water law does not contain any specific provision concerning IBTs, it has reached, to some extent, the point of containing certain principles and criteria for measuring their permissibility, which cannot be found easily in other legal systems, as it was also demonstrated by the examination of the three IBT schemes implemented in different parts of the world. Such a development has to be viewed also in conjunction with the partial change of 'paradigm' in water law. Moreover, the relevant CJEU ruling in the *Acheloos* case is significant in terms of determining the critical provisions for judging the permissibility of IBTs mainly under WFD. Furthermore the contribution of the EU environmental law is also critical in terms of providing certain legal instruments, which are crucial for assessing in advance the environmental impacts of the various options for water supply, including IBTs, (EIA) and of the relevant plans and programmes which set the directions for their authorisation (SEA). Despite the progress which has been made concerning the development of the relevant regulatory concepts, certain issues can, though, be raised first because the Directives introducing the assessment instruments are highly procedural. Subsequently, the quality of the assessments, which constitute the basis for the decisions concerning the development of major infrastructure projects, cannot always be ensured. Moreover, the procedural character of the provisions of the WFD in conjunction with the discretion left to Member States concerning the application of the vague formulated derogation provisions can result in the possible misuse of the exceptions as a basis for decisions concerning the development of water infrastructure, such as IBTs. In such circumstances and if the relevant decisions are challenged, the role of the national courts is crucial for reviewing the relevant decisions mainly from the standpoint of the exercise of the discretion by the authorities, while certain substantive criteria concerning the achievement of a certain level of protection can also be taken into consideration.[106]

The second conclusion, which is drawn after the systematic overview of the critical provisions of the EU water and environmental law and in line, in large

[106] *S. van Holten* & *H.F.M.W. van Rijswick*, *supra* note 90, pp. 43, 45.

terms, with their interpretation within the framework of the CJEU ruling, is that the authorisation of IBTs is hardly compatible with the relevant EU regulatory framework and is, thus, subject to very strict conditions. Such conditions become even stricter and more complicated, when the relevant project, as was the case with the Acheloos diversion project, affects also Natura 2000 sites, so that the permission for the project implementation may require the cumulative application of both derogations regimes (Article 4(7) of the WFD and Article 6(4) of the Habitats Directive).[107] This can be the case when mitigation measures for preventing the deteriorating effects on the integrity of the protected site were already implemented and 'failed' to avert such effects, as the derogation provision of Article 6(4) of the Habitats Directive is applied only in such a constellation, while the derogation provision of the WFD does not explicitly presupposes the prior adoption of mitigation measures.[108] In this context, an IBT project can be permissible under the derogation provision of the WFD, when the following conditions are satisfied: (i) all the practicable steps for the mitigation of the adverse effects on the status of water bodies are taken; (ii) the reasons for the project implementation are extensively explained in the RBMP, while it is also ensured that the requirements set in Article 4(8) and (9) are observed; (iii) the project serves a reason of overriding public interest which is restrictively defined or it provides benefits to the society and the environment which outweigh the benefits of achieving the environmental objectives; and (iv) the positive effects of the project could not be achieved by other more environmental friendly alternatives due to reasons relating to their technical feasibility or the disproportionately high cost. Furthermore, in the case of the cumulative application of the derogation provision of the WFD with that of the Habitats Directive, certain requirements have also to be fulfilled for the permission of an IBT scheme, which are mainly even more stringent and divergent from the conditions of the Article 4(7) of the WFD. These requirements relate to the absence of less harmful alternatives in comparison to water infrastructure, which have to be defined without any economic considerations, the existence of very significant reasons justifying the project implementation, which are determined in accordance with the protection level of the habitat to be affected by the project implementation and the adoption of compensatory measures.[109] It becomes, thus, obvious that IBTs should be seen as a last resort, when all possible alternatives fail, as it is also persuasively recognised in the clear hierarchy established in the EU Strategy on Water Scarcity and

[107] *P. de Smedt & H.F.M.W. van Rijswick, supra* note 90, p. 426 claiming persuasively that in accordance with Article 4(9) of the WFD the application of the derogation provision of Article 4(7) cannot be used to jeopardise the conservation objectives of the Habitats Directive, unless both derogation regimes are applied in a cumulative way.

[108] *P. de Smedt & H.F.M.W. van Rijswick, supra* note 90, pp. 427, 428.

[109] *N. de Sadeleer, supra* note 74, p. 17 et seq.; *P. de Smedt & H.F.M.W. van Rijswick, supra* note 90, pp. 429, 430, analysing the relationship between the public interest requirement of Article 4(7) of the WFD with that of the derogation provision of the Habitats Directive.

Droughts. Moreover, this thesis is supported by the relevant practical experience gained by the implementation of such projects worldwide.

The third conclusion drawn by the *Acheloos* case is that the insufficient planning of a large-scale diversion project, the fragmented implementation of the gradually developing legislation, the very weak governance arrangements and the lack of compensation to those affected, led to a long-term dispute between the citizens of the recipient area from the one side and the citizens from the donor area and the environmental NGOs from the other side, which was resolved after many years in a court room. The role of the jurisprudence of the Council of State has been critical to a large extent in terms of employing methods of dynamic interpretation of the relevant national framework and setting limits to the implementation of a project with significant environmental impact, although certain issues of judicial activism could be raised. In this context, it can also be argued that despite the divergences that can be observed and the issues that can be raised by the use of policy discretion left to Member States, the relevant frameworks, which have been introduced at the national level for the transposition and implementation of the WFD and other pieces of EU Environmental Legislation, include certain criteria, guidelines and instruments by which plans for developing water infrastructure can be adequately assessed. Moreover, such frameworks were not in place at previous stages of the development of the EU legislation. Subsequently, under such circumstances the *Acheloos* case could either not have 'existed' or developed at such a stage, as the relevant issues could have been resolved at earlier stages of the planning procedure. Furthermore, the effective implementation of the public participation provisions included in the WFD and in other pieces of the EU environmental legislation (EIA and SEA Directives) could have played a significant role in such circumstances, as it can substantially contribute to reaching legitimate and fair decisions. Effective public participation, though, also presupposes an administration familiar with openness and capable of copying with the challenge of organising participation procedures where the key interests are represented. Finally, departing from the thesis that access to justice constitutes the 'ultimum refugium' for the protection of those affected by the relevant decisions and of the environment *per se*, it is vital, also in these constellations, that national procedural systems ensure effective legal protection mainly by recognising broad standing criteria for the individuals and NGOs to challenge the alleged violations of the critical rules and by providing remedies responding to the particularities of the environmental litigation.

PART V
NATURE

CHAPTER 13

ASSESSMENT AND AUTHORISATION OF PLANS AND PROJECTS HAVING A SIGNIFICANT IMPACT ON NATURA 2000 SITES

Nicolas DE SADELEER

1. INTRODUCTION

The continuing loss of biodiversity is an issue of global concern. Europe's biological diversity, in addition to displaying a number of important ecological characteristics, is testament to the millennial symbiosis between man and his natural environment. In effect, more than on any other continent, human activities have been shaping biodiversity over centuries. Ecosystems were relatively stable until the agricultural and industrial revolutions of the past two centuries.[1] Today, however, biodiversity faces a major crisis at both global and European levels, the implications of which still have not been fully appreciated. Biodiversity is indeed passing through a period of major crisis. Most natural or semi-natural, continental and coastal ecosystems are now subject to significant modifications as a result of human activities (land use changes, intensification of agriculture, land abandonment, urban sprawl, climate change, etc.). Scientists expect that these disruptions will cause an unprecedented drop in the wealth of specific and genetic diversity.[2]

In order to reverse these negative trends, in 1979 the EU enacted the Birds Protection Directive,[3] and in 1992 a sister directive, Council Directive 92/43/EEC of 21 May 1992 on the conservation of natural habitats and of wild fauna and flora (the Habitats Directive). In addition, under the Convention on Biological Diversity, the EU agreed in 2001 to a global target of 'significantly reducing the current rate

---

1 *EEA*, Progress towards halting the loss of biodiversity by 2010, 2006, p. 8.

2 *F. Ramade*, Le grand massacre, 1999.

3 Council Directive 79/409/EEC of 2 April 1979 on the conservation of wild birds, OJ 1979 L103/1, replaced by EP and Council Directive 2009/147/EC of 30 November 2009 on the conservation of wild birds, OJ 2010 L20/7.

of biodiversity loss by 2010'. After this failed attempt to stop biodiversity loss,[4] the European Commission adopted a new strategy to halt biodiversity loss in the EU by 2020.

The Birds Directive makes it a requirement for Member States to 'preserve, maintain and re-establish sufficient diversity and area of habitats for all wild birds' and in particular to designate a range of Special Protection Areas (SPAs). The aim of the Habitats Directive is to contribute towards ensuring biodiversity through the conservation of natural habitats and of wild flora and fauna throughout the Member States.[5] Accordingly, measures taken pursuant to the Directive must be designed to 'maintain at or restore to', a favourable conservation status, natural habitats and species of wild flora and fauna 'of Community interest'.[6] It is thus 'an essential objective of the Directive that natural habitats be maintained at and, where appropriate, restored to a favourable conservation status'.[7] Given the continuing deterioration of natural habitats, Member States are called on to designate and to protect the most appropriate natural sites as Special Areas of Conservation (SACs). The following table highlights the two regimes.

Legal Acts	**Natura 2000 protected areas**	**Scope of ambit**
EP and Council Directive 2009/147/EC	SPAs	Annex I rare and vulnerable bird species as well as migratory species
Council Directive 92/43/EEC	SACs	Sites of Community Importance contributing significantly to the maintenance or restoration at a favourable conservation status of a natural habitat type (200 types) or of a species (over 1,000 animal and plant species)

Against this background, both SPAs and SACs are the backbone of the so-called Natura 2000 network of protected sites.[8] Being the biggest ecological network in the world, the Natura 2000 network has become the cornerstone of EU nature conservation policy. In 2015, the network has over 26,000 sites and covers over

4 The Commission as well as the EEA have repeatedly been acknowledging that the EU was unable not achieve its global target of significantly reducing biodiversity loss by 2010. For example, *European Commission*, A mid-term assessment of implementing the EC Biodiversity Action Plan, COM(2008) 864 final; *European Commission*, Communication on options for an EU vision and target for biodiversity beyond 2010, COM(2010) 4 final; *EEA*, *supra* note 1; *EEA*, The European Environment, 2010, pp. 49–50.

5 Article 2(1).

6 Article 2(2).

7 AG Sharpston opinion in Case C-258/11 *Peter Sweetman* [2012] EU:C:2013:220, para. 40.

8 Nothing prevents Member States to designate the same site as both a Special Protected Area (SPA) and a Special Area of Conservation (SAC). As a result, such areas fall within the ambit of both the Birds and the Habitats Directives.

1 million km^2. 18% of the land surface and 4% of the EU waters (territorial seas and EEZs) have been designated. These sites are located on a diverse range of land use types ranging from agriculture, forests, mountains, to wilderness areas. Accordingly, this network has been hailed as the key instrument that aims to effectively prevent Noah's Ark from sinking.

Among the different provisions of the Habitats Directive, Article 6 – which applies to both SPAs and SACs[9] – has been given rise to a steady flow of cases. It requires Member States to protect designated habitats, and provides for specific procedural requirements whenever projects or plans are likely to threaten those protected habitats.[10] Accordingly, this provision has not only halted ill-conceived development projects but has also encouraged developers to find ways to reduce damaging effects of their projects. The four paragraphs of that provision require a few words of explanation.

As regards the conservation of natural habitats, the two first paragraphs of this provision provide for necessary conservation measures to be established in relation to SACs (Article 6(1)) and for steps to be taken to avoid the deterioration of those habitats (Article 6(2)).

In particular, the first paragraph ensures that positive steps are taken with a view to maintaining and/or restoring habitats.[11]

The second paragraph 'imposes an overarching obligation to avoid deterioration or disturbance'.[12] The general binding regulatory framework intends to cover the whole set of human activities capable of causing:

1. 'deterioration of natural habitats and the habitats of species', irrespective of their nature; and
2. 'disturbances of species', where such disturbances are significant.

---

9 Account must be made that pursuant to Article 7 of the Habitats Directive, Article 6(2) to (4) of that directive replaces the first sentence of Article 4(4) of the Birds Directive as from the date of implementation of the Habitats Directive or the date of classification by a Member State under the Birds Directive, where the latter date is later (see, in particular, Case C-418/04 *Commission v Ireland* [2007] ECR I-10947, para. 173).

10 *N. de Sadeleer*, Habitats Conservation in EC Law: From Nature Sanctuaries to Ecological Networks, Yearbook of European Environmental Law, 2005 (5), pp. 215–252.

11 Article 6(1) requires the adoption of 'necessary conservation measures' for habitats located within a SAC. Special conservation measures relating to the habitats of a SAC consist of the adoption of 'appropriate management plans specifically designed for the sites or integrated into other development plans'. Management plans are vitally important as they set the Site Conservation Objectives (SCOs). The SCOs therefore play an important role in the Appropriate Impact Assessment (AIA) procedure (*infra*).

12 Article 6(2) of the Directive obliges the Member States to take 'appropriate steps to avoid, in the special areas of conservation, the deterioration of natural habitats and the habitats of species as well as disturbance of the species for which the areas have been designated, insofar as such disturbance could be significant in relation to the objectives of this Directive'. The CJEU has on several occasions offered clarifications relating to the implementation of Article 6 of the Habitats Directive. The following cases deal with the transposition of Article 6 of the Habitats Directive: Case C-374/98 *Commission v France* ('*Basses Corbières*') [2000] ECR I-10799; Case C-324/01 *Commission v Belgium* [2004] ECR I-11197; Case C-75/01 *Commission v Luxembourg* [2003] ECR I-1585; and Case C-143/02 *Commission v Italy* [2003] ECR I-2877.

The Court of Justice of the European Union (CJEU), has described paragraph 2 as 'a provision which makes it possible to satisfy the fundamental objective of preservation and protection of the quality of the environment, including the conservation of natural habitats and of wild fauna and flora, and establishes a general obligation of protection consisting in avoiding deterioration and disturbance which could have significant effects in the light of the directive's objectives'.[13] Accordingly this preventive obligation has to be read as an obligation of result.[14] In order to establish a failure to fulfil the preventive obligations within the meaning of Article 6(2), the Commission does not have to prove a cause and effect relationship between the project or the operation at issue and significant disturbance to the protected species found on the site. In effect, it is sufficient for the Commission 'to establish the existence of a probability or risk that that operation might cause significant disturbances for that species'.[15]

However, the preventive obligation encapsulated in Article 6(2) is not an absolute one. The 3rd and 4th paragraphs set out a series of procedures to be followed in the case of plans or projects that are not directly connected with or necessary to the management of the site. Accordingly, these two paragraphs are not concerned with the day-to-day operation of the site.[16]

Under Article 6(4) a plan or project may, in spite of a negative assessment of the implications for the site and in the absence of alternative solutions, be carried out for imperative reasons of overriding public interest, including those of a social or economic nature, if the Member State takes all compensatory measures necessary to ensure that the overall coherence of Natura 2000 is achieved. Such derogations are applicable only *after* the implications of the project or the plan have been assessed pursuant to the conditions laid down under Article 6(3). Accordingly, an Appropriate Impact Assessment (AIA) must be conducted thoroughly in order to ascertain that the plan or the project is not likely to impair the site's integrity.

The obligation to carry out a genuine AIA is of utmost importance for the sake of habitats conservation. Firstly, as a matter of principle, negative conclusions preclude the adoption of the plan or the granting of the licence. Secondly, in case the proposal is likely to be authorised in accordance with overriding interests, experts must assess whether alternatives exist which have a lesser adverse effect on the area. Thirdly, experts can determine the compensatory measures that are likely to be required in case the development is taking place in accordance with Article 6(4).[17] It flows from that that the experts conducting the AIA must

13 Case C-226/08 *Stadt Papenburg* [2010] ECR I-131, para. 49.

14 Case C-308/08 *Commission v. Spain* [2010] ECR I-4281, paras. 53 and 54; Case C-517/11 *Commission v. Greece* [2013], para. 43. See *N. de Sadeleer & C.-H. Born*, Droit international et communautaire de la biodiversité, 2004, p. 516.

15 Case C-241/08 *Commission v. France* [2010] ECR I-1697, para. 32; Case C-2/10 *Azienda Agro-Zootecnica Franchini and Eolica di Altamura* [2011], para. 41; Case C-404/09 *Commission v. Spain* [2011] ECR I-11853, para. 142.

16 Opinion AG Sharpston in Case C-258/11 *Peter Sweetman* [2012] EU:C:2013:220, para. 45.

17 Opinion AG Kokott in Case C-304/05 *Commission v. Italy* [2007] ECR I-7495, para. 54.

show a high level of competence with respect to nature conservation issues. As a consequence, questions arise as to their independence as well as to the quality of their assessment.

Given the importance of the AIA procedure for achieving the biodiversity conservation objectives, the question arises as to whether the traditional EIA is taking into account this particular procedure. It must be noted that Article 2(3) of Directive 2011/92/EU as amended by Directive 2014/52/EU of 16 April 2014 requires:

> 'In the case of projects for which the obligation to carry out assessments of the effects on the environment arises simultaneously from this Directive and from Council Directive 92/43/EEC ... Member States shall, where appropriate, ensure that coordinated and/or joint procedures fulfilling the requirements of that Union legislation are provided for.'

In shedding the light on the procedural requirements laid down under Article 6(3) and (4) of the Habitats Directive, a key provision for implementing the EU's system of protecting and preserving biological diversity in the Member States, this article attempts to emphasise the extent to which this atypical procedure reinforces the obligations stemming from the EIA and the SEA Directives.[18] It should at this point be noted that in sharp contrast to these two directives, that are entirely dedicated to impact assessments, only two sentences in Article 6(3) of the Habitats Directive relate to the appropriate assessment.

The discussion will be structured in the following manner. Given that Article 6(3) distinguishes two procedural stages, sections 2 and 3 examine subsequently the assessment procedure and the authorisation scheme. Section 4 is dedicated to the possibility for the Member States to authorise a plan or a project adversely affecting the integrity of a protected site. Last but not least, there will be a discussion in section 5 of the relationship between the different impact studies provided for under EU environmental law.

---

[18] Directive 2014/52/EU of the European Parliament and of the Council of 16 April 2014 amending Directive 2011/92/EU on the assessment of the effects of certain public and private projects on the environment; Directive 2001/42/EC of the European Parliament and of the Council of 27 June 2001 on the assessment of the effects of certain plans and programmes on the environment. Regarding the scope of these two directives, see *N. de Sadeleer*, L'évaluation des incidences environnementales des programmes, plans et projets : à la recherche d'une protection juridictionnelle effective, RDUE, 2014 (2), pp. 1–56.

2. APPROPRIATE IMPACT ASSESSMENT (ARTICLE 6(3) FIRST PHRASE)

2.1. INTRODUCTORY COMMENTS

In order to preserve classified habitats from development or other activities likely to alter their ecological integrity, Article 6(3) provides for a *sui generis* prospective impact study of the environmental effects applicable to 'any plan or project not directly connected with or necessary to the management of the site but likely to have a significant effect thereon, either individually or in combination with other plans or projects'.[19] In other words, the AIA procedure applies to either plans or projects that:

1. have no relationship with the management of the site; and
2. create a risk of a significant effect on the site.

According to the CJEU, Article 6(2) cannot be applied concomitantly with Article 6(3).[20]

For clarity, we shall use the acronym AIA ('appropriate impact assessment') in order to distinguish that assessment from the broader EIA ('environmental impact assessment' in Directive 2014/52/EU) and SEA ('strategic environmental assessment' in Directive 2001/42/EC[21]).

2.2. WHICH PLANS AND WHICH PROJECTS ARE SUBJECT TO AN AIA?

2.2.1. Broad Interpretation of the Concepts

The Habitats Directive has defined neither the concept of plan nor the concept of project. According to the CJEU, the definition of project laid down under the EIA Directive is relevant to defining the concept of project as provided by the Habitats Directive given that both directives are aiming to prevent activities which are likely to damage the environment from being authorised without prior assessment of their impact on the environment.[22] Pursuant to Article 1 of the

---

19 Article 7 of the Birds Directive, which applies to SPAs designated under the Birds Directive, makes clear that the provisions of Article 6(3) apply.

20 Case C-127/02 *Landelijke Vereniging tot Behoud van de Waddenzee, Nederlandse Vereniging tot Bescherming van Vogels v Staatssecretaris van Landbouw, Natuurbeheer en Visserij* ('*Waddenzee*') [2004] ECR I-7405, para. 38.

21 European Parliament and Council Directive 2001/42/EC on the assessment of the effects of certain plans and programmes on the environment OJ 2001 L197/30.

22 Case C-127/02 *Waddenzee*, para. 27.

EIA Directive, the concept of project is defined as 'the execution of construction works or of other installations or schemes and 'other interventions in the natural surroundings including those involving the extraction of mineral resources'. Account must be made of the fact that the concepts of 'project' under the EIA Directive has been interpreted broadly by the CJEU.[23] What is more, in sharp contrast to the EIA Directive, the Habitats Directive does not introduce any threshold as to the nature, the location, the size, the level of impact of the projects and plans falling within its scope. As a matter of law, where the EU lawmaker wishes to limit the obligation to carry out an EIA, it makes express provision to that end in laying down specific thresholds.[24]

As far as plans are concerned, they are broadly defined under Article 3(2) of the SEA Directive. They can cover policies relating to 'agriculture, forestry, fisheries, energy, industry, transport, waste management, water management, telecommunications, tourism, town and country planning or land use'.

The concepts of 'project' and 'plan' must be interpreted broadly due, on the one hand, to the wording of Article 6(3) covering 'any plan or project', and, on the other hand, the conservation objectives on the strength of which SACs are set up.[25] It follows that whilst plans and projects which are directly related to or necessary for the management of a site are not subjected to an impact study (e.g. the woodcutting foreseen in the management plan for a Natura 2000 forestry site), all other plans or projects capable of having a significant effect on the area must be assessed in accordance with procedures set in place by the Member States.[26] For instance, national courts as well as the CJEU have been holding that the following activities qualify as 'plans or projects' for the purposes of this provision:

- amendments of territorial management plans allowing for the operation of a rubbish dump;[27]

---

23 Regarding the scope of the EIA Directive, the CJEU has stated on numerous occasions that its scope is very wide. See Case C-72/95 *Kraaijeveld and Others* [1996] ECR I-5403, para. 31; Case C-435/97 *WWF and Others* [1999] ECR I-5613, para. 40; Case C-2/07 *Abraham and Others* [2008] ECR I-0000, para. 32; and Case C-142/07 *Ecologistas en Accion-Coda v Ayuntamentio de Madrid* [2008] ECR I-9097, para. 28. However, projects must alter the physical aspects of a site. See Case C-275/09 *Brussels Hoofdstedelijk Gewest* [2011] ECR I-1753, para. 24. That prompts the question whether emissions into water or air are likely to qualify as a project under the EIA Directive. See *H. Schoukens*, Ongoing Activities and Natura 2000. Biodiversity Protection vs Legitimate Expectations?, JEEPL, 2014 (11:1), p. 21.

24 Case C-133/94 *Commission v Belgium* [1996] ECR I-2323, paras. 26–27. Regarding the importance of thresholds to determine the scope of the EIA Directive, see Case C-531/13 *Marktgemeinde Straßwalchen* [2015] C:2015:79.

25 Opinion AG Fennelly in Case C-374/98 *'Basses Corbières'*, para. 33; and Opinion AG Kokott in Case C-127/02 *Waddenzee*, para. 30.

26 The issue of ongoing activities within SPAs and SCAs is giving rise to debate. See *B. Gors & L. Vanskick*, Le contrôle par le juge européen des activités en cours sur ou à proximité des sites Natura 2000, Amén.-Envt, 2014 (4), pp. 42–54; *H. Schoukens*, *supra* note 23.

27 Belgian Council of State, *Wellens*, n. 96.198, 7 June 2001.

- annual permits to fish cockle in a SPA;[28]
- dredging works in a navigable channel;[29]
- open-cast coal mine;[30] and
- alteration to an urban development plan comprising a series of industrial construction projects.[31]

Several Member States took the view that projects or plans not subject to national authorisation schemes are falling outside the ambit of Article 6(3). In effect, the first phrase of that provision merely requires that 'any plan or project' shall be subject to appropriate assessment without requiring a formal development consent procedure. However, given that the second sentence of that paragraph requires that 'the competent national authorities shall agree to the plan or project', a formal consent procedure is implicitly required. In effect, a consent procedure should be required to ensure that, firstly, reasons are given as to why environmental damage is being permitted, and secondly, so these reasons can be used to guide appropriate compensatory measures. What is more, given that developers are required to limit their impacts on the site's integrity as much as possible, formal consent is needed in order to properly set out the mitigation measures.[32]

2.2.2. Projects and Plans that Are Likely to Have a Significant Impact

Only plans and projects that are 'likely' to have a 'significant' effect on the area are subject to the AIA. This calls for a few words of explanation.

- *Interpretation of the terms 'likely to occur'.*

Firstly, the effect is 'likely' to occur. The first question to answer is thus whether the plan or project is 'likely' to have an effect.

As regards the transposition of Article 6(3), the CJEU has held that that paragraph makes the requirement for an AIA of the implications of a plan or

28 Case C-127/02 *Waddenzee*, paras. 21–29.
29 Case C-226/08 *Stadt Padenburg* [2010] ECR I-131.
30 Case C-404/09 *Commission v. Spain* [2011] ECR I-11853.
31 Case C-179/06 *Commission v. Italy* [2007] ECR I-8131.
32 Mitigation measures are those that are part of the plan or programme: for example, in building a highway, tunnels could be made so as not to obstruct the movement of small mammals; or highways could be insulated to reduce noise impacting upon bird breeding areas. On the other hand, compensatory measures can be carried out outside the immediate scope of the plan or programme. For example, developers may purchase land elsewhere to 'compensate' for the damage caused by putting a highway through an area used by various species of birds for feeding or nesting. See *H. Schoukens & A. Cliquet*, Mitigation and Compensation under EU Nature Conservation Law in the Flemish Region: Beyond the Deadlock for Development Projects?, Utrecht Law Review, 2014 (10:2); *D. McGillivray*, Compensatory Measurse under Article 6(4) of the Habitats Directive, in C.-H. Born et al. (ed.), The Habitats Directive in its EU Environmental Law Context, 2015, pp. 101–118.

project conditional on there being 'a probability or a risk that that plan or project will have a significant effect on the site concerned'.[33]

However, the terms 'likely to have [an] effect' used in the English-language version of the text appear to be stricter than the ones used in the French version (*'susceptible d'affecter'*), the German version (*'beeinträchtigen könnte'*), the Dutch version (*'gevolgen kan heben'*), and the Spanish version (*'pueda afectar'*). According to AG Sharpston, each of those versions suggests that the test is set at a lower level than under the English-language version.[34] As a result, the English terms 'likely to' have to be interpreted in line with the other EU official languages. Accordingly, they mean 'possible' or 'potential' and must not be understood as requiring absolute proof that a risk will occur.

The question arises as to how to determine the likelihood or the probability of a significant effect. According to the CJEU, '[i]n the light, in particular, of the precautionary principle, such a risk exists if it cannot be excluded on the basis of objective information that the plan or project will have a significant effect on the site concerned'.[35]

– *Interpretation of the term 'significant'.*

The second requirement that the effect in question be 'significant' exists in order to lay down a *de minimis* threshold.[36] In other words, 'significance' operates as a threshold for determining whether an appropriate assessment of the implications of the project should be conducted. In contrast, plans or projects that are deemed not to have such effects could proceed without further procedural requirements.

Given that there is no legal definition of the term 'significant', the question arises as to how the plan or project is determined to fall below a threshold of 'significance'. The issue of significance is of the utmost importance and can give rise to heated debates.

'Significance' is a legal standard rather than a rule. Given that a standard does not lay down any precise legal test, it merely requires the exercise of judgment on specific grounds, according to the specificities of the individual case. From an ecosystemic perspective, the impact would become significant where the ecosystem has lost his ability to reorganise itself in order to provide the same ecological functions. The CJEU has expanded upon that standard in the *Waddenzee* case: a plan or project is deemed not to entail significant effect where 'it is considered not likely to adversely affect the integrity of the site concerned and consequently, not likely to give rise to deterioration or significant disturbances within the meaning of Article 6(2)'.[37]

---

33 Case C-6/04 *Commission v. United Kingdom* [2005] ECR I-9017, para. 54; and Case C-418/04 *Commission v. Ireland* [2007] ECR I-10947, para. 226.

34 Opinion AG Sharpston in Case C-258/11 *Peter Sweetman* [2012] nyr, para. 46.

35 Case C-127/02 *Waddenzee.*

36 Opinion AG Sharpston in Case C-258/11 *Peter Sweetman* [2012] EU:C:2013:220, para. 48.

37 Case C-127/02 *Waddenzee*, para. 36.

The fact that the Habitats Directive requires assessment of the projects likely to have significant effects is not merely a question of drawing the line between small and large projects. As the CJEU already stated with respect to the EIA procedure 'even a small-scale project can have significant effects on the environment if it is in a location where the environmental factors ..., such as fauna and flora, soil, water, climate or cultural heritage, are sensitive to the slightest alteration'.[38]

One should thus take into account that 'significance' can vary tremendously according to the size and the vulnerability of the area. In effect, small habitats containing unusual and particularly delicate species may react much more sharply than other less 'sensitive' protected sites to a given type of external effect.[39] For example, the loss of $100m^2$ of chalk grasslands can have significant implications for the conservation of a small site hosting rare orchids, whereas a comparable loss in a larger site (such as a steppe) does not necessarily have the same implications for the conservation of the area.[40] The *Sweetman* judgment offers a typical illustration of the soundness of that interpretation. In effect, the CJEU ruled that a road scheme involving the permanent loss of a small percentage of a site harbouring a priority habitat (limestone pavement) had an impact on the integrity of the site.[41]

Last, given that opinions may vary regarding whether or not there is a significant effect, it may be necessary at this preliminary stage to invite the public or stakeholders as well as nature conservation experts to express their opinions. In other words, the assessment of the significance could be made the subject of a statement of reasons, consultation of specialised authorities and enhanced public participation.

– *The determination of the 'significance' of the effects.*

The 'significant' nature of the impact of the plan or project must be interpreted objectively in light of the Site Conservation Objectives (SCOs), the particular characteristics and the environmental conditions of the protected site. SCOs are 'the specification of the overall target for the species and/or habitat types for which a site is designated in order for it to contribute to maintaining or reaching favourable conservation status'.[42] Management plans adopted under Article 6(1) are vitally important as they set these objectives. The SCOs are thus essential to

---

38 Case C-392/96 *Commission v. Ireland* [1999] ECR I-5901, para. 66.

39 Opinion AG Tizzano in Case C-98/03 *Commission v. Germany* [2006] ECR I-53, para.38.

40 *European Commission*, Managing Natura 2000 Sites: The provisions of Article 6 of the 'Habitats' Directive 92/43/EEC, 2000, p. 35.

41 Case C-258/11 *Peter Sweetman.*

42 *European Commission*, Note on Setting Conservation Objectives for Natura 2000 Sites, Final Version 23/11/2012.

streamline the management of the site and to assess whether or not the project or plan has a 'significant' impact upon the site.[43]

Accordingly, the CJEU has held that any activity compromising the SCOs, which apply to the area, is assumed to have a significant effect.[44]

- *Projects and plans not having significant effect on the integrity of the site are subject to Article 6(2) preventive obligations.*

Last, given the extra costs incurred by AIAs, developers are often intent upon avoiding this procedure in claiming that their projects are not falling within the scope of Article 6(3). That prompts the question whether avoiding the AIA procedure amounts to a Pyrrhic victory. In effect, though projects and plans not having significant effect on the integrity of the site are not subject to the AIA requirements laid down by Article 6(3), their implementation nevertheless falls within the scope of Article 6(2).[45] Indeed, given that paragraphs 2 and 3 of Article 6 'are designed to ensure the same level of protection of natural habitats and habitats of species', these two paragraphs have been construed 'as a coherent whole in the light of the conservation objectives pursued by the directive'.[46]

2.2.3. Screening: Prior Assessment of the Plan or Project's Significance

As indicated above, in order to be assessed the plan or project must be likely to have a 'significant' effect. Given that thousands of project categories could have an impact on sites, the question arises as to which criteria are needed to assess them. Most of the Member States do have screening devices aiming at determining which projects have to comply with the AIA procedural requirements.

Screening can be seen as the preliminary stage of the assessment. It can be defined as the process through which the experts are assessing whether the plans or projects at issue are likely to have a significant impact. In doing so, the experts decide whether a full assessment should be conducted. In other words, the ability at that stage to determine whether the plan or the project is likely to have a significant impact triggers the whole AIA process.

---

43 There are several references to the term 'conservation objectives' in the preamble of the Directive as well as an explicit mention of it in Article 6(3). As far as national laws are concerned, in Germany Article 33(3) of the *Bundesnaturschutzgesetz* (NtSchG) (Federal Nature Protection Law) requires that the 'protection declaration' shall set out the protection purpose (*Schutzzweck*) in accordance with the SCOs. In France, the '*document d'objectifs*' (the management plan) sets SCOs and indicators in order to assess their fulfilment. In the UK, the SCOs are 'the starting point from which management schemes and monitoring programmes may be developed as they provide the basis for determining what is currently or may cause a significant effect'. In the Walloon Region of Belgium, SCOs (called 'active management objectives') are adopted in the Natura 2000 site designation decree and have statutory force.

44 Case C-127/02 *Waddenzee*, para. 48. See also Opinion AG Kokott also in *Waddenzee*, para. 85.

45 Case C-226/08 *Stadt Papenburg* [2010] ECR I-131, paras. 48 and 49; Case C-404/09 *Commission v. Spain* [2011] ECR I-11853, para. 125.

46 Case C-127/02 *Waddenzee*, para. 32.

One could draw a distinction between the screening exercise seen as a prior assessment and with that of the full assessment (AIA) (see the table below).

Prior assessment	Screening *in abstracto*	Determine whether there is likely to be a significant effect triggering the full assessment
Full assessment	Screening *in concreto*	Determine the extent to which the impact is significant

It must be stressed that such broad screening does not jeopardise the project; it just requires the authorities to assess whether a full assessment of the effects of the project has to be conducted from a preventative perspective.

It must also be kept in mind that in screening the likely significance of the impacts, the authority cannot take into account the proposed compensatory measures. The potential impacts of the plan or project must be assessed in their own right, irrespective of further measures that could compensate for their potential adverse effects. As AG Kokott rightly pointed out: 'compensatory measures can be considered only when adverse effects have to be accepted in the absence of any alternative, for overriding reasons of public interest. The preservation of existing natural resources is preferable to compensatory measures simply because the success of such measures can rarely be predicted with certainty'.[47] By way of illustration, a developer cannot claim that his or her project would not have a significant adverse effect considering the habitat restoration proposals on a locally distinct site. This reasoning is predicated on the assumption that the design of the nature, location and size of mitigation and compensatory measures can only be dealt with at the AIA level.

2.2.4. *Advantages and Drawbacks of Screening Methods*

There are two main ways in which the screening could be operated. Regarding the implementation of the Habitats Directive, the 'significance' criterion is usually determined either by a case-by-case approach or in laying down thresholds or criteria.[48]

1. The quantitative approach: setting thresholds or criteria.

    (a) *Advantages*: enhances legal certainty in reducing the authority's discretion.
    (b) *Drawbacks*: This first option is more controversial as it is very difficult, from an ecological point of view, to guarantee that the plans and projects will never have a significant impact. For instance, given that the thresholds

47 AG Kokott's opinion in Case C-239/04 *Commission v. Portugal* [2006] ECR I-10183, para. 35.

48 See also Article 4(2) EIA Directive.

might be too high, or inaccurate, many projects or plans that may have a significant impact could escape the full assessment procedure.[49]

2. The qualitative approach: case-by-case analysis.

   (a) *Advantages*: given that the impacts of a plan or project are highly contingent/variable, their significance is likely to increase with respect to many factors, for instance, proximity, the size of the project, or additional or cumulative effects of pre-existing projects. As far as these cumulative effects are concerned, the CJEU confirmed in the *Waddenzee* case that Article 6(3) first sentence requires the significant effect to be taken into account not only 'individually' but also 'in combination with other plans or projects'. As a result, the cumulative impact with other projects must be considered. That can be done only through a case-by-case approach. For instance, an additional highway in an area honeycombed with roads will slightly modify the ecology of the site whereas the construction of a minor road in a pristine road-less area is likely to have a significant impact. To conclude with, a qualitative (not quantitative) approach is better suited for Natura 2000 sites.
   (b) *Drawbacks*: a case-by-case approach might be seen as a somewhat cumbersome procedure because the likely significance of the plan or project must be established before the full AIA is conducted. In other words, it requires the authority to ensure that at this preliminary stage some assessment is conducted.

According to CJEU case law, the discretion left by the Habitats Directive does not preclude judicial review of the question as to whether Member States have exceeded their margin of appreciation.[50] Indeed, it is settled case law that national authorities cannot rely exclusively on abstract criteria to decide whether the project or plan needs to be assessed or not. In that respect, several CJEU judgments are crystal clear:

- In Case C-256/98 *Commission v. France* the CJEU held that the French regime providing that an AIA could be waived because of the low cost of the project or its purpose was inconsistent with the Directive.[51]
- In Case C-98/03 *Commission v. Germany* the CJEU held that the restriction of AIA to projects subject to notification or authorisation procedures were

49 In establishing criteria and/or thresholds at a level such that, in practice, all projects of a certain type would be exempted in advance from the requirement of an impact assessment the Member States would exceed the limits of their discretion. See Case C-392/96 *Commission v. Ireland* [1999] ECR I-5901, paras. 75 and 76.

50 See, by analogy, Case C-72/95 *Kraaijeveld* [1996] ECR I-4503, para. 59.

51 Case C-256/98 *Commission v. France*, para. 35.

inconsistent with Article 6 requirements.[52] As a result, Germany had to amend the *Bundesnaturschutzgesetz*: every activity affecting a Natura 2000 site must now be regarded as a project.

- In Case C-241/08 *Commission v. France* the CJEU took the view that a Member State cannot grant a general exemption for fishing and hunting activities on the account that one cannot consider that these activities will never cause significant disturbance.[53]

To sum up, one is driven to the conclusion that the dispensation to conduct an AIA must be granted on a case-by-case basis and not in accordance with a general list of exemptions.

2.2.5. Splitting of Plans and Projects

With the aim of avoiding the assessment procedure, developers might be willing to split the project or the plan into several smaller units (highway or motorway being split in a series of 2km long projects to avoid a 2.5km EIA threshold), neither of which individually requires a permit as they are deemed not to entail significant effects. However, the cumulative impacts of a flurry of small projects can be significant. Viewed individually these projects may fall below the significance threshold; however, seen in combination with other projects (tyranny of small decisions phenomenon), they may have significant impacts.

As a matter of EU law, one must not consider the project in isolation if it can be regarded as an integral part of more substantial development. Accordingly, the CJEU took the view that: '[n]ot taking into account of the cumulative effect of projects means in practice that all projects of a certain type may escape the obligation to carry out an assessment when, taken together, they are likely to have significant effect on the environment'.[54] This points to the conclusion that any administrative practice allowing a splitting of projects or plans that could be regarded as an integral part of a specific development is inconsistent with the objectives of the Habitats Directive.[55]

52 Case C-98/03 *Commission v. Germany* [2006] ECR I-53, paras. 42–45.

53 Case C-241/08 *Commission v. France* [2010] ECR I-1697.

54 Case C-392/96 *Commission v. Ireland* [1999] ECR I-5901.

55 It must be noted that the CJEU ruled that various splitting practices were inconsistent with the EIA Directive: Case C-431/92 *Commission v. Germany* [1995] ECR I-2189; and Case C-142/07 *Ecologistas en Accion-Coda v. Ayuntamentio de Madrid* [2008] ECR I-6097, para. 20.

2.3. CONTENT OF THE AIA

2.3.1. Background Against which the Appropriate Assessment Must Be Carried Out

The authority is called upon to assess the significant impact of the plan or project in terms of:

- 'its implications for the site in view of the sites SCOs';[56] and
- the site's integrity, as defined in the SCOs.

Firstly, the assessment has to identify the SCOs, and second to assess the manner in which the project or plan could jeopardise the realisation of these objectives. Secondly, under Article 6(3), second phrase, the effects on the integrity of the site have to be assessed. Given that the requirement of 'integrity' is set out in the second sentence of Article 6(3) of the Habitats Directive, we shall provide a more detailed analysis of this second requirement in the next section.

By way of illustration, the main SCO of Glen Lake SPA in Ireland is to protect the Whooper Swan (*Cygnus cygnus*), a species listed under Annex I of the Birds Directive. The CJEU held that drainage works carried out within the SPA adversely affected the integrity of the site within the meaning of the second sentence of Article 6(3). The Court reached the conclusion that 'since conservation of the whooper swans' wintering area is the principal conservation objective of the SPA, its integrity was adversely affected within the meaning of the second sentence of Article 6(3) of the Habitats Directive'.[57]

2.3.2. Soundness of the Appropriate Assessment

The Natura 2000 assessment must be 'appropriate' having regard to the SCOs of the particular site (Article 6(3)).[58] The CJEU has already pointed out that 'the provision does not define any particular method for carrying out such an assessment'.[59] That does not mean that the experts are endowed with unfettered discretion. According to AG Kokott, this term should also be understood in the sense of 'proper' or 'expedient'. Accordingly, 'an assessment is not merely a formal procedural act, but rather it has to achieve its aims. The aim of the assessment is to

---

56 It is settled case law that 'where a plan or project not directly connected with or necessary to the management of a site is likely to undermine the site's conservation objectives, it must be considered likely to have a significant effect on that site.' See Case C-127/02 *Waddenzee*, para. 49; and Case C-258/11 *Peter Sweetman* [2012], para. 30.

57 Case C-418/04 *Commission v. Ireland* [2007] ECR I-1094, para. 259.

58 On the concept of appropriate evaluation, see the Opinion of Advocate General Kokott in *Waddenzee*, paras. 95–98.

59 Case C-127/02 *Waddenzee*, para. 52; case C-304/05 *Commission* v *Italy* [2007] ECR I-7495, para. 57; and case C-43/10 *Nomarchiaki Aftodioikisi Aitoloakarnanias* [2012], para. 111.

establish whether a plan or project is compatible with the specified conservation objectives for the particular site'.[60] It follows that the AIA must be carried out in such a manner that 'the competent national authorities can be certain that a plan or project will not have adverse effects on the integrity of the site concerned, given that, where doubt remains as to the absence of such effects, the competent authority will have to refuse development consent'.[61]

In analysing the rationale of Article 6 as well as the Directive's objectives it is possible to highlight a number of components of an 'appropriate' assessment. Of importance is that the scope and content of an AIA depends upon:

- the intensity of the impacts according to the nature, location (current use of the land, relative abundance of the natural resources) and size of the proposed plan or project;
- the extent of the impacts of the project on the ecosystems and the scale of the works involved;[62]
- the vulnerability of the habitats or species under protection (resilience, regenerative capacity, absorption capacity); and
- the level of existing threats.

In particular, the CJEU has been stressing the need to conduct AIAs as sound as possible: 'the assessment … cannot have lacunae and must contain complete, precise and definitive findings and conclusions capable of removing all reasonable scientific doubt as to the effects of the works proposed on the protected site concerned'.[63] Accordingly, the assessment is not deemed to be appropriate where reliable and updated data are lacking.[64] This statement requires a few words of explanation.

2.3.3. Best Scientific Knowledge in the Field

The CJEU has stressed that the assessment must be carried out 'in the light of the best scientific knowledge in the field'.[65] Thus, the experts conducting

60 Opinion AG Kokott in Case C-441/03 *Commission v. Netherlands* [2005] ECR I-3043, paras. 11–12.

61 Case C-304/05 *Commission v. Italy* [2007] ECR I-7495, para. 58.

62 Case C-43/10 *Nomarchiaki Aftodioikisi Aitoloakarnanias et al.* [2012] C:2012:560, para. 132.

63 Case C-404/09 *Commission v. Spain* [2011] ECR I-11853, para. 100; and Case C-258/11 *Peter Sweetman* [2012], para. 38.

64 Case C-127/02 *Waddenzee* [2004] ECR I-7405, para. 54; Case C-404/09 *Commission v. Spain* [2011] OJ C25/3, para. 100; and Case C-43/10 *Nomarchiaki Aftodioikisi Aitoloakarnanias et al.* [2012] C:2012:560, para. 128.

65 Case C-127/02 *Waddenzee*, para. 54. By the same token, Member States are required to adopt conservation measures in favour of endangered bird species using the most up-to-date scientific data. See Case C-355/90 *Commission v. Spain* [1993] ECR I-4221, para. 24; and Case C-418/04 *Commission v. Ireland* [2007] ECR I-10947, para. 47. With respect to the designation of protected sites, it must be noted that public authorities do not always have a monopoly

the assessment must show a high level of competence with respect to nature conservation issues. As a matter of fact, failure to take into account the whole set of impacts from a genuine scientific perspective will lead to a narrow assessment which fails to provide the competent authority with the relevant information.[66] Therefore, such an assessment should be deemed inconsistent with the concept of 'appropriateness' required by the Habitats Directive.

However, neither the lawmaker nor the CJEU require that scientific advice must be based on the principles of excellence, independence, and transparency.[67] Given that in a number of Member States assessors are appointed and paid by the operator or the developer itself, the question arises as to whether the assessors are independent of the vested interests. This prompts the question whether the methods applied by the experts are reliable.[68]

In this connection, the recent *Seaport* judgment is a good case in point regarding the absence of independence of assessors under the Strategic Environmental Assessment (SEA) Directive. When asked whether an authority responsible for drawing up a development plan may be designated as the sole scientific authority to be consulted under the SEA Directive, the Court of Justice held that the directive did not prevent the authority from wearing two hats.[69] It follows that whilst the obligation to consult must be functionally separated, it need not be institutionally separated. By adopting such a minimalist approach to the obligation to consult provided for under the directive, the Court departed from the opinion of Advocate General Bot. It is clear that the Court's reading of the SEA Directive does not satisfy the objective of transparency in the national decision-making process pursued by the EU legislature. Indeed, it is the contribution of external expertise to that of the authority that creates and fuels debate, results in constructive criticism, and even offers alternative solutions to the planned project. Requesting the authority adopting the plan or the programme to be an independent expert in the procedure to which it is a party may appear to be somewhat schizophrenic.

The imperative lesson to be learned here is that strict and independent control of the quality of AIAs must be organised before the consent to the plan project is delivered. This guarantees that the assessment, *in fine*, may be considered

---

over scientific knowledge. For instance, a review of the classification by national authorities of natural habitats for wild birds may be made by reference to scientific inventories drawn up by NGOs. See Case C-3/96 *Commission v. Netherlands* [1998] ECR I-3031; and Case C-418/04 *Commission v. Ireland* [2007] ECR I-10947, paras. 51 and 55.

66 See the different cases discussed in Directorate-General for Internal Policies, Citizens' Rights and Constitutional Affairs of the European Parliament, National Implementation of Council Directive 92/43/EC of 21 May 92, 2009, 74 p.

67 Regarding food safety, the EU courts have been setting out such a requirement. See Case T-13/99 *Pfizer* [2002] ECR II-3305, para. 158.

68 *E. Truihlé-Marengo*, How to cope with the unknown: a few things about scientific uncertainty, precaution and adaptive management, in C.-H. Born et al. (ed.), The Habitats Directive in its EU Environmental Law Context, 2015, p. 341.

69 Case C-474/10 *Seaport* [2011] OJ C362/10.

appropriate and allows the competent authority to have 'ascertained that [the plan or project] will not adversely affect the integrity of the site concerned'. Many techniques exist in this perspective. Independent technical analysis committees or environmental consultative organs can assess the quality of AIAs submitted by the developer of a project. By the same token, independent inspectors can be appointed by the authorities to hold a public inquiry and to report back to them with recommendations. Furthermore, the certification of the experts by an environmental agency is likely to improve the quality of the AIA.

2.3.4. Material Range of Effects

In assessing the intensity of the impacts, the AIA must in particular take into account the following effects:

- the *specific*, and not abstract, *effects* of the plan or project on every habitat and species for which the site was classified;
- the *indirect effects* of the project, impacts which are not the direct result of the project, but the result of complex pathways;[70]
- the *interrelated effects*, the interactions between the impacts stemming from other projects within or outside the area;
- the *short and long-term effects* of the plan or the project;[71]
- the *reversible and irreversible effects* of the plan or the project;[72]
- the *cumulative effects* of the project with other proposed or existing projects must also be taken into consideration. Even the cumulative effects of more negligible impacts have to be taken into account. These impacts result from incremental changes caused by other past, present, and future actions interacting with the project at issue. The 'in combination' requirement (Article 6(3), first sentence) means that the content of the assessment should not be restricted to the effect arising from the project in consideration, but also the effects stemming from existing plans or projects not under consideration in the approval procedure. Likewise, the CJEU has stressed in the *Waddenzee*

[70] In view of the overall assessment of the effects of projects required by the EIA Directive, it 'would be simplistic and contrary to that approach to take account, when assessing the environmental impact of a project or of its modification, only of the direct effects of the works envisaged themselves, and not of the environmental impact liable to result from the use and exploitation of the end product of those works' (Case C-2/07 *Abraham and Others* [2008] ECR I-1197, paras. 42 and 43; Case C-142/07 *Ecologistas en Accion-Coda v. Ayuntamentio de Madrid* [2008] ECR I-6097, para. 39).

[71] For instance, the impacts of climate change on habitats are just emerging and their impacts have not yet been fully recognised.

[72] Regarding the irreparable destruction of a priority habitat, see Case C-258/11 *Peter Sweetman* [2012], para. 43.

case the need to take into account 'the cumulative effects which result from the combination of that project with other plans or projects';[73]

- Since it is important to consider the possibility of *alternative solutions* to the plan or project (required under paragraph 4), the assessor could also determine – though this is not compulsory under paragraph 3 – whether such solutions do in fact exist, including the alternative of cancelling the project entirely (zero option);[74]
- Last but not least, the assessor could also propose an *appropriate compensation package* – though this is not compulsory under paragraph 3 – depending on the circumstances of the case.[75] These measures must envisage the prevention, reduction and where possible the offset of any significant impact on the site's integrity. These measures may allow the objections to the project to be overcome.

The following table sets out the different effects that should be dealt with.

Sort of impacts to be assessed	**Provisions**
Specific, and not abstract, effects	Article 6(3), first sentence
Indirect effects	By analogy to the case law on the EIA Directive
Interrelated & cumulative effects	Article 6(3), first sentence; C-127/02, *Waddenzee*, para. 53
Short and long-term impacts	*Ratio legis* of Article 6
Reversible and irreversible impacts	*Ratio legis* of Article 6
Alternative solutions and mitigation measures	Not required under para. 3 but implicitly from para. 4

2.3.5. *Uncertain Effects*

Although the conductors of AIAs seem unable or reluctant to identify, according to the precautionary principle (Article 192(2) TFEU), even those impacts which are still uncertain,[76] this author's view is that uncertainty should prompt the authority to err on the side of caution in requiring at the screening stage a full

[73] Case C-127/02 *Waddenzee*, para. 53. Regarding the cumulative effect of open-cast mining operations on the conservation of the capercaillie (*Tetrao urogallus*), see Case C-404/09 *Commission v. Spain* [2011] ECR I-1185.

[74] The authorities are called upon to examine 'solutions falling outside' the site: Case C-239/04 *Commission v. Portugal* [2006] ECR I-10183, para. 38. What is more, under Article 5(1) of the SEA Directive that applies to plans affecting Natura 2000 sites, experts are called on to take into consideration 'reasonable alternatives'.

[75] *European Commission*, Managing Natura 2000 Sites: The provisions of Article 6 of the 'Habitats' Directive 92/43/EEC, 2000, p. 38.

[76] See National Implementation of Council Directive 92/43/EC, *supra* note 66.

assessment. Indeed, since the AIA must cover plans and projects 'likely' to affect a site, the conductor of the impact study must be able to identify, in accordance with the precautionary principle, even those damages which are still uncertain.[77] Therefore, uncertainty should naturally involve the search of further information as to the real existence or extent of a risk.

2.3.6. *Geographical Range of Effects*

The geographical range of the AIA is not only limited to activities carried out in protected areas, but must also cover any plan or project located outside the site which is likely to have a significant effect on the conservation status of the classified area. Thus, even more distant polluting activities (for example, polluting activities located upstream from a protected wetland) must be subject to an AIA provided there is a probability or a risk of significant impact. Accordingly, the material nuisances caused outside the protected sites have to be taken into account.[78] It goes without saying that the radius of the zone where the projects and plans are likely to affect the integrity of the protected sites is likely to vary according to the nature of each plan and each project.[79]

2.3.7. *Concluding Remarks*

To conclude with, the information gathered in the course of the assessment must be characterised by its predictive quality. Put simply, the assessment is an exercise in prediction. Given that the assessment might become more complex while dealing with synergetic and long-term risks, the experts should extrapolate (from the information gathered) the level of risk with a view to triggering an anticipatory approach (e.g. the authorisation cannot be granted unless mitigation measures are endorsed).

3. SUBSTANTIVE DECISION CRITERION (ARTICLE 6(3) SECOND PHRASE)

3.1. INTRODUCTORY COMMENTS

Article 6(3) provides that 'in the light of the conclusions of the assessment of the implications for the site and subject to the provisions of paragraph 4, the

[77] Case C-127/02 *Waddenzee*, para. 44.

[78] Case C-418/04 *Commission v. Ireland* [2007] ECR I-1094, para. 232; and Case C-98/03 *Commission v. Germany* [2006] ECR I-53, para. 51.

[79] *F. Haumont*, AIA: the key to effective integration of nature conservation issues into land-use planning, in C.-H. Born et al. (ed.), The Habitats Directive in its EU Environmental Law Context, 2015, p. 94.

competent national authorities shall agree to the plan or project only after having ascertained that it will not adversely affect the integrity of the site concerned'. The aim of this third section is thus to explore some of the key issues arising in the implementation of this requirement.

3.2. IMPACT OF ARTICLE 6(3) OF THE HABITATS DIRECTIVE ON NATIONAL PROCEDURAL LAW

3.2.1. *Express Authorisation*

Under Article 2 of the EIA Directive, the concept of 'project' is linked with the requirement of development consent. In sharp contrast, the Habitats Directive does not require that all plans and projects covered by Article 6(3) have to be authorised by an express act, subject to various conditions, which will determine the rights and obligations of the parties involved.[80] That would be the case of projects subject to a notification scheme. It must be noted that in the majority of the Member States, so far no specific Natura 2000 licensing regimes have been adopted yet. To make matters worse, activities such as grazing, hunting, fishing, camping and canoeing are not always subject *per se* to authorisations.[81]

Although they do not fall within the scope of an authorisation regime, these projects are nonetheless subject to an AIA. Indeed, the Member Sate is called on to ensure that installations not subject to authorisation comply with the duty laid down in Article 6(3) of the Directive.[82]

We are nonetheless taking the view that the lawmaker should require the competent authorities to expressly mark their agreement on the project or plan. Indeed, where a risk of significant impact on the site of plans or projects must be assessed, it must also be necessary for the developer or operator to obtain the authorisation or express and written (and reasoned) approval of the relevant authority. In other words, the developer must obtain a permission giving him or her the right to develop in accordance with the conditions laid down by the public

[80] *Ibid.*

[81] However, the Swedish Environmental Code provides for a specific Natura 2000 authorisation, which must be granted in addition to traditional urban or environmental licences. A similar system has been set out in the UK. Under French law, the competent authority may request a specific licence for activities that are, as a matter of law, not subject to a permit (Article L 414–4, IV French Environmental Code). In the Belgium Walloon Region, the Government may request that any activity, which is not yet subject to a 'traditional' licence, be subject to a specific permit (like farm or forestry practices or recreational activities). Accordingly, land consolidation, drainage or contour modification operations impinging upon the conservation of SPAs and SACs must all be submitted for assessment and authorisation, even if they would not otherwise be submitted to such procedures under national law.

[82] Case C-98/03 *Commission v Germany* [2006] ECR I-53, para. 43.

authorities.[83] If it were not the case, it would be much more difficult for the public authorities to require mitigation measures. It follows that implicit authorisation regimes that would render any impact study irrelevant are incompatible with the requirements of Article 6(3).[84]

3.2.2. Stage at which Formal Consent Must Be Granted to the Developer

Attention should also be drawn to the fact that consent procedures can be somewhat burdensome. A phased project might be carried out provided it is subject to several consents (e.g. planning permission, industrial operations consent, water extraction or water discharge consent, etc.). The following questions arise: which of these decisions properly constitute development consent and, as a result, trigger the procedural requirements in paragraph 3? Should the screening assessment or the full assessment apply at every stage and for any decisions? Or, should the assessment requirements apply exclusively at a particular stage?[85] The Habitats Directive does not offer any answer to these questions. Reasoning by analogy, it is worth noting that the CJEU held, in *Wells*,[86] that where a consent procedure comprises several stages, the EIA requested under the EIA Directive must be carried out as soon as possible.

3.2.3. Circumventing Formal Administrative Consent by Legislative Acts

Another problem can occur when the legislature confers a legislative force to individual permits in order to prevent administrative or judicial review of the project. Such a system is provided in Belgium by Flemish and Walloon laws in order to allow major projects to be implemented without any control from the Belgian *Conseil d'Etat* (supreme administrative court).[87] This option not only puts the separation of powers at stake but is also in breach of the Aarhus Convention and related EIA Directives.[88] Furthermore, the Article 6 obligations are incumbent on the Member States regardless of the nature of the national authority with

83 The EIA Directive defines the consent as 'the decision of the competent authority or authorities which entitles the developer to proceed with development'.

84 Here an analogy can be drawn with Court's jurisprudence on so-called tacit permits: Case C-360/87 *Commission v. Italy* [1991] ECR I-791, paras. 30 and 31; and Case C-131/88 *Commission v. Germany* [1991] ECR I-825, para. 38.

85 Case C-201/02 *Wells* [2004] ECR I-723, para. 54.

86 *Ibid.*

87 *M. Delnoy & R. Snal*, La délivrance ou ratification par le législateur de permis d'urbanisme ou d'environnement au regard du droit européen et de la Convention d'Aarhus, JDE 2014, pp. 50–53; *L. Lavrysen*, Justice constitutionnellle et Natura 2000, in C.H. Born & F. Haumont, Natura 2000 and the Judge, 2014, pp. 136–143.

88 Case C-128/09 *Boxus* [2011] ECR I-9711, para. 39; and Case C-182/10 *Solvay and Others* [2012] C:2012:82, para. 52.

competence to authorise the plan or project concerned. Consequently, the legislative authority has to comply with the AIA requirements.[89]

3.3. PLAN AND PROJECT THAT CAN BE AUTHORISED IN AS MUCH AS IT WILL NOT AFFECT SITE'S INTEGRITY

3.3.1. *No Adverse Effects on Site's Integrity*

In order for the project to be authorised, Article 6(3) requires that the competent authority additionally ensures that 'it will not adversely affect the integrity of the site concerned and, if appropriate, after having obtained the opinion of the general public'. In appraising the scope of the expression 'adversely affect the integrity of the site' in its overall context, the CJEU has made clear that 'the provisions of Article 6 of the Habitats Directive must be construed as a coherent whole in the light of the conservation objectives pursued by the directive.'[90] In other words, a plan or a project may be agreed to insofar as the authorities are convinced that the site's integrity will not be adversely affected.[91] It therefore follows that a negative assessment obliges authorities to refuse consent for the project that is likely to deteriorate the site's integrity. Put it differently, the authority must be convinced that the negative effects will not occur.

However, it is not at all clear what is meant by the obligation to assess the significance of the effects in the light of the integrity of the site. Whereas, a number of language version (English, French, Italian) use an abstract term (integrity), some other language versions are more concrete. Thus, the German text refers to the site '*als solches*' (as such). The Dutch version speaks of the '*natuurlijke kennmerken*' (natural characteristics) of the site.[92]

Until the *Sweetman* case was decided by the CJEU, there was little guidance from the courts on what an adverse effect on site integrity was. In that case, the Court was asked to rule on whether the loss of 1.5ha of limestone pavement could be qualified as an adverse effect on the integrity of the Irish Natura 2000 site, regardless of the fact that it only amounted to 0.5% of the actual surface of limestone in the whole site. According to the Irish planning authority, the road bypass at issue was not so severe as to adversely affect the integrity of the Natura 2000 site.

---

89 Case C-182/10 *Solvay and Others* [2012], para. 69.

90 Case C-258/11 *Peter Sweetman*, para. 32.

91 In Case C-127/02 *Waddenzee*, the CJEU stressed that the national authorities are to be 'convinced', and that they can grant consent only if they have made certain that it will affect the integrity of the site (para. 59).

92 Opinion AG Sharpston in Case C-258/11 *Peter Sweetman* [2012], para. 53.

Notwithstanding those linguistic differences discussed above, AG Sharpston took the view that it is 'the essential unity of the site that is relevant'. As a result, in her view, the notion of 'integrity must be understood as referring to the continued wholeness and soundness of the constitutive characteristics of the site concerned.'[93]

The CJEU endorsed in *Sweetman* the AG's reasoning: 'in order for the integrity of a site as a natural habitat not to be adversely affected for the purposes of the second sentence of Article 6(3) of the Habitats Directive the site needs to be preserved at a favourable conservation status; this entails … the lasting preservation of the constitutive characteristics of the site concerned that are connected to the presence of a natural habitat type whose preservation was the objective justifying the designation of that site in the list of SCIs, in accordance with the directive.'[94] It must be noted that the Court paid heed to the irreversible damage caused to the protected habitat: once destroyed by the road, it could not be replaced.[95]

The Court's interpretation of site integrity has been welcomed since it provides an additional safeguard for the EU's most vulnerable habitats in particular with respect to the accumulation of adverse impacts on biodiversity. Such an interpretation should help decision-makers to eschew the risk of the so-called 'death by a thousand cuts' phenomenon.[96]

Along the same lines, the CJEU held recently in *Briels* that a motorway project which will impair the protected natural habitat type molinia meadows, due to drying out and acidification of the earth caused by increases in nitrogen deposits, adversely affect the integrity of the site within the meaning of Article 6(3) of the Habitats Directive.[97] The creation of new habitat with a view to off-setting the losses had to be categorised as a 'compensatory measure 'within the meaning of Article 6(4). Accordingly, they could not be taken into consideration in the assessment of the impact on the integrity of the site.

Further guidance has been provided by the European Commission. The meaning of the concept must be understood in the light of a number of criteria, including:

- coherence of the ecological structures;
- resilience of the habitats to change;
- ability of the habitats to evolve in a sense favourable to conservation;

93 *Ibid.*, para. 54.
94 Case C-258/11 *Peter Sweetman* [2012], para. 39.
95 *Ibid.*, para. 45.
96 *D. McGillivray*, The ruling of the court of Justice in Sweetman: How to avoid a death by a thousand cuts?, ELNI Rev., 2014 (1), p. 1.
97 Case C-521/12 *Briels* [2014] C:2014:330, paras. 23 and 24.

- inherent potential for meeting SCOs; and/or
- self-renewal without external management support.[98]

As a result, the AIA does provide a positive means by which the granting of permission may either be refused or made conditional. Put simply, the assessment's conclusions shape the substantive outcomes of the decision. The site's integrity comes first, development second. This reasoning is predicated on the assumption that most of the land in the Member States is subject to development whereas only a small percentage falls within the ambit of the Natura 2000 network. As a result, development occurring in the protected areas must be subject to a web of procedural conditions with a view to reducing the adverse effects as much as possible. This legal reasoning stands in stark contrast to the EIA Directive, which does not prevent the authority granting permission despite the fact that the conclusions of the assessment are negative.[99]

3.3.2. *Precautionary Decision-Making*

The precautionary principle has been proclaimed in EU primary law with the principles of prevention, rectification at source and the polluter pays in Article 191(2) TFEU, a provision obliging institutions to base their environmental policies on a set of principles. It is however not defined in Treaty law, even though there are various definitions in international environmental law.[100] In short, precaution is testament of a genuine paradigm shift. While prevention is based on the concept of certain risk, the new paradigm is distinguished by the intrusion of uncertainty. Precaution does not posit a perfect understanding of any given risk: the absence of full evidence does not preclude the authorities to act in face of uncertainty. In this respect, precaution aims to bridge the gap between scientists working on the frontiers of scientific knowledge and decision-makers willing to act to prevent environmental degradation.

The precautionary principle came to centre stage in the field of environment policy in response to the limitations of science in assessing complex and uncertain ecological risks. With respect to assessing the impacts of projects on ecosystems, uncertainty may arises as a result of the inherent complexity of ecosystems, the distance in time and space between sources and damages, the cumulative and synergistic effects of other impacts (acidification, eutrophication, climate change, invasive species, etc.), the unpredictable reactions of some ecosystems (potential resilience), and the incomplete knowledge of the effectiveness of mitigation

98 *European Commission*, Managing Natura 2000 Sites: The provisions of Article 6 of the 'Habitats' Directive 92/43/EEC, 2000.

99 See AG Elmer's opinion in Case C-431/92 *Commission v. Germany* [1995] ECR I-2209, para. 35.

100 See also our previous works on this topic: Environmental Principles: from Political Slogans to Legal Rules, 2002; Implementing Precaution. Approaches from Nordic Countries, the EU and USA, 2007.

measures.[101] The lack of knowledge is compounded by methodological difficulties in assessing these risks such as:

- the lack of opportunity for experimental testing;
- the lack of scope for comparative analysis; and
- the lack of long-term data sets.[102]

Accordingly, there is a strong deficit in predictive capability with respect to the functioning and the resilience of ecosystems.

The CJEU has been fleshing out the environmental principle with respect to the AIA procedure. In effect, it is settled case law that authorisation can only be given where the AIA demonstrates the absence of risks in relation to the integrity of the site. If there is any lingering uncertainty over the subsequent manifestation of risks, the term 'ascertain' would require, according to CJEU case law and in line with the precautionary principle, that the competent authority refrain from issuing the authorisation.[103] It follows that an assessment made under Article 6(3) of the Habitats Directive 'cannot be regarded as appropriate if it contains gaps and lacks complete, precise and definitive findings and conclusions capable of removing all reasonable scientific doubt as to the effects of the works proposed on the SPA concerned'.[104] In other words, where there is any reasonable doubt or where there is incomplete knowledge over the absence of any effects, authorities must refrain from issuing authorisations.[105] Put it simply, where the information is insufficient, the project can't go along. *In dubio pro natura*, as the saying goes. That being said, in accordance with the logic of the precautionary principle, authorities can order additional investigations in order to remove the uncertainty (if needed).

Lastly, the precautionary principle does not prompt a reversal of the burden of proof from the project opponent to the authority authorising the project or plan.

---

101 *J. & R. Kasperson* (ed.), Global Environmental Risk, 2001.

102 *G. Tucker & J. Treweek*, The Precautionary Principle and Impact Assessment, in R. Cooney & B. Dickson (eds.), Biodiversity & the Precautionary Principle, 2005, p. 75.

103 Case C-127/02 *Waddenzee*, para. 67; Case C-6/04 *Commission v. UK* [2005] ECR I9017; Case C239/04 *Commission v. Portugal* [2006] ECR I-10183, para. 24; Case C404/09 *Commission v. Spain* [2011], para. 99.

104 Case C-304/05 *Commission v. Italy* [2007] ECR I-7495, para. 69; Case C-404/09 *Commission v. Spain* [2011] ECR I-11853, para. 100.

105 Regarding the risks entailed by hazardous substances, see, by analogy: Case T-229/04 *Sweden v. Commission* [2007] ECR II-2437; and Cases C-14 and 295/06 *Parliament and Denmark v. Commission* [2008] ECR I-1649.

3.3.3. Participatory Decision-Making

Contrary to the EIA Directive that entitles individuals to express their opinion as to the likely significance of a project, Article 6(3) does not automatically ensure public participation. This is left to each Member States' discretion. It should be noted here that this is a grey area and does not align with recent developments in international law: Member States are parties to the UNECE Convention on Access to Information, Public Participation in Decision-making and Access to Justice in Environmental Matters adopted on 25 June 1998, that requires them to organise public participation for a wide array of projects and plans.

Even when public participation is not provided for, it can be wise to provide opportunities for the wider public to take part in the public debate. As a matter of law, there are numerous ways in which public participation could be organised (conference, consultation, public debate, public inquiry, etc.). Moreover, public participation should be organised as early as possible, if possible at screening level.

Finally, in most of the national legal orders, the fact that someone participates in the decision-making process reinforces his or her right to standing and therefore in challenging the authorisation that will be issued. Furthermore, participation enhances the correct implementation of EU law, given that the public might raise questions as to the correct implementation of the Habitats Directive. Moreover, when a plan or a programme is subject to an AIA, it must also be subject to an SEA, which expressly entails a participatory process.[106]

3.3.4. Statement of Reasons

It goes without saying that the duty to state the reasons as to the weighing of conflicting interests narrows the discretion on the part of the authorities. Accordingly, the authority should disclose the rationale behind their decision. For instance, if an alternative option is not deemed to be possible, it must provide specific explanations as to which factors led it to choose the proposed development. However, there is no express obligation to state the reasons similar to the one laid down under Article 9 of the EIA Directive. Nonetheless, when the project falls within the ambit of the EIA Directive the authority is also being called upon to state the reasons.

---

106 See Article 3(2) SEA Directive.

4. DEROGATORY REGIME (ARTICLE 6(4))

4.1. INTRODUCTORY COMMENTS

4.1.1. Derogation Mechanism Following Negative Findings in Assessment

Environmental protection has more often given way to socio-economic considerations. For instance, in cases involving the overlap of administrative regulations, the solutions adopted by the national courts generally lean in favour of economic development rather than the conservation of natural resources.[107] Nature has thus paid a weighty tribute to the absence of any incorporation of environmental requirements into other policies. In adopting the Habitats Directive, the EU lawmaker struck a balance between the competing interests.

Where it transpires that the AIA shows that the project threatens the integrity of the site, in principle no authorisation can be issued. An exception is however provided for by Article 6(4) which is testament, according to Advocate General Kokott, to the principle of proportionality.[108]

Optimum environmental protection is assured by both procedural and substantive guarantees contained in Article 6(4) of the Directive. Projects can only be implemented where:

- there are no alternative measures;
- their completion is justified by specific interests;
- moreover, where a challenged project is accepted, the Member States must implement compensatory measures in order to off-set the losses of habitats and guarantee the global consistency of the Natura 2000 network.

These conditions warrant special attention.

---

[107] For the convenience of representation, the impact of transport infrastructures on protected habitats have been chosen. For example the construction of a highway across a Natura 2000 site in order to alleviate traffic was deemed to be an imperative reason of overriding public interest that justifies, by virtue of Art. 6(4) of the Habitats Directive, encroachments on priority habitats and species (BVerwG A 20,05 of 17 January 2007, BVerwG 128 1). By the same token, the enlargement of a protected area within an existing industrial plant in order to complete the production of a jumbo jet was deemed to fulfil an imperative reason of overriding public interest on account that 'the German authorities have demonstrated that the project is of outstanding importance for the region of Hamburg and for northern Germany as well as the European aerospace industry (Commission, C(2000) 1079 of 14 April 2000).' In spite the fact that a number of specimens of the most endangered mammal in Europe, the Iberian lynx (*Lynx iberica*), were killed due to an increase in traffic, the conversion of a by-road into a regional motorway across a national park did not infringe the Habitats Directive's obligations on the protection of that rare species (Case C-308/08 *Commission v. Spain* [2010] ECR I-4281).

[108] Opinion AG Kokott in *Waddenzee*, para. 106.

4.1.2. *First Condition: Absence of Alternative Solutions*

The Habitats Directive makes the issuance of authorisations dependent on the absence of alternative solutions.[109] First, only in the absence of alternative solutions could the authority allow for derogations under paragraph 4. Member States must therefore be able to demonstrate, where appropriate, that the AIA has found there to be no viable alternative.[110] Developers should therefore demonstrate that they have fully considered alternative solutions.

Given that the obligation to seek the least damaging alternative[111] encapsulates a preventative approach,[112] the specific importance of that obligation is not difficult to fathom. However, given the traditional emphasis upon developers' rights, one can expect a fair amount of resistance from the authorities to seek the least damaging alternative.

Considering the useful effect (*effet utile*) of the Directive, it is appropriate to give, keeping in mind the *effet utile* of the EU legislation, a broad interpretation to the obligation to seek out the least damaging alternative for the conservation of the site.[113] The obligation to seek the least damaging alternative should be at the heart of every AIA, with the particular aim of reducing the potential impact on the Natura 2000 site. Strictly speaking, it should be considered as a key feature of the assessment. As soon as it becomes possible for the Member State to achieve the same objective in a way that causes less damage to the conservation of the protected habitat, the initial project must be abandoned in favour of the alternative project. This means that it should not be possible to invoke the higher costs of alternative projects as a reason for excluding less damaging projects, except where the costs are disproportionately high.[114]

Nonetheless, the assessors have to overcome a number of hurdles, including:

- the difficulty in obtaining the relevant information, for example as needed for assessors to have something to compare and contrast; and

109 In sharp contrast, the EIA Directive is not as crystal clear. Annex III of Directive 85/337/EEC provides, 'where appropriate' that the developer study 'an outline of the main alternatives'.

110 Case C-21/08 *Commission v. France.*

111 Case C-239/04 *Commission v. Portugal* [2006] ECR I-10183, paras. 38–39.

112 *J. Holder*, Environmental Assessment, 2004, p. 148.

113 On the obligation to privilege the alternative which is least prejudicial to ecological interests, see Judgment of 12 December 1996 in Case C-10/96 *Ligue royale belge pour la protection des oiseaux* [1996] ECR I-6775, para. 18. Cf. the Commission's favourable opinion of 24 April 2003 on the construction of a railway line in Northern Sweden where the available alternatives did not entail higher costs.

114 The European Commission considers that economic criteria do not take precedence over ecological criteria when selecting 'alternative solutions'. Cf. *European Commission*, Managing Natura 2000 Sites: The provisions of Article 6 of the 'Habitats' Directive 92/43/EEC, 2000, p. 43.

- the difficulty in comparing the ecological value of the development site and the proposed mitigation site given that developers' property rights are usually limited to the site proposed for development.

Besides, the obligation to seek the least damaging alternative prompts a number of questions:

1. What range of alternatives should be covered? The solutions could involve an array of measures ranging from alternative locations, alternative processes, different scales or design, or the zero-option or do-nothing alternative.
2. What is the appropriate level of comparison? This raises the question of the level at which the comparison of alternatives should take place. For instance, it makes more sense not to compare the different routes that a motorway could follow but to compare different means of transportation.
3. How should alternatives be compared? According to the Commission's documents: 'economic criteria cannot be seen as overruling ecological criteria'.[115]
4. Technical feasibility: Which are the reasonable sites for the proposed development? Must all alternatives be viable? Are the alternatives likely to be suitable? Are the alternative sites available?
5. Territorial dimension: Should the assessor focus exclusively on a particular site or should he set out a broader approach? For instance, when assessing the opportunity of a harbour development, should the experts assess the port capacity with respect to other projects around the country, around the EU or around the globe (e.g. development in Tangier or in Singapore)?

4.1.3. Second Condition: Weighing Interests

In addition to the obligation to adopt the least damaging alternative possible, the advantages of the project must be carefully balanced against its damaging effects for the conservation of natural habitats. The proportionality principle plays a key role in this balancing of interests: a project justified by a fundamental interest with only a relatively minor negative impact will be more readily accepted than a particularly damaging project in which public interest is marginal. A fundamental distinction must, however, be established between habitats where protection is deemed to be important and those where it is not.

[115] *Ibid.*, p. 43.

4.1.3.1. Non-Priority Habitats and Species

For *non-priority habitats and species,* 'imperative reasons of overriding public interest, including those of a social or economic nature' will justify the execution of the project.

However, it would not be viable to give too broad an interpretation to 'reasons of a social or economic nature' which would run the risk of depriving the protection regime of any substance. Although in *Lappel Bank* the Court took care not to make any express statements on the range of 'imperative reasons of overriding public interest, including those of a social or economic nature', paragraph 41 of the judgment ('economic requirements, as an imperative reason of overriding public interest') nonetheless indicates that a restricted interpretation of 'economic requirements' must prevail. In any case, it is evident from the wording of Article 6(4) that economic requirements cannot be directly equated with 'imperative reasons of overriding public interest'.[116] This means that the enlargement of a harbour or the construction of a road network cannot be authorised for the simple reason that it satisfies particular economic requirements (e.g. job creation or local economic development) but rather because it is intended to satisfy an overriding public interest (e.g. the opening up of a particularly isolated region, the necessity of substantially raising the standard of living of the local population). This interpretation has been endorsed in *Solvay*. The CJEU ruled that: 'an interest capable of justifying, within the meaning of Article 6(4) of the Habitats Directive, the implementation of a plan or project must be both 'public' and 'overriding', which means that it must be of such an importance that it can be weighed up against that directive's objective of the conservation of natural habitats and wild fauna and flora.'[117] As a result, the mere construction of infrastructure designed to accommodate a management centre cannot constitute an imperative reason of overriding public interest within the meaning of Article 6(4).[118]

4.1.3.2. Priority Habitats and Species

On the other hand, greater weight has been given to ecological interests when the site hosts so-called *priority habitats or species.*[119] Accordingly, the Member State's margin of appreciation is more limited since 'the only considerations which may be raised are those relating to human health or public safety, to beneficial consequences of primary importance for the environment or, further to an

116 In the context of modifications to SCAs, any pre-eminence of economic over ecological interests must be tempered in virtue of Article 3 TEU as well as of Article 11 TFEU. These provisions put economic and environmental objectives on an equal footing. See *N. de Sadeleer*, EU Environmental Law and Internal Market, 2014.

117 Case C-182/10 *Solvay and Others* [2012], para. 75.

118 *Ibid.*, para. 78.

119 Neither the Birds nor Habitats Directives, however, indicate whether wild birds are to be considered as priority species.

opinion from the Commission, to other imperative reasons of overriding public interest' (Article 6(4)). The authority can only grant the permission on the ground of this narrow set of interest.

The fact that social or economic reasons are not expressly included in this second exception indicates that they are not covered by it. Therefore, Member States may not authorise the passing of a motorway through a nature reserve classified as a special conservation area hosting priority species where the impact study shows that the project will damage the integrity of the site.

The CJEU has already taken the view that health protection objectives may prevail over those relating to nature protection. For instance, a project jeopardising a wild bird sanctuary protected under the Wild Birds Directive can be authorised insofar as it wards off the risk of floods.[120]

Although it adversely affects the integrity of a Natura 2000 site, the conversion of a natural fluvial ecosystem into a largely man-made structure in Northern Greece can be justified on the ground that it 'may, in some circumstances, have beneficial consequences of primary importance for the environment'.[121] Indeed, irrigation and the supply of drinking water can be of such an importance that such projects can be weighed against the Habitat Directive's objective of conservation of natural habitats and wild fauna.[122] Given the severity of the impact of irrigation projects on the natural environment, the position of the Court on this question is controversial.[123]

The position of the CJEU on this issue is slippery. Framed in restrictive language, these grounds of derogation are to be interpreted strictly insofar as they depart from the principle that authorisations not be granted to plans or projects when assessments demonstrate that they would have negative ramifications for the conservation of the site (Article 6(3)). It is therefore necessary to understand the phrase 'other imperative reasons of overriding public interest' as referring to a general interest superior to the ecological objective of the Directive.

4.1.3.3. Derogations Interpreted in the Light of the Objective of Sustainable Development

The concept of sustainable development is recognised as one of the main objective pursued by the EU.[124] That being said, it is characterised by a strong degree of

---

120 Case C-57/89 *Commission v. Germany* [1991] ECR I-883, paras. 20–23.

121 Case C-43/10 *Nomarchiaki Aftodioikisi Aitoloakarnanias et al.* [2012], para. 125.

122 *Ibid.*, paras. 121–122.

123 Indeed, 'irrigation and drainage projects invariably result in many far-reaching ecological changes', some of which 'cover the entire range of environmental components, such as soil, water, air, energy, and the socio-economic system'. See the *Food and Agriculture Organization (FAO) and Overseas Development Administration (ODA)*, FAO Irrigation and Drainage Paper 53, 1995, p. 1.

124 The concept is currently enshrined in Articles 3(3)–(5) and 21(2)(d)–(f) TEU, Article 11 TFEU, as well as Article 37 EUCFR. See also the 6th recital of the preamble to the TEU. See *N. de*

indeterminacy. Though few authorities and undertakings will contend with the proposition that development should be sustainable, they might disagree on how to flesh out this proposition in individual cases. Accordingly, the main attraction of this concept is that 'both sides in any legal argument will be able to rely on it'.[125]

The interpretation given by Advocate General Léger to sustainable development in his Opinion in *First Corporate Shipping*, a case on development taking place in protected birds habitats, is testament to a conciliatory approach. Indeed, the Advocate General stressed that 'the concept 'sustainable development' does not mean that the interests of the environment must necessarily and systematically prevail over the interests defended in the context of the other policies pursued by the Community... On the contrary, it emphasises the necessary balance between various interests which sometimes clash, but which must be reconciled'.[126] Against this backdrop, some scholars have been taking the view that nature conservation law has not always be capable to facilitate sustainable development on the ground that Article 6 requires 'merely a dogmatic approach focusing on ecological criteria'.[127]

Recently, the impact of sustainability on the procedural requirements set out under Article 6 has been gathering momentum. In *Nomarchiaki Aftodioikisi Aitoloakarnanias*, the Greek Council of State sought to ascertain whether the Habitats Directive, interpreted in the light of the objective of sustainable development, could allow the conversion of a natural fluvial ecosystem into a largely man-made fluvial and lacustrine ecosystem, irrespective of the negative impacts on the integrity of sites that are part of the Natura 2000 network. The CJEU took the view that the Habitats Directive, and in particular its Article 6(3) and (4) interpreted in the light of the objective of sustainable development, permits such project.[128] Nonetheless, the Court stressed that such a project can be authorised inasmuch as the conditions for granting the derogation were satisfied – conditions which have so far been interpreted rather narrowly.[129]

Our view is that sustainable development cannot water down basic environmental requirements. As noted previously, the assessment and decision-making procedures are framing the balance between the competing interests. Moreover, pursuant to Article 3(3) TEU and Article 191(2) TFEU, the manners in which these procedures apply include the requirement to attain a 'high level of protection and improvement of the quality of the environment'.

Sadeleer, Sustainable Development in EU Law. Still a Long Way to Go, in Jindal Global Law Review. Special Issue on Environmental Law and Governance, 2015 (6:1), pp. 1–7.

125 *P. Birnie, A. Boyle & C. Redgwell*, International Law and the Environment, 3rd ed., 2009, p. 124.116.

126 Opinion AG Léger in Case C-371/98, *First Corporate Shipping* [2000] ECR I-9235, para. 54.

127 *F.H. Kistenkas*, Rethinking European Nature Conservation Legislation: Towards Sustainable Development, JEEPL, 2013 (10:1), p. 75.

128 Case C-43/10 *Nomarchiaki Aftodioikisi Aitoloakarnanias et al.* [2012], paras. 134–139.

129 Case C-538/09 *Commission v. Belgium* [2011] OJ C211/5, para. 53.

4.1.3.4. Procedural Requirements

As far as projects justified by 'other imperative reasons of overriding public interest' are concerned, a favourable opinion from the Commission is required in all cases. This requirement is drawn up in similar terms to Article 37 of the Euratom Treaty. According to the Commission's position on the Euratom Treaty, the approval required for development affecting priority sites does not have binding force.[130] However, a failure to request the Commission's opinion or the implementation of a project in spite of a Commission refusal would constitute a default on the obligations contained in the Habitats Directive, which should be punished both by the competent national or Community authorities as well as by the national courts.

Be that as it may, several authors contend that many of the Commission's opinions do not fulfil the applicable derogation requirements set about by Article 6(4).[131]

4.1.4. Mitigation Measures

The conservation of the area having been established in principle, any derogations that can be made must be interpreted strictly. As Article 6(2) requires Member States to take appropriate measures to avoid the deterioration of natural habitats and significant disturbances to species in these areas, they must therefore mitigate as far as possible any negative impacts of any project authorised pursuant to an impact study.[132] The view of this report is that these considerations should be dealt with in the AIA with the aim of reducing the negative impacts on the integrity of the site.

The adoption of mitigation measures also limits the importance of compensatory measures.[133]

---

130 Case C-187/87 *Saarland v. Minister for Industry* [1988] ECR I-5013.

131 The Commission's practice seems to be *a priori* favourable to requests from Member States. See the commentary by *A. Nollkaemper*, Habitat Protection in European Community Law: Evolving Conceptions of a Balance of Interests, Journal of Environmental Law, 1997 (9), p. 271; *L. Krämer*, The European Commission's Opinions under Article 6(4) of the Habitats Directive, J. Environmental Law, 2009 (21); *D. McGillivray*, Compensating Biodiversity Loss: the EU Commission's Approach to Compensation under Art. 6 of the Habitats Directive, Journal of Environmental Law, 2012 (3), pp. 417–450; *L. Krämer*, Implementation and Enforcement of the Habitats Directive, in C.-H. Born et al. (ed.), The Habitats Directive in its EU Environmental Law Context, 2015, pp. 236.

132 It should be noted that the EIA Directive only provides for the adoption of mitigation measures where strictly procedural pre-requisites are satisfied (see Annex IV, section 5).

133 See the mitigation measures for the passage of the A20 motorway through the '*Peene*' protection area (anti-noise barriers, headlight-blocking screens). For example, Commission Opinion 96/15/EC of 18 December 1995, para. 4.3.

4.1.5. *Compensatory Measures*

If a project is justified because there are no available alternatives and it satisfies the interests outlined above, it can be implemented subject to the obligation to take 'all compensatory measures necessary to ensure that the overall coherence of Natura 2000 is protected. [The Member State] shall inform the Commission of the compensatory measures adopted'. Regarding the scope of this obligation, AG Sharpston noted:

> 'The legislation recognises, in other words, that there may be exceptional circumstances in which damage to or destruction of a protected natural habitat may be necessary, but, in allowing such damage or destruction to proceed, it insists that there be full compensation for the environmental consequences. The status quo, or as close to the status quo as it is possible to achieve in all the circumstances, is thus maintained.'[134]

In *Briels*, the Court was asked whether Article 6(3) of the Habitats Directive must be interpreted as meaning that a motorway project in the Netherlands which provides for the creation of an area of equal or greater size of the same natural habitat type within the same site, has an effect on the integrity of that site and, if so, whether such measures may be categorised as 'compensatory measures' within the meaning of Article 6(4) thereof. The Court took the view that the creation of an area of the same natural habitat type were aiming at compensating for the negative effects of the project on the Natura 2000 site. Accordingly, these compensatory measures could be taken into account in the assessment of the implications of the project provided for in Article 6(3).[135] The judgment deserves a warm welcome. Indeed, it does not make sense to eschew the assessment on the account that compensatory measures belittle the impact of the project on the Natura 2000 site. These measures have to be carved out in a second stage, when the risks have been clearly ascertained by the experts thanks to an AIA.

5. AIA, EIA, AND SEA: HOW TO SQUARE THE CIRCLE?

The obligation to carry out an AIA does not preclude the obligations to conduct:

1. a traditional EIA under the EIA Directive; or
2. a SEA under SEA Directive 2001/42/EC.

---

134 Opinion AG Sharpston in Case C-258/11 *Peter Sweetman*, para. 64.
135 Case C-521/12 *Briels* [2014], para. 29.

These procedural obligations are indeed autonomous and cumulative.[136]

Of importance is to note that when a plan or programme is subject to an AIA in accordance with Article 6(3), it must also be subject to an SEA. Article 3(2) of SEA Directive runs as follows:

> 'Subject to para. 3, an environmental assessment shall be carried out for all plans and programmes,
>
> ...
>
> (b) which, in view of the likely effect on sites, have been determined to require an assessment pursuant to Article 6 or 7 of Directive 92/43/EEC.'

The SEA Directive has added value on the account that it enhances a more upstream approach. For instance, inasmuch as land planning regulations allow the realisation of public or private projects, environmental concerns must be taken into account at the earliest stage, when conceiving the land-planning regulation, not at the time of construction. It is certainly more effective first to assess the overall impact of all the roads encapsulated in a highways project than to single out every road without any broader assessment.

The CJEU ruled recently that the examination carried out to determine whether the plan is not subject to an SEA 'is necessarily limited to the question as to whether it can be excluded, on the basis of objective information, that that plan or project will have a significant effect on the site concerned.'[137] Accordingly, where a plan subject to an AIA, it is consequently subject to an SEA.

That being said, it ought to be remembered that there is a difference in substance between the different assessments. Given that the bulk of the information in the AIA relates to ecosystemic data, the Habitats AIA is more targeted as well as far less multidisciplinary than the traditional EIA or the SEA.[138] Conversely, the AIA provides a much clearer picture, and a more in-depth analysis of the impacts on habitats. It is therefore not necessary to take into consideration all the environmental impacts of the project (effects on archaeological resources, cultural heritage or human health, etc.) as it needs only to 'be subject to appropriate assessment of its implications for the site in view of the site's conservation objectives'.

Moreover, the negative conclusions of an AIA do bind the competent authorities whereas the conclusions of either an EIA or a SEA dot not entail specific requirements. Accordingly, neither an EIA nor a SEA can replace a genuine AIA.

---

136 *N. de Sadeleer,* L'évaluation des incidences environnementales des programmes, plans et projets : à la recherche d'une protection juridictionnelle effective, RDUE, 2014 (2), pp. 1–56.

137 Case C-177/11 *Sillogos Ellinon Poleodomon kai Khorotakton* [2012], para. 24.

138 Case C-256/98 *Commission v. France*, the Court held that the object of the French impact study regime was not sufficiently 'appropriate' having regard to the conservation objectives of the sites (para. 40).

The EIA Directive 2011/92/EU as amended by Directive 2014/52/EU of 16 April 2014 takes into account to a greater extent than in the past the need to conserve the biodiversity.

The preamble of the new directive states:

> 'The measures taken to avoid, prevent, reduce and, if possible, offset significant adverse effects on the environment, in particular on species and habitats protected under (the Habitats Directive 92/43/EEC) and (the Birds Directive 2009/147/EC), should contribute to avoiding any deterioration in the quality of the environment and any net loss of biodiversity, in accordance with the Union's commitments in the context of the Convention and the objectives and actions of the Union Biodiversity Strategy up to 2020 laid down in the Commission Communication of 3 May 2011 entitled 'Our life insurance, our natural capital: an EU biodiversity strategy to 2020'.

Furthermore, Article 2(3) of Directive 2011/92/EU as amended by Directive 2014/52/EU of 16 April 2014 requires coordination between the EIA and the AIA procedures. That provision reads as follows:

> 'In the case of projects for which the obligation to carry out assessments of the effects on the environment arises simultaneously from this Directive and from (the Habitats Directive 92/43/EEC and the Birds Directive 2009/147/EC) ... Member States shall, where appropriate, ensure that coordinated and/or joint procedures fulfilling the requirements of that Union legislation are provided for.'

Paragraph 37 of the preamble of Directive 2011/92 offers some clarification :

> 'In order to improve the effectiveness of the assessments, reduce administrative complexity and increase economic efficiency, where the obligation to carry out assessments related to environmental issues arises simultaneously from this Directive and (the Habitats Directive 92/43/EEC and the Birds Directive 2009/147/EC), Member States should ensure that coordinated and/or joint procedures fulfilling the requirements of these Directives are provided, where appropriate and taking into account their specific organisational characteristics.'

Pursuant to Article 2(a) of Directive 2011/92/EU as amended by Directive 2014/52/EU, the Commission is called on to provide guidance regarding the setting up of any coordinated or joint procedures for projects that are simultaneously subject to assessments under the EIA Directive and the Habitats Directive 92/43/EEC and the Birds Directive 2009/147/EC.

In addition, the wide scope of the EIA has to include, in virtue of Article 3 of the EIA Directive the assessment of 'biodiversity, with particular attention to species and habitats protected under' the Habitats Directive.[139]

Last but not least, where Member States have to subject projects listed under Annex II to an EIA, they have to take into consideration the criteria set out in Annex III. Among these criteria, the Member States have to take into consideration 'the environmental sensitivity of geographical areas likely to be affected by projects must be considered, with particular regard to: ... areas classified or protected under national legislation; Natura 2000 areas designated by Member States pursuant to Directive 92/43/EEC and Directive 2009/147/EC'.[140]

That being said, one should bear in mind that the SEA and EIA Directives expressly entail a participatory process whereas the Habitats Directive does not require compulsory public inquiries.

Nonetheless, nothing stands in the way of establishing more targeted Habitats Directive assessments as it is seen as a specific sub-assessment within the broader (general) assessment regime. Given the size and the nature of infrastructure projects (harbours, motorways, etc.), most of the AIAs are part of much broader EIAs conducted pursuant to national regulations implementing the EIA Directive.

Last but not least, as a matter of practice, it must be noted that there are a huge number of projects not encompassed within the EIA and the SEA Directives' scope of ambit. As a result, the EIAs and SEAs cannot serve as an ersatz for the vast majority of plans and projects threatening the conservation of Natura 2000 sites.

6. CONCLUSIONS

Halting biodiversity loss has become a key objective of the EU. It requires a strict application of AIA requirements. Indeed, the AIA is a critical biodiversity management tool as it ensures that the effects of developments within, or next to, Natura 2000 sites are fully assessed before consent is given. In addition, negative conclusions preclude the adoption of the plan or the granting of the licence. As a result, the site's integrity comes first, development second.

139 Pursuant to Article 3(1)(b) of the EIA Directive, 'the environmental impact assessment shall identify, describe and assess in an appropriate manner, in the light of each individual case, the direct and indirect significant effects of a project on the following factors: biodiversity, with particular attention to species and habitats protected under Directive 92/43/EEC and Directive 2009/147/EC'.

140 Annex II, 2, c, v).

In spite of its key role in conserving biodiversity in the EU, Article 6 is still dogged by controversies.[141] The extension of ports[142] and of mining activities,[143] the development of renewable energy projects,[144] the irrigation of intensive agriculture,[145] or the construction of major infrastructure works such as railways,[146] motorways[147] and tourist facilities[148] increasingly collide with the protective regime enshrined in the Habitats Directive. Moreover, a few lawyers argue that this 'rigid' piece of legislation excludes social and economic interests to the detriment of sustainable development.[149] That being said, it must be noted that the vast majority of projects still go ahead, even when they seem hardly reconcilable with the conservation objectives pursued by the directive.

What is more, there are serious grounds for concern that Member States are not sufficiently implementing the Directive.[150] So far the vast majority of the cases adjudicated by the CJEU concern situations where there has been no appropriate assessment.[151] Additionally, many SPAs and SACs have merely been designated for the purpose of reporting to the Commission and are not yet protected with proper regulatory regimes or management plans. Most of the SACs which have not been or are in the process of being designated are still lacking a proper management plan. In addition, there are no sets of scientific indicators that could be used with the aim of assessing whether the SCOs are being realised. These sites are, as a result, extremely vulnerable to development.

The question is whether this cornerstone of nature legislation will become the victim of the Better Regulation creed. On Tuesday 16 December 2014, the new Juncker Commission announced to the European Parliament its Work Programme 2015. The Commission's power to initiate is exclusively focused on creating job opportunities. In relation to environmental policy any new vision

---

141 The huge amount of complaints sent to both the Commission and the European Parliament's Petition Committee signifies the frustration among citizens as well as national nature protection NGOs regarding unsatisfactory processes.

142 Case C-44/95 *Royal Society for Protection of Birds* (*'Lappel Bank'*) [1996] ECR I-3805; Journal of Environmental Law (9:3), 139, note J.D.C. Harte.

143 Case C-404/09 *Commission v. Spain* [2011] ECR I-11853.

144 Case C-2/10 *Azienda Agro-Zootecnica Franchini and Eolica di Altamura* [2011].

145 Case C-202/00 *Commission v. France* (*'Plaine des Maures'*); case C-43/10 *Nomarchiaki Aftodioikisi Aitoloakarnanias* [2012].

146 Case C-182/10 *Solvay and Others* [2012].

147 Case C-239/04 *Commission v. Portugal* [2006] ECR I-10183; Case C-142/07 *Ecologistas en Accion-Coda v. Ayuntamentio de Madrid* [2008] ECR I-9097; Case C-258/11 *Peter Sweetman* [2012].

148 Case C-304/05 *Commission v. Italy* [2007] ECR I-7495.

149 *S. Borgström & F. Kistenkas*, The Compatibility of the Habitats Directive with the Novel EU Green Infrastructure Policy, EEELR, 2014 (23:2), p. 40.

150 The EC Commission has initiated an infringement procedure against Romania, because the SPAs designation is inconsistent with the Important Birds Area (IBA) and fewer and smaller areas have been designated.

151 Case C-179/06 *Commission v. Italy* [2007] ECR I-8131; Case C-241/08 *Commission v. France* [2010] ECR I-1697; Case C-226/08 *Stadt Papenburg* [2010] ECR I-131; and Case C-182/10 *Solvay and Others* [2012].

is missing. Here, the Commission only looks at existing legislation and pending proposals asking if they are 'fit for purpose' or are still topical. In particular, the Commission is intent upon proposing the lawmaker the merger of the Habitats and the Birds Directives with the aim of assuaging the fears of developers and some Member States. Accordingly, the sensible but sustained compromise between environmental and economic interests achieved in EU nature protection law may be blurred if the Natura 2000 directives are tested in terms of economic efficiency within a new regulatory framework. Given the significant and continuing loss of biodiversity across Europe, it is of utmost importance that the lawmaker keeps in mind the cardinal importance of the Natura 2000 network.

CHAPTER 14

COMPENSATORY MEASURES FOR LARGE-SCALE PROJECTS IN EUROPEAN NATURE CONSERVATION LAW AFTER THE *BRIELS* CASE

Geert Van Hoorick

1. INTRODUCTION

The Wild Birds and Habitats Directives[1] are the cornerstones of EU nature conservation law, aiming to achieve the conservation of the Natura 2000 network, a network of protected sites under these directives, and the protection of species. The protection regime for these sites and species is not absolute: Member States may, under certain conditions, allow plans or projects that can have an adverse impact on nature. In this case compensatory measures can play an important role in safeguarding the Natura 2000 network and ensuring the survival of the protected species. In this contribution we will discuss the obligations of the Member States under the Wild Birds and Habitats Directives to compensate for biodiversity loss within the framework of Article 6(4) of the Habitats Directive. This provision requires the Member States to take compensatory measures to ensure the coherence of Natura 2000 in cases where plans or projects causing negative impacts on a Natura 2000 site have been allowed because of overriding public interests. For a long time, there was no European case law regarding the characteristics of compensatory measures, but in 2012 the *Acheloos River* case in Greece came before the Court of Justice[2] on a reference for a preliminary ruling, and in 2014 the issue arose again in the *Briels* case, a preliminary reference

[1] Directive 2009/147/EC of 30 November 2009 on the conservation of wild birds, OJ L20, 26.01.2010, p. 7; Council Directive 92/43/EEC of 21 May 1992 on the conservation of natural habitats and of wild fauna and flora, OJ L59, 08.03.1996, p. 63; see *M. Blin*, Les directives oiseaux et habitats, Revue Juridique de l'Environnement, 2009 (1), pp. 115–119; *N. de Sadeleer*, Habitats Conservation in EC Law – From Nature Sanctuaries to Ecological Networks, Yearbook of European Environmental Law, 2005 (5), pp. 215–252.

[2] Case 43/10, *Nomarchiaki Aftodioikisi Aitoloakarnanias v. Ipourgos Perivallontos* [2012] ECLI:EU:C:2012:560.

from the Netherlands.[3] Therefore we will focus on these two cases (in particular on the *Briels* case), which regard on the one hand to the relationship between compensation, mitigation, and conservation (usual nature conservation measures, nature development measures), and the assessment of alternative solutions, and on the other hand to the naturalness of compensation.[4]

2. TEXT OF ARTICLE 6(4) OF THE HABITATS DIRECTIVE

The obligation relating to compensatory measures in Article 6(4) of the Habitats Directive[5] is formulated as follows:

> 'If, in spite of a negative assessment of the implications for the site and in the absence of alternative solutions, a plan or project must nevertheless be carried out for imperative reasons of overriding public interest, including those of a social or economic nature, the Member State shall take all compensatory measures necessary to ensure that the overall coherence of Natura 2000 is protected. It shall inform the Commission of the compensatory measures adopted.
>
> Where the site concerned hosts a priority natural habitat type and/or a priority species, the only considerations which may be raised are those relating to human health or public safety, to beneficial consequences of primary importance for the environment or, further to an opinion from the Commission, to other imperative reasons of overriding public interest.'

The provision aims at taking compensatory measures in case of damage to Natura 2000 sites when plans or projects have been allowed despite a negative assessment because of overriding public interests.

For the interpretation of the obligation relating to compensatory measures, besides the two mentioned judgments of the Court of Justice, there is a Commission Guidance document on Article 6(4)[6] that can be useful. However, it merely reflects the views of the Commission services only and is not of a binding nature. Nevertheless, it can be very helpful and we can be certain that the Court of Justice tends to look at such guidance documents.[7] Up until now the Commission

---

3 Case 521/12, *T.C. Briels and others v. Minister van Infrastructuur en Milieu* [2014] ECLI:EU:C:2014:330.

4 See for an outline before the Briels case was judged *G. Van Hoorick*, Compensatory Measures in European Nature Conservation Law, Utrecht Law Review, 2004 (10:2), pp. 161–171.

5 See *J. Bonichot*, L'article 6 de la directive habitats et la CJCE, Revue Juridique de l'Environnement, 2009 (1), pp. 127–129.

6 European Commission (2007), Guidance document on Article 6(4) of the 'Habitats Directive' 92/43/EEC, http://ec.europa.eu/environment/nature/natura2000/management/docs/art6/guidance_art6_4_en.pdf (last visited 23 March 2014).

7 e.g. Case 182/10, *Solvay and Others* [2012] ECLI:EU:C:2012:82, para. 28.

has issued 20 opinions under Article 6(4)(2),[8] and although these opinions are difficult to evaluate for an outside observer, they at least provide an insight into how the compensation obligation is dealt with in practice.[9] There also exists some legal doctrine[10] about the topic, and in some Member States also national case law.[11]

3. COMPENSATORY VS. MITIGATION MEASURES – THE *BRIELS* CASE

The term compensatory measures is not defined in the Habitats Directive. In the Guidance document[12] a distinction is made between mitigation measures (those measures which aim to minimise, or even cancel, the negative impacts on a site that are likely to arise as a result of the implementation of a plan or project) and compensatory measures (those measures which are independent of the project, including any associated mitigation measures, and are intended to offset the negative effects of the plan or project so that the overall ecological coherence of the Natura 2000 Network is maintained). Let us give an example: if the plan or project is the construction of a motorway, an ecoduct or wildlife crossing to connect the populations of the negatively affected species amounts to 'mitigation', the creation of a new habitat for the affected species is 'compensation'. The meaning of mitigation here is close to the definition used in the European doctrine:[13] minimisation, such as limiting or reducing the degree, extent, magnitude or duration of adverse impacts, by scaling down, relocating or redesigning elements of a project. In the Commission's opinions, for example, the following measures were regarded as mitigation measures: an extension of a bridge over a river to reduce the impact on alluvial forests,[14] noise barriers,[15] a 300m viaduct,[16] anti-collision barriers of 4m for bats,[17] the removal of temporary construction roads

8 http://ec.europa.eu/environment/nature/natura2000/management/opinion_en.htm.

9 See *L. Krämer*, The European Commission's Opinions under article 6(4) of the habitats directive, Journal of Environmental Law, 2009 (21:1), pp. 59–85; *D. McGillivray*, Biodiversity loss: the EU Commission's approach to compensation under article 6 of the Habitats Directive, Journal of Environmental Law, 2012 (24), pp. 417–450.

10 e.g. *F. Haumont*, L'application des mesures compensatoires prévues par Natura 2000, ERA Forum, 2009 (10), pp. 611–624; *D. McGillivray*, *supra* note 9, pp. 417–450.

11 See e.g. *H. Schoukens & A. Cliquet*, Mitigation and Compensation under EU Nature Conservation Law in the Flemish Region: Beyond the Deadlock for Development Projects?, Utrecht Law Review, 2014 (10:2), pp. 194–215.

12 Guidance document, *supra* note 6, p. 10.

13 *K. Rundcrantz & E. Skärbäck*, Environmental compensation in planning: a review of five different countries with major emphasis on the German system, Eur. Env., 2003 (13:4), p. 206.

14 Opinion in *Motorway A 49.*

15 Opinion in *Peene.*

16 Opinion in *TGV East.*

17 Opinion in *Motorway A 20.*

after completion,[18] collecting and relocating protected species (e.g. bulbs and reptiles),[19] prohibiting construction activities at night[20] or dredging activities during spawning times,[21] postponing the time frame for felling trees during the breeding season,[22] and speed limits for ships to reduce the intensity of their waves.[23] The measures which the Commission regarded as compensatory were in all cases the creation or restoration of the affected habitat types or species' habitats. In contrast, contrary to the European approach, 'mitigation' in the USA includes 'compensation by replacement or substitution'.[24]

The clear distinction in the EU, which distinguishes mitigation from compensatory measures, is not only of academic value but necessary so as not to jeopardise a sound assessment of the adverse effects of the plan or project and of the alternative solutions, and not to circumvent the application of Article 6(4) in cases of a negative impact. Otherwise, combining an environmentally damaging plan or project with strong compensatory measures could supersede a less damaging alternative plan or project combined with weak compensatory measures, or could even be allowed without need to apply the derogation regime of Article 6(4). This cannot be the purpose of the Habitats Directive, because, as stated in the Guidance document,[25] it is widely acknowledged that it is highly unlikely that by taking compensatory measures the conservation status of the related habitats and species can be reinstated to the level they had before the damage by a plan or project. Mitigation measures, however, are an integral part of the specifications of a plan or project.[26]

Thus, compensatory measures should be considered only after having ascertained a negative impact on the integrity of a Natura 2000 site.[27] Specifically, the logic and rationale of the assessment process require that if a negative impact is foreseen then an evaluation of alternatives should be carried out as well as an appreciation of the importance of the plan or project in relation to the natural value of the site. Once it is decided that the plan or project should proceed, then it is appropriate to move on to a consideration of compensatory measures.[28]

---

18 Opinion in *Motorway A 49*.

19 Opinion in *Györ*.

20 Opinion in *Motorway A 20*.

21 Opinion in *River Elbe*.

22 Opinion in *River Main*.

23 Opinion in *River Elbe*.

24 e.g. *J.B. Zedler*, Ecological issues in wetland mitigation: an introduction to the forum, Ecological Applications, 1996 6(1), pp. 33–37.

25 Guidance document, *supra* note 6, p. 17.

26 Guidance document, *supra* note 6, p. 10.

27 Case 182/10, *Solvay and Others* [2012] ECLI:EU:C:2012:82, paras. 73 and 74; Case C-258/11, *Sweetman and Others* [2013] ECLI:EU:C:2013:220, para. 35.

28 Guidance document, *supra* note 6, p. 11; Opinion given by the Advocate General in Case 239/04, *Commission v. Portuguese Republic*, para. 35; In conformity therewith in Belgium the Raad van State (this is the highest administrative court in Belgium) (RvS 29 November 2011, no. 216.548, *vzw Natuurpunt Limburg and others*; RvS 29 March 2013, no. 223.083, *vzw Natuurpunt Limburg and others*, www.raadvst-consetat.be) ruled that nature development

In its judgment in the *Briels* case, the Court of Justice supports this vision. This case was brought to the Court by a request for a preliminary ruling from the *Raad van State* (Council of State) of the Netherlands.[29] The *Raad van State* wanted to know if the phrase 'not adversely affect the integrity of the site' in Article 6(3) has to be interpreted as follows: when the project adversely affects the area of a protected natural habitat type within the site, the integrity of the site is not adversely affected if in the framework of the project an area of that natural habitat type of equal or similar size is created within that site. In other words, the question is whether compensation measures may be taken into account when assessing the project.

The case was about the widening of the A2 motorway towards Eindhoven, which was assessed as being likely to have a negative impact on the Natura 2000 site Vlijmens Ven, Moerputten & Bossche Broek. This was designated for, in particular, the natural habitat type molinia meadows, which is a non-priority habitat type. The assessment concluded that the A2 motorway project would cause the drying out and acidification of molinia meadows (acidification due to nitrogen deposits). As a result of this assessment the Dutch government adopted hydrological measures in another molinia meadow within the proposed development area, which would then develop into a high-quality habitat. The question was whether these measures should be seen as mitigation, preventing the application of Article 6(4), or as compensation in the sense of Article 6(4). The project itself had meanwhile been completed.

Briels and others brought an action before the referring court against two ministerial orders approving the project. In their viewpoint the Minister could not lawfully adopt the orders for the A2 motorway project, given the negative implications of the widening of the A2 motorway for the Natura 2000 site in question. They argued that the development of new molinia meadows on the site, as provided for in the ministerial orders at issue in the main proceedings, could not be taken into account in determining whether the site's integrity was affected. They submitted that such a measure cannot be categorised as mitigation, a concept which is, moreover, non-existent in the Habitats Directive.

The Court rejected the view of the Dutch government and regarded the measures as being compensatory measures. The Court held that the application of the precautionary principle in the context of the implementation of Article 6(3) required the competent national authority to assess the implications of the project for the Natura 2000 site concerned in view of the site's conservation objectives and to take into account the protective measures, forming part of the project, that aimed to avoid or reduce any direct adverse effects upon the site, in order

measures (the creation of habitats by the expropriation of agricultural land) accompanying a motorway project could not be seen as mitigation measures to take away the negative effects of the plan or project, and therefore could not be taken into account in the appropriate assessment. These measures were clearly compensatory measures.

29 Case 521/12, *supra* note 9; ABRvS 7 November 2012, 201110075/1/R4 en 20120185/1/R4.

to ensure that it does not adversely affect the integrity of the site.[30] The Court clearly refers here to mitigation measures, however without expressly stating so. The Court adds that protective measures provided for in a project which are aimed at compensating for the negative effects of the project on a Natura 2000 site cannot be taken into account in the assessment of the implications of the project provided for in Article 6(3).[31] The Court's main reason for adopting this viewpoint is that the positive effects of the future creation of a new habitat are difficult to forecast and will be visible only several years into the future.[32] As second reason for its viewpoint the Court points out that it is seeking to avoid a situation where competent national authorities allow so-called 'mitigating' measures, which are in reality compensatory measures, in order to circumvent the specific procedures provided for in Article 6(3) and thereby authorise projects which adversely affect the integrity of the site concerned.[33] Authorisation for the project therefore needs to be given in accordance with the procedure for compensation measures, provided for in Article 6(4).

4. COMPENSATORY MEASURES VS. USUAL NATURE CONSERVATION MEASURES

It is obvious, as is stated in the Guidance document,[34] that compensatory measures should go beyond the normal or standard measures required for the protection and management of Natura 2000 sites. But because space is limited and 'naturalising' agricultural or other intensively used land often meets strong opposition from farmers and other people, governments sometimes prefer to take qualitative compensation measures within existing Natura 2000 sites, thus enhancing their ecological value.

It is not always easy to determine in a real case what the normal or standard measures required for the protection and management of Natura 2000 sites are. A clear criterion could be the conservation status of the related habitats and species in the Natura 2000 site where the compensatory measures are taken: in principle, as long as the conservation status of the related habitats and species in this site is not favourable, 'compensatory measures' in this site cannot be regarded as going beyond the normal or standard measures for the protection and management of Natura 2000 sites, and the Member State should have the burden of proving the opposite.[35]

---

30 Case 521/12, *supra* note 9, para. 28.

31 Case 521/12, *supra* note 9, para. 29.

32 Case 521/12, *supra* note 9, para. 32.

33 Case 521/12, *supra* note 9, para. 33.

34 Guidance document, *supra* note 6, p. 10.

35 In Belgium there was a case before the Raad van State (RvS 30 July 2002, no. 109.563, *Apers and others*, www.raadvst-consetat.be) in which it was determined that nature development measures at a proposed site of Community interest under the Habitats Directive could not be

5. COMPENSATION BEFOREHAND; COMPENSATION VS. NATURE DEVELOPMENT MEASURES AND HABITAT BANKING

In practice there is a need for a more comprehensive and proactive approach towards compensation, in which negative assessments of several (succeeding or territorially close) plans and projects in a certain region (e.g. a seaport) and also the relevant compensatory measures are bundled together and handled early on during the planning phase. But questions arise as to whether the Wild Birds and Habitats Directives can deal with this need for flexibility and whether this approach could possibly endanger the Natura 2000 network.

In the Guidance document it is mentioned several times[36] that a case-by-case approach is appropriate, but by using the word 'plan', Article 6(3) of the Habitats Directive provides some room for a comprehensive approach: several (succeeding or territorially close) projects can be included in one plan (e.g. for the development of a seaport). The Guidance document states that best efforts should be made to assure compensation is in place beforehand[37] (i.e. before the damage to Natura 2000 is caused), thus not prohibiting a proactive approach, and in recent opinions[38] the Commission has considered it necessary that the compensatory measures are completed before the damaging activities begin. But there seem to be limits as to how long beforehand the compensation should be in place. Given the link with the damage that will be caused, the appropriate assessment, and the strict requirement that compensation should ensure the coherence of the Natura 2000 network, it seems that there is only limited room for prior nature development measures to be regarded as compensatory measures under Article 6(4) of the Habitats Directive. This also applies to habitat banking,[39] as

---

seen as compensatory measures in the sense of Article 6(4) of the Habitats Directive for the destruction of a special protection area under the Birds Directive because of overriding public interests, given that the Habitats Directive itself obliges the Member States to ensure a sound management of these sites. This judgment gave rise to some critical remarks in legal doctrine (*H. Schoukens et al.*, Handboek natuurbehoudsrecht, 2011, p. 226) because, as mentioned, the Habitats Directive and the Guidance document do not exclude such compensatory measures as such. Assuming that it was not evident that in the Belgian case the compensatory measures did go beyond the normal or standard measures required for the protection and management of Natura 2000 sites, the judgement of the Raad van State can be seen as being correct.

36 e.g. Guidance document, *supra* note 6, pp. 17 and 19.

37 Guidance document, *supra* note 6, p. 13.

38 e.g. opinion in *Granadilla* and *Motorway A 20.*

39 *G. Van Hoorick*, Innovative legal instruments for ecological restoration, in I. Boone et al. (eds.), Liber Amicorum Hubert Bocken. Dare la luce, 2009, pp. 483–488. Two studies commissioned by the Commission have been made on this topic: REMEDE, Compensation in the form of Habitat Banking. Short Case Study Report, 2008, www.envliability.eu/docs/D12CaseStudies/D12CaseStudies.html; *EFTEC, IEEP et al.*, The use of market-based instruments for biodiversity protection – The case of habitat banking – Summary Report, 2010, www.ieep.eu/work-areas/biodiversity/2010/02/the-use-of-market-based-instruments-for-biodiversity-protection-the-case-of-habitat-banking.

the Guidance document[40] considers it as being rarely useful in the framework of compensation. This does not have to discourage Member States from proactively taking nature development measures or setting up habitat banking schemes for Natura 2000 sites. In practice these measures can enhance the conservation status of the related habitat and species, and by doing so, make them less vulnerable to damage, i.e. thereby requiring a higher damage level to qualify the effect of the plan or project as significant within the meaning of Article 6(3) of the Habitats Directive. In light of the above discussed requirements for compensatory measures, the nature development measures or the newly developed habitats in the habitat banking system have to be operational a considerable time before the plan or project affecting Natura 2000 is put in place; only under these circumstances can the result of these measures legally play a role in the appropriate assessment.

6. BIOLOGICAL INTEGRITY VS. MAN-MADE NATURE – THE *ACHELOOS RIVER* CASE

The Guidance document stresses the importance of the biological integrity of Natura 2000. Compensatory measures under the Habitats Directive must be established according to the characteristics of the biological integrity of the site that is likely to be lost or damaged, and according to the likely significant negative effects that would remain after mitigation. Biological integrity can be defined as all those factors that contribute to the maintenance of the ecosystem including structural and functional assets. In the framework of the Habitats Directive, the biological integrity of a site is linked to the conservation objectives for which the site was designated as part of the Natura 2000 network.[41] Once the biological integrity likely to be damaged and the actual extent of the damage have been identified, the measures in the compensation programme must specifically address those effects, so that the elements of integrity contributing to the overall coherence of the Natura 2000 network are preserved for the long term.[42] The area selected for compensation must have – or must be able to develop – the specific features attached to the ecological structure and functions, and required by the habitats and species populations. This relates to qualitative aspects like the uniqueness of the assets impaired and it requires that consideration be given to local ecological conditions.[43] In recent cases[44] submitted for a Commission opinion it seems that Germany has delivered detailed explanations, per habitat type, also quantitatively, of the proposed compensatory measures.

---

40 Guidance document, *supra* note 6, p. 16.
41 Guidance document, *supra* note 6, p. 15.
42 Guidance document, *supra* note 6, p. 16.
43 See Guidance document, *supra* note 6, p. 18.
44 e.g. opinions in *Karlsruhe Airport*, *Lübeck Airport*, etc.

In 2012 the case of the *Acheloos River* in Greece was brought before the Court of Justice[45] on a reference for a preliminary ruling (as a result of no less than 14 questions by the Greek Council of State). The controversial Acheloos diversion scheme is more than 80 years old and is a huge project, altering the course of the Acheloos River and making it flow into the Aegean instead of the Ionian Sea. The river has its source in the Pindus mountains, it flows through Natura 2000 sites and has a delta that has considerable nature conservation value. Despite actions by environmental groups, numerous judgments annulling Government decisions by the Greek Council of State and even a discontinuation of the allocation of EU Structural Funds for the project in the 1990s by the EU Commission, parts of the project, consisting of the construction of hydro-electric dams and associated reservoirs and tunnels, have already been completed in the last couple of decades, destroying many landscapes around the river and leading to a dramatic drop in the water supply by the river in the delta. The river water is being diverted to the Thessaly plains for drinking water supply and mainly to irrigate maize and cotton crops.[46]

In the legal proceedings the question arose whether the government measures leading to the partial diversion of the Acheloos river for water supply and electricity generation purposes was in conformity with *inter alia* the EU Water Framework Directive[47] and Habitats Directive. Although the Court's judgment allowed the Greek Council of State to uphold their cessation of the project, which seems now to be definitely abandoned by Greek government,[48] its interpretation of Article 6(4) of the Habitats Directive can give rise to some comments. Not controversial is that the Court acknowledged that the supply of drinking water, one of the reasons that Greece relied upon for justifying the project, can be seen as an imperative reason of overriding public interest relating to human health in the sense of Article 6(4) of the Habitats Directive. But the Court also viewed irrigation as being an imperative reason of overriding public interest though not related to human health, and moreover stated that, in general, irrigation could be considered to be related to beneficial consequences of primary importance for the environment.[49] However, this must be seriously doubted if, as in this case, it is for the cultivation of maize and cotton. Particularly interesting for this contribution, is the Court's judgment in relation to the compensatory measures adopted. On

---

45 Case 43/10, *supra* note 2; See *P. De Smedt*, Heikele toepassingsvragen bij de Kaderrichtlijn Water, in relatie tot de Habitatrichtlijn, naar aanleiding van een omstreden Griekse rivieromleiding (annotation Case 43/10), Tijdschrift voor Milieurecht, 2013 (2), pp. 153–169; *H. Schoukens*, Omlegging Griekse rivier: de mythe van "groene" infrastructuurprojecten, Tijdschrift voor omgevingsrecht en omgevingsbeleid, 2013 (1), pp. 67–69.

46 www.balcanicaucaso.org/eng/Regions-and-countries/Greece/Greece-fight-for-the-soul-of-the-Achelous-River-128205.

47 Directive 2000/60/EC of 23 October 2000 establishing a framework for Community action in the field of water policy, OJ L327, 22.12.2000, p. 1.

48 www.wwf.gr/en/component/joomblog/post/an-ancient-myth-turned-into-a-modern-victory-for-nature.

49 Case 43/10, *supra* note 2, para. 125.

the one hand, the Court stated that the extent of the diversion of water and the scale of the works involved in that diversion are factors that must be taken into account in order to identify with precision the adverse impact of the project on the site concerned and, therefore, to determine the nature of the necessary compensatory measures required to ensure the protection of the coherence of Natura 2000.[50] Thus it seems that in this case huge compensatory measures would have had to be taken. On the other hand, the Court ruled that the compensation obligation laid down in Article 6(4), interpreted in the light of the objective of sustainable development,[51] as enshrined in Article 6 TFEU, permits, in relation to sites which are part of the Nature 2000 network, the conversion of a natural fluvial ecosystem into a largely man-made fluvial and lacustrine ecosystem provided that the conditions are met to ensure the protection of the overall coherence of Natura 2000.[52] With this last statement, i.e. that a natural ecosystem may be compensated by a man-made ecosystem, the Court did not really adhere to the requirements for biological integrity and ecological functionality in the Guidance document, and has slipped from its usual requirement that Member States should implement high environmental standards. The question even arises whether it is *a contradictio in terminis* that conversing natural ecosystems in man-made ecosystems one can ensure a long-term protection of the coherence of Natura 2000. Certainly, in contrast to the Court's view, this is not the purpose of sustainable development[53] (perhaps except for saline deserts when there is no longer a more natural alternative).[54] But avoiding and minimising human encroachment upon natural ecosystems certainly is.[55]

7. CONCLUSIONS

The obligation to take compensatory measures under Article 6(4) of the Habitats Directive, as interpreted by the Court of Justice and by the Commission's guidance and practice appears to create a strong legal duty for the Member States.

50 Case 43/10, *supra* note 2, para. 132.

51 Sustainable development is only ensured when both intergenerational (environmental protection) and intragenerational (fair economic and social development) equity is ensured and equally considered through the decision-making (*V. Barral*, Sustainable development in international law: nature and operation of an evolutive legal norm, EJIL, 2012 (23), pp. 380–381).

52 Case 43/10, *supra* note 2, para. 139.

53 Compensatory habitat creation can probably be used in some wetlands and intertidal environments, but the prospects for success in many terrestrial situations are far less certain (*R. Morris et al.*, The Creation of Compensatory Habitat – Can it Secure Sustainable Development?, J. Nat. Conserv., 2006 (14), p. 106).

54 See *D.A. Jones et al.*, Sabah Al-Ahmad Sea City Kuwait: development of a sustainable man-made coastal ecosystem in a saline desert, Aquatic Ecosystem Health & Management, 2012 (15:1), pp. 84–92.

55 See also *H. Schoukens*, Omlegging Griekse rivier: de mythe van 'groene' infrastructuurprojecten, Tijdschrift voor omgevingsrecht en omgevingsbeleid, 2013 (1), pp. 67–69.

Compensatory measures differ from mitigation, former nature development, and usual nature conservation measures. Recent case law of the Court in the *Briels* case supports this view. By doing so, the Court emphasises that compensatory measures have an added ecological value. They do not jeopardise an appropriate assessment of alternative solutions, nor are they means to circumvent an appropriate assessment of the project's negative impacts. Recent case law of the Court in the *Acheloos River* case, however, allows too much room for the creation of man-made ecosystems as compensatory habitats. We hope that the relevant passage of the judgment is a passing fad and that the Court continues to contribute to a sound interpretation of European nature conservation legislation.

PART VI

LAND USE

CHAPTER 15

LAND USE REGULATION IN THE UK AND THE ROLE OF THE COURT

Elizabeth Dunn*

1. INTRODUCTION

This chapter provides an overview of land use regulation in the UK, access to justice and the role of the courts. It focuses on the system that operates in England and Wales and highlights its relationship with European jurisprudence. Although broadly similar, Scotland has its own system with its own terminology. That said, a version of this chapter was delivered as a presentation and there was significant interest in the likely outcome just over a week before the referendum on Scottish independence. At the time this was too close to call, and in the event the narrow majority in favour of remaining as part of the UK[1] may have only been secured as a result of the additional devolution of powers promised. This is of relevance to the debate as, in considering the system that currently operates in England and Wales, the recent passage of the Planning (Wales) Act 2015[2] through the Welsh Government will bring further change and further limit the current control exercised by Westminster.

In order to put the recent changes to the process into context, this article sets out an overview of the planning process in England and Wales and the interrelation and interdependencies between statute and the common law. In a system where the decision-maker for land use planning consents is often the same body as sets the policy against which such decisions are taken it explores in detail the key case of *Alconbury* and the reasoning that led to the House of Lords' affirmation regarding the separation of powers, access to justice and compliance

---

* Partner, Burges Salmon LLP.

1 The final result saw Scotland voting against becoming an independent country by 55% to 45%.

2 The Planning (Wales) Act introduces early community consultations on major developments that planning applications for development of national significance to Wales will be decided by Welsh Ministers and strategic development plans prepared by strategic planning panels comprising representatives of local authorities, community, environmental and business interests.

with the European Convention on Human Rights (ECHR) within the planning system. The importance of the role of the Courts within this system has grown significantly, even since *Alconbury*.

The wider tensions between the aims and objectives of European jurisprudence, their effect on the judicial review process and the delivery of development are also explored. 'Judicial review has grown from an exceptional remedy of last resort to the predictable next step for a determined objector'[3] and it is impossible to separate the growth in European legislation from the marked increase in judicial review challenges in England and Wales over the past 15 years. Also considered are the ways in which the Courts have sought through the development of case law to effect necessary change.

An analysis of recent government reforms to the judicial review system is provided. Some of these changes may be considered controversial in light of considerations as to whether the planning system sufficiently allows access to justice. During the recent House of Lords debate on the Criminal Justice and Courts Bill, Lord Pannick stated that: 'judicial review is a vital means by which central and local government and other public bodies can be held to account to ensure the legality of their actions before independent judges in public ... when proposals for amendment of judicial review are brought forward by Ministers – who are, after all, the main defendants in such litigation – the proposals require the most careful scrutiny by the House'.[4] This underlines the view that the fundamental principles of judicial review are not an historical anachronism, but remain a central tenet of the UK legal system. If challenged, Parliament will protect these principles, even against its own Government.

2. OVERVIEW OF PLANNING IN ENGLAND AND WALES

As the UK remains a common law jurisdiction, statute only forms part of the framework for planning regulation, with the interpretation of relevant legislation being left to case law established through the courts. This provides a degree of flexibility not available in codified systems, but places substantial power in the hands of the judiciary. In his lecture 'Judicial and Political Decision Making – the uncertain boundary'[5] Jonathan Sumption QC states that: 'the decisions of the Courts on the abuse of discretionary powers are based, far more often than the Courts have admitted, on a judgement about what it is thought right for

3 *S. Ricketts*, Heroes and Villains – Challenge and Protest in Planning: What's a Developer to Do?, JPL, 2014 (13), p. OP11.

4 Lord Pannick, Lords Hansard Text for 27 October 2014, Criminal Courts and Justice Bill.

5 *J. Sumption QC*, Judicial and political decision making: The uncertain boundary, JR, 2011 (16:4), p. 301.

parliament to wish to do'.[6] This 'uncertain boundary' is explored in further detail throughout this chapter, in the context of proposed reforms.

Land use planning in England and Wales is primarily regulated by the Town and Country Planning Act 1990 (TCPA) and the Planning Act 2008 (the Planning Act). The Planning Act clearly reflects the current drive for devolution; it takes some important controls from Westminster and gives them to the Welsh Government. This process of devolution in planning matters is being taken further through the recently passed Planning (Wales) Act 2015.

The TCPA contains the statutory framework for the regulation and management of development and empowers the local planning authority and the Secretary of State to make planning decisions within the policy framework they have put in place. Decisions are to be made in accordance with the adopted development plan unless 'material considerations' indicate otherwise.[7] The courts have both a supervisory role over this decision-making process and provide a significant level of judicial interpretation that shapes key concepts like 'material considerations' which has no statutory definition. This also places significant power in the hands of the judiciary.

In recognition of some of the issues which have developed within the planning process in England and Wales, in particular the time and cost of appeals and public inquiries into major infrastructure projects, the Labour Government introduced the Planning Act in 2008.[8] This sets out the consenting framework for a class of development identified as Nationally Significant Infrastructure Projects (NSIPs) covering energy, waste, transport, water and waste water projects above certain thresholds.

The Planning Act was designed to be a 'one-stop shop', allowing applicants to include a wide scope of works and powers within their consent (known as a 'development consent order') which takes the form of secondary legislation. This includes compulsory acquisition powers, highways powers and may also include consents such as environmental permits, which would otherwise have to be secured separately from another decision-maker. The Planning Act was set up to be administered by an independent body, the Infrastructure Planning Commission (IPC), which, through appointed inspectors, was empowered to determine applications for NSIPs.

Whilst the Planning Act requires that such decisions are to be taken in accordance with National Policy Statements ratified by Parliament (where these are in place), when originally set up there was no direct input by the Government into the decision-making process. Whilst some welcomed the independence of the IPC, to others it was a non-elected and unaccountable quango.[9] Placing

---

6 *Ibid.*, p. 307.

7 Section 70, Town and Country Planning Act (1990).

8 The Planning Act received Royal Assent on 26 November 2008.

9 *Department for Communities and Local Government*, Localism Bill: major infrastructure projects, Impact assessment, 2011, p. 1.

decision-making for NSIPs back into ministerial control was one of the first actions of the Coalition Government under David Cameron.[10] The reluctance to place decision-making power in the hands of unelected bodies and a desire to strictly maintain a separation of powers is also a fundamental issue in relation to judicial review and is explored further in this article. This can be seen as part of a wider drive by the Government to restrict the discretion of non-elected bodies and is at the heart of the reforms discussed in section 6.

3. PRINCIPLES OF HIGH COURT CHALLENGES

In the majority of land use cases judicial review will be engaged when an administrative decision has been taken by a public authority and the object of the challenger is to reverse that decision.

Generally, in the UK judicial review is not an application to the court to make a decision in place of the original decision-maker. In the case of a challenge to the grant of planning permission by a local authority, the effect of a successful challenge will be only that the decision is quashed and remitted to the planning authority for redetermination. The courts' reluctance to engage with the merits of a particular planning application is an example of adherence to the doctrine of the separation of powers which is discussed further throughout this article.

There are two distinct types of challenge. The first is not strictly judicial review but rather a statutory challenge whereby a person aggrieved by the decision of a body who has been granted authority by virtue of a statutory provision may apply within a specified time limit to the High Court for the decision to be quashed. An example of this is under section 288 of the TCPA which conveys a power to challenge the decision of the Secretary of State (or one of his Inspectors) to grant planning permission on appeal.

Statutory challenges are closely modelled on the process of judicial review, and in light of recent reforms, there is increasingly little distinction between the two, but judicial review, properly defined, is not a creature of statute at all. It derives from a much older jurisdiction based in the common law, and the Courts' inherent jurisdiction to review the powers of officials if it has been alleged they have exceeded those powers. If there is an official action being undertaken (for example the grant of planning permission) but there is no other means of redress available to a person alleging that power has been improperly carried out, judicial review is the appropriate challenge route.

Judicial review grounds are often summarised as falling into one of three categories: illegality, procedural impropriety and irrationality. However, echoing the words of Lord Donaldson: 'judicial review is a rich tapestry of many strands

[10] The IPC was abolished in 2012 after the passing of the Localism Act 2011 and the relevant Secretary of State now makes the final decision on NSIP applications.

which cross and recross and blend to produce justice,[11] for the purposes of this chapter, two broad groups are considered; those challenges which are 'procedural' (i.e. they derive from the requirement to meet any specified procedural steps that are set out in legislation) and those which are on the grounds that the authority has acted beyond its powers.

Procedural challenges are one area where European legislation has had an important influence over the review process via the imposition of a number of both discretionary and mandatory procedural requirements. Planning in itself is not an EU competence except to the extent that member states are required to implement measures in relation to environmental protection.[12] However, many environmental measures imposed through EU legislation (for example the Environmental Impact Assessment (EIA) Directive) have had a direct impact on the planning system in the UK. One example (which will be explored in further detail later) is the requirement that the classes of development set out in Schedule 1 of the EIA Regulations[13] must have an EIA to accompany any application for planning permission. In the case of an application for 'Schedule 1' development where an EIA has not been submitted, planning permission cannot be granted. In relation to discretionary matters, such as whether a particular development falls within Schedule 2 of the EIA Regulations and as a result requires EIA, then the issue to be considered would be whether there has in fact been the proper exercise of that discretion.

The scope of procedural challenges is wide ranging and extends to requirements such as:

(a) the decision-maker taking account of all relevant material;
(b) the decision-maker not taking into account any irrelevant material;
(c) the duty for a decision-maker to give reasons for any decision and for those reasons to be clear and intelligible. This does not oblige the decision-maker to refer to every single matter put before them, but any significant issues should be referred to;
(d) the duty to act fairly between parties. This is reflected in the established concepts of natural justice and legitimate expectation, which require that parties are given a fair opportunity to be heard and to challenge any evidence put against their interests; and
(e) the duty to act reasonably within the margin of discretion available. This is often known as being 'Wednesbury' reasonable, deriving from a case involving Wednesbury Council[14] in the West Midlands.

---

11 Lord Donaldson, *R. v. Secretary of State for the Home Department, Ex parte Oladehinde* cited in 'Overview of Judicial Review', Richards, Harwood and Wald, September 2010, para. 92.
12 Article 192(2) TFEU, OJ 2012 C326/49.
13 The Town and Country Planning (Environmental Impact Assessment) Regulations 2011.
14 *Associated Provincial Picture Houses Ltd v. Wednesbury Corporation* [1948] 1 KB 223.

Challenges relating to acts beyond the authority's powers (often known as substantive *ultra vires*) could be as simple as a local authority granting planning permission for an electricity generating station with a rated capacity of over 50 MW – something which can only be done by the Secretary of State for Energy and Climate Change.[15]

3.1. HOW DO HIGH COURT CHALLENGES WORK?

As a starting point in judicial review (and statutory challenge) proceedings the courts have discretion whether or not to grant relief.

The court can decide that there has been some error in the way the decision has been made, but can also conclude that no real harm has come of it and that the same result would have occurred even if the error had not been made. As discussed in section 6 there are changes proposed to the operation of their discretion.

Judicial discretion is important in establishing a number of the characteristics of judicial review:

(a) there is uncertainty for the challenger as to whether they will be granted relief (normally the quashing of the decision in question) even if there has been a breach of due process;
(b) there is almost always a defence to a judicial review on the grounds that the error would not have led to a different decision being made; and
(c) by approaching its discretion in this way the courts may be encouraging challenges that seek to engage the concept of 'fairness'.

The court's starting point in judicial challenge cases is that it will uphold the administrative decision if it is capable of doing so. The burden of proving that there is a problem, and that without that problem a different decision would have been made, rests firmly on the challenger. If matters are evenly balanced the courts will uphold the administrative decision. In practice, the position will be stronger than this; unless the decision is shown to be clearly flawed, the courts are very likely to uphold it for the simple reason than that it is not persuaded there has been an error. This rule is likely to be strengthened by recent proposed reforms.

Consequently, it can be difficult to bring a successful challenge. As a Government consultation response published in 2013 highlighted; of the 7,600 applications for permission to bring judicial review proceedings considered by the courts in 2011, only around 16% were granted. By the time the case reaches a substantive hearing, success rates are closer to 44%.[16] The courts' objective to maintain the status quo wherever possible lies behind these statistics.

---

15 Section 15, Planning Act 2008.
16 Reform of Judicial Review: the Government response, April 2013, Cm 8611.

3.2. PERMISSION

A judicial review claim cannot be considered in full without the permission of the Court. Normally this is done on the challenge papers submitted by the claimant and any defence submitted by the decision-maker and any interested parties which in the planning context will include the beneficiary of any planning permission.

The judicial review permission stage is intended to act as a filter to weed out unmeritorious claims that would otherwise clog up court timetables and involve all parties in unnecessary costs and delay. However, it is almost certainly not the case in practice that only meritorious cases get through to a full hearing. This issue has prompted the recent review of the judicial review process for planning cases.

For statutory challenges, (including those made under section 288 of the TCPA), recent amendments have introduced a permission stage.[17] This change was introduced as the process 'has been seen as a political tool and blocking device'.[18] The Criminal Justice and Courts Act 2015 which introduced the changes has been justified on the basis that it will minimise the 'unmeritorious cases ... brought, with no chance of success, in order to delay the implementation of public decisions and to gain publicity'.[19] The recent reforms are discussed in more detail in section 6 of this chapter including the potential impacts on an individual's ability to have their case heard.

The test that the permission judge reviewing the papers will apply is whether there is an 'arguable case'. When defending a challenge there is an obvious tension between restricting the permission stage to brief facts and argument with the aim of fairly and finally disposing of a challenge in the shortest period of time, and exploring the challenge in greater detail at an earlier stage in the hope that it will shorten the overall time for determining the challenge and making any final ruling more robust.

3.3. REMEDIES

As discussed above, the most common remedy sought from the court is for a decision to be quashed. However, an alternative may be to force a local authority to take a step that it is refusing to carry out by way of interim injunction. In planning cases, careful consideration should always be given to injunctions because they

17 Criminal Justice and Courts Act, Schedule 16.
18 *A. Samuels*, Judicial Review and the New Law: The Criminal Justice and Courts Act 2015, Journal of Planning Law, 2015 (7), p. 754.
19 *Ibid.*

are difficult to obtain, can be costly and carry a significant additional cost risk[20] if they are not upheld.

3.4. SEPARATION OF POWERS IN ENGLAND AND WALES AND THE RULE OF LAW

Arguably, 'judicial review has been one of the most remarkable, and remarkably successful, constitutional innovations in the English Legal system ... judicial review has restrained abuse by public authorities, produced a vast body of public law, and greatly promoted the rule of law'.[21] Judicial review is borne out of the doctrine of separation of powers between the three distinct functions of Government: 'the legislative, executive and the judicial – which should be discharged by three separate agencies ... no individual should be a member of more than one of them'.[22]

Consequently the judiciary strictly maintain 'belief in the unfettered judicial curb on the Executive – to ensure legality, to ensure that Ministers believe and act legally – and in the continuation of the long-standing judicial discretion which is the bastion for the maintenance of the rule of law.'[23] This has always been an important feature of judicial review cases in England and Wales and highlights the important role the Courts have to play in facilitating access to justice in the planning system.

Although it is long established that 'the British constitution, though largely unwritten, is firmly based on the separation of powers',[24] it can be argued that over the last 15 years, since the coming into force of the Human Rights Act, 'only now that the positive assertion of the rights and liberties contained in the European Convention on Human Rights is possible in domestic Courts is a more formal separation of powers being realised in the UK constitution.'[25] This can be seen very clearly in a number of cases since 2000, including *Alconbury* as the fair and impartial hearing required by Article 6 of the Convention can arguably only be achieved when this doctrine is upheld (discussed further in section 4 below). Although *Alconbury* was heard in the House of Lords in 2001, almost 15 years ago, it remains a leading authority on the doctrine of the separation of powers within the judicial review system.

---

20 As it will be necessary to give a cross-undertaking in damages to cover any losses incurred in the event that on full hearing the Court does not grant the injunction.

21 *A. Samuels*, *supra* note 18, p. 754.

22 *E. Barendt*, Separation of powers and Constitutional Government, Public Law, 1995, p. 592, 601.

23 Lord Morris of Aberavon, Lords Hansard Text for 9 December 2014, Criminal Courts and Justice Bill.

24 *Duport Steels Ltd v. Sirs* [1980] 1 WLR 142 at 157.

25 *R. Masterman*, Determination in the Abstract? Article 6 (1) and the Separation of Powers, EHRLR, 2005 (6), p. 628.

It is worth noting that, 'while the European Court ... has consistently stated that ECHR does not demand the maintenance of any "theoretical constitutional concepts as such", the notion of the separation of the executive, legislative and judicial power can be said to have achieved a certain prominence'[26] and the Courts have engaged with this on a number of occasions pre and post *Alconbury*.

4. THE EUROPEAN CONVENTION ON HUMAN RIGHTS AND HIGH COURT CHALLENGES

4.1. *ALCONBURY* AND THE RIGHT TO A FAIR AND PUBLIC HEARING

The 2001 case of *Alconbury*[27] was, in the words of Lord Nolan, 'one of great practical and constitutional importance for this country, and of importance also for the development of human rights law both in this country and abroad'.[28]

The case dealt with the potential conflict in the UK planning system between the role of the Secretary of State as policy maker and his role as decision taker and, in particular whether this was compliant with Article 6 of the ECHR and the Human Rights Act 1998. The fundamental basis of the UK planning system was challenged.

Four conjoined cases were brought before the (then) House of Lords on appeal by the Secretary of State from the High Court. The following powers of the Secretary of State had been challenged, with claims that they were incompatible with Article 6 of the ECHR:

(a) the power to call-in planning applications under section 77 of the TCPA;
(b) the power to 'recover' planning appeals under sections 78 and 79 and paragraphs 3 and 4 of Schedule 6 of the TCPA;
(c) the powers to make orders relating to the construction and operation of a railway, to authorise compulsory purchase of land and to grant planning permission under sections 1, 3 and 24 of the Transport and Works Act 1992; and
(d) the powers to make decisions in relation to the building of roads and related compulsory purchase orders under the Highways Act 1980 (sections 14, 16, 18, 125 and Schedule 1) and the Acquisition of Land Act 1981.

---

26 *Ibid.*, p. 634.

27 *R (on the application of Holding & Barnes plc) v. Secretary of State for the Environment, Transport and the Regions* [2001] UKHL 23.

28 *Ibid.*, para. 58.

Article 6(1) of the ECHR states:

> 'In the determination of his civil rights and obligations ... everyone is entitled to a fair and public hearing ... by an independent and impartial tribunal established by law ...'

The essence of the complaints was that the Secretary of State could not be regarded as 'independent and impartial' when it came to taking decisions relating to matters on which he, or his department, had laid down policy and guidance.

The decision in the High Court went against the Secretary of State, and effectively the planning system as a whole, with the Court finding that the powers set out in the TCPA were in fact incompatible with Article 6. Had the House of Lords upheld this decision, the UK planning system would have required major reform.

In fact, the Lords ruled the other way. Despite the fact that the Secretary of State was found not to be 'independent' for the purposes of Article 6, this was not objectionable under Article 6 given the supervision of the decision-making process by the Courts through judicial review.

There were several key factors that contributed to the decision of the House of Lords outlined below. The judgment acts as a useful explanation of the function which judicial review exercises in the UK's planning system.

4.2. THE ROLE OF DEMOCRATIC ACCOUNTABILITY

Much emphasis in *Alconbury* was placed on the fact that the Secretary of State is answerable to Parliament and, ultimately, to the electorate.

The Courts are keen to avoid straying into the realms of political decision-making and a key point established in *Alconbury* was that decisions about what the general interest requires (such as granting planning permission) are to be made by democratically elected bodies or persons accountable to them.[29] Lord Nolan said, 'Parliament has entrusted the requisite degree of control to the Secretary of State, and it is to Parliament which he must account for his exercise of it. To substitute for the Secretary of State an independent and impartial body with no central electoral accountability would not only be a recipe for chaos: it would be profoundly undemocratic.'[30] When considered in the context of the institution of the original IPC (see discussion at section 2), this view was clearly shared by the Coalition Government in its decision to re-instate the role of the Secretary of State in determining NSIPs.

---

[29] See *J. Sumption QC*, *supra* note 5, p. 308.

[30] *R (on the application of Holding & Barnes plc) v. Secretary of State for the Environment, Transport and the Regions* [2001] UKHL, para. 60.

This approach has also been a feature of more recent cases such as *Rooney v. Secretary of State for Communities and Local Government*[31] which concerned a statutory challenge involving an alleged breach of Article 8 of the ECHR. In *Rooney* the Court placed emphasis on the fact that it was removed from the planning decision-making process, having not seen the site or heard detailed evidence, and therefore would not be in a position to conduct a review of the merits.[32] That said, the determination of a decision's lawfulness and its merits is often difficult to separate and some commentators believe that 'decisions on the abuse of discretionary powers are based, far more often than the Courts have admitted, on a judgement about what it is thought right for Parliament to wish to do.'[33]

In terms of the incorporation of the ECHR in domestic law, there has been strong feeling that 'litigation founded on these rights almost always turns ... on the question of what inroads into them are justifiable in the public interest. This involves a difficult balance between competing ... interests [which] we have transferred ... out of the political arena altogether and into the domain of judicial decision making where public accountability has no place'.[34] One can see that for the courts to take such a decisive step (as the District Court had in that case) and determine that the will of Parliament was incompatible with convention rights would sit uneasily with the notion of public accountability.[35]

Building on the approach of his fellow judges in *Alconbury*, Lord Hoffman, stated that 'it is the business of the Secretary of State, aided by his civil servants, to develop national planning policies and co-ordinate local policies. These policies are not airy abstractions. They are intended to be applied to actual cases. It would be absurd for the Secretary of State, in arriving at a decision in a particular case, to ignore his policies and start with a completely open mind.'[36] However, it was openly acknowledged that whilst the Secretary of State was democratically accountable, on a narrow and literal reading of Article 6, it would be easy to conclude that his actions were incompatible with the ECHR.

Consequently, the Court in *Alconbury* accepted that the Secretary of State did not constitute an impartial and independent tribunal. However, the judges took a pragmatic approach in finding that the planning system 'as a whole' is compliant with Article 6. In support of this, it was established that Article 6 does not require full independence at all stages of the decision-making process. Lord Clyde helpfully summarised this in his judgment:

---

31 *Rooney v. Secretary of State for Communities and Local Government* [2011] EWCA Civ 1556.

32 *Ibid.*, para. 22.

33 See *J. Sumption QC, supra* note 5, p. 307.

34 *Ibid.*, p. 308.

35 For further discussion on the adherence to ECHR generally see *J. Sumption QC, supra* note 5.

36 *R (on the application of Holding & Barnes plc) v. Secretary of State for the Environment, Transport and the Regions* [2001] UKHL, para. 123.

> 'It is possible that in some circumstances a breach in one respect can be overcome by the existence of a sufficient opportunity for appeal or review ... In the civil context the whole process must be considered to see if the article has been breached. Not every stage need comply. If a global view is adopted one may then take into account not only the eventual opportunity for appeal or review to a Court of law, but also the earlier processes and in particular the process of public inquiry at which essentially the facts can be explored in a quasi-judicial procedure and a determination on factual matters achieved.'[37]

In any planning appeal or call-in, the role of the inspector and the existence of the public inquiry are important. An inspector's report makes findings of fact and gives the parties the opportunity to put their case forward in a quasi-judicial setting. Lord Slynn in *Alconbury* acknowledged that the inspector 'provides an important filter before the Secretary of State takes his decision'.[38] Subsequent case law has reinforced the concept that 'albeit employed by the Secretary of State ... inspectors nonetheless have independence akin to that provided for judges ... they should adopt the same approach that judges would adopt.'[39]

This 'investigation of fact' could not be allowed to be compromised by a pre-disposition for or against particular types of development or alternatives, unless robustly supported by evidence. Therefore, the Parliamentary process adopted must review the information in detail, hear evidence from stakeholders and come to a considered view.

In terms of accountability and separation of powers, the House of Lords' decision put in the strongest terms that whilst the final decision on any development project is essentially political, and rightly so, that was only supportable if the political decision was based on a sufficiently rigorous investigation of fact.

Following this means of proceeding, and accepting the fact that the Secretary of State is not an independent or impartial tribunal, in *Alconbury*, the question was then whether there is a sufficient judicial control to subsequently ensure a determination by an independent and impartial tribunal. This is explored further below.

4.3. THE SCOPE OF JUDICIAL REVIEW – WHAT IS 'FULL JURISDICTION'?

When ministers or officials make decisions affecting the rights of individuals, they must do so in accordance with the law. The legality of their actions must be subject to review by independent and impartial tribunals. Without the supervisory role

[37] *Ibid.*, para. 152.
[38] *Ibid.*, para. 46.
[39] *R. on the application of Ortona Ltd v. Secretary of State for Communities and Local Government* [2008] EWHC 3207, para. 55.

the courts play in the process, the planning system of England and Wales would not be compliant with the European Convention of Human Rights.

As previously discussed, judicial review gives the reviewing court jurisdiction to quash the Secretary of State's decision if it finds that he (or she) acted *ultra vires*, or failed to meet important procedural requirements such as those outlined in section 3.

It is also well established that the principles of judicial review give effect to the rule of law. They ensure that administrative decisions will be taken rationally, in accordance with a fair procedure and within the powers conferred by Parliament.[40] Nevertheless, it is clear that Article 6 does not require the courts to substitute their own judgment in planning matters for that of democratically accountable planning authorities.[41] The function of judicial review is to provide 'subsequent control by a judicial body which has full jurisdiction'.[42]

'Full jurisdiction' at first sight might seem to require in every case an exhaustive and comprehensive review of the facts as well as the law. If that were so, a remedy by way of a statutory appeal or an application to the supervisory jurisdiction of the courts in judicial review would be inadequate. However it is evident that full jurisdiction means a full jurisdiction in the context of the case.[43]

Although giving effect to the ECHR in the courts of England and Wales has been described above as potentially removing areas of policy from democratic accountability,[44] often the jurisprudence of the European Court of Human Rights works in parallel with principles of domestic law. For example, the European court has stressed that it is a frequent feature throughout Member States that in specialised areas of the law such as judicial control of administrative decisions, the review by a court of law does not extend to a review of the decision on its merits.[45] As highlighted previously, this is also a key principle of the doctrine of the separation of powers.

---

40 *R. (on the application of Holding & Barnes plc) v. Secretary of State for the Environment, Transport and the Regions* [2001] UKHL, Lord Hoffman, para. 73.

41 Also supported by *Ringeisen v. Austria (No 1)* (1971) 1 EHRR 455 and *Zumtobel v. Austria* (1993) 17 EHRR 342.

42 *Albert and Lecompte v. Belgium* (1983) 5 EHRR 533.

43 *R. (on the application of Holding & Barnes plc) v. Secretary of State for the Environment, Transport and the Regions* [2001] UKHL Lord Clyde, para. 154.

44 *J. Sumption QC, supra* note 5, p. 314.

45 *Bryan v. UK* (1995) 21 EHRR 342.

4.4. ACCESS TO A FAIR AND PUBLIC HEARING POST-*ALCONBURY*

4.4.1. *Separation of Powers*

Alconbury has remained the leading authority on the separation of powers in the planning context over the last 14 years, and is still being applied in the courts today. In *Moore and Coates*[46] a claim was made following action taken by the Secretary of State to recover decisions on planning appeals relating to caravan pitches in the green belt which resulted in significant delay in the decision of these appeals. The case in question involved caravan pitches for travellers and in this case the Court went further than *Alconbury*, stating that Article 6 requires a hearing to be held within a reasonable time in order to ensure compliance.[47] The challenge therefore succeeded on this ground. The Court reaffirmed that *Alconbury* should not be departed from, and the planning system as a whole is compatible with Article 6.

Moore and Coates is also a recent example of the courts' strict adherence to the separation of powers doctrine. In the UK, the Secretary of State has broad discretion to recover the determination of appeals under the TCPA. The claimants did not succeed in their arguments that the Secretary of State was irrational in seeking to recover all appeals. The Court acknowledged that it was standard practice for Secretaries of State to formulate policy by recovering a set of appeals in order to establish a standard approach which will then carry significant weight in future decisions.[48]

The central ground of challenge in *Moore and Coates* was, however, to the Secretary of State's recovery of traveller appeals, and this was not upheld by the courts. Although the Court reaffirmed that the Secretary of State had both maintained an undisclosed policy on the level of traveller appeals and published a revised policy part way through the period in which appeals were being recovered, the Court determined that this was not unlawful, stating that, 'although I can understand why some may cavil at the use of an undisclosed policy, my task is to determine whether a decision made in its application is unlawful. It is not for this Court to determine whether it was appropriate from the SSCLG and his minister to have acted on a policy which had not been disclosed to Parliament. That is a matter for Parliament, not this Court'.[49]

---

[46] *Moore and Coates v. Secretary of State for Communities and Local Government* [2015] EWHC 44.

[47] *Moore and Coates v. Secretary of State for Communities and Local Government and Bromley LBC and Dartford LBC and the Equality and Human Rights Commission*, Case Law Reports, [2015] JPL, paragraph 148.

[48] *Ibid.*, para. 18.

[49] *Ibid.*, para. 168.

Whilst some may see the intervention by the Secretary of State in recovering appeal decisions as offending the principle of the separation of powers established in *Alconbury*, this is clearly not the view taken by the Court.

4.4.2. Planning Act 2008 Challenges

The Planning Act 2008 system in relation to larger infrastructure projects has been developed post-*Alconbury* to provide a 'sufficiently rigorous investigation' of fact by the examining authority prior to the Secretary of State making a decision on the NSIP application.

Under the Planning Act 2008 regime, between 13 October 2011 (the date on which the first NSIPs decision was issued in respect of Rookery South Energy from Waste Facility) and September 2015, only one application (for the Preesall saltfield underground gas storage facility) had been refused. A challenge was launched by the developer, Halite Energy Group, on a number of grounds, including the fact that the examination process had not allowed them sufficient opportunity to address key issues (relating to geology). The original decision was quashed by the Court which stated that: 'It is critical that the examination process is undertaken in a way which achieves the objectives of the examining authority but is fair to all parties throughout'.[50]

The Court made it clear that the examination process only works where all parties receive a 'fair crack of the whip'[51] and the *Halite* case is an example of where the lack of fair process[52] provided good grounds for challenge. The *Halite* case[53] is also the only NSIP-related action brought by the promoter of a project rather than an objection group prior to September 2015.

The inquisitorial process used in examination is designed to allow key issues to be aired and ideally resolved prior to a decision being made, the result being that in all other NSIP challenges to date, the courts have not found sufficient grounds to quash a decision. However, *Halite* is proof that within the Planning Act system, the courts, in their supervisory role, will quash a decision where the 'investigation of fact' was not conducted fairly.

5. DEVELOPMENTS IN JUDICIAL REVIEW AND EUROPEAN INFLUENCE

This section looks at the use of the judicial review system over the last 15 years and provides the context for the UK Government's recent reforms. Over this period

---

50 *R. (on the application of Halite Energy Group Limited) v. Secretary of State for Climate Change and Energy* [2014] EWHC 17 (Admin), para. 79.

51 *Ibid.*, para. 39.

52 *Ibid.*, para. 102.

53 *Ibid.*

we have seen the introduction of human rights legislation in the UK, enshrining the ECHR in domestic law, and the firm establishment of regular and widespread EU environmental controls through processes like EIA.

At the start of that period, there existed a very settled procedure in the UK planning system which had been in place since its post-war inception in 1947 and judicial review at this time, could reasonably have been categorised as a high hurdle for the challenger to take on. 'In previous generations, large scale development has been achieved largely without recourse to the Courts and without direct action on the part of objectors ... the final decision was usually, indeed, final'.[54] Through many case law decisions the obstacles to bringing a challenge, and then to succeeding, were formidable. There were a number of reasons for this:

(a) the courts would not hear an argument that was purely academic; a real practical decision had to turn upon its judgment;
(b) the courts would not use judicial review if another form of appeal would offer a remedy; judicial review could only be used as a last resort where no other appeal was available;
(c) a claimant had to show a genuine connection with the case, to a high level of proof;
(d) a claim would often be struck out for not being brought in time, even if it was within the absolute cut off period for such claims; and
(e) a claimant faced the full weight of the opposing side's legal costs (and sometimes more than one set of costs) if a challenge was unsuccessful.

Over the past 15 years the trend has been decidedly in favour of encouraging judicial review litigation, in many cases by relaxing the constraints set out above. A number of changes have also been brought about in a direct response to the treaties and legislation of the European Union.

5.1. STANDING

As well as the claimant and defendant, in judicial review claims there may also be a class of 'interested parties' who are automatically entitled to participate in the claim. These could include the developer or promoter and anyone with a statutory role in the process. In addition to these parties, any objector or supporter group may bring or participate in a challenge.

This raises the question of 'standing' (or *locus standi*). This can be an important factor in any judicial review and derives from the established principle that the right to bring a claim is not open to just anyone who seeks to do so. In

[54] *S. Ricketts, supra* note 3, p. OP9–10.

order to be considered to have 'standing' a claimant has to show that they have a 'sufficient interest' in the matter to which the claim relates.[55]

15 years ago standing was an important consideration in any judicial review as it was a hurdle that a claimant could easily fall at, and challenges were frequently rejected because the claimant lacked an adequate connection with the issues. However, the trend in decisions is now decisively toward taking an inclusive approach to claims.[56] The position can now be summarised as being that if a party has taken any part in the planning process (for example having written a letter of objection) the court is likely to allow it to challenge, even if the basis of the challenge is not something that it identified or raised in its participation in the decision.

When this approach is added to the fact that the courts now appear willing, should, for example, a claimant run out of funds, to allow a substitute claimant to take on a judicial review challenge mid-case[57] it is perhaps not surprising that parties spend less time seeking to question issues of standing. As a result the focus has moved to managing costs and court time, even in borderline cases. Legislative reforms were recently proposed in order to generally restrict the parties who were considered to have standing to bring a claim however this was met with fierce opposition, by those citing the rights of citizens to challenge 'bad authority'[58] and the need to uphold the rule of law (see section 6 for former discussion). Reforms have however been introduced so that third party interveners (which often include non-government organisations (NGOs) and charity organisations such as Greenpeace) will be required to bear their own costs. These may have an effect in practice on the number of interested parties able to participate in the process. This is discussed further below.

5.2. EUROPEAN MANDATORY REQUIREMENTS

As discussed at section 3 above, procedural requirements in the determination of land use consents are a fertile ground for judicial challenge. Mandatory requirements might on their face appear more important than discretionary ones, but even with a discretionary power it is as much a flaw to have failed to consider a discretionary matter when required to do so or not to have given any indication of how that discretion was exercised fairly as it is to have failed to follow a required process.

In the planning context, nothing has matched European legislation for creating a mix of mandatory and discretionary requirements. Starting with

55 Supreme Court Act 1981, Section 31(1).

56 e.g. *R. (Edwards) v. Environment Agency (No 1)* [2004] EWHC 736 (Admin) and *R. (Feakins) v. Secretary of State for the Environment, Food and Rural Affairs* [2003] EWCA Civ 1546.

57 *River Thames Society v. First Secretary of State* [2006] EWHC 2829 (Admin).

58 *A. Samuels*, *supra* note 18, p. 758.

Environmental Impact Assessment in the late 1980s, the Species and Habitats Directives which were brought together into the Habitats Regulations[59] from the early 1990s and most recently Strategic Environmental Assessment (SEA) from 2004[60] – all share a common approach in that they impose a range of procedural assessment hurdles, and in some cases mandatory tests that have to be applied if development is to be permitted.

This creates a clear issue: 'the more rules, the greater the opportunity for objectors to argue that there have been infringements and more so when rules are unclear or constantly changing.'[61] Alleged non-compliance with the EIA Directive is used frequently as a ground of challenge by objectors to controversial development proposals.

It is clear that the introduction of European mandatory requirements has had a powerful influence on judicial review in the UK. Cases such as *Berkeley v. Secretary of State for the Environment*, decided in 2001, established that non-compliance with these requirements is not something that could be subject to the exercise of the courts' discretion.[62] However, in a recent decision, *R. (on the application of Champion) v. North Norfolk District Council*,[63] involving a lorry park development which posed a risk of polluting in a nearby river (also an SAC), the Supreme Court exercised discretion regarding non-compliance with EU requirements (in this case a defective screening opinion). The Court found that although the application should have been subject to assessment under the EIA regulations, the failure did not prevent the fullest possible investigation of the proposal and the involvement of the public. There was no reason to think that a different process would have resulted in a different decision and the claimant's interests had not been prejudiced. The Supreme Court set out clear guidance: 'in future cases, the Court considering an application or permission to bring judicial review proceedings should have regard to the likelihood of relief being granted, even if an irregularity has been established.' This decision has suggested that judges are increasingly prepared to exercise their discretion, even in cases of non-compliance with EU requirements. It could mark a significant shift in approach by the UK courts from cases like *Berkeley*.[64]

---

59 The Conservation of Habitats and Species Regulations 2010.

60 Environmental Assessment of Plans and Programmes Regulations 2004.

61 S. *Ricketts*, *supra* note 3, p. OP12.

62 *Berkeley v. Secretary of State for the Environment and another* [2001] 2 AC.

63 *R. (on the application of Champion) v. North Norfolk District Council* [2015] UKSC 52.

64 *Berkeley v. Secretary of State for the Environment and another* [2001] 2 AC.

5.3. AARHUS[65] CONVENTION

The Aarhus Convention has imposed an international baseline requirement that the public in each signatory state has access to a clear system of environmental justice as part of a wider objective to ensure the informed participation of the public in environmental decision-making. This has proved an important catalyst in both litigation and national policy. Some of the practical consequences of Aarhus in terms of judicial review in the UK are described below.

5.3.1. Time Limits for Judicial Review

Aarhus has impacted on the time limit within which a judicial review claim can be brought.

The time periods for bringing challenges are different for different types of claim. For judicial review the standard period for bringing a challenge is three months from the date of the relevant decision. However from 1 July 2014, in an attempt to stimulate development, for planning cases, the period has been reduced to six weeks. For statutory challenges in the planning context the applicable period is also six weeks.[66]

For challenges to the Secretary of State's decisions on NSIPs, the Planning Act confirms that these are to proceed by way of judicial reviews, with a time period of six weeks. This ensures that these challenges are subject to a permission stage, and that they continue to follow the process that applied under the previous consenting regimes.[67] Recent amendments (discussed further below) have clarified that the time runs from the day after the order was made. This was following challenges to NSIP decisions which were struck out on the basis that the application was made out of time.[68]

It was, however, not sufficient for a judicial review challenge to have simply been lodged within the relevant time period. To deter last minute challenges, and to provide some certainty to developers, it was a requirement that a claim was brought 'promptly and in any event within three months'.[69] The effect of this was that, even if challenge was lodged within the three-month period, it could be dismissed if it could be shown that the claimant had not acted 'promptly'.[70]

Two recent decisions have confirmed that, in light of the Aarhus Convention requirements that the public has access to a clear system of environmental justice

65 The UNECE Convention on Access to Information, Public Participation in Decision-making and Access to Justice in Environmental Matters (the 'Aarhus Convention').
66 Town and Country Planning Act 1990, sections 288 and 289.
67 i.e. orders under the Transport and Works Act 1992 and Electricity Act 1989 consents.
68 See for example *Blue Green London Plan v. Secretary of State for Environment, Food and Rural Affairs* [2015] EWHC 495 against the Thames Tideway Tunnel Order 2014, where the six-week period was counted from the day the order was made.
69 Civil Procedure Rules, Rule 54.5(1).
70 *Finn-Kelcey v. Milton Keynes Council* [2008] EWCA Civ 1067.

that is not prohibitively expensive (which is discussed in more detail below), the requirement for promptness was non-compliant with EU law.[71] Currently this only applies to challenges which engage Aarhus and involve environmental issues, drawing in any projects subject to EIA, SEA, or Habitats Assessment.

It has always been the case that, in exceptional circumstances the Courts may waive the need to issue a judicial review claim within the challenge period. For example, in *Gerber*,[72] a challenge against a solar farm development succeeded despite the substantive decision having taken place some two years before. The claim passed the permission stage on the basis that the claimant was unaware of the planning permission until a year after it had been granted due to the local authority's failure to notify him of it at the relevant time. One of the grounds of challenge was that the local authority's screening decision for EIA was flawed both as to its substance and reasoning. Notwithstanding the very substantial financial prejudice caused to the developer, as the scheme had already been constructed, and taking into account the loss of government subsidy by the removal of the installation, the Court held that the appropriate course of action was to quash the planning permission.

This can be contrasted with the decision in *Champion,* where the Court was keen to emphasise the fact that fullest possible investigation had been undertaken and the claimant's interests were not prejudiced by the decision. Nevertheless, whilst there are clear differences in the facts of each of these cases, as a Supreme Court decision, *Champion* has established that a breach of an EU requirement does not require a decision to be quashed. Given the substantial prejudice to the developer in allowing a claim to be brought out of time and quashing consent for a constructed project, it will be interesting to see how much weight the Court of Appeal places on the *Champion* decision in rehearing *Gerber.*

5.3.2. Costs

The courts have the power to make awards of costs at various stages during a judicial review challenge. Such awards tend to be made following a substantive hearing, and the starting point for the court is that the approach to costs in judicial review should be the same as in other civil proceedings.[73] The court has a wide discretion under section 51 of the Senior Courts Act 1981 'to determine to whom and to what extent the costs are to be paid.' This legislation is supplemented by the rules contained in Parts 43–48 of the Civil Procedure Rules 1998 (the CPR) and Practice Direction 11 – General Rules about Costs.

The Courts are also given an unqualified power to 'take any other step or make any other order for the purpose of managing the case and furthering the

[71] C-406/08 *Uniplex (UK) Ltd v. NHS Business Services Authority* and UN-ECE Aarhus Compliance Committee ruling ACCC/C/2008/33 (the 'Port of Tyne case').

[72] *Gerber v. Wiltshire Council* [2015] EWHC 524 (Admin).

[73] *R. (Smeaton) v. Secretary of State for Health* [2002] EWHC 886, para. 8.

overriding objective'[74] which is to ensure that the parties are on an equal footing and that the case is dealt with fairly in order that the courts may deal with cases justly.[75]

In practice, an unsuccessful claimant would generally be liable for not only their legal costs, but also the defendant's costs, and vice versa where the claim is successful. In circumstances where there are multiple defendants (for example the Secretary of State and the local planning authority), an unsuccessful claimant's costs exposure could be extensive. In practice, the courts would usually only award one set of costs for any substantive hearing unless there are exceptional circumstances that justify a further award.[76]

As with other forms of civil litigation, the costs regime and risk of costs for an unsuccessful claimant or defendant have, in conjunction with the permission stage, acted as a natural filter on the number of challenges that are considered by the courts. As a result, in England and Wales, Protective Costs Orders (PCOs) have become increasingly common as a means for a claimant to restrict its potential costs exposure in the event that a challenge does not succeed.

The principles on which PCOs could be granted were set out by the Court of Appeal in the *Corner House* case.[77] These principles have evolved considerably over the past ten years, resulting in three tests required to be met for a PCO to be granted:

(a) that the case has some merit;
(b) that having regard to the likely costs of the case it is fair and just to make the order; and
(c) if the order is not made the claimant is likely to discontinue the challenge.

In addition, changes were recently introduced to the costs regime for environmental cases (proceeding by way of judicial review), bringing it into line with Aarhus Convention requirements. The effect of these changes are that for individual claimants in the event that the challenge is unsuccessful their exposure to the defendant's costs is limited to £5,000; if successful they are only entitled to recover up to £35,000 of their own costs. For an organisation recoverable costs are fixed at £10,000. As the risk of an adverse costs award was a deterrent to would-be judicial review claimants, these changes to the costs regime can only lead to an increase in the number of challenges to planning decisions involving EIA, SEA or human rights.

---

74 CPR, Rule 3.1(2)(m).

75 CPR, Rules 1.1 and 1.2.

76 e.g. bringing something to the proceedings that could not have been covered by the main parties, such as evidence on a crucial issue. See *Bolton Metropolitan District Council v. Secretary of State for the Environment* [1995] 1 WLR 1176, 1178–1179.

77 *R. (Corner House Research) v. Secretary of State for Trade and Industry* [2005] 1 WLR 2600 (CA).

Currently, under domestic law, section 288 applications do not fall under Aarhus as CPR 45.41, which confers discretion to grant a PCO, excludes statutory appeals and only applies to judicial review. The applicable rules in such cases are therefore the *Corner House* principles rather than those contained in CPR 45.41.[78] The courts have recently explicitly recognised that this 'two tier' costs regime is 'flawed in terms of Aarhus compliance'[79] but, in applying the doctrine of the separation of powers, have noted that this inconsistency is for Parliament to resolve. On this point a recent case comment on *Venn v. Secretary of State for Communities and Local Government* notes that 'once it is accepted that the exclusion of statutory appeals and applications from CPR 45.41 was not an oversight but a deliberate expression of legislative intent, it followed that it would have been inappropriate (possibly unconstitutional?) to use judicial discretion so as to sidestep a limitation deliberately imposed by secondary legislation'.[80] In relation to recent reforms, some of which are of relevance to costs and PCOs, Parliament appears to have missed an opportunity to ensure that this non-compliance with Aarhus is rectified, although we may see further changes being made over the next few years.

5.4. SOCIAL INFLUENCES

It is not just changes within the legal system itself which have exerted an influence over the nature of judicial review challenge in England and Wales. Influences from a wider social context have also placed considerable pressure on the planning system. From the availability of documents online to the power of freedom of information and environmental information requests, information is more freely and readily available than ever before and those wanting to prevent development are becoming increasingly resourceful when it comes to taking action against a proposal. This has increased the number of challenges being brought.

Social media campaigns are also starting to have a material impact on planning decisions: 'via social media we can readily show our frustrations and organise ourselves quickly, establishing a strong presence … sharing data and knowledge. It is much easier for objectors to turn up the heat on individuals via Twitter and Facebook from the comfort of their smartphone'.[81]

There are reports of a judicial review action against Whitemoss landfill extension, a consented nationally significant infrastructure project, being crowdfunded[82] via 'Crowdjustice', a website founded on the premise that 'everyone

---

78 *Secretary of State for Communities and Local Government v. Venn* [2014] EWCA Civ 1539.

79 *Ibid.*, para. 34.

80 Case Comment: *Venn v. Secretary of State for Communities and Local Government*, JPL, 2015 (5), 573–583.

81 *S. Ricketts*, *supra* note 3, p. OP10.

82 www.bbc.co.uk/news/uk-33785461.

should have access to the law, and that funding shouldn't stand in the way'.[83] This site was launched earlier this year, promoting the 'power of the community to create change'[84] and funding targets have already been reached for a number of potential challenges. Sites such as this have the potential to revolutionise the way claims are made, on the one hand allowing more challenges to proceed that would otherwise be prevented by the cost of such action; but on the other hand presenting a clear and significant risk of an increase in 'spurious litigation'.[85]

This ease of access to the courts for individuals also has far reaching implications for developers, even if the challenge is successfully defended. In relation to Whitemoss, the owner of the site has commented that 'crowdfunding and social media are like a force multiplier. You've got maybe fifty people who can appear to be a thousand people. Something that might have been dealt with in a relatively reasonable timeframe is dragged on. If the delay to the extension continues, in the worst case, we could lose all of our existing customers, which it has taken us twenty years to build up.'[86]

This increase in knowledge and the willingness of individuals to challenge planning decisions has had a significant impact on the planning system as a whole. The final decision from a local authority or Secretary of State no longer provides certainty. When coupled with the courts' inclusive approach to standing, and the grounds on which to bring a challenge widening, it is easy to see how the volume of challenges has increased over recent years and as a result, the time taken to resolve them has also increased. The Government's recognition of this and the resulting reforms are discussed in section 6.

6. REFORM OF THE JUDICIAL REVIEW PROCESS AND THE NEW PLANNING COURT

6.1. ORIGINS

Increasingly, as discussed above, 'judicial review has been seen as a political tool and blocking device [and] commercial bodies have sought to derail commercial proposals brought forward by their competitors'.[87] There has been a rise in concern that challenges to decisions granting consent for development were being made as a way of delaying unpopular and controversial development taking place, rather than as a way to resolve a substantial legal flaw with the decision-making process. This was perceived by the Government as the reason why development

83 www.crowdjustice.co.uk/#cases.

84 www.crowdjustice.co.uk/#cases.

85 www.bbc.co.uk/news/uk-33785461.

86 www.bbc.co.uk/news/uk-33785461.

87 *A. Samuels, supra* note 18, p. 754.

was not coming forward as quickly as it should have been.[88] There is also a more fundamental concern that genuinely aggrieved individuals with a right of recourse to the courts are being caught up alongside claims brought purely to delay development and are having to wait for long periods of time before their cases are heard. In December 2012 the Government commenced consultation on proposals for reforming the judicial review system in England and Wales. Three key changes were identified and implemented as part of the Government's response to the consultation:

(a) a reduction in the time limit for bringing a claim from three months to six weeks for planning cases;
(b) the introduction of a new fee for an oral renewal hearing where the claimant does not accept a refusal of permission on the papers and asks for the decision to be reconsidered at a hearing; and
(c) the removal of the right to an oral hearing where the case is assessed as 'totally without merit'.

A further consultation was launched in September 2013 with the objective of finding further ways to reduce the time and money spent on 'unmeritorious' judicial review challenges. The outcome of this consultation has been two-fold. Firstly, changes have been introduced following royal assent of the Criminal Justice and Courts Act 2015 (CJCA). The Government policy underpinning the reforms brought about the CJCA can be summarised as a desire to reduce delay, dissuade and prevent unmeritorious applications, prevent reconsideration of the substantive merits or minor technical points, protect the winning public authority from being unable to recover costs and make interveners bear their own costs.[89] There has been some debate about whether the provisions also have a negative impact on administering justice for example, Nicholas Lavender QC, chairman of the Bar Council had urged peers to reject the Government proposals and said: 'The fact that the Government of the day sometimes disagrees with the judges does not justify a claim that the judges lack common sense or are allowing the system to be abused. It is certainly not a reason for using an act of Parliament to curtail the judges' discretion to do right in individual cases or to direct the judges how to decide particular cases.'[90]

As a result of the fierce debate, some of the more controversial aspects of the proposed reforms brought about by the CJCA, were dropped prior to the bill becoming law.[91]

88 For example, see the foreword to the Government consultation paper, Judicial Review: Proposals for Reform, December 2012.
89 See *A. Samuels, supra* note 18, p. 754.
90 www.theguardian.com/uk-news/2014/dec/09/house-lords-rejects-government-plans-restrict-judicial-review-access.
91 www.independent.co.uk/voices/editorials/rule-of-law-is-still-our-defence-10061673.html.

Secondly the 'Planning Fast Track' was introduced in the Administrative Court in July 2013 which had the aim of ensuring that important planning cases were heard quickly before specialist judges. Shortly after this the Planning Court came into existence on 6 April 2014 which created a specialist list for judicial review and statutory challenges relating to planning issues previously dealt with in the Administrative Court. An analysis of the key changes is discussed further below.

6.2. REFORMS

6.2.1. *The Criminal Justice and Courts Act 2015 (CJCA)*

Despite the criticisms, the CJCA still made a number of significant changes to the judicial review and statutory challenge procedures some of which are detailed below. Despite the fierce opposition, the effects of the changes will be significant both in terms of the role the courts play in the planning process and the limiting of judicial discretion.

6.2.1.1. Making a Challenge

A permission stage has been introduced for statutory challenges to planning decisions under section 288 of the TCPA bringing it into line with the judicial review procedure. It is argued that this change will restrict the ability of aggrieved persons to bring a statutory challenge and will lengthen the process, with more information being required upfront. The statistics presented in section 3 relating to the success of judicial review claims highlight the impact the introduction of a permission stage could have on the number of section 288 challenges made; we would expect to see the volume of full hearings reduce.

6.2.1.2. Financing a Challenge

New provisions have been introduced which prevent judicial review cases from proceeding in the absence of information about the financing of the challenge. The reforms have been proposed to identify where a costs capping or PCO may be appropriate. However, this reform runs contrary to the spirit of the automatic costs cap for Aarhus claims, has also been met with opposition and 'might prejudice the giving of leave on the merits'.[92]

Costs capping orders may only be granted when certain criteria such as whether proceedings are in the public interest or are of public importance, or

[92] *A. Samuels, supra* note 18, p. 755.

whether without the order proceedings may be withdrawn.[93] Provisions are included that would allow the Courts to apply different criteria for environmental cases, using reference to ECJ principles.[94] It is unclear what exactly these criteria will be at this stage and it will be interesting to see how this secures compliance with Aarhus.

There are now limitations on the discretion of the judge to require either a claimant or defendant to pay costs for third party interveners (such as Greenpeace) to exceptional circumstances only. Third parties will instead be required to bear their own costs. This could significantly impact on the way challenges are made; claimants may find it more difficult to achieve the backing of a third party, and developers (who are a third party themselves in this type of action) will find themselves unlikely to be able to recover their costs.

6.2.1.3. Determining a Challenge

Judges are now prevented from granting permission in judicial review actions if they consider it highly likely that the defendant's conduct would not have affected the outcome for the applicant, unless there are exceptional public interest reasons for granting permission. Opponents of the new provision have argued that 'the citizen must be entitled to challenge authority [and] denial of an oral hearing can give rise to a deep sense of injustice'.[95] Furthermore, it may require the case to be put in more detail at the permission stage which may lengthen the process and potentially increase costs (see section 3 above). The Supreme Court in *Champion*[96] sent a clear message that caution should be exercised in a case where there is a clear procedural defect but it is unlikely that a different decision would have resulted if the defect had not occurred. The Court in *Champion* was arguably bringing its decision-making process in line with Government aims, acknowledging the need for a claimant to have access to a fair and impartial hearing but recognising that a procedural defect in itself may not merit the granting of relief.

As noted above, the passage of the Bill through the Houses of Parliament was not as smooth as the Government must have hoped it would be and triggered a fierce debate surrounding the separation of powers.

Reports from national newspapers further indicate the scale of the concern in the House of Lords (where a number of ex-judiciary now reside) and the challenge the Government faced to make the proposals acceptable to Parliament:[97]

---

93 See for further information; sections 88–90 of the Criminal Justice and Courts Act 2015 which set out the full statutory code for determining whether to grant a costs capping order.

94 See for example *R. (on the application of Edwards) v. Environment Agency* [2013] UKSC 78.

95 *A. Samuels*, *supra* note 18, p. 755.

96 *R. (on the application of Champion) v. North Norfolk District Council* [2015] UKSC 52.

97 See e.g. www.theguardian.com/uk-news/2014/dec/09/house-lords-rejects-government-plans-restrict-judicial-review-access.

> 'In the debate, Lord Beecham, the Labour peer, observed: 'The Government, itself a possible defendant in these cases, seeks to restrict the exercise of judicial discretion in its own interests, and on the basis of the flimsiest evidence of the abuses it affects to detect in the working of the system and the decisions of the Courts ...'

Among the rebels was Baron Deben, the former Conservative MP John Selwyn Gummer, who told the Lords: 'Ministers ought to be embarrassed if they break the law. People will not respect the law if they think ministers have a special arrangement. If we are not here to uphold principles of this kind, then we should not be here at all.'[98]

Overall, although proposals to directly restrict those with standing to bring a judicial review claim were dropped, the effect of other reforms such as the requirement to provide information about financial resources and increasing the risk of costs will have the effect of restricting some individuals' ability or desire to make a claim.[99] This could be seen as an erosion of the concept of democratic accountability and has been seen by some as an attempt by the Government to reduce the remit of the judiciary and arguably the entitlement of the citizen to challenge authority.

6.2.2. *The Introduction of the Planning Court*

In contrast to the changes brought about by the CJCA earlier this year, the reforms which resulted in the introduction of the Planning Court have more clearly improved access to justice by speeding up the processing of claims and have decisions made by experts in planning law. In addition, the new case management powers allow the judge discretion over the management of the process.

The Planning Court deals with judicial review claims and statutory challenges which involve planning (including policy), highways, compulsory purchase, EU environmental matters, village greens and any other matters the planning judge considers appropriate.

The Court has the objective of preventing claims which are without merit being made purely to delay development, and to ensure that those claims with merit are properly considered. Planning Court claims are managed by a specialist 'Planning Liaison Judge'.

---

98 www.theguardian.com/uk-news/2014/dec/09/house-lords-rejects-government-plans-restrict-judicial-review-access.

99 See *A. Samuels*, *supra* note 18, p. 755.

6.2.2.1. 'Significant Cases' and Target Timescales

With the introduction of the Planning Court came the introduction of Practice Direction 54E of the Civil Procedure Rules. This sets out the definition of 'significant' cases and target timescales for their determination. While significant cases are to be heard by specialist planning judges they are also to be resolved within strict timetables thereby seeking to ensure that development is not unnecessarily delayed. To be considered 'significant' a claim must:

(a) relate to commercial, residential, or other developments which have a significant impact either at a local level or beyond their immediate locality;
(b) raise important points of law;
(c) generate significant public interest; or
(d) by virtue of the volume or nature of technical material, are best dealt with by judges with significant experience of handling such matters.

It is open to any party to make representations as to whether their claim should be characterised as significant and, in the event that it is, the Court will endeavour to determine the claim according to prescribed timescales.[100]

The target timescales should mean that the time to determine a judicial review from filing to substantive hearing should be up to five months (or six months if an oral hearing is required). Under the previous system it could take that long for an application for permission for a judicial review to be considered on the papers.

It is also possible for the Planning Liaison Judge to expedite any Planning Court claim if it is considered necessary to deal with the case justly. This should further reduce the time for determination of the claim.

The target timescales are subject to the overriding objective of the interest of justice but the recent case of *London and Henley*[101] shows that the timescales will be enforced quite rigorously. Lindblom J while granting an adjournment of a substantive hearing took the opportunity to remind parties that this would be an exceptional move in the Planning Court and that counsel's availability would not necessarily be a reason for hearing a case significantly outside the target timetable.

Arguably, since the provisions were introduced, the process has become more front loaded, with parties using rolled up hearings (which combines the permission stage and full hearing) to expedite the process. More time and money is therefore being required upfront but the case should be concluded more quickly.

100 Practice Direction 54E – Planning Court Claims, Civil Procedure Rules, para. 3.4.

101 *London and Henley (Middle Brook Street) Limited v. Secretary of Estate for Communities and Local Government* [2013] EWHC 4207 (Admin).

6.2.2.2. New Case Management Powers

The Planning Court also has new powers to be able to direct that any party intending to contest a claim must file summary grounds of defence explaining the position that they are taking.

This is an important power as defendants of statutory applications or appeals, such as those under section 288 of the TCPA, were not previously required to disclose their case until they filed their skeleton submissions in anticipation of the substantive hearing; potentially some months after the claim had been filed. This meant that there was no way to assess the merits of the claim, nor any impetus for the defendant (usually the Secretary of State) to consider the case in detail until after potentially significant cost and delay had been incurred by the claimant, any interested party and the courts.

Experience is showing that the new Planning Court is taking a proactive and robust approach to judicial review and statutory planning challenges, and as planning law is a niche area the consideration and determination of challenges is being greatly assisted by the availability of a specialist planning judge who understands the intricacies and inter-relationships between the law, policy and procedure.

However, as it continues to operate within the established judicial review process and the Administrative Court, the Planning Court will neither operate as a court of first recourse for the determination of complex land use development consents nor seek to unify the existing consent regimes by extending its present jurisdiction to offer some form of arbitration of land use decision-making. These aspects will remain within the existing jurisdiction of the Planning Inspectorate and the Lands Chamber in the Upper Tribunal respectively.

It is hoped that the deployment of specialist and experienced judges to planning cases should lead to a more consistent series of high quality judicial decisions.[102] This will ensure the establishment of a reliable body of case law which can be used in the following ways to assist the operation of the Planning Court:

(a) by practitioners in assessing and advising upon whether to bring claims;
(b) by the Planning Liaison Judge in considering cases on the papers; and
(c) by the Judiciary when considering and determining claims.

[102] To put this into context, Richard Harwood QC has noted that, prior to the introduction of the Planning Court, there was a concern over the quality of the decision-making, given that the judges in the Administrative Court often did not have extensive public law experience, see *R. Harwood QC*, Legal update: what have been the key issues emerging from cases over the past year?, Journal of Planning Law, 2014, 13 Supp (Power to the People?), pp. OP139-OP165.

7. CONCLUSION

There are a number of key elements to the operation of the judicial oversight of the UK planning process. This area of law is best described by the title 'judicial review' because the unifying feature of its different manifestations is that the courts have the ability to review a decision and either uphold it or return it for reconsideration, but not to substitute its own decision.

The jurisprudence of Strasbourg recognises that in a democracy, where the courts have jurisdiction to conduct a judicial review of the lawfulness and fairness of a decision, a Government minister can be both a policy maker and a decision-taker without there being a violation of Article 6 of the ECHR. A minister can properly perform the functions of both policy maker and decision taker because he is answerable to Parliament as regards the policy aspects of his decision and answerable to the High Court as regards the lawfulness and fairness of his decision-making process.

The role of the Secretary of State in determining planning applications of whatever magnitude is an exercise of the political mandate given to the elected Government. It has been found to be correct that such decisions should be taken as an exercise of political authority.

The safeguards imposed by the ECHR do not require that political role to be relinquished by Government but rather require that safeguards be put in place to ensure that the process which leads to that political decision is independent of any political pre-determination.

A combination of increasing mandatory assessment rules in planning procedures and an increasingly benign environment to those wishing to bring challenges has fuelled a major increase in judicial review litigation which has consequently increased the importance of the role of the courts in the planning process. The range of topics vulnerable to challenge encompass all major development initiatives many of which are hugely politically contentious. Whilst the challenge regime is directed at protection of public rights, not private property, in practice it is accepted that private individuals will often be the mouthpiece of wider public concern.[103]

With so much commercial and economic need for development meeting so much informed and motivated public opinion a radical initiative has been needed to, in the view of the Government, render the challenge process fit for purpose, through the changes to the judicial review system and the new Planning Court.

The introduction of the Planning Court has been broadly welcomed and experience is showing that, although still in its infancy, the Court is engaging with projects and taking an active role in both their case management and determination. These changes, along with the opportunity to develop an

103 See for example the House of Lords Hansard texts debating the Criminal Justice and Courts Bill.

informed and consistent body of planning case law, can only be welcomed by all those involved in the process.

To date, however, much of the remainder of the Government's judicial review reforms are facing a less positive reception. The changes are clearly an attempt to control the significant increase in judicial review litigation that has taken place over the past decade which is evidence of 'the considerable impact that EC law has had on domestic public law'.[104] In the context of the current tensions between the UK Government and Europe, it will be interesting to see whether, assuming the UK elects to remain within the EU, the tension that is inherent in the European and UK approaches can be managed or whether ultimately it will result in open conflict with either the UK courts or the European Parliament as each seeks to uphold and defend its own system.

[104] *R. Gordon* QC, Using EC law in Environmental Judicial Review, Journal of Planning Law, 2007, p. 834.

CHAPTER 16

PUBLIC PARTICIPATION IN LAND MANAGEMENT LAW-MAKING PROCESS IN THE BASQUE COUNTRY:

Effects on Soil and Other Natural Resources

Iñaki Lasagabaster and María del Carmen Bolaño*

1. INTRODUCTION

Member States' land management law must comply with European Union's policies and regulations. Land management law's principal objective is to set land uses according to both soil type and quality. Soil provides the main foundation for human activities and it is a matter of transversal nature.[1] It affects issues of widely different kinds, e.g. water, habitats or birds protection. In fact, there is a link between land management and water legislation: land management plays a main role in the protection of aquifers. According to land management regulations, there are a number of land uses that cannot be set in areas of aquifers. It is understood that those land uses may have a negative effect on water quality.

* Dr Iñaki Lasagabaster, Professor of Administrative Law at the University of the Basque Country, Faculty of Economics and Business Studies, and Dr María del Carmen Bolaño, Lecturer and researcher of Administrative Law at the University of the Basque Country, Faculty of Economics and Business Studies.

1 In relation to environmental soil concept and its protection in the Basque Country, see *M.C. Bolaño Piñeiro*, Concepto ambiental de suelo y normativa reguladora, Ingurugiroa eta Zuzenbidea, 2014 (12), pp. 13–45; *M.C. Bolaño Piñeiro*, Registros administrativos e inventarios en material de suelos contaminados, Revista Vasca de Administración Pública/Herri-Arduralaritzako Euskal Aldizkaria, 2014 (98), pp. 17–48; *M.C. Bolaño Piñeiro*, La aplicación retroactiva de las leyes 22/2011 y 1/2005, en referencia a la obligación de recuperar los suelos declarados contaminados o alterados en la Comunidad Autónoma del País Vasco, Revista Aranzadi de Derecho Ambiental, 2014 (28), pp. 223–249.

The restrictions, prohibitions and requirements of the regulations have also the objective of protecting the areas ruled by the Habitats or Birds Directive.[2]

The essential issue is that most land management regulations are approved by public authorities, not by Parliaments, and that they have a direct effect on local councils. This is a fundamental fact because councils can permit land uses that are in contradiction with the European Union's regulations. However, this unwanted practice can be prevented by an appropriate land management law, which must be implemented by councils.

Land management in the Basque Country is regulated by the *Land Management Law.* The Land Management Law is divided into three different categories. The most general regulations are the *Guidelines for Land Management,* which govern spatial planning in the whole Autonomous Community of The Basque Country. These Guidelines have a legal nature and they are hierarchically superior to Urban Planning Regulations. The Guidelines for Land Management classify land into different types and, according to this classification, these rules determine all the different possible uses of each type of land. Thus, every part of the territory of the Autonomous Community is classified as a specific land category as well as connected to some specific uses. The Land Management Guidelines establish which land uses are forbidden, which are admissible and which are adequate. In accordance with what is established in the *Land Management Act,* the Guidelines for the Land Management's purpose is to oversee and establish land uses in the Autonomous Community.

In addition to the Guidelines, the Basque Land Management Law set the *Land District Plans,* which rule the land management of a concrete area, and the *Land Sector Plans,* which rule the protection of some natural resources as well as the development of some traditional activities. For instance, some *Land Sector Plans* set the standards and the rules of the use of the rivers, in order to protect not only the bank of the river but also the waters.

One of the principal objectives of Land Management Law is to provide some limits on the use of land. Despite the progress made by the Guidelines of the Land Management in achieving a proper occupancy of the land, the most remarkable obstacle found is that these regulations do not apply to some large projects since, in reality, those projects affect completely land's development. The example of a high speed railway project is, undoubtedly, par excellence.[3]

---

2 *I. Lasagabaster Herrarte & A. Garcia Ureta,* Las relaciones Plan Especial – planeamiento general y la Directiva 79/409. Comentario a la STSJPV 1033/2000, de 16 de octubre, Revista Vasca de Administración Pública, 2001 (59), pp. 301–326.

3 The High Speed Railway project Vitoria-Bilbao-San Sebastián will connect the Basque Country with the Baiona-Burdeos-Paris line. Firstly it was said that a journey Vitoria-Bilbao-San Sebastián would take 35 minutes. Now, they say it will take 55 minutes. The project was widely criticised because of the lack of public participation in its making process. Moreover, public authorities gave some misleading information. For instance, they made up some data that was not proved, e.g., that the number of trucks in the Basque motorways would decrease exponentially. But some studies have shown just the contrary. The HSR has a huge impact on

The Basque ruling approach has had some positive and remarkable effects on land management but less than desired.

2. CLARIFICATION OF THE MEANING OF LAND MANAGEMENT

Before analysing land management, there is a need to clarify its terminological concept.[4] Sometimes, when we talk about land management it is not really clear what we want to mean by this term, especially if we take into account that it is used from very different perspectives and by completely different players. From a non-technical point of view, land management refers to everything which is related to territory. Thus, land management can be analysed from various perspectives: politically, economically, demographically, etc. Because of this, without getting embroiled in academic arguments about land management concept, there is a need to determinate the meaning or the content we designate to it in this work. We will connect land management with other issues this term goes hand in hand with, for example, urbanism or environment.[5]

By land management we mean human beings' decisions which affect the land and have been adopted because of a previous idea of the reasons and consequences they were thought to involve. A motorway through the Pyrenees could be useful to connect people from isolated areas with other populated areas, although it could be understood that a major project like this implies an unbearable environmental cost. A high speed railway line could be seen as an infrastructure with beneficial effects bringing improvements to transport and communications, etc. However, those advantages are thought to be not enough to justify the environmental degradation these kinds of undertakings imply.

This essay is based on a legal perspective. That is, the instruments of land management that are at the service of land management are going to be analysed. A legal analysis cannot forget that reality does not end in the law and that the

---

the environment and, in the case of the Basque Country, is being built in some of the few virgin areas the Basque Country maintains. It is also criticised that the HSR will not be a solution for the Basque Country because of its dispersed population. It will not be cost-effective. The Basque authorities do not have information about the cost of the tickets and the connection with the European HSR has been postponed until 2032. See, *I. Lasagabaster Herrarte*, Información administrativa y transparencia en la ordenación del territorio y el medio ambiente, Revista Vasca de Administración Pública, 2009 (83), pp. 183–215.

4 *I. Lasagabaster Herrarte*, La Ordenación del Territorio: qué es y algunas ideas sobre lo que debería ser, Instituto Robles-Arangiz, Bilbao, 2008. See also *I. Lasagabaster Herrarte & J.I. Cubero Marcos*, La ordenación del territorio y el urbanismo en los Pirineos, in I. Lasagabaster Herrarte (ed.), El Régimen jurídico de protección de los Pirineos, Universidad del País Vasco/Euskal Herriko Unibertsitatea, Bilbao, 2012, p. 87–114; *I. Lasagabaster Herrarte & I. Lazcano Brotons*, Protección del paisaje, ordenación del territorio y espacios naturales protegidos, Revista Vasca de Administración Pública, 2005 (70), pp. 125–187.

5 *A.M. García Ureta*, Urbanismo y Red Natura 2000. Ley 8/2007 y alteración de zonas protegidas, Revista Vasca de Administración Pública, 2007 (78), pp. 113–152.

law has influence on reality. Both perspectives of analysis should be taken into account, giving each of them the relevance they deserve.

In order to introduce the topic of this work some history is needed. Human activity was not regulated at first. Landowners could build or do whatever they desired, without limits. There were no rules which obliged or stopped them from doing what they liked. This way, cities started to grow chaotically with no regulation apart from some minor rules, such as the Right of Lightening and Views, which governed construction with the aim of respecting neighbour's rights. However, cities reached a point in which unplanned development became unsustainable. Eventually, the expansion of cities started to be planned, establishing wide city avenues, geometric grid systems, etc. In other words, councils started to set some mechanisms of control. Those requirements were which now we call urban planning or urbanism,[6] although this last word could be also used to describe a city or to analyse building typology.

Urban planning is a set of rules and techniques that establish cities' development. These regulations are crucial for dwellers because they provide (a) how the city grows; (b) in which part of the city this growth is possible; (c) who benefits from city's growth; (d) how the city is structured, that is to say, where schools, health centres, cultural and religious facilities, green areas, etc., will be settled; or (e) how communication between neighbourhoods is solved. These regulations, among more others, unquestionably affect people's standard of living.

Urban planning has developed very differently from one place to another.[7] Moreover, the same rules have had very different results due to a variety of reasons: the size of the city, the city's strategic importance – depending on, for example, its location – close to natural resources or near a communications hub – etc. Frequently, some regions' balanced and harmonious development has taken place due to a way of living and feeling 'city's culture'. Likewise, although there is not a direct and proven link between richness and balanced urbanism, wealth often affects development. Poverty is not a good companion, although a big budget does not equate with adequate development – it depends on other reasons as well, e.g. climate.

Over the years, urban planning has been almost incomprehensible in some areas. This is the case of, for instance, Mediterranean urban planning and that of the Autonomous Community of Castilla-La Mancha, among others. Low exchange rates combined with a complex law system – no transparent and

6 *I. Lasagabaster Herrarte & I. Lazcano Brotons*, Una introducción general sobre la Ley vasca del Suelo y Urbanismo, Ley 2/2006, de 30 de junio, Revista de Urbanismo y Edificación, 2006 (14); *I. Lasagabaster Herrarte*, Breve nota a la Resolución del Parlamento europeo relativa a los abusos producidos como consecuencia de la aplicación de la Ley de la actividad urbanística de Valencia, Ingurugiroa eta Zuzenbidea, 2006 (4), pp. 71–80.6, pp. 23–38; *I. Lasagabaster Herrarte & I. Lazcano Brotons*, Protección del paisaje, ordenación del territorio y espacios naturales protegidos, Revista Vasca de Administración Pública, 2005 (70), pp. 125–187.

7 *T. Quintana López*, De la conservación de las edificaciones a la regeneración de la ciudad existente. Claves de la evolución, Revista de urbanismo y edificación, 2011 (24), pp. 41–60.

extremely permissive with some abusive practices – have led to an abhorrent state of affairs.

Urban planning has typically been a local power.[8] This means that decisions made on city growth, the way in which the city develops and the facilities determined, among others, are defined by each council. In democracy, local autonomy – given local authorities are elected by citizens – finds its highest expression in the power to adopt urban plans. This fact is of great importance. On the one hand, it is true that during the administrative procedure to approve urban plans local councils have to comply with a lot of requirements and conditions. Those controls give the impression that some mechanisms are in place to guarantee that councils act properly. But, on the other hand, this local power clearly shows major deficiencies. One of these deficiencies is that the land is limited to the council's space. A local council is entitled to decide how to develop its land but it cannot forget that neighbouring councils have also necessities and the right to plan their territory. They must take into account that some facilities such as means of transport, water supply, energy and other large infrastructures – airports or similar – have to be provided jointly or in cooperation with other authorities

As city councils found it impossible to plan the space, land management law was put forward. Land management tried to respond to the need of determining the form and the uses which will have a particular area, through the coordination of the council's development and the relations with superior territorial areas. The land management can make reference to a region, a historic territory, an Autonomous Community, Europe, etc. On each case the land management had a specific role and specific regulatory instruments.

3. LAND MANAGEMENT IN THE BASQUE COUNTRY

Land management in the Basque Country is regulated under the *Land Management Act*[9] (LMA). This Act does not define what is supposed to be understood by land

[8] In relation to environment and local powers, see: *T. Quintana López*, Las competencias de las corporaciones locales en materia de protección ambiental. Referencia a Castilla y León, Cuadernos de derecho local (17), 2011, p. 7–19; *T. Quintana López*, Régimen urbanístico de la implantación de grandes establecimientos comerciales en Castilla y León, Revista Jurídica de Castilla y León, 2011 (24), pp. 35–61.

[9] Basque Territory Management Act 4/1990 (Spanish: Ley 4/1990, de 31 de mayo, de Ordenación del Territorio del País Vasco). See: *I. Lasagabaster Herrarte*, La Ordenación del Territorio: qué es y algunas ideas sobre lo que debería ser, Instituto Robles-Arangiz, Bilbao, 2008; *I. Lasagabaster Herrarte*, En torno al valor jurídico de las Directrices de Ordenación Territorial. Nota a la Sentencia del Tribunal Superior de Justicia del País Vasco 1033/2000, Revista Vasca de Administración Pública, 2001 (60), pp. 239–260; *I. Lasagabaster Herrarte & I. Lazkano Brotons*, Régimen jurídico de la Ordenación del Territorio en Euskalherria, HAEE/IVAP, Oñati, 1999; *I. Lasagabaster Herrarte*, La inconstitucionalidad de la Ley de Ordenación

management. The Act just provides (a) the regulatory instruments which will govern territory management; (b) the procedures to adopt them; and (c) the competent authorities to pass the regulations. Likewise, the Act establishes the relation amid those instruments and urban plans. Three are the regulatory instruments ruled in the Act: (a) the Guidelines for Land Management; (b) the Land Sector Plans; and (c) the Land District Plans. The following is a further description of each of those legal instruments so that we can understand their content and value. There is a need to highlight there is a hierarchical relation among them and, in turn, these plans are hierarchically superior to Urban Plans.

3.1. GUIDELINES FOR LAND MANAGEMENT

The Guidelines for Land Management are the 'framework of reference'[10] and they must be respected by the other territory management regulatory instruments. The first Guidelines for Land Management were adopted by Decree 28/1997, of 11 April. This framework of reference has three main functions: (a) it shall formulate from a global and an interacting point of view the rules which would set the establishment of economic and social activities of either public or private agents; (b) the management and the usage of territory to implement public authorities' sector policies, including urban planning; and (c) it shall foresee regional actions that require joint implementations with the State or other Autonomous Communities, serving as an instrument to adopt the corresponding cooperation agreement.[11] In order to accomplish all the functions, the Guidelines for Land Management must contain some provisions, e.g. a detailed land assessment, social situation, unemployment rate, location for farming, location for infrastructures or percentage of social housing.[12]

---

del Territorio del País Vasco (Comentario a la STC 149/1998, de 2 de julio, BOE 181, de 30 de julio), Revista Vasca de Administración Pública, 1998 (52), pp. 363–372.

10 Article 4 LMA.

11 Article 5 LMA.

12 (a) A detailed evaluation of existing problems and ways of solving them. They will probably be related to territory or environment. It would be advisable to take the rate of unemployment into account in this analysis; (b) general criteria to solve those problems; (c) precise location of areas needing special protection because of environmental, cultural or economic reasons, ensuring rational exploitation of natural resources according to their specific regulations. Allocation of land reserved for farming; (d) listing of areas to be regulated by district Territory Plans, establishing the criteria for their management. Those areas shall be called functional areas in the Land Management Guidelines; (e) identification of the most adequate lands for the settlement of large projects, and the necessary measures to give a solution to the environmental problems; (f) ascertain the extent of social housing and non-officially sponsored houses, stating the criteria for their location and the parameters that shall be taken into account by urban planning; (g) facility deficiencies in each area; (h) assessment of work necessary to restore historic and artistic heritage by area; (i) establishment of information systems between different public authorities that ensure the effectiveness of Land Management Guidelines and the other legal instruments; (j) the scenarios and the reasons for modifying Land Management Guidelines (Article 6 LMA).

As can be easily derived, the previsions established in the Guidelines range from descriptions of the physical environment to generic proposals or particular determinations that oblige or prevent public authorities from adopting some decisions. In reality, some of those functions have not been carried out or, if so, only partially and unsuccessfully. In some cases, the content has not been set with the firmness that should be desired. On the other hand, the Guidelines are too general and lack substance. They set few objectives and not detailed enough. Social housing is a case in point. The Guidelines contain few provisions that can be directly applicable. This is the case of the prohibition of setting houses on non-building classified land. The land classified as non-building cannot be used for building cities. This is, housing is banned on non-building classified land. The importance of the Guidelines lies on the fact that they must be complied by urban planning regulations. On the other hand, their implementation must be controlled and it has not been done.

It is worth mentioning that the Land Management Law in force at that time was not capable of giving solutions to the problems that emerged from massive urbanisation occurred before the crisis which started in 2007.

3.1.1. *Specific Analysis of the Land Use Matrix*

One of the most innovating instruments contained in the Guidelines is the Land Use Matrix. The Land Use Matrix works as follows: In the abscissa axis the typology of land is detailed. In the ordinate axis the uses that are adequate, admissible or forbidden are listed. Additionally, the matrix sets which uses necessarily require a licence to be carried out. For example, as it can be verified, in a flooding area it is forbidden to build isolated houses (number 3 is assigned), but it is allowed to settle infrastructures connected with pre-existent urban areas.

Table 1. Land Use Matrix

		LAND USE								LAND USE														
		Environ-mental protection		Entertainment and leisure			Exploitation of primary resources			Exploitation of primary resources			Infrastructures						Building uses					
		Conservation	Environmental improvement	Extensive recreation	Intensive recreation	Hunting and fishing activities	Agriculture	Greenhouses	Livestock	Forest area	Agrarian industry	Extractive activities	Transport	Overhead wires	Underground lines	Type A constructions	Type B constructions	Solid waste landfills	Growing housing in pre-existing urbanised areas	Growing housing in no pre-existing urbanised areas	Constructions of public interest	Isolated farms	Isolated housing	Dangerous systems
LAND TYPOLOGY	Organisation categories																							
		Areas of special protection	1	1	2*	3	2*	3	3	2*	2*	3	3	3	2*	2*	3	2*	3	3	3	2*	3	3	3
		Environmental improvement	1	1	2	2*	2*	3	3	2*	2*	2*	2*	2*	2*	2*	3	2*	2*	2*	3	2*	3	3	3
		Forestry area	2	2	2	2*	2*	2*	3	2*	2*	2*	2*	2*	2*	2*	2*	2*	2*	2*	3	2*	2*	3	3
		Farming areas and countryside	2	2	2	2*	2*	1	2*	1	2*	2*	2*	2*	2*	2*	3	2*	2*	2*	3	2*	2*	3	2*
		Montane pastures	1	1	2	2*	2*	3	3	1	2*	3	3	2*	2*	2*	2*	2*	3	3	3	2*	3	3	3
		Land with no defined use	2	2	2	2*	2*	2	2*	2	2*	2	2*	2*	2*	2*	2*	2*	2*	2*	2*	2*	2*	3	2*
		Surface waters' protection	1	1	2	2*	2*	2*	2*	2	2*	3	2*	2*	2*	2*	2*	2*	3	3	3	2*	3	3	3

LAND TYPOLOGY	Determining factors	Aquifers' vulnerability				2*	2*	2*	2		2	2*	2*	2*	2*	2*	2*	2*	3	2*	2*	2*	2*	3	2*
		Erodible areas				2*	2*	2*	2		2*	2*	2*	2*	2*	2*	2*	2*	2*	2*	2*	2*	3	3	2*
		Floodable area				2*	2*	2	2*		2*	2*	2*	2*	2*	2*	2*	2*	2*	2*	2*	2*	3	3	2*
		Protected Natural Spaces and Urdaibai Biosphere Reserve				2*	2*	2	2*		2*	2*	2*	2*	2*	2*	2*	2*	2*	2*	2*	2*	2*	3	2*

1. Appropriate project.
2. Acceptable project.
3. Forbidden project.
* Plans adopted after the development of the Guidelines for Land Management

The Land Use Matrix, if properly implemented, might be useful. However, very often it has not been enforced as it should have because of the manipulation of the requirements by Public Authorities. Nevertheless, proper land classification, with a well thought out typology and precise designation of possible land uses would be an interesting and valuable instrument for correct land management.

3.2. LAND DISTRICT PLANS

Land District Plans are adopted for each of the fifteen regions of the Basque Country. The content of those plans is established in the LMA and, in turn, they are an implementation of the Guidelines for Land Management.[13] In relation to the content, the most remarkable requirements to be determined in a plan are the objectives, the location of large infrastructures and public facilities and the location of the land reserved for social housing.

Up to now, a number of Land District Plans have been adopted.[14] It can be assured that some of them have had a multiplying effect regarding land occupancy and the development of housing has been neither justified nor controlled. The target period is essential. If the Land District Plans are in force for sixteen years, it would be inadmissible if the growing rates for this period were completed in four years.

The Land District Plans could have been an appropriate tool to establish the percentage of land that can be built. The land is a natural resource of great importance and there is a need to preserve it. However, the weaknesses of the Land District Plans lie on the fact that the rules are not detailed enough, especially because some large municipalities oppose to be governed by a superior entity.

---

13 Article 12 LMA. This is their content: (a) definition of management objectives based on an analysis of the territory, its socio-economic situation and its development possibilities; (b) location of major infrastructures; (c) location of community facilities for the area; (d) establishment of the criteria, principles and general rules to be taken into account by urban planning; (e) identification of areas in need of modernisation, regeneration or renovation in order to prevent them falling into disrepair or disuse, or to give them a change of use, setting up programmes to develop them and support to carry them out; (f) delimitation of the land to be reserved for social housing in its current and future modalities; (g) a record of publically authorised industrial land for industrial/trading estates; (h) the establishment of the necessary criteria, rules and principles for the development of Territory Management Guidelines. As can be seen, this is a very broad provision, it has a wide scope, although it should be understood that the Land district Plans are there to put into effect Territory Management Guidelines. In accordance with this the Territory district Plans seek comprehensive land management, but within the district. The formal content of the Land District Plans is also set in the LMA: (a) reports and information maps; (b) explanatory memorandum of the Plan; (c) economic-financial study; (d) an implementation programme divided into four stages; (e) management maps and rules; (f) any other document considered relevant.

14 An analysis of the Basque coast planning can be seen in: *I. Lazkano Brotóns & X. Arzoz Santisteban*, La ordenación, planificación y gestión del litoral en el País Vasco, in *M. García Pérez & F.J. Sanz Larruga* (eds.), Estudios sobre la ordenación, planificación y gestión del litoral: hacia un modelo integrado y sostenible, 2009, pp. 287–298.

Before the crisis which started in 2007, they did not want to be told about the percentage of land they were allowed to occupy to carry out with urbanisation projects.

3.3. LAND SECTOR PLANS

Land Sector Plans are adopted by the Basque Government or the Regional Governments of Bizkaia, Araba or Gipuzkoa. As their name reflects, these Plans regulate a particular sector. Up to now, these are the Land Sector Plans that have been adopted:

(a) the Territory Sector Plan for Coastal Protection and Management in the Basque Country;
(b) the Territory Sector Plan for the Road Network;
(c) the Territory Sector Plan for the Rail Network in Bilbao's Metropolitan Area and other Municipalities;
(d) the Territory Sector Plan for the Creation of Land for Business and Business Premises;
(e) the Territory Sector Plan for the Basque Country's Wetlands;
(f) the Territory Sector Plan for the Basque Country's Wind Power;
(g) the Territory Sector Plan for the Basque Country's Rail Network;
(h) the Territory Sector Plan for the Basque Country's River Banks and Streams' Management (Mediterranean region);
(i) the Territory Sector Plan for Biscay's Road Network; and
(j) the Territory Sector Plan for the Basque Country's River Banks and Streams' Management (Cantabrian region).

4. PRACTICAL ANALYSIS OF THE LAND MANAGEMENT SET IN THE BASQUE LEGAL INSTRUMENTS

4.1. ENERGY POLICY AND WIND FARMS

The adequacy of the Guidelines for the Land Management and, specifically, the Land Use Matrix can be analysed in relation to the policy on the construction of wind farms. To do so, we will analyse a real case in which it was of major importance the compliance with Birds Directive – the wind farm was to be built in a Special Protection Area for Birds (SPAB).[15] In this case, Land Management Law

[15] Directive 2009/147/EC of the European Parliament and of the Council of 30 November 2009 on the conservation of wild birds (codified version of Directive 79/409/EEC as amended).

served to highlight that the location was within the scope of the Birds Directive and the wind farm could not be carried out.[16]

The Basque Government approved a Land Sector Plan on Basque Country's wind power following the line of policy established in the Special Plan for Elgea's wind farm.[17] This Special Plan was set before passing the Land Sector Plan on Basque Country's wind power but after the Guidelines adoption. The construction of Elgea's wind farm raised the question about its compatibility with Land Use Matrix. The land in which the wind farm was to be located was classified as 'montane pasture' – see the Land Use Matrix. On this type of land, the construction of type A infrastructures was forbidden and type B permitted. According to the Guidelines of Land Management, type A infrastructures were defined as A wide range of facilities such as large outdoor areas for car parking, water purification and water treatment plants, large reservoirs or water tanks, electric power stations, transformer stations larger than 100m^2, gas-fired generating stations, sewage systems, solid waste treatment plants and any other facility of general interest which had the same impact on the environment". In turn, type B infrastructures are defined as: 'A range of facilities such as towers, antennas, radio sending and receiving stations, television and communication via satellite, lighthouses, radio beacon stations and any other communication facilities with the same impact on the environment'.

In view of both definitions it has to be determined whether Elgea's wind farm is a type A or a Type B infrastructure. All reports pointed out that wind farms were a type A infrastructure. However, when the Land Sector Plan on wind power was approved the Government understood that wind farms were type B infrastructures. Firstly, the Basque Court of Justice delivered that they were type A infrastructures but, secondly, they also understood that they were type B. In this manner, it can be clearly deduced that the Guidelines' functionality is very limited because of the way in which the Basque Authorities interpret them. When the Public Authorities find a definition inconvenient for their interests they simply ignore it. This way, a wind farm is equated with an antenna or a radio station, as if the impact on the environment – in this case, the landscape – was similar. Moreover, the Guidelines do not mention wind farms in the whole text. It can be understood that this is a deliberate lack of prevision.[18]

16 *I. Lasagabaster & A. Garcia, supra* note 2.

17 *I. Lasagabaster Herrarte*, Consideraciones jurídicas sobre la planificación de instalaciones eólicas en la Comunidad Autónoma del País Vasco, Ingurugiroa eta Zuzenbidea, 2013 (11), pp. 13–28; *I. Lasagabaster Herrarte & I. Lazcano Brotons*, El Plan Territorial Sectorial eólico: análisis crítico de su regulación, Revista Vasca de Administración Pública, 2002 (64), pp. 145–192.

18 *A.M. García Ureta & I. Lazkano Brotóns*, Parques eólicos, red Natura 2000 e impacto ambiental: comentario a la sentencia del Tribunal Superior de Justicia del País Vasco de 18 de febrero de 2011 (proyecto de parque eólico de Ordunte), Revista Vasca de Administración Pública, 2011 (91), pp. 233–256.

4.2. POLICY ON LARGE PROJECTS AND THE TRADE ACT

Over the last twenty years, because of the policy that the Basque Government has developed on large projects, these buildings have gone from being nonexistent to taking up large areas of the territory.[19] Thus, they have not considered the negative impact that those infrastructures have on the environment, especially, as a consequence of the huge movement of people they cause. The Guidelines say nothing about this matter – remember that the Guidelines were adopted in 1997 – and, although the Trade Act was in force, some large projects, especially large supermarkets, were settled without any plan. The self-interested and biased interpretations of the rules by Public Authorities can be illustrated by some examples.

Gorbeia Shopping Centre was built in a neighbouring town to Vitoria because, at that moment, the city council of Vitoria did not allow those large constructions to be built. The absence of such regulation in that town permitted the construction of Gorbeia Shopping Centre, which had not been feasible in the capital city. Sustainability is the criterion which firstly goes against the construction of big supermarkets. It has been proven that the shopping centres built in Barakaldo Council's territory imply five million displacements by private car every year. Every shopping centre constructed there was built without any kind of supra-municipal planning.

In other cases, territory consumption, which the construction of malls implies, breaks the dynamic of 'creating city'. In the Council of Durango, the large surface occupied by shopping centres has broken the harmonious interaction between it and its neighbouring town Abadiño. It would have been more appropriate a smaller surface occupation in another location, further from both population nuclei. In addition, the external illumination used to display advertise these shopping centres has a huge visual impact on landscape, as happens in the area of Durango and Matiena which are located closed to Urkiola Nature Park.

The consequences of building these types of premises have not been taken into consideration in the different land management legal instruments. The public authorities are more in favour of addressing the problems once they are built than subjecting their construction to a public decision procedure. Once again, the public authorities have enforced a fait accompli policy.

[19] In connection with large projects in the Autonomous Community of Castilla y León, see: *T. Quintana López*, Claves de la evolución del urbanismo comercial: la implantación de grandes establecimientos comerciales en Castilla y León, Revista jurídica de Castilla y León, 2011 (23), pp. 67–104.

4.3. CONSTRUCTION OF GOLF COURSES

The construction of golf courses is one of the most common practices to carry out with what, otherwise, would be economically unworkable urban developments.[20] Golf requires the construction of facilities that consume large surfaces and big amounts of water. Moreover, the use of fertilisers and chemical products has an important impact on the environment – on soil quality and, consequently, on groundwater. Because of those reasons, such sport facilities should be constructed in non-building land and they should be ruled by a supra-municipal planning, taking the consumption of water into account. Moreover, it cannot be forgotten that the maintenance of golf courses is highly costly and, in the majority of cases, not cost-effective.

The golf course construction project in Labastida Council is a clear example of illegal actions that the construction of private sport facilities often hides. In the case of Labastida, the golf course was to be built, partly, in a Nature Protection Area. Public Authorities tried to present the project as compatible with environmental protection of the area. They wanted to sweep under the carpet (a) the amount of water that golf courses need for their maintenance; (b) golf courses' effect on water quality by the use of fertilisers – in terms of contamination – and (c) the compulsory compliance with the European Union Water Framework Directive's requirements.[21]

Before summarising the case of Labastida, there is a need to explain briefly how urban planning in Labastida has evolved. Currently, owners of a one-hectare-building-land are entitled to establish two single-family houses. According to the urban planning in force some years ago, that rural land could only have been used for farming. However, once it was reclassified by the Town Council it got the rating of 'building land' and, thus, the economic value increased. However, owners had to transfer some surface so that it could be urbanised – that is, for the construction of streets, roads, parks, etc. Likewise, owners would have to pay for the electricity, the gas, the water supply, amid others – the so-called urbanisation costs. In the following lines Labastida golf course's case is briefly explained.

In Labastida it was planned to construct 800 houses which were to be built at the same time as a golf course, this is, in the same urban operation. Following the explanation above, the buyers of those houses would have had to pay not only for the house but also for the golf course. The golf course was to be constructed at the buyers of the houses' expenses, although it would be a private golf course just for the members of the golf club. They would not only pay for the golf course but also for its deficit for ten years, which was estimated at 3 million euros. This operation

[20] *I. Lasagabaster Herrarte,* Dotaciones públicas, sistemas generales y algunas perversiones del sistema urbanístico, Ingurugiroa eta Zuzenbidea, 2008 (6), pp. 35–53; *I. Lasagabaster Herrarte,* El suelo, ¿un bien público sin protección?, Ingurugiroa eta Zuzenbidea, 2007 (5), pp. 47–56.

[21] Directive 2000/60/EC of the European Parliament and of the Council establishing a framework for the Community action in the field of water policy.

would have implied that the buyers would have had to pay 24 million euros for a golf course which would have been completely private.

The golf course is an example of the business – clearly illegal – that is behind some development projects. The Urban Planning Law in the Basque Country does not include the cost of building a golf course or similar infrastructures as urbanisation costs.

4.4. PRIVATISATION OF URBAN PLANNING AS A PUBLIC SERVICE

Urban planning constitutes a public service. This means that authorities are responsible for the development of both the territory in general and the city in particular. Recent changes to rules have allowed private individuals a role in urban planning, one that they did not have before. The direct consequence is that the initiative goes from the public authorities to individuals, and for individuals read urban developers, connected with political parties and public authorities. As is well known, many politicians are employed by construction companies.

Some very important urban development is taking place as a result of dubious agreements. An important question to be raised is: Should local councils be allowed to let private developers drive a city's expansion by building *urbanizaciones* (private housing estates)?[22] Such is the case of some sport facilities. They occupy large spaces not by creating a harmonious city but conditioning the transport in it and generating ghettos. Private urbanisations do not create city and involve the enriching of some landowners or construction companies that obtain from public authorities the reclassification of the land – principally, from a non-housing land to a housing land – never mind how far from the city centre the land is or whether there are appropriate facilities.

Sometimes, local authorities are weak and, in other cases, do not have the necessary means to stop unfair practices. Construction businesses and landowners condition cities development. Urban plans constitute a *fait accompli* policy, in which public debates and citizens' participation are reduced to a minimum. It is not unusual for public authorities to be actively involved in these dealings. Of course, this affirmation does not mean that every local authority should always be challenged. Most public authorities do their job in an unbiased way. However, what we want to mean is that transparency in the process of approving urban plans is essential. Urban planning process should guarantee an adequate development of urbanism as a public service.

---

22 *T. Quintana López, S.J. González-Varas Ibáñez & A.B. Casares Marcos*, La iniciativa particular en la creación de infraestructuras y en la oferta de suelo edificable en el sistema concesional español, Estudios de construcción y transportes, 2005 (102), pp. 99–112.

5. URBAN AND TERRITORY PLANS: PARTICIPATION AND INFORMATION

The authorities should take measures to make land management more accessible to the public. In our view, the followings are some examples that would help people to participate more on all important issues that so directly affect society:

1. Clarity of documents both in substance and in form. Land and Urban Planning have become a form of public intervention that frightens citizens. In most cases, rules are unintelligible and, at the same time, they hide or mask their true motives. Because of this, we need to demand clarity in all documents referring to Urban and Territory Planning.
2. The steps involved. Each step in the process and who does what in the process of territory management should be clearly laid out. It does not appear logical to adapt fundamental decisions without giving the chance to citizens to participate. The citizens – those who the process affects – must be able to participate before decisions are taken.
3. Forms of participation. Councils should clearly set out how the public can take part in the process. This participation must be real and effective and not a mere formality.
4. In the face of complexity, equality is the key. Participation requires that people and population groups need to understand the policies in order to choose the ones that match their needs. One solution would be to make neutral and independent expertise easily available for citizens, paid for out of the public purse. This would enable citizens to understand the policies properly and take part in the process on an equal footing.[23]

6. CONCLUSION

As it has been shown, land planning is a fundamental tool for society's development and plays an important role regarding land use and environment. Planning what land is used for in all the Autonomous Community of the Basque Country involves a great deal of consideration. Some guidelines for land management would prohibit a certain activity, e.g. building houses on non-housing land. Other rules define some compulsory criteria which are open to interpretation, depending on what is compatible. Compatibility requires motivation to make clear what is understood as compatible and incompatible land use. The land use

---

[23] *I. Lasagabaster Herrarte*, Información administrativa y transparencia en la ordenación del territorio y el medio ambiente, Revista Vasca de Administración Pública, 2009 (83), pp. 183–215; *I. Lasagabaster Herrarte & M.C. Bolaño Piñeiro*, Medio ambiente y obligación de difusión, Ingurugiroa eta Zuzenbidea, 2009 (7), pp. 21–34.

matrix, with a few modifications, could be the basis of a more efficient land use policy in the Basque Country.

Some of those decisions should be analysed from the perspective of their consequences. It cannot be declared every piece of land as natural area without weighting up the effects of such a declaration.[24] Traditional activities of the area should also be taken into account. Likewise, if they decide to build houses or set up industries in a certain area, they also have to predict what the speculative impact of such decisions will be. Moreover, public authorities should have an active role in land acquisition.[25] Similarly, it should be a clear policy to preserve land for agriculture and farming.

Different public authorities implement land management law. This situation requires the existence of adequate inspection and control tools. Land management law is an important tool in order to implement and comply with European Union Law on issues such as water protection, birds, habitats[26] or waste.[27] The well-known saying 'everything holds up on paper' is particularly relevant here. The law can be properly implemented if, apart from the tools for control and inspection, there are more possibilities for citizens and associations to take part in the making process. Transparency and accessibility on land planning policies are a must. The legal and political importance of public participation has been revealed through a number of acts, most of them State acts, e.g. State Act 27/2006 on access to environmental information, public participation in decision-making and access to justice[28] and the Act 1/2008 on Environmental Impact Assessment. The latter is the one that regulates more thoroughly public participation.

In spite of the importance of these regulations their enforcement has been deficient. On the one hand, there are a number of rules of very different origin. On the other hand, public authorities do not act transparently and public participation is almost impossible. Moreover, there are not established legal consequences when legislation on public participation is not complied by public authorities. Because of this, social sectors have to keep more than an eye on public authorities when approving land management plans.

---

24 In relation to natural areas, see: *I. Lazkano Brotóns*, Espacios naturales, in I. Lasagabaster Herrarte (ed.), Derecho Ambiental Parte Especial I. Espacios Naturales, Flora y Fauna, Montes, Paisaje, LETE, 2010, pp. 37–288.

25 *T. Quintana López*, Algunas cuestiones sobre el régimen de los patrimonios públicos del suelo: la Ley 8/2007, de 28 de mayo, de Suelo, Revista jurídica de Castilla y León, 2007 (13), pp. 113–136; *T. Quintana López*, La regulación de los patrimonios municipales del suelo como fuente de controversia, Revista Española de Derecho Administrativo, 2004 (121), pp. 83–89.

26 Council Directive 92/43/EEC of 21 May 1992 on the conservation of natural habitats and of wild fauna and flora, consolidated version of 1 January 2007.

27 Council Directive 99/31/EC of 26 April 1999 on the landfill of waste.

28 This act implemented Directive 2003/4/EC of the European Parliament and of the Council of 28 January 2003 on public access to environmental information, and Directive 2003/35/EC of the European Parliament and of the Council providing for public participation in respect of the drawing up of certain plans and programmes relating to the environment.

The Autonomous Community of the Basque Country's experience regarding Land management has shown good and bad points. The main criticisms have been the following: (a) construction of wind farms in privileged areas of the country; (b) building of a number of shopping centres, especially on the left bank of Bilbao's river, and in Araba on the outskirts of Vitoria-Gasteiz, which have had an incredible impact on both the land and environment; (c) the speculative urbanism in the Mediterranean seems to have been copied in the Basque Country by the construction of golf courses under the disguise of housing; and (d) housing developments built thanks to agreements between local authorities and property developers, which limits the power of public authorities to plan land use appropriately. This was the case of Elordigane neighbourhood in Mungia, as well as the case of private housing behind the airport in Sondika. Infrastructures such as the high speed railway, the so-called '*supersur*' motorway or the expansion of Pasaje's port are carried out without the participation of citizens or some Public Authorities. Citizens can participate, but only after the decision has been taken. So, criticism over policy-making process is unavoidable.

For the purposes of this article, the main conclusions can be summarised as follows: (a) there is a need to set a number of binding and non-binding rules on land management depending on the different needs and situations; (b) ways to make participation real and democracy effective should be established; (c) consequences of land management policies should be thoroughly analysed; (d) they should be reinforced by giving them more importance, both economically and organisationally, in the Basque Territorial and Environmental Public Administration; and (e) regulatory instruments should be a tool to comply effectively with European Union environmental law.

CONCLUSION

Reconciling Conflicting Values: A Call For Research on Instruments to Achieve Quasi-Sustainability

Lorenzo SQUINTANI and Bernard VANHEUSDEN

Sustainable development and sustainability are in this second EELF Conference book central terms that recur in the contributions. Unfortunately, various contributions also indicate that this goal of sustainability is often hampered by conflicting values. As already stated in the introduction to the first EELF Conference book, '[f]ocusing on the European Union, the Union itself and each of its Member States has to balance economic welfare, social welfare and environmental welfare, i.e. they have to find "*sustainability*"'.[1] At first glance, sustainable development ranks high in the list of objectives of the European Union. Indeed, the European Union is 'determined to promote economic and social progress for their peoples, taking into account the principle of sustainable development'.[2] More explicitly, '[i]t shall work for the sustainable development of Europe based on balanced economic growth and price stability, a highly competitive social market economy, aiming at full employment and social progress, and a high level of protection and improvement of the quality of the environment'[3] and '[i]t shall contribute to peace, security, the sustainable development of the Earth'.[4]

A closer reading of the Treaties, however, reveals that this policy goal is not operationalised by a specific legal framework. Its relevance in the shaping of the decision-making process at EU level is mediated by the principle of integration. First, Article 7 Treaty on the Functioning of the European Union (TFEU) states that '[t]he Union shall ensure consistency between its policies and activities, taking

---

1 *H. Vedder & L. Squintani* with *M. Reese & B. Vanheusden*, Sustainable Energy United in Diversity – Challenges and Approaches in Energy Transition in the EU, European Environmental Law Forum Book Series, Vol. 1, 2014, p. 1.

2 Preamble of the Treaty on European Union (TEU).

3 Article 3(3) TEU.

4 Article 3(5) TEU.

all of its objectives into account and in accordance with the principle of conferral of powers.' Second, Article 11 TFEU states that '[e]nvironmental protection requirements must be integrated into the definition and implementation of the Union's policies and activities, in particular with a view to promoting sustainable development'. If we define sustainable development as 'development that meets the needs of the present without compromising the ability of future generations to meet their own needs',[5] it can be doubted whether Articles 7 and 11 TFEU ensure the achievement of sustainable development under European Union law. Article 11 TFEU only focuses on one of the three 'P's of the sustainability paradigm, namely the planet,[6] and Article 7 TFEU makes the integration of all EU objectives, including sustainable development, conditional upon the fulfilment of the principle of conferral.

Whether the principle of conferral renders sustainable development possible under the Treaties can be questioned. Under the principle of conferral, 'the Union shall act only within the limits of the competences conferred upon it by the Member States in the Treaties to attain the objectives set out therein.' This means among others that, the Union action in the field covered by Title XX TFEU shall aim at a high level of protection of the environment while contributing to the pursuit of: (a) preserving, protecting and improving the quality of the environment; (b) protecting human health; (c) prudent and rational utilisation of natural resources; and (d) promoting measures at international level to deal with regional or worldwide environmental problems, and in particular combating climate change. As stated under Article 191(3) TFEU, '[i]n preparing its policy on the environment, the Union shall take account of: ... c) the potential benefits and costs of action or lack of action, and d) the economic and social development of the Union as a whole and the balanced development of its regions.' The reference to economic and social development in Article 191(3) TFEU allows striking a balance between the three 'P's of the sustainability paradigm, while being in keeping with the principle of conferral, as required by Article 7 TFEU.

Yet, from the perspective of sustainable development, Article 191 TFEU seems to rank environmental protection higher than economic and social values. While environmental protection *shall be aimed at*, social and economic development *shall be taken into account*. A quick look at the case law of the Court of Justice concerning the review of the legality of acts of the European Union in light of the principle of conferral shows that the difference between these two formulas is not merely a linguistic one. In order to be based on Article 192(1) TFEU, European Union legislation must *mainly* aim at environmental protection.[7] Even

---

5 *World Commission on Environment and Development*, Our Common Future, 1987.

6 The three 'P's are: People, Planet and Profit.

7 For example, the seminal judgments in Case C-300/89 *Commission v. Council of the European Communities*, ECLI:EU:C:1991:244 and Joined Cases C-164/97 and C-165/97 *European Parliament v. Council of the European Communities*, ECLI:EU:C:1999:99.

if a 'high level of environmental protection' does not mean the highest possible,[8] the manner in which the Court of Justice interprets European Union measures based on Article 192(1) TFEU clearly shows a preference for environmental values. Provisions contributing to the achievement of the environmental goals of a decision, directive or regulation are interpreted extensively.[9] The principle of conferral, as applied in practice, creates a hierarchical relationship between the three 'P's of the sustainability paradigm. No such hierarchy is visible under the Brundtland Report definition.[10]

The manner in which environmental concerns are taken into account while formulating and adopting actions under policy areas other than the environmental one, e.g. transport, follows a similar pattern to that indicated under Article 192 TFEU. Article 11 TFEU requires integrating environmental concerns into other policy areas. Yet this does not mean that the environment ranks equal to economic development or social protection, as showed by the contributions of *Marcin Stoczkiewicz* in the field of State aid, of *Delphine Misonne*, as regards noise-related operating restrictions at Union airports, of *Ludwig Kramer* in the field of Trans-European Networks, and of *Yixin Xu* with regard to CDM forest projects. As stated in Marcin Stoczkiewicz's contribution in this book: 'Environmental objectives cannot change the notion of what State aid is and therefore cannot be taken into account in the assessment of whether a particular measure constitutes State aid in the meaning of Article 107(1) of the TFEU. Environmental rules must be considered in the scope of the assessment of compatibility of the State aid measure with the internal market pursuant to Article 107(3) of the TFEU, if the measure has an environmental goal.' Once again, thus, we see an implicit hierarchy between the various 'P's of the sustainability paradigm, a hierarchy which is visible also in the case law of the Court of Justice interpreting the provisions on EU State Aid.[11] Delphine Misonne is on this point

[8] Case C-284/95 *Safety Hi-Tech Srl*, ECLI:EU:C:1998:352, para. 49. It should be noted that this statement of the Court of Justice is not linked to the need of balancing environmental protection with socio-economic development. It is linked to the division of competences between Member States and the EU in the field of environmental protection.

[9] See the explicit words of the Court of Justice in Cases C-418/97 and C-419/97 *ARCO Chemie Nederland Ltd v. Minister van Volkshuisvesting, Ruimtelijke Ordening en Milieubeheer (C-418/97) and Vereniging Dorpsbelang Hees, Stichting Werkgroep Weurt and Vereniging Stedelijk Leefmilieu Nijmegen v. Directeur van de dienst Milieu en Water van de provincie Gelderland (C-419/97)*, paras. 39 and 40. For a recent application of this approach see, for example, Case C-416/13 *Bund für Umwelt und Naturschutz Deutschland eV v. Bundesrepublik Deutschland*, ECLI:EU:C:2015:433, paras. 34–51.

[10] Of course, it could be argued that such a hierarchy is desirable, see *O. Woolley*, Ecological Governance – Reappraising Law's Role in Protecting Ecosystem Functionality, 2014, p. 71, and *R.A. Giljam*, Towards a Holistic Approach in EU Biomass Regulation, Journal of Environmental Law, 2016 (28:1). Yet these readings of the sustainability paradigm are not (yet) generally accepted and cannot, therefore, be used to understand the concept of 'sustainability' under the Treaties.

[11] C-487/06P *British Aggregates Association v. Commission of the European Communities and United Kingdom*, ECLI:EU:C:2008:757, paras. 81–39. In Case T-57/11 *Castelnou Energía, SL v. European Commission*, ECLI:EU:T:2014:1021, para. 189 the General Court explicitly stated

even more explicit, when she concludes that '[t]hese elements demonstrate a narrow-minded approach to how transport policies integrate the protection of the environment and of citizen's health against noise'. Indeed, her close analysis of the Regulation shows that operating restrictions under Regulation 598/2014 are treated as 'the exception' rather than 'the rule'. As regards Trans-European Networks, the little consideration of environmental concerns is evident also in the context of public participation in environmental matters. As stated in Ludwig Kramer's contribution in this book '[i]f one takes this legal requirement of EU policy [Article 11 TFEU] seriously, one will have to admit that the consultation of the citizens concerned only after the adoption of Regulation 347/2013 on energy infrastructure, Regulation 1391/2013 on energy projects of common EU interest and Regulation 1315/2013 on transport infrastructure comes too late.' Finally, Yixin Xu indicates that the environmental sustainability of CDM forest projects can sometimes be questioned because they may cause harm to local lands and biodiversity conditions by the plantation of harmful trees or by unintentionally increasing illegal logging in unprotected forests. To promote the sustainability of CDM forest projects in terms of biodiversity conservation and poverty alleviation, Xu proposes to enhance the current CDM sustainability assessment regulation and practices from a law and economic perspective. Within the EU, the European Commission has already required that individual and public projects and programmes co-financed by the EU have to comply with the EIA and SEA Directives. However, this seems to have a limited effect. Therefore, Xu suggests that the EU Member States could extend the scope of EIA and SEA practices to CDM projects financed by their domestic investors.

The lack of a fully developed legal framework to achieve sustainable development at EU level seems to be paired with a growing wish by (at least) some Member States to reshape the balance between environmental and economic interests reached at EU level under environmental legislation. This tendency clearly emerges out of the various contributions included in this book which focus on the national level. This tendency was highlighted in the field of public participation with the contributions of *Viviana Molaschi*, *Hendrik Schoukens* and *Jose Cubero Marcos* and *Unai Aberasturi Gorriño* showing that Italy, Belgium, the UK and Spain (the Basque Country) see public participation rules as 'one of the main triggers of the 'excessive' administrative burden and cumbersome delays large infrastructural projects are facing across Europe these days' (Molaschi). In Belgium, the UK and Spain (the Basque Country), such a perception seems at the basis of the use of legislative validation to circumvent public participation requirements. In the field of environmental impact assessment, *Glen Wright*'s contribution shows that the UK is quite 'creative' in developing instruments,

that the 'protection of the environment does not constitute, per se, one of the components of that internal market'. Without arguing that this approach is right, it is explicative of the relationship between the principle of conferral and that of integration and how such a relationship shapes the legal reasoning of the Court of Justice and the General Court.

such as the 'Rochdale Envelope' and the 'Deploy and Monitor' approaches, aiming at allowing economic development despite uncertainties conceding the environmental impact of projects. The tension in the relationship between environmental protection and economic development in the field covered by the EIA Directive is also highlighted in *Medhi Piri Damagh*'s contribution. His in-depth analysis of the manner in which, in particular, Germany, Denmark, Sweden and Finland, but also Estonia, Latvia, Lithuania and Poland, cooperated in the establishing of an EIA Report for the Nord Stream Gas Pipeline shows that environmental protection was less than optimal due to the lack of willingness to go beyond the requirements of the Epsoo Convention and the EIA Directive. Rather than performing several national EIAs, a single transboundary EIA could have led to better environmental protection. This, however, would have been gold-plating, which, as known, is not a priority of Member States, to put it mildly.[12]

If we focus on the 'vertical sectors' of EU environmental law, the contributions of *Vicky Karageorgou, Lisa Löffler*, and *David Salm* highlighted shortcomings in the implementation of EU water law. The contribution of Vicky Karageorgou exposes the unwillingness of Greece to cope with the requirements stemming out from the Water Framework Directive in the context of the Interbasin Water Transfer concerning the Acheloos River. Lisa Löffler's contribution argues about a widespread tendency among the Member States not to recognise the binding force of the Water Framework Directive requirements as regards the deadline for the phasing-out of priority hazardous substances. Similar findings can be seen in the contribution of David Salm, who shows how Germany misinterprets/ed the concept of 'no deterioration' under the Water Framework Directive.

In the field of nature conservation, the contributions of *Nicolas de Sadeleer* and *Geert Van Hoorick* show that several Member States have insufficiently implemented the Habitats Directive. In particular, the Netherlands seems to have been quite 'creative' in finding what, from the perspective of the Dutch Government, can be considered a solution to the need of lowering the regulatory burdens deriving from the Habitats Directive to speed up economic development (Van Hoorick).

Finally, in the context of land use and planning law, the contribution of *Elizabeth Dunn* puts the UK, once again, at the table of those Member States willing to encourage economic development at the cost of environmental protection. As indicated by Dunn, various amendments introduced in 2015 to the rules of procedures regulating challenges to planning decisions, arguably with the exception of the creation of a specialised court, aim at preventing judicial review of planning decisions in order to spur on economic development. Administrative practice in Spain (the Basque Country) shows a similar tendency.

12 *J.H. Jans, L. Squintani et al.*, 'Gold Plating' of European Environmental Measures?, JEEPL, 2009 (8:4), pp. 417, 418; *L. Squintani*, Gold-Plating of European Environmental Law, PhD thesis, Groningen, 2013; and *H. Anker Tegner et al.*, Coping with EU environmental legislation: transposition principles and practices, Journal of Environmental Law, 2015 (27:1), p. 17.

The contribution of *Inaki Lasagabaster* and *Maria Del Carmen Bolaño* reports several cases in which provisions aiming at environmental protection were set aside by public authorities in the name of economic development.

The impressionistic appraisal in this book hence suggests the existence of a red line throughout the EU. Member States are not at ease with the EU environmental acquis. The Better Regulation Agenda can be seen as the EU dimension of Member States' concerns.[13]

This leads to the question of how EU environmental law can meet Member States' request for more flexibility as regards the balance between the three 'P's of the sustainability paradigm without endangering the need for a high level of environmental protection. As stated above, a full-fledged sustainability approach at EU level requires amending the Treaties. Only when the EU abandons the principle of conferral or develop a specific policy and legal framework to achieve sustainable development will it be able to pursuit sustainability within the meaning of the Brundtland Report. There is no sign that such intrusive changes in the EU constitutional structure will occur any soon. A quasi-sustainable approach must, consequently, be sought within the actual framework provided by Titles XX and XXI of the TFEU.

A close look at the EU environmental legislative practice over the last three decades shows a series of instruments deployed by the EU legislature to cope with this challenge. Self-regulation, especially in the form of labelling requirements, cap-and-trade instruments, especially in the form of emissions trading schemes, and the so-called programmatic approach[14] are exemplary in this context. They all aim at reducing the rigidity of EU environmental goals and requirements and enhance cost-effectiveness. Labelling requirements allow industry to compete on the level of environmental friendliness. Well-informed consumers, rather than regulators, set the standard by means of their informed choice. Environmentally sensitive consumers will choose environmentally friendly products which will then become the standard, enabling the green revolution. At least, this is the theory. Emissions trading schemes allow polluters to choose the most cost-effective route to reduce emissions. A polluter can meet environmental standards either by improving its performance or by purchasing allowances from competitors. A rational polluter will choose the least expensive route and therefore maximise efficiency. Finally, the programmatic approach recognises

[13] *L. Squintani*, Gold-Plating of European Environmental Law, PhD thesis, Groningen, 2013, pp. 96 and 97.

[14] Under this approach, national public authorities adopt a plan or programme indicating how and when a certain environmental standard or goal will be achieved. On this concept see *F. Groothuijse & R. Uylenburg*, Everything according to plan? Achieving environmental quality standards by a programmatic approach, in M. Peeters & R. Uylenburg (eds.), EU Environmental Legislation, Legal Practice on Regulatory Strategies, 2014, pp. 116–145.

a 'wide leeway' in how to implement EU requirements.[15] Such flexibility can be used to foster innovative, sustainable development, and the functioning of the preventive and polluter-pays principles and a fair allocation of room for economic development.[16] Moreover, flexibility can be used to cope with socio-economic and environmental development, on the one hand, and developments in the state of knowledge, on the other. This latter aspect is referred to as adaptability or adaptiveness.[17] More generally, the programmatic approach is consistent with the subsidiarity principle.[18]

Each of these three instruments fit well within the so-called Sustainable Development Governance Regime and, thanks to their enhanced cost-effectiveness, is potentially capable of achieving quasi-sustainability within the framework offered under Titles XX and XXI of the TFEU.[19] Yet they all come with severe shortcomings.

The success of labelling requirements depends upon the sensitivity of consumers and the willingness of producers to invest in environmentally friendly technologies. In certain fields, the benefits of environmentally friendly technologies will be visible only over a long period of time, such as in the fields covered by the Labelling Directive[20] and the Energy Performance of Buildings Directive.[21] Given that the high investment costs required under these two Directives will be recouped only over a long period of time, purchasing decisions do not seem to be informed by labelling.[22] Moreover, producers do not seem

---

15 This terminology is mutated from *I. von Homeyer*, The Evolution of EU Environmental Governance, in J. Scott (ed.), Environmental Protection – European Law and Governance, 2009, pp. 1–26, at 20.

16 As regards the two latter effects, see *C.W. Backes & H.F.M.W. van Rijswick*, Effective environmental protection: towards a better understanding of environmental quality standards in environmental legislation, in L. Gipperth & C. Zetterberg, Miljörättsliga perspektiv och tankevändor, Vänbok till Jan Darpö & Gabriel Michanek, 2013, pp. 19–50 and *C.W. Backes, Andrea M. Keesen & H.F.M.W. van Rijswick*, Effectgerichte normen in het omgevingsrecht – De betekenis van kwaliteiteitseisen, instandhoudingsdoelstellingen en emissieplafonds voor de bescherming van milieu, water en natuur, 2012, p. 130.

17 *L. Squintani & H.F.M.W. van Rijswick*, Improving legal certainty and adaptability in the programmatic approach (submitted to Journal of Environmental Law).

18 *F. Groothuijse & R. Uylenburg*, *supra* note 4, p. 143.

19 *I. von Homeyer*, *supra* note 14, pp. 18–24. This regime is characterised by four elements: (a) concrete targets are formulated during the implementation phase (see for example Article 4 of the WFD); (b) long time spam for implementation (twenty and more years); (c) wide leeway in how to implement the EU requirements; and (d) the possible lack of binding requirements in respect of certain important aspect.

20 Commission Directive 2010/30/EU of the European Parliament and of the Council of 19 May 2010 on the indication by labelling and standard product information of the consumption of energy and other resources by energy-related products, OJ 2010 L153/1.

21 Directive 2010/31/EU of the European Parliament and of the Council of 19 May 2010 on the energy performance of buildings, OJ 2010 L153/13.

22 For the latest publication on this issue, see *H. Vedder*, Energy Efficiency, in E. Woerdman, M. Roggenkamp & M. Holwerda, Essential EU Climate Law, 2015, pp. 157–179, at 178, with further references.

willing to cooperate in deploying energy saving technologies.[23] Finally, in those cases in which the producers themselves assess the energy efficiency of products, the quality of the assessment is not always impeccable, to put it kindly.[24]

Similar problems affect the EU Emissions Trading Scheme (ETS). Stakeholders' concerns and the lack of ambitions of the EU political class have led to a legal regime which needed, and in certain cases still needs, important reforms. Recently, Woerdman listed five implementation problems: (a) over-allocation; (b) windfall profits; (c) new entrants and closures; (d) allowances prices and structural reforms; and (e) tax fraud and allowance theft.[25] These problems have been addressed by the EU legislature, but it can be questioned whether this has been done in a satisfactory manner. The establishment of an EU-wide cap serves to resolve the issue of over-allocation, but the emissions surplus is already so high that this reforming measure will need a long time before it is effective.[26] The same can be said for the issues of windfall profits and of new entrants and closures. The increasing percentage of emissions being auctioned, instead of being allocated for free, will eliminate the tendency of allowances owners to pass opportunity costs over to the final consumers and cure the inefficiencies associated with benchmarking.[27] Yet the increase in the amount of allowances being auctioned occurs at a slow rate. It will take a long time before auctioning can solve these two problems. More intrusive reforms are blocked by the lack of political will. Moreover, some problems seem to derive from an overall lack of coherence within the EU climate law policy framework, with the three pillars of the '20–20–20' target being partially incompatible.[28] As a result, the effectiveness of the structural reforms presented by the Commission has been questioned.[29]

Also as regards the programmatic approach, it is possible to highlight many shortcomings, to an extent that the effectiveness of such an instrument to achieve a high level of environmental protection is doubtful. Initial research concerning the pieces of EU environmental legislation prescribing a programmatic approach shows relevant differences among the various regimes.[30] Not all the differences can be explained at the hand of the differences between the environmental fields.

---

23 *Ibid.*, p. 177.

24 e.g. *L. Squintani*, Regulation of emissions from non-ETS sectors, in E. Woerdman, M. Roggenkamp & M. Holwerda *supra* note 22, pp. 96–124, at 113–121, with reference to the testing requirements of vehicle emissions.

25 *E. Woerdman*, The EU greenhouse gas emissions trading scheme, in E. Woerdman, M. Roggenkamp & M. Holwerda *supra* note 22, pp. 43–75, at 64–73.

26 *Ibid.*, p. 66.

27 *Ibid.*, pp. 66–69.

28 *B. Görlach*, Emissions Trading in the Climate Policy Instrument Mix: Understanding and Managing Interactions with Other Policy Instruments, Energy and Environment, 2014 (25), pp. 733–749.

29 *E. Woerdman*, *supra* note 25, pp. 69–73. Furthermore, the measures adopted to prevent allowance theft do not seem to have weakened crime in this area, see Case T-317/12 *Holcim (Romania) SA v. European Commission*, ECLI:EU:T:2014:782.

30 *F. Groothuijse & R. Uylenburg*, *supra* note 4, pp. 116–145, focusing on the Water Framework Directive and the Air Quality Directive. *L. Squintani & H.F.M.W. van Rijswick*, *supra* note 17,

For example, it is unclear why only the Water Framework Directive requires the joint establishment of a joint river basin plan, including one or more programmes of measures, in case of transboundary pollution,[31] while the Air Quality Directive just establishes an option in this regard.[32] Moreover, public participation is regulated under water management law but not under air quality law.[33] Besides, the linkage between environmental goals and individual decisions seems to vary from one regime to another. The *RWE* case shows that the emission limit values under Article 4 of the NEC Directive can hardly be used to review the legality of specific, individual decisions.[34] They serve only to review the legality of national emissions programmes. Differently, the *Weser* case shows that the quality standards under Article 4 of the Water Framework Directive can be used to review the legality of specific individual projects affecting water quality, regardless of the content of a programme of measures.[35] It is still unclear what the rule is under the Air Quality Directive as regards this aspect of the programmatic approach.[36] Legal certainty is not well served by such a lack of clarity.

More generally, there seem to be deficiencies affecting all regimes. Most notably, no EU environmental measure prescribing the use of a programmatic approach regulates judicial protection against plans or programmes. This is not in line with the Aarhus Convention (Articles 6 and 7 in conjunction with Article 9). Moreover, none of the EU measures prescribing a programmatic approach regulates the manner in which the effectiveness of programmes must be assessed. This renders it extremely difficult, if not impossible, to review Member States' implementation of the quality standards and related programmes.

The brief appraisal of the three exemplary instruments developed by the EU legislature to achieve quasi-sustainability shows several shortcomings. The alleged effectiveness of these instruments cannot, therefore, be taken for granted. From a legal perspective, there seem to be at least two recurring problems. First, there is a lack of legal certainty. Many core aspects of the three instruments mentioned above are unclear or under-regulated. The assessment methods under the labelling and programmatic approach instruments are framed in such a way

focusing on the Water Framework Directive, the Air Quality Directive, the Nitrates Directive and the National Emission Ceilings Directive.

31 Directive 2000/60/EC of the European Parliament and of the Council of 23 October 2000 establishing a framework for Community action in the field of water policy, OJ 2000 L327/1, Articles 3 and 13.

32 Directive 2008/50/EC of the European Parliament and of the Council of 21 May 2008 on ambient air quality and cleaner air for Europe, OJ 2008 L152/1, Article 25.

33 See Article 14 of the Water Framework Directive. The Air Quality Directive is completely silent on this issue.

34 Joined Cases C-165/09 to C-167/09 *Stichting Natuur en Milieu and Others v. College van Gedeputeerde Staten van Groningen (C-165/09) and College van Gedeputeerde Staten van Zuid-Holland (C-166/09 and C-167/09)*, ECLI:EU:C:2011:348.

35 Case C-461/13 *Bund für Umwelt und Naturschutz Deutschland*, ECLI:EU:C:2015:433.

36 *C.W. Backes & H.F.M.W. van Rijswick*, Annotation to the Weser case, JEEPL, 2015 (3–4), pp. 363–377.

that enforceability is basically impossible. Second, shortcomings in the design and implementation of these instruments require legislative reforms. Adaptability, i.e. the power to cope with new developments including those in the understanding of the functioning of these instruments, is not automatic. EU legislative reforms, however, do not seem capable of fully solving the problems that emerged during the implementation of the instruments, the reforms of the ETS Directive being exemplary on this point.

These findings justify a call for fundamental research on the shortcomings of the EU legal framework in light of the sustainability principle in general, and of the various instruments to achieve quasi-sustainability in light of the high level of environmental protection principle in particular. It is not only the EU dimension that should be covered. As shown by the contributions in this book, Member States are developing 'creative' approaches to balance environmental, social and economic values. Comparative research can reveal the strengths and weaknesses of these approaches. The contributions presented at the Second EELF Conference, including those published in this book, show the urgency of such research. The economic crisis has only intensified the wish for reshaping the EU environmental acquis. The ongoing REFIT process of EU nature conservation law could not have taken place in a worse economic climate.[37] Given the lack of clarity about the instruments mentioned above, we can only hope that the species and habitats protection will not serve as a guinea pig for the EU legislature. We simply know too little about the effectiveness of instruments to achieve quasi-sustainability to afford ourselves the luxury of experimenting in a field of environmental law known for its fragility.

Given the extent of a research programme capable of shedding light on (quasi-)sustainability, a broad EU-steered call for research is needed. We cannot expect individual Member States to have the capacities, interest and the financial motivation to finance such a research programme, let alone individual universities or research centres. It is therefore regrettable that the DG Research political agenda under the Horizon 2020 funding programme is based on market-driven innovation and does not allow room for fundamental research. If the EU and the national legislators do not want academia to continue playing the role of 'Jiminy Cricket' in the quest for (quasi-)sustainability, it is time to put fundamental research back at the top of DG Research's agenda.

---

37 See the proceedings on this process at http://ec.europa.eu/environment/nature/legislation/fitness_check/index_en.htm.

www.ingramcontent.com/pod-product-compliance
Ingram Content Group UK Ltd.
Pitfield, Milton Keynes, MK11 3LW, UK
UKHW051919100926
8556IPUK00021B/1259

9 781780 683812